PRAISE FOR ROBERT GORDON AND
IT CAME FROM MEMPHIS

Memphis Zoo, circa 1959. Photo by Ernest Withers.

it
CAME
from
MEMPHIS

Robert Gordon

POCKET BOOKS
New York   London   Toronto   Sydney

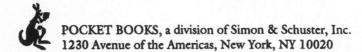

POCKET BOOKS, a division of Simon & Schuster, Inc.
1230 Avenue of the Americas, New York, NY 10020

ISBN-13: 978-0-7434-1045-8
ISBN-10:   0-7434-1045-9

First Pocket Books trade paperback printing November 2001

10 9 8 7 6 5 4 3

POCKET and colophon are registered trademarks of
Simon & Schuster, Inc.

For information regarding special discounts for bulk purchases, please contact
Simon & Schuster Special Sales at 1-800-456-6798 or
business@simonandschuster.com

Cover design by Brigid Pearson
Front cover photo credits: top row, left to right: Jim Dickinson, Rick Brumbraugh,
Jim Dickinson, William Eggleston: bottom: PhotoDisc

Printed in the U.S.A.

For Tara
With love

We knew what it was like to be born in the old world. We had everything to consume and nothing to conquer. We had to invent everything ourselves.

Godard
Jean Collet

Contents

⮜—⮞

Foreword

FOR THE LAST TWENTY-FIVE YEARS, MORE OR LESS, I'VE BEEN WALKING the streets of Memphis looking for ghosts, listening for echoes, trying to construct a vision in my mind of *what it must have been like.* I must admit, I was egged on by Stanley Booth and Jim Dickinson, I was prompted by the lure of history (Sun, Stax, and beyond)—but until I met Robert Gordon I was beginning to think I was crazy. And now I'm not so sure which one of us is.

I don't know how old Robert is exactly, and I don't want to suggest in any way that he has lived other lives or possesses what is called an "old soul"—but there's something going on here. Because Robert *is* possessed by an imaginative grasp of history, he does see and hear ghostly footsteps, he is a young writer/filmmaker/musical avant gardist/Memphis literateur living very much in the present who is no less connected to the past.

I first met Robert not long after I started work on my Elvis Presley biography, when I saw the film he codirected, *All Day & All Night: Memories from Beale Street Musicians*. Not long after that he started showing me his Memphis. We went to the Antenna Club. We went to the Paradise. We went to Green's Lounge. And we went to Riverside Park. That was where I disappointed Robert. We went out there because that was where Elvis and his friends hung out as teenagers. I wanted to find the location of the pavilion area and Rocky's Lakeside refreshment stand. Searching for someone who might remember, we went into the golf course clubhouse. Not only did we find someone who knew: we met Rocky's wife. But I was too embarrassed to reveal myself. I don't think Robert ever looked at me the same way again: *he* knew that a good reporter doesn't get embarrassed.

Robert proves to be not only a good reporter but a wonderful raconteur and host in the pages of this book. He introduces me to people I have never met and to people I have met many times—to my equal edification. He presents the spirit of Memphis—an equal parts mix of genius, orneriness, and individuation—without trying to bottle it. He tells a good story—he tells *a lot of good stories*—without ever abandoning the free-flowing, Shandyan form of digressive discourse that seems so well-suited to Memphis. He captures Memphis, and he captures an era, for the very reason that he does not seek to capture it. As Randall Lyon says, of a movement that would be rightfully insulted if you called it a movement: "We had what you would call in rhetoric *eroico furore,* poetic furor. We were inspired, we were in a frenzy. . . . I always figured that was the best thing that could happen to you, to be caught up with a group of people with enthusiasm for what they're doing. And how it's received was beyond our consideration."

I've had a lot of fun with Robert. And I expect to have a lot more fun. But I've never had more fun than reading the pages of this remarkable book.

—*Peter Guralnick*

Acknowledgments

I WROTE THIS BOOK WITH THE LOVE OF MY PARENTS, WHOSE DEVOTION and support has shaped my life. With the love of my brother. Of Odessa Redmond, a lifelong inspiration.

Memphis: Jim Dickinson and his family. Dickinson prefers the dark corners, and there he is a light. Mud Boy and the Neutrons: Sid Selvidge, Lee Baker, Jimmy Crosthwait, Dickinson. Belinda Killough, wittiest transcriber in the west. Adam Feibelman, diligent research. Susan Thomas. The history staff, the arts and music staff at the main library. All of those kind enough to let me interview them, especially those whom I did not quote. And everyone else who made the music.

The writers who sparked my interest: Walter Dawson, Stanley Booth, Robert Palmer, Greil Marcus, and writer Peter Guralnick, who was instrumental in bringing this book to light. Dick McDonough, stalwart agent. Betsy Uhrig, encouraging editor. Rob Bowman, Stax man. Stu Abraham.

I imposed this manuscript on several opinionated readers, and I am indebted to each of them: Joy Tremewan, Bobby Caudle Rogers, Joe Purdy and Donna Rifkin, my parents, and RJ Smith, an astute and insightful editor and a good friend.

John Fante, in *Full of Life*, must have been thinking of Tara McAdams when he wrote: "My prose, such as it was, derived from her. For I was always quitting the craft, hating it, despairing, crumpling paper and throwing it across the room. But she could forage through the discarded stuff and come up with things, and I never really knew when I was good, I thought every line I ever wrote was no better than ordinary."

Introduction

THE WORLD IN WHICH WE TRAVELED, THOUGH I COULD NOT KNOW IT AT the time, was like the spaces between the latticework of the existing world. A serpentined, lush, and tangled growth wove its way through this other place—a culture at once more dank and more vital than its counterpart. For decades, access to this other world had been unfettered and democratic, and I was lucky, stumbling onto, recognizing, a portal in the 1970s. Seeing blues giant Furry Lewis sweeping Beale Street—can, broom, pushcart, wooden leg—was even more likely in the 1950s and 1960s. Some chose to talk to the garbageman, some chose to fill his can. Furry Lewis still played the blues.

Toward the end of this book, two characters who witnessed the cultural collision of Memphis in the 1960s are talking, and one tells the other, "You were fortunate enough to witness the end of something truly great, and intelligent enough to understand some of it." History continues to confirm that what happened in Memphis was "something truly great," and if what they witnessed was the end, what I saw was the light from a dead star, limning the exchange of great ideas at work and at play. I didn't appreciate my good fortune at the time; I didn't yet realize that my experience was not shared by everyone. I witnessed the witnesses, and understood some of it, and remember most of it.

That star died, but others have appeared in its darkness. The world between the latticework still exists, populated by new faces, new old souls.

I laughed aloud during most of the writing of this book, bonked in the head again and again by the bravura and the dignity of these wild men and women. The art these people created is among the most liberating ever made. Upon rereading their story, nothing seems undoable after their accomplishments.

Murder and medical mayhem have slain the mighty since this book was first published. I dedicate this second edition to the memories of Randall Lyon, Lee Baker, Robert Palmer, and Fred Ford, and also to the ongoing artistry of the Jim Dickinson family—all with love and respect.

It Came from Memphis

CHAPTER ONE

The Dream of a Common Language

THE ROLLING STONES INTRODUCED ME NOT TO THE BLUES, BUT TO THE bluesmen. The players. On a sweltering Fourth of July, 1975, the summer before I entered ninth grade, they delayed their Memphis performance by placing a wooden stool at stage center and then bringing out a fragile black gentleman with a guitar. The crowd of 50,000 was hot and impatient, but Furry Lewis came up playing medicine shows in the 1920s and he knew more than a little about entertaining. Though solo blues wasn't what a lot of weary rednecks wanted to hear, I'm sure I was not the only new fan he won.

The next time I saw Furry, the crowd numbered less than fifty. At the end of tenth grade, an upperclassman brought him to school during lunch. He sat on a porch near a parking lot and played for a small gathering. A hat was passed. I asked how the performance had been arranged and was given Furry Lewis's phone number. So within two years of being one in 50,000 to see him at a Rolling Stones concert, I did exactly what Mick Jagger and Keith Richards had done—I phoned Furry Lewis. He invited this unknown voice to visit him, accepting my offer to bring whiskey. His brand was Ten High.

Within a year, the phone list on the linen closet door of my parent's house included the names of guitarists, piano players, Sonny "Harmonica" Blake, Saxman Brad's business card, and various schoolmates who liked to kick a soccer ball. These phone numbers were not trophies, though having them made me feel cool. I was a gangly suburban teenager, middle-class, the braces finally removed from my teeth. My neighborhood was like a thousand others across the country. The blues musicians were giving me a geographical and historical grounding in Memphis. Their lives were the product of this particular place.

At the end of eleventh grade, some friends and I pitched in to bring the piano player Mose Vinson for a lunchtime performance. When Mose rests his hand on a table, his fingers look like rows of a furrowed field. I've since learned he was the janitor for Sam Phillips at Sun Records during the pre-Elvis days, and several of his previously unreleased recordings appeared on the *Sun Blues Box*. In 1977, Vinson was a regular at a bar called Birth of the Blues. So were we, getting drunk on Billy Beer and leading parades around the club with salt shakers as castanets. Furry also played there, and the owner booked a handful of other local giants. I think the club was open less than a year.

On the morning when Mose was to perform at school, he arrived late and drunk. Our friend who'd picked him up found him half-lit and had to coax him into the car with more beer. The quick refurbishment during the ride had produced a head rush in the elderly man: He entered the auditorium staggering and slobbering. I think the end-of-lunch bell rang as his hands reached for the first notes. He could not form words. When he tried to speak or sing, he emitted deep-throated moans and grunts. Drool accumulated around his fingers on the keys. I remember the reaction of a squat senior from a rich family, a kid who could make a difference: He cackled loudly.

I still hate that kid. Perhaps because in his action I saw a part of me, that sense of detachment. In Mose Vinson's talent, I was finding meaning in this particular place on Earth, a meaning that also encompassed this student, the son of a cotton baron. The very cotton bolls which formed Mose Vinson's piano style paid this ingrate's private school tuition. The lack of respect in his life's breath exposed the disparities upon which Memphis is founded. This kid would inherit his father's civic influence and power, and the city would remain divided as his family sees it, not between rich and poor, but between whites and "niggers."

The evil behind that word lives and breathes in Memphis. The city was built on that word. Rock and roll is a response to that word. Rock and roll rejected the idea of enforced segregation, mixing cultures as it mixed musical genres. On the streets today, the populations mix, but it's a surface politeness, a charming civic trait. Oppression is not unique to Memphis, though it is neatly encapsulated here. It's the sort of environment where great art develops in obscurity. The ideas are strong because, like weeds growing in a concrete sidewalk, they must force themselves through.

Concrete sidewalks have proliferated in these times of urban sprawl. Walking out the front door to a landscape that could be anywhere has taken a new meaning since the microchip met the fiber-optic cable: Walking out the front door is no longer necessary. Today, particulars everywhere are made generalities. There is as much Cajun cooking in a Long Island fast-food joint as there is Americana at Euro-Disney. "Authenticity" is mass-produced.

This age of access, however, has not erased history and cannot completely remove an area's innate characteristics. Natural light in California is conducive to filmmaking, hot peppers grow next to fish ponds in southern Louisiana, cattle and cowboys come from the Midwest because the prairies are there. If aerial photographs could reveal energy the way infrared photographs reveal heat, Memphis would be surrounded by vectors pointing toward it: This is the place.

Memphis was founded on a Mississippi River bluff, safe from the flooding which defines the Delta south of it. Before clothing the world in cotton, the region's fertility fed Native Americans. Sun Studio, the site where black and white cultures merged as rock and roll, stands on what was a river trail heavily traveled by the Chickasaw Indians. Sun's current proprietor has the receipts from T-shirt sales to prove that people will always pass by his door.

Memphis is the capital of the large rural region that surrounds it. You can drive two hundred miles in any direction before hitting another city of size. There are small towns, and smaller ones. The Ozark Mountains are to the west; the distant Appalachian range cascades eastward from across the state, flattening into farmland before finally spilling into Memphis and the river; the Mississippi Delta sprawls south in the shape of a chicken leg, and the conversion of crops to cash has always taken place in Memphis. As a natural crossroads, the city has been influenced by many cultures, but its insulation has deterred European sophistication.

Since its founding in 1819, Memphis has been a place for innovation. Among its contributions are such ubiquitous concepts as the supermarket (Piggly Wiggly, 1916), drive-in restaurants (Fortune's, 1906), motel chains (Holiday Inn, 1952), and efficient overnight package delivery (Federal Express, 1972). Recording music is another part of Memphis's entrepreneurial spirit. The audio recording process was successful here even before the equipment was locally available. Field recordings were made of fife and drum music, work songs, field hollers, and other African expressions that mutated in the Delta. Once facilities in Memphis were available and flourishing, the artists traveled instead of the equipment. Sam Phillips gambled his cozy job recording radio transcriptions of big bands for a shot with an independent label and a new kind of music. He recognized the business of music, and his maverick attitude pointed the industry in a new direction. Oldies radio, alternative rock, and the other stops on today's dial remain a response to or re-working of the ideas he assembled under the aegis of Sun Records.

In Memphis, the studios generated human cultural collisions, not just the inanimate interactions between the listener and circular vinyl spinning at seventy-eight rotations per minute. The initial area recordings were the fiber optics of their time, enabling people to experience another culture without leaving home to do it. Though Delta blues could be imitated by anybody any-where who heard a recording, Delta bluesmen could be imitated only by those with whom they interacted. They defined regionality, the product of a distinct place.

The blues is a sophisticated music. The Delta musicians created art that was fully realized, that when assessed needs no handicap or critical crutch. As West-ern scholarship has explored broader horizons, reckoning with the subjectivity and imperialistic attitudes that distorted previous investigations, it has recog-nized the complexity of expressions once thought "primitive," recognized the traditions and heritage that produced the blues. Unlike other immigrants, when Africans came to these shores they were not permitted to preserve their culture in the new land. Africans underwent a forced transformation. Slave-owners imposed the breakup of families, the mixing of tribes, the acceptance of Christianity. What was produced was something new. Rather than a sterile hy-brid, a vibrant, vital culture emerged. Memphis has enslaved this culture; Memphis has nurtured it.

Co-opt, preempt, recycle. I first heard that description of popular culture from a Memphis musician named Jim Dickinson. Like a sponge, pop culture can absorb anything, defying the context of whatever it takes and making it part of the here and now. That's fine and dandy for the pop scene, but it's not neces-sarily good for what's being absorbed. As pop music, rock and roll has co-opted blues, gospel, and country, preempted the original artists, and recycled their techniques and ideas. We all have a story of learning that our favorite song by the Rolling Stones, Rod Stewart, or Michael Bolton did not originate with these artists; likewise, we know that Arthur "Big Boy" Crudup lan-guished in poverty while Elvis Presley got rich singing his songs. The "original artists" are crassly exploited. Diluted imitators reap fame and fortune, while the preempted musicians receive neither, nor even acknowledgment. The popularizers are not legally obligated to pay homage to their predecessors, only royalties, and often they avoid paying even those. (Chris Strachwiz, of the Arhoolie label, once suggested implementing a Miranda act for musicians, reading bluesmen their rights before they sign a contract.) Even right-minded, moral "disciples" who have tried to remunerate their predecessors have found their way thwarted by thieves calling themselves publishers who wield shady contracts that allow them to divert money. The pop industry, of which the music industry is only a part, is founded on concepts of exploitation and greed. Recycling ideas can be both a tribute and a sham.

Pop culture is novelty-hungry, and the cultural divides between the races are a quick source for new trends. When the rock and roll sound was pioneered by black artists like Ike Turner and Roy Brown, both black and white audiences perceived it as a part of rhythm and blues; there was no novelty in blacks revving up R&B. White imitations of it, however, were freakish. Whites were unable to exactly mimic black music, and their failure created another hybrid. People of all colors gawked. This interaction is really what's being discussed when people ask the question, Can whites play the blues? That phrasing misses the point. What's meant is, What do we call it when whites try to play the blues? As a definition for rock and roll, I suggest: Rock and roll was white rednecks trying to play black music. Their country music background hampered them and they couldn't do it. That's why we don't call what they made rhythm and blues.

In the 1950s, with Elvis as an icon, white audiences were ready for new artists like Little Richard and established artists like Ike Turner, whom they'd previously missed. Though rock and roll now sells everything from hamburgers to presidential candidates, white society did not readily embrace such interracial, intercultural concepts. Segregation was still the law of the land in the 1950s, and anyone who respected black culture was given the same treatment as blacks: second-rate. Only when white eyes witnessed blacks laying down their lives for their country in World War II did some begin perceiving blacks as their allies. That slight opening of the door coincided with a push from the other side. Black witnesses to their brothers' deaths—deaths for a country that enforced apartheid—moved their community to rebel en masse: the Civil Rights movement and desegregation. Despite the passage of laws and the enforcement of various race-mixing programs, this conflict is still being resolved today. Welfare, substandard housing and education, prejudice from the bank's loan desk—the violence that is a response to this covert domination is a testament to the chasm that still runs beneath our society.

This same lack of understanding between the races is responsible for the innovation of rock and roll. Most of the machinery for recording and manufacturing was owned by the whites, and when they got in the studio with blacks, a bridge had to be established. An example of the cultural collision is cited by the aforementioned Jim Dickinson. "There's a box set of Little Richard outtakes that's out on CD, with Earl Palmer on the drums. Brilliant drummer, one of the most influential in early rock music. You hear the first take of, I think, 'Lucille,' and they run it down several times till they get the master. Lee Allen, the sax player, plays the same solo from the first cut to the last. But Earl Palmer starts out playing a shuffle! He's not playing the eighth note thing that became Little Richard's signature. He's shuffling. You also hear these insets of white voices on the talkback, and one of 'em is Cosmo Matassa, the engineer, and the other one must be the producer Art Rupe. And Rupe is saying the most insensitive, typically white things. But those had to be said in order to make the shuffle into what we now know as rock and roll. The racial collision, it has to be there."

The forces of cultural collision struck thrice in the Memphis area, first with the Delta blues, then with Sun, then Stax. These sounds touched the soul of society; unlike passing fads, these sounds have remained with us. By definition, most of popular culture is disposable, but Memphis music has refused to disappear. In electrified civilization, even when stripped of the particular racial and social context in which it was born, what happened in Memphis remains the soundtrack to cultural liberation.

Jim Dickinson has another saying that goes something like this: The best songs don't get recorded, the best recordings don't get released, and the best releases don't get played. It's the antithesis to corporate music mentality, and it also explains why Memphis is so full of treasures. Though no city has had more of a lasting impact on modern culture, Memphis has never been a company town. The forces have all been independent, renegade. Dickinson's maxim defends obscurity by attacking popular culture's drive toward mediocrity. Reaching the most people through the lowest common denominator denigrates individuality, destroys artistry. There is no reason that every song has to be a hit, but there's every reason for the song to *be*.

In 1978, a depressed girl I was dating recommended an album to me, *Big Star 3rd*. It so happened that Big Star was from Memphis, though I was not familiar with them or their first two albums. *3rd* had been recorded in 1974 and languished on a shelf for four years after being roundly rejected by record companies. Everything about it was mysterious. The company that released it was so small that the label on one side of the vinyl listed all of the songs and the label on the other side was a generic design. Yet a major name like Steve Cropper, playing guitar, was printed right there on the back. I recognized a couple of the other musicians, most from Memphis and among them two of my favorites, Lee Baker and Jim Dickinson. The record came with an extensive essay full of references I didn't know. When I played the album, it was un-like any I'd ever heard. One side began with backward-sounding strings and the other with something like cartoon music. Neither opening song sounded like the beginning of an album. Entering *Big Star 3rd* was like entering a movie after it's begun.

Which, in a way, it was. The band leader was Alex Chilton, who had found fame eleven years earlier at sixteen when he first entered a studio and recorded "The Letter" with the Box Tops. By the time of *3rd's* release, his interest had moved to other types of music. *3rd,* I came to understand, was a response to his career to date: the commercial success and artistic frustration of the Box Tops, the artistic success and commercial frustration of Big Star. It was a record of introspection. The darkness of the music was immediately gripping, and the elusiveness of the lyrics encouraged repeated listenings. It was almost three years—I was by then unhappy in college—before I discovered the lines, "Get me out of here/I hate it here/Get me out of here." That I cannot readily name the song is indicative of the record's lasting beauty.

Since 1978, *Big Star 3rd* has been rereleased at least twice. (As per Dickin-son's maxim, one of the best songs, "Dream Lover," was not included until the second issue.) The band's other two albums, widely praised, poorly dis-tributed, and long out of print, have also been made newly available. The influence of Alex Chilton and this once-overlooked group has become so widespread that Big Star practically defines a category in modern rock. *3rd's* sound may have been a generation removed from cultural collision, but its re-sult reverberated with the bluesmen: obscurity. The bluesmen did not stop making music after the 1920s and 1930s; they were just no longer recorded. Their material did not hinge on the critical acclaim they may have briefly en-joyed. Rather, it was an extension of their being, and if a record man was will-ing to part with a ten-dollar bill to hear them do their thing, that was fine. But if not, it didn't stop the music. With their lives and not just their words the blues artists had taught those following them to trust their ideas. The audi-ence's response becomes secondary.

The rediscovery of the Delta blues artists began in the later 1950s, shortly after the introduction of Elvis and rock and roll. The first rock and roll audi-ence was also the first blues renaissance audience, and those listening—the witnesses—bore the dual responsibilities of keeping an old tradition alive and of creating a new genre. By the middle and late sixties, the audience had so ex-panded and the industry become so secure that, although less than ten years earlier the witnesses couldn't imagine a career in music, by Chilton's genera-tion it was every kid's dream. The difference, in a word, was the Beatles.

For me, the Beatles were a Saturday morning TV cartoon long before I appreciated their social impact. They allowed my generation to take for granted the possibility of a career in rock music, or even rock music journalism. In my rock and roll youth, the music was losing its social meaning and becoming a service industry, becoming, in fact, a cartoon. But in Memphis, I'd felt the bluesmen's power.

In May 1978, when my sense of place was solidifying and I was distressed that such great music as Furry Lewis and *Big Star 3rd* seemed available only to locals, I was exposed to a Memphis band called Mud Boy and the Neutrons. Rock and roll witnesses all, their music was the missing link between the Rolling Stones and Furry Lewis. Mud Boy and the Neutrons were four white guys who fused the washboard, the electric guitar, and field hollers; where the Stones had come up emulating blues records, Mud Boy emulated bluesmen. I saw them perform as part of a two-day music festival honoring the city's heritage. Gospel music, rock and roll, blues, and country all shared the same stage. Part of the event's pleasure was experiencing the common spirit in such diverse music.

On the main stage, a Delta blues group was winding up their set. Alex Chilton was in the artist's tent and, though not scheduled to play, he'd been inspired. The event was loose enough to allot him some time, and several members of Mud Boy joined him. Their impromptu set, including a menacing run-through of Chilton's hit, "The Letter," introduced punk rock to Memphis at large. Before Mud Boy began, a member of their entourage, Guru Biloxi, came out carrying a spear and ranting, pushing the energy cautiously high. Wound up tight like a heart attack, stomping the stage, Chilton introduced the band—"some very good friends, some very close personal friends of mine," he shouted like a man about to pull the trigger—and Mud Boy kicked into Chuck Berry's "Little Queenie." The four core members were backed by a drummer and a bassist; three dancing girls were part of the act.

"Dancing" doesn't convey what I saw these women do. I was seventeen and so drunk on cheap white wine that I had to put my hand over one eye to rightly hear what was going on. The music was rumbling the way a house shakes when a heavy truck passes out front. There was a sense to the chaos, a sense not so much based on beat or rhythm, though this music was as full of both as any could be without exploding—but a sense based on emotion. The women were dancing, yeah, they were dancing all right. They were fucking the music. They were slithering up and down that rumble. This was fuck music. Not the wet sensuality of Al Green, not the sultry innuendo of the early blues queens. This was the guttural howl of the bump and grind, the madness of urge, the flaunting of that which we've been taught to repress. The power of the blues—the violence, the energy, the sex—was laid bare.

The plug was pulled on their performance. The band was one song into what was the set of a lifetime when the authorities decided it was too much truth for the public good. Johnny Woods and Prince Gabe had each performed that day on the same stage, and they had told the truth. Grandma Dixie Davis would perform parlor piano later on that same stage, and she would tell the truth. Phineas Newborn Jr.—God rest his weary soul—would speak the gospel; B. B. King, Big Sam, Carla Thomas. But only Mud Boy's truth was censored.

The band revolted. There was a shouting match, a sit-in. The audience responded with raised fists. Oho Mick Jagger, oho Johnny Rotten, the real shit went down that day. Rock and roll busted loose from its chains and wasn't a commodity to place between radio commercials or at the top of charts. Music came back to life that afternoon with all the energy of Elvis Presley's 1954 hips.

Mud Boy, for the most part, revels in their obscurity. They continue to perform occasionally, and in 1993, seven years after their first album, twenty-one years after their inception, they even graced their audience with a second record. Naturally, it's on a small French label and difficult to find in the United States. Personally, that no longer frustrates me. If people need to find this band, they will. Those who have continue to come out of the woodwork when they perform, responding to the tribal shamans who call on our behalf to the spirit voice in the woods.

Memphis music is an approach to life, defined by geography, dignified by the bluesmen. This is the big city surrounded by farmland, where snug businessmen gamble on the labor of fieldhands, widening the gap between them, testing the uneasy alliance. Memphis has always been a place where cultures came together to have a wreck: black and white, rural and urban, poor and rich. The music in Memphis is more than a soundtrack to these confrontations. It is the document of it. To misquote W. C. Handy's "Beale Street Blues," If the Mississippi River could talk, a lot of great folks would have to get up and walk.

One summer day, before I entered the twelfth grade, I spotted a couple of tourists downtown. Bullish on Memphis, I stopped to offer assistance. They were French, in town only for the day, and expressed an interest in Memphis music. They got in my car and, though it was my custom to phone first, we showed up unannounced at Furry Lewis's rundown duplex. Over the past year I'd visited him regularly enough that he and his lady friends recognized me when I appeared. This was 1978. Furry was near eighty. I was seventeen. Furry was black. I was white. The French tourists were wearing short pants.

There were hellos all around as we were welcomed, and, once seated, the question was raised about Furry playing the guitar. Seems like he might could play the tourists a song, uh-huh. Did my friends drink whiskey, he wanted to know. I was translating. I didn't speak French, but their schooling hadn't prepared them for Furry's accent. One tourist asked for water, but then decided he'd drink with us. There was a liquor store around the corner, and a friend of Furry's volunteered to get the bottle for us, how much did we want, a half gallon? It was about four in the afternoon. Furry had his guitar out, tuning. Beautiful. I recently found a cassette recording of all this. Thinking only of myself, and only of the present, a half gallon seemed a bit much. Don't try to take *me*. When we sent the friend off for our whiskey with just two dollars, enough for a half pint, barely a swallow all the way around, Furry put the guitar down and said, "The rheumatism got me this afternoon, I can't get myself together."

French wasn't the only language I was learning that day.

CHAPTER TWO

Tell 'Em Phillips Sentcha

WHEN NIGHT SETTLED ON THE TOWN IN 1949, MEMPHIS, DESPITE ITS big-city aspirations, was as quiet as a distant country crossroads. Citizens sighed in the glow of their American happiness. In November of that year, after months of test patterns, Memphis's first TV station began filling homes with the warmth that radiated from their newfangled sets. "We the People," "Circus Animals," and the puppet show "Kukla, Fran & Ollie" all confirmed that life after World War II was good.

In the older medium of radio, 1948 had been a watershed year. In late October, the city's sixth station, WDIA, confronted the audience's lack of interest in yet another place on the dial playing country, pop, and light classical. With nothing to lose but their failing year-old operation, owners Bert Ferguson and John Pepper enlisted Nat. D. Williams, a nationally syndicated black Memphis journalist, as host of a forty-five-minute afternoon show. The response was so overwhelming—including the mandatory bomb threats—that by the summer of 1949 WDIA was the first station in the United States with an entire cast of black disc jockeys.

The impact was enormous. The bullets of World War II had recognized no color, and the movement toward civil rights was fomented by the returning servicemen and their demands for equality. In an era of condoned, organized racism, WDIA became a community bulletin board, a public institution that celebrated instead of insulted 40 percent of Memphis's population.

"I remember when the black ambulances could not haul white people," says Gatemouth Moore, the station's first gospel programmer. "They had a white company, I'll never forget, called Thompson's. I was on my way to the station, and when I come around the curve there was the ambulance from

11

S. W. Quall's with the door open, and there was a white lady laying in the ditch, bleeding. And they were waiting for Thompson's to come and pick her up. Quall's couldn't pick her up. I guess I waited thirty or forty minutes and still no ambulance. They tell me that the lady died. So I came to WDIA and told the tale. I said, 'Look here.' I said, 'Black folks put their hands in your flour and make your bread, they cook the meat, they clean up your house, and here's this fine aristocratic white lady laying in the ditch bleeding and they won't let black hands pick her up and rush her to the hospital.' And the next week, they changed that law where a black ambulance could pick up anybody. I got that changed on WDIA."

In a few years, WDIA would be the most powerful station in Memphis, but the repercussions of its format were felt immediately. WHBQ, an older station also in financial straits, put economics before apartheid and, when "the mother station of Negroes" went off the air at sunset, WHBQ began broadcasting rhythm and blues. Not ready to hire a black personality, they relied instead on one of their dulcet-toned announcers, Gorden Lawhead. He named the program after a Broadway play, "Red, Hot & Blue," but it was none of those. Lawhead epitomized the white radio announcer of the era, as innocuous as its pop music: Perry Como's "Some Enchanted Evening," Evelyn Knight's "A Little Bird Told Me," Gene Autry's "Rudolph the Red-Nosed Reindeer." Lawhead neither understood nor appreciated R&B.

In the spacious night, after parents retreated to the soothing murmur of TV, the baby boomers found comfort in their radios. They kept the volume low enough not to attract attention, and the light from the dial fought off the total darkness. A little fiddling with the tuner brought in creatures from another dimension. Many of the local stations vanished with the sun, leaving chasms filled by voices from Mexico, from Nashville, from alien places that played alien music. Pop had a certain glide to it, but this music went *thump*. *Thump thump*. It was mysterious how far the sound traveled to reach beneath the cotton blankets.

The distance was twice what these future witnesses to the birth of rock and roll realized. Many of these records originated right in their own town but had to travel to distant radio stations to achieve their popularity. Howlin' Wolf. Rosco Gordon. Junior Parker's "Mystery Train." The music sounded crazy when border radio stations sent it through the reaches of dark night, but that paled beside the frightening live performances of the artists, just a few miles away and tanked on bad whiskey. Beale Street was in downtown Memphis, and it was the Mississippi Delta's largest plantation. It was where black people could relax, unencumbered by Jim Crow because few whites patronized Beale. Those who did were mostly landlords, and they liked to see a busy place.

Beale Street and the surrounding neighborhood was the mid-South's African-American commerce center, adjacent to downtown Memphis, the white commerce center. Beale was more compact and always hopping. This is the street where the zoot suit was created, where a single amateur night produced Rufus Thomas, B. B. King, Bobby Bland, and Johnny Ace, and the clubs launched Howlin' Wolf, Hank Crawford, and Phineas Newborn Jr. "Wide open" is the term usually applied to Beale.

"Gambling, drinking, policy shaking—had a joint on every corner," recalls pianist Booker T. Laury, born in 1914. "They had a restaurant in the front, you get hot dog and fish sandwiches, and ladies in the next room had a little place set aside for a dance hall. Every crap house had a dance hall. On back a little further, they had a dice table, and the men leave the women up there to be entertained whilst I'd play the blues to 'em. The men would be back there shooting a few craps. Every day, that was the routine. The doors didn't close. They stayed open all night. Changed shifts from twelve to twelve."

The multitude of clubs on Beale Street established the thriving music scene in the city and, by attracting and nurturing regional talent, was directly responsible for both Sun and Stax Records. The core of venues on Beale spawned other clubs around town and also across the river in West Memphis, Arkansas. There was plenty of work for a large number of bands, orchestras, and soloists, and the constant flow of people in and out of Memphis assured an audience. The variety of styles, the opportunities to mix them together, and the plenitude of venues helped forge the groundwork for a musical aura in Memphis that remains to this day.

In 1949, eleven years after Orson Welles's "War of the Worlds" demonstrated the power of radio, another voice from outer space chewed up Memphis and spit it back in its ear. Channeling the same spirit that had lain dormant since tuning Robert Johnson's guitar at the crossroads, a white disc jockey interrupted the satiny WHBQ broadcast. "Dee-gaw!" the radio squawked, and it chilled the parents' bones because they heard something different and knew it meant change. "Dee-gaw!" the detached voice drawled, and the kids leaned closer to the speaker. They heard a jumble of words that was like Captain Midnight's code; you had to listen closely to keep up. Dewey Phillips wasn't coming in for a landing; he was taking off. The excitement was intensified by this alien's proximity. Broadcasting from right downtown "on the magazine—uh, mezzanine floor of the Chisca Hotel," he was no farther away than where a visiting relative or a father's war buddy might stay.

Elvis Presley and Dewey Phillips at WHBQ radio, circa 1956. Photo courtesy of Jim Dickinson.

Thump. Thump thump.

Daddy-O Dewey. He is best known as the first disc jockey to play Elvis Presley, but the legacy of Dewey Phillips is every attempt by a white Memphis kid to play black music, from the first generation of rock and roll right through Stax Records. His listeners learned not to distinguish between races or genres. He demonstrated that the boundaries of "normal" were arbitrary and heralded a freedom that society shunned. Many took heart in the realization that they might be able, like Dewey, to parlay their own particular weirdness, oddity, or eccentricity into a career. Nowhere else in society was such nonconformist thought publicly condoned. It has taken forty years of corporate rock and roll to rebuild the walls Dewey Phillips broke down.

The very fact that Dewey got on the air indicates the force of his character. He was everything that a deejay in 1949 was not. He had been spinning records in the phonograph department at W. T. Grant's in downtown Memphis, howling over the store's intercom and causing a roo-kus. Rocking and rolling. People, including Sam Phillips (no relation), would come in just to listen to his mad ramblings. Management found that Dewey was unmanageable, but they couldn't argue with the crowds he drew. Something about whatever it was he was doing worked.

Grant's was on Main Street, near WHBQ's Gayoso Hotel location. Lawhead and the other radio announcers were more than familiar with Dewey, who accosted them regularly, excited and impassioned, stepping on their feet, sputtering while he pushed whatever new release had caught his ear—and, he was sure, would catch ears all over Memphis if one of the deejays would just play it on the radio. And kindly plug his department at Grant's.

"Dewey was not physically well organized," says Lawhead. But he got what he wanted. It's said that Dewey, yearning for an on-air time slot, visited "Red, Hot & Blue" one night and, pained by how wrong Lawhead was for the job, stepped into the hallway beyond the announcer's sight and set a trash can aflame. When Lawhead ran for the fire extinguisher, Dewey jumped for the microphone. Callers phoned in their support. Lawhead says, "I thought, God, has radio come to this? That we're putting this character Dewey on the air?"

Dewey began with forty-five minutes but soon commanded a three-hour show, five nights a week: "Red, Hot & Blue," nine to midnight. Dewey always called it "The hottest thing in the country."

"As screwed up as he eventually got," says Jim Dickinson, a fan he inspired who would record with the Rolling Stones, "Dewey never lost that warm and almost loving feeling when he was broadcasting. You could tell it was an act of communion between you and this crazy guy. And that he was really playing this music for a purpose, unlike all the other insincere bastards at the time."

For a decade, Dewey reigned supreme. And supremely insane. According to Charles Raiteri, who has chronicled much of Dewey's life and produced an album of his radio shows (*Red Hot & Blue*, Zu-Zazz Records), "B. B. King called him Daddy-O. The [Howlin'] Wolf, to whom all whites were suspect, called him 'brother.' He played draw poker with Johnny Ace. And he and Ike Turner shared co-billing as talent scouts for Sam's Sun label." That's heavy company in an era when sipping cool water from the wrong fountain on a hot day could cost a life.

By 1954, when Sam Phillips cut his acetate of Elvis's first single, "That's All Right," Dewey was the natural test market. He had the kids' ears. The story goes that Dewey screened it over the air and liked it so much that, while playing it continuously—yakking his patter over it all the while—he phoned Elvis's mom to find the kid and bring him to the station. When he showed up, Dewey told him not to cuss. He surreptitiously opened the mike but acted like he was spinning a record, and casually began asking questions. Dewey first established what high school Elvis went to, indirectly informing the listeners that no matter how black the record sounded, the kid was a honky. When it was all done, Elvis asked, "Aren't you going to interview me, Mr. Phillips?"

A white kid sounding black was perfect for Sam Phillips, and perfect for Dewey Phillips. Sam knew he could market it; Dewey liked the confusion. While other deejays kept to a mellifluous format, he made car wrecks of genres, defying the pop charts by whimsically counting down his own top ten, Dewey's Top Ten, the hottest ten records in Dewey country at this very moment in time—and changing fast.

"It was years before I figured out that this stuff I heard on Dewey Phillips's show wasn't popular music," says Dickinson. "I certainly didn't realize that he was playing things that nobody else played. Like 'Red Hot' by Billy Lee Riley —I didn't realize that wasn't a hit until I moved to Texas for college. He'd play Little Richard, then he'd play Sister Rosetta Tharpe. He'd play a country song, he'd play a rock song, he'd play a blues song. And the mindset I learned, listening to that music, is what has enabled me to make a living in the music business."

Indeed, the Dewey Phillips mindset, a reflection of the city's geographic and economic crossroads, defined Memphis music for years to come. He could propel a song like Carl Perkins's "Blue Suede Shoes" to national attention, where it became the first song to simultaneously top the pop, country, and R&B charts. His fans—and almost without exception every Memphis musician raised during his era was a fan—knew no boundaries. Do not tune in now for three hours of light classical; do not tune in now for three hours of down-home blues; do not tune in now with expectations of any sort whatsoever, because never has so untamed a person had so much broadcast power behind him, and whatever happens in the next three hours will be completely different from whatever you heard last week and bear little or no similarity to what you will hear next week, podnuh podnuh.

"I was fourteen and I didn't realize that Dewey wasn't being heard all over America," says Don Nix, who, along with his schoolmates, would capture the Dewey energy in the Mar-Keys, a band of white boys who broke racial barriers playing the black circuit in 1961. "I thought everybody in every town had a disc jockey that in one night, three hours, you could hear anything you wanted to hear. I wasn't allowed to listen to the radio at night, so my brother and I used to sneak the radio under the covers and listen after my parents went to bed. He played Little Walter and Johnny Ace, but also Frank Sinatra, Nat King Cole, and Jimmy Reed. I listened to WDIA too, but not as much, because WDIA played only one kind of music. Dewey played it all."

Dewey played what he liked, and if he liked something a lot, he'd repeat it. "One of the things I remember most, and anybody who listened to Dewey back then will tell you, was a record called 'Tell Me Why You Like Roosevelt' by a gospel guy named Otis Jackson," says Milton Pond, a longtime Memphis record retailer and collector. "It was never on the charts anywhere, but Dewey made it a hit. He liked it and played it on his program every night." Dewey made hits of such contrasting songs as a gospel number called "Down on My Knees" and an R&B song called "Drunk." When Dewey said, "It's a hit," there was no other authority to defy him.

Future Sun musician Randy Haspel remembers Dewey "unashamedly" playing "Heartbreak Hotel" twenty times in a row. Conversely, as record producer Jim Blake adds, what Dewey didn't like, he wouldn't play. "He'd pick up records in the middle, screech 'em off, 'Well that ain't gonna get it.'"

What got it was that the kids—and anybody else who dared to listen— could hear a real person playing real records and could pick up on the enthusiasm. "Nobody knew what Dewey looked like," continues Blake. "We imagined he looked like a fucking Martian. And when he got his TV show [in late 1956] and we saw him, he *was* a Martian. Dewey was hip, he was beat, he was everything all at the same time."

"I didn't listen to black music but I listened to Dewey," says Roland Janes, the legendary Sun guitarist. "He played all kinds of records, but you listened to Dewey as much for Dewey as for the music he played."

Dewey's patter was integral to his show. An offhand phrase one night would become street lingo the next day. He tumbled through a roster of characters, drawing from popular Red Skelton sketches and from people he met on Beale Street. He'd do poor imitations of Tennessee Ernie Ford or Dizzy Dean and fumble with crude sound effects. He'd whip his head from position to position carrying on conversations with himself, each personality occupying a particular place in his mind. The attentive listener heard a song somewhere between the one-man dialogue. This is a straight transcription, Dewey doing all the voices, and beneath him some poor vocalist fighting to be heard: "Ain't that right, Diz? That's right. Did you call Sam, podnuh? No, I gotta call Sam, Diz. [Screeching:] Hi, Phillips, how you, Phillips? How you getting along, Lucy Mae, what's the matter w'you? I'm looking for my husband, Phillips. I ain't seen your husband. You'd better call Sam."

"Mostly what I remember about Dewey," says Jimmy Crosthwait, Memphis's premier white washboard player, "was his beer ads. Falstaff was a sponsor, and he'd say, 'If you can't drink it, freeze it and eat it. Open up a rib and pour it in.'"

Another of Dewey's sponsors was Poplar Tunes, a record store on Poplar Avenue run by Joe Cuoghi, John Novarese, and Frank Berretta. Poplar Tunes's early success allowed the owners to branch out, with Cuoghi founding Hi Records—home to Ace Cannon and Bill Black, and later, under the guidance of Willie Mitchell, home to Al Green; Novarese established a jukebox agency; and Berretta ran the store, which sold retail to the public, wholesale to jukebox operators, and served smaller stores as a one-stop (the middle man who carried recordings from all the various distributors). Cuoghi was a private man, and much to his chagrin, Dewey loved to say his name on the air, embellishing it as far as he could stretch it. "Go on down to Poplar Tunes, get you a wheelbarrow full of—full of—[searching] full of mad dogs, see Papa Joe-Joe Da-Coogie [dramatic pause before yelling] and tell 'em Phillips sentcha."

Milton Pond thought he was the luckiest guy in the world to get a job at Poplar Tunes when he was seventeen. He remembers: "Dewey had made Joe Cuoghi legendary, a household name. But Joe Cuoghi didn't want to be famous. He used to hate whenever Dewey would come in the store because he created such chaos. Dewey'd get back behind the counter and handle records, put 'em on the turntable, didn't care if there was two or two hundred people in the store. He'd say, 'Joe! Come here, buddy boy, I want you to hear this. Hottest record in the country!' He'd crank the volume up, Joe would say, 'Turn that goddamn shit down, there's customers in here.'" "Every time Dewey was in Poplar Tunes," adds Jim Blake, "Cuoghi's asshole would clamp up and he'd chomp down a little harder on that cigar."

"Dewey was great to introduce you to stuff," says the Memphis painter Charlie Miller, "but he'd talk all through the songs. I really wanted to listen to the music, so I liked WDIA better." Many of Dewey's coworkers never adjusted to his style. "The guys at HBQ didn't like Dewey," Pond says. "He did more by accident than a lot of those guys did on purpose. That's what really bothered them. They said, 'Look at this guy, he's a goddamn lush, he's a pill-head, he doesn't know what the fuck he's doing. Yet people love him and he's breaking records. How can Dewey do this and we can't?'"

Dewey was a pillhead, an addiction resulting from injuries suffered in a couple of car wrecks. But when he was successful, not even pain pills could slow him down. Riding high in late 1956, Dewey began an afternoon simulcast on radio and TV. "Phillips' Pop Shop" aired daily from 3:30 to 4:30, and the soda fountains didn't know what hit them. Instead of hanging out there, the kids raced home after school to catch Dewey's act on TV. It's an exaggeration to say that Dewey's show made Ernie Kovacs, the great madman of early 1950s television, look like a funeral, but not by much. Certainly Dewey was the rock and roll Kovacs, whether sticking his face in the camera or walking behind it to bust the fourth wall. He was unscripted, unplanned, untethered, and completely live on two media. His breakaway times for each were not simultaneous, and he loved the confusion of not knowing which audience he was addressing. He kept his nighttime radio slot throughout his TV reign, and though it would have been easier, "Pop Shop's" director says they never considered losing the radio simulcast. Dewey enjoyed the pay and the power.

"Pop Shop" aired before there was a concept for playing records on television. The national broadcast of "American Bandstand" was not until the late summer of 1957, and making short films to illustrate the music was decades away from popularity. Dewey's show originated from the same studio as local TV wrestling, and it drew from the same muse. The magic of rock and roll was capturing the manic moment, and instead of music television, or phonograph or lip-synch television, Dewey created rock and roll television. He let the music inspire him, and the show's object was to seize the inspiration.

"Dewey Phillips on television was one of the strangest things I think I've ever seen, anywhere," says Memphis recording executive John Fry. "They would make technical operations very apparent, violating the cardinal rule of broadcasting. They spent half the time on television dragging the cameras out in front of the audience. And Dewey would carry on arguments with the guy at the radio station about when they were going to do a commercial. They would argue back and forth on the air. It was crazy."

The dynamics of the TV show grew from Dewey's relationship with his assistant, Harry Fritzius. By the time "Pop Shop" debuted, Dewey was thirty years old, a large man and somewhat avuncular. Fritzius was twenty-four, scrawny and vigorous. Both had instinctual timing and a flair for the absurd, and like many great partnerships, theirs fed on mutual disdain.

Fritzius had moved to Memphis from Blytheville, Arkansas, when he was eighteen to attend the Memphis Academy of Arts. The school had sought him, offering an unsolicited scholarship. At the end of his first term, serious Harry Fritzius won his class prize. Shortly thereafter, his first solo painting exhibition nearly sold out and drew a rave review from Memphis's daily newspaper, the *Commercial Appeal*. Several pieces were mentioned in the article, and one, *The Young Artist,* was reproduced. "*The Young Artist,*" the critic wrote, "was inspired by a quotation which is by the artist himself: 'I wander through deserted rooms where memories hang like tattered things upon the walls . . . and loneliness is always at my side.' Here, the gaunt, ashen-faced young artist sits alone under the dreadful glare of a bare light bulb in a deep brown room which is like a recess in the mind, and on the walls are the curled parchment-like scraps of paper, the tattered memories."

Hardly the makings for a manic sidekick.

Upon completion of his art degree, Fritzius took a job at WHBQ-TV, working as a set designer, floor director, and director. His innate ability and creativity were quickly recognized, making his transition onto "Pop Shop" easy. "We were all on camera," says Durelle Durham, the show's director. "We were required to fill an hour's time with video, and you couldn't just follow Dewey around. So it was up to the studio crew to make stuff up. We'd show engineers working on equipment, people climbing the light grid—anything to have something crazy going on while Dewey spun the record. Harry just carved himself a permanent slot in the show."

Serious Harry loosened up. Concrete would loosen after enough time around Dewey. "Whatever his medium," the *Commercial Appeal* said of Harry's second solo art show, "whatever his approach to his subject, he attacks the matter with complete originality." For "Pop Shop" Harry created "Harry," a character that Durham describes as Fritzius's alter ego, as distant from the artist's nature as could be imagined. "Harry" wore a lecherous trench coat, rubber boots, a hunter's hat, and a mask that was either a cockeyed ape or a caveman. This character did not speak; he just acted, pantomimed, and ran amok. To transform himself, Harry entered the dressing room alone; Durham remembers that he never took off the mask even in front of the studio crew.

"Harry" put Fritzius on Dewey's level. Crew members agree that Harry and Dewey did not particularly get along; Harry felt Dewey was beneath him. "Everybody felt superior to Dewey," says one crew member. "He was a coun-

Dewey Phillips and company. Left to right: Harry Fritzius, Dewey Phillips, rockabilly star Billy Lee Riley, Phillips's associate Claude Cockrell, Sam Phillips. Photo courtesy of Dot Phillips.

try boy that people liked. He had a mass appeal to the kids with his craziness, but you wouldn't ascribe much to his intelligence."

"Dewey played records, and Harry was the creative artist on the show," Durham says. "Harry was quite an actor, quite an improviser. You never knew what he was going to do. We interviewed people like Jane Russell and just every star that came to town would be a guest on Dewey's show. We had a starlet there one day and Harry got a chocolate pie and told her to hit him with it. As she was reaching to slam it into his face, he grabbed her wrist and smashed it right into her face. When he put that mask on, he became an entirely different person. It was just uncanny. He was two personalities, he was truly that personality that he was playacting.

"One of his routines was to open mail on the air. Harry would stomp on these packages, kick them around, and then see what he had smashed. One day there was a round tube, like a Quaker Oats container, that he beat up and then held up to the lens and pulled the top off. It was a hornet's nest with live hornets in it. When the cameramen fled, no one was sure they would come back. It turned out that Harry had sent it to himself. We all had cans of bug spray the rest of the week, and that became a running gag."

Another time, Harry took a cameraman up to the building's roof. At his instruction, the camera tilted up from him to the sky, then back down. Harry was gone. People watching at home figured he had jumped off the roof and

someone called the fire department's rescue team. When they showed up un-
expectedly, Harry put them on the air.

Harry Fritzius, tech crew, made appearances on the show as floor director.
His hair was getting a little longer, he grew sideburns, and there was a glint of
craziness in his eye. The edge of live TV, where there is no safety net, appealed
to him. He also continued his work on the station's other shows. On Christmas Eve, WHBQ broadcast Christmas carols to the image of Harry Fritzius,
not as madcap sidekick but as serious art student, painting a Madonna and
child live in the studio. Over the course of a few hours, he created the classic
image and when he was done, the station went off the air. Jim Dickinson, an
ardent fan of "Pop Shop" ("I never saw anything funnier on television, period"), went to the studio to look at the painting. "On television, it was black
and white and looked perfectly straight. At the studio, I saw that the faces
were green, the hair was orange, there was purple in it—he'd Harry'ed it. And
never cracked a smile."

When "American Bandstand" went national in August of 1957, ABC pres-
sured WHBQ to run it in the after-school time slot occupied by Dewey. The
affiliate was forced to defy the network. "Pop Shop" was too popular. The
network feed still came into the station, and whenever Dewey or the show's
director felt like incorporating a taste of "Bandstand," which had yet to debut
in Memphis, they didn't hesitate to cut in. "They'd punch up the picture por-
tion off the network and you'd see these kids in Philadelphia dancing," says
John Fry. "You had no idea where it was coming from, and they were dancing
to a different song so it was all out of time. For a period of months we'd see
this bizarre live television picture coming from somewhere without having
any idea what it was. He made pieces of 'American Bandstand' just another ingredient that he put into the stew."

"I remember watching 'Pop Shop' when they cut in Jerry Lee Lewis from
'Bandstand,'" says Dickinson. "I'm sure Dewey felt like he owned the Memphis artists and had the right to show it." He used the same proprietary air to
justify stealing a test pressing from Elvis in California. The singer was working
on *Jailhouse Rock,* his third film, when he paid Dewey's way to visit him. On the
MGM lot, they met the actor Yul Brynner. "You a short mother, ain'tcha?" was
Dewey's response, and his ticket home.

While there, he'd pilfered a copy of "Teddy Bear," still weeks away from
release. Back on his TV show, Dewey boasted about his connections with the
superstar and announced that he was going to give Memphis a preview of ol'
Elvis. And, against all rules, he played the unreleased test pressing. Never one
for understatement, he repeated the preview the next day, as he no doubt in-

tended to do for as long as he was the only disc jockey with a copy. While Dewey was building up to spinning it, the costumed Harry appeared at his side. Harry looked down at the turntable, looked up at the camera, manipulated a quizzical look on his mask, and as Dewey's face turned to disbelief, Harry put the record in his mouth and chewed it into little pieces.

After six months of resistance, WHBQ finally yielded to ABC. On Monday, January 6, 1958, Dewey's show was rescheduled to midnight and renamed "Night Beat." "American Bandstand" assumed its "rightful" time. After a solid dose of Dewey Phillips, Dick Clark was completely unhip.

On Thursday, January 9, the fourth night of the new show, "Night Beat" was abruptly cancelled. "Harry" had gotten out of hand. The incident involved a life-size cutout of Jayne Mansfield that hung on the set behind the turntables. During the usual mayhem, the costumed Harry stood in front of it, his back to the camera, and, according to the evening *Press Scimitar*, "carried on some foolishness." In popular lore, his actions have become grander, more outrageous and suggestive. Director Durelle Durham was there: "He pinched her on the rear and turned his back to the camera, loosened his belt and his zipper, you've done it yourself a million times, and retucked his shirt. He did it with his back to the camera and that was construed as him unzipping himself and playing with that life-size cutout. But it was pressure from ABC that really put Dewey off the air. We all knew the midnight show didn't have the same spunk that it had in the afternoon. We were a very, very popular program."

An old movie ran the following night in Dewey's time slot. TV manager Bill Grumbles fired Fritzius and was quoted in the *Press Scimitar* as saying, "This has been the most miserable week I've spent in broadcasting." Of Harry, he said, "He is very talented, if he could just discipline his talent."

Fritzius could not be reached for comment, but a friend quoted him: "This is probably the best thing that ever happened to me. I'm twenty-five, and it's time I found something to do with my life." The article continues, "The same friend said: 'He can be a very nice person when he doesn't get into one of his moods, and then he lets the pixie part of him overrule his better judgment.'"

True to his word, Harry Fritzius left Memphis, to pursue his artistic career in New York. A play he wrote, *Summer Is a Game We Play*, won a competition and was performed off-Broadway. Then he moved to the West Coast, taking a minor role in the TV series "The Alaskans," and painting.

In the mid-1980s, when Charles Raiteri, who worked at WHBQ for nearly two decades, was seeking information on Harry for a screenplay about Phillips, everyone he encountered spoke of him with the highest respect. Raiteri says, "When rumors were floating around the station that Harry was gay, he called his crew together one night, took them down the street to the Normal Tea Room [named for the neighborhood], and explained to them all about what being gay was and that he was gay. And they accepted that and that was the end of it.

"Anybody who ever worked with Harry described him as a genius. They never talked about anybody else that way. They all thought he was the most talented guy that ever lived. When I was trying to find him, I heard rumors that he was preaching in Greenville, Mississippi, that he'd fallen off an oil barge, things like that. Eventually, a friend of mine found him in San Francisco. I had seen a review of an art show that Harry had there, and the tone of this review made him sound like a very respected, well-known artist. His stuff was also being shown in Europe. This friend said Harry was living in a great big loft, and he had these gigantic paintings all over the place, lying on the floor, everywhere. And he was drinking vodka from the bottle and smoking continuously, and he would finish a cigarette and flick it across the room on his paintings. At that time, this guy said that he didn't think Harry had much more than a year to live. He soon had a heart attack and died."

After "Pop Shop's" demise, WHBQ's only local music program was a Saturday afternoon show hosted by Wink Martindale, later of "Tic Tac Dough" fame. "Every kid resented Wink Martindale hosting 'Dance Party,'" explains Jim Blake, "because we remembered him on 'Space Patrol.' That had been a kiddie program where you sat in a rocket ship and Wink showed Flash Gordon serials. Seeing him trying to be hip didn't work because we all thought of him in his space suit."

Dewey began falling out of favor with radio when contrivances like structured playlists and rigorous formulas were introduced. Gearing itself more toward selling advertising than pleasing listeners, radio needed predictability and fixity. Dewey was nothing if not spontaneous, and unfortunately he became nothing.

In 1958, when Phillips and WHBQ parted ways, it was as if his life became untethered. He began drifting until a new station, WHHM, hired him, hoping to capitalize on his name. They went bankrupt. More drifting, a marital separation, more drinking and pill-popping. He settled for a time at a small station outside Memphis. The fans who had been raised on him and now had their own bands hired Dewey to spin records during the breaks at their dances. He enjoyed a small burst of popularity, developing a new audience while reacquainting himself with his original one.

Dewey's injury, or the pills he took, prevented him from driving. "I used to drive him home from the dances," says Randy Haspel. "Those of us who knew the Dewey Phillips story from childhood were eager to overlook his faults. We ignored the ever-present bottle and the vials of pain pills. We assumed it was part of the Phillips persona and we were too naive to recognize his abuses."

Haspel remembers the night Dewey called and invited him and three friends out to meet Elvis. "We thought he was joking but he insisted he was not. Dewey had said, 'Say something, Elvis,' and a voice sounding remarkably like Presley's came over the telephone and invited us to Graceland that very night. We picked Dewey up at his house, thanking him profusely for this tremendous favor. We stopped four miles before Graceland at the Manhattan Club, a very popular night club featuring Willie Mitchell and the Four Kings as the house band. Dewey informed us that Elvis was sending someone down in a Cadillac to meet us and we would follow him up to the house. In the meantime, Dewey waited inside the bar. We were not yet seventeen, so we waited in the car. Nearly two hours passed. No Cadillac ever stopped for us. We decided to go home. Dewey would not hear of it and in a final act of bravado, he jumped into the front seat and told us to drive to Graceland. Events happened mercifully fast after that as we anxiously watched Dewey confront the gatekeeper outside the Presley mansion. I remember angry words, defiant gestures, and Dewey, red-faced and frustrated from the ordeal, stalking rapidly away from the driveway with his loping stride.

"He rode back with us silently, humiliated in front of a bunch of idolizing kids when all he really wanted was a ride to the Manhattan Club."

Roland Janes says, "One night someone was supposed to pick him up down at my studio. It was bitter cold then, like ten degrees outside, and Dewey said, 'Well I'm gonna wait out here for a minute and they'll be by to get me.' I thought he was gone. Thirty minutes later when I locked up and was going home, I walked out and he was still standing out there. He knew what was happening. I said, 'Dewey, what the hell you still doing out here?' and he said, 'Oh, so-and-so's gonna be by here in a minute to get me.' I said, 'Nah, he ain't coming, c'mon get in the car.' There was a lot of that happening during the later days."

"He lived with his mother," says Milton Pond. "He had this prescription that he could get filled anytime he needed it. He'd come by Pop Tunes late, when I was working till nine, and ask me if I could give him a ride. I'd say, 'Sure, no problem,' because I thought that was nice. He was one of my heroes. He would always say, 'Now don't forget, Elvis'—by then he was calling everyone Elvis—'on my way home, I've got to stop by Doc's.' He'd stop at Doc Russell's pharmacy and run in and get his prescription filled."

On September 28, 1968, the forty-two-year-old Dewey went to sleep at his mother's house and didn't wake up. He'd helped bring musicians into this world, and musicians helped carry him out. Among his pallbearers were the songwriter Dickie Lee, Sam Phillips, and Sam's two sons, Knox and Jerry.

CHAPTER THREE

The World's Most Perfectly Formed Midget Wrestler

━┥┝━

THE LINK BETWEEN THE EXPANSE OF THE DELTA AND THE TWELVE-INCH pieces of black vinyl that recorded the region's sound is peanuts. Beale Street would have drawn Howlin' Wolf from the country, stinking like a mule and covered in mud. Wolf might have established himself as a performer in the clubs and enjoyed a career, in Memphis or Chicago, thrilling audiences with his powerful persona. But getting that power onto vinyl, and getting the vinyl to places where people could hear it and buy it, was the direct result of what easy-listening, big-band fan Buster Williams learned as a young man selling peanuts.

In 1949, the same year Dewey Phillips went on the air, Williams established Plastic Products, Inc., an independent, nonaffiliated record pressing plant. Just two weeks earlier, a plant on Long Island, New York, became the first independent. Williams was the second, but in Memphis he was far from the controlling influence of the major labels on either coast. His empire already included jukeboxes (Williams Distributors) and record distribution (Music Sales). The Quonset hut called Plastic Products completed the system that would lay the physical groundwork for the growth of rock and roll.

"What it boils down to," says the soft-spoken Leon "Mack" McLemore, who, as manager of the record distributorship, was at the nucleus of Williams's web, "is that Buster knew that through Music Sales putting the records out on our jukeboxes, we could sell enough to get our money back for pressing costs. We had all these machines and routes spanning three or four states, and if a record was playing in one jukebox, another guy would want that record too and he would have to get it from us. A thousand was easy, and if you sold that thousand, the label got a little money, Buster got paid, and they

27

could press another thousand. He could gamble on a thousand records, extending credit, and not stand the chance of losing any money." Buster helped Sun Records, Chess Records in Chicago, and later Stax in Memphis, and a host of other independent labels across the country come to their ultimate fruition: getting their music on vinyl, their vinyl into customers' hands.

Buster Williams was born January 14, 1909, in the appropriately named city of Enterprise, Mississippi. At age twelve, he began selling peanuts at high-school football games. The business drained his mother, who was slave to the roaster the day of the event. His first innovation was to replace the paper bag with wax paper, sealing a piece of string along the edge to create an easy open pull-tab. It kept the peanuts fresher, allowing his mother to spread the roasting over a couple days. At sixteen, he had made enough money from peanuts to buy a drugstore, and the profit he made from the store's coin-operated machines led him to jukeboxes and Williams Distributors. "There were some snack machines and several slot machines in that drugstore," says Robert Williams, Buster's son. "He saw what kind of profits those slot machines turned, and soon he had a route for those all over this four-state area. Jukeboxes were a natural thing from the coin machines."

Before the prevalence of radio, jukeboxes were the primary outlet for exploiting a record. Wherever there was a jukebox, there was a crowd. And there was money. After the war, Williams could afford to establish the Music Sales record distributorship and pay himself, essentially, to move records from the wholesale side of the warehouse to the retail side. Independent labels could now get their record in a store as well as on a jukebox. "When he opened the record distribution, it wasn't for local artists or local labels," says his son. "At that time there wasn't anything happening in Memphis. He was looking at a much wider geographic scope. He soon had offices in New Orleans, Shreveport, St. Louis, and Chicago and was shipping independent records all over the country."

The majors also controlled the pressing plants. Independents could bring them work, but outside jobs received lower priority than the in-house jobs; subject to the whims of the factory, it was impossible for a small label to plan a release date and maintain stability. Plastic Products was the next logical step for Williams, completing his control of manufacturing, distribution, and the means of consumption.

As Chess Records in Chicago was developing, Leonard Chess realized the importance of dependable pressing. He came to Memphis on a bus—"Dad picked him up at the bus station"—and after a meeting with Williams, left with a credit line and the understanding that when Chess could pay, Plastic

Products would be at the top of the list. According to Robert Williams, there was no contract, nothing written on paper. And that became the standard. As their business relationship blossomed, the Williams family and the Chess family became close-knit. "The first time I ever had gone to Chicago, I must have been eight or nine years old," remembers Robert. "Leonard had his offices in a rough area but, as you can imagine, he was well connected. The cab pulled up and dropped us off in front of the offices there. Dad put the bags out and turned around to pay and when he turned back, the bags were gone. He walked in and told Leonard, and we had the bags back in about twenty minutes. I mean, they were delivered back with apologies."

The Chess account became a bedrock for the pressing plant, which fed Williams's record distribution and jukebox companies. "Once Music Sales got established in retail stores, we did a whale of a business," says McLemore. "One thing that helped establish us was acquiring MGM as a client. People had to have Hank Williams. We'd tell 'em, 'You buy some of my records, I'll sell you some Hank Williams.' Aside from just the popular stuff, the shops had a section on R&B music and country music. We handled all that."

"These record distributors supported a lot of us little guys," says Roland Janes, whose labels included Rolando, Renay, and Rita Records (the original "Mountain of Love"). "They could almost assure us to break even on our little releases, which would give us an opportunity to work the radio stations and try to get some recognition there. Buster Williams helped everybody, and not just locally." On a runaway hit, Mack McLemore says, they could unload fifty thousand singles between their jukeboxes and retail shops.

In 1961, Williams outgrew the Memphis plant and opened a much larger one in Coldwater, Mississippi. By 1973, he had reopened in Memphis and was running both plants with three shifts, twenty-four hours a day to meet the demand. (He also bought into Eastern Manufacturing, a pressing plant in Philadelphia.) When they were at their peak, Plastic Products's southern plants could press over 150,000 singles a day; they also pressed twelve-inch albums. By the early 1970s, the pressing plant's major clients included Stax, Atlantic, Chess, ABC-Paramount, and MGM. "We shipped a lot of records by air back then," says McLemore. "Tonnage-wise, Coldwater was the largest shipper that Delta Airlines had for a couple of years. We'd send a truckload of records into the airport every night. We had ninety-seven presses at one time down there. Sure it's incredible."

One day in 1966, Buster phoned Mack and told him that he was shutting down the Music Sales distributorship. "I was kind of taken by surprise. We had a real steady business going. But Buster owned the company and if he decided he wanted to close, he'd just close." Thirty years later, McLemore still says with pride that he was able to find new distributors for nearly all the labels they handled. He stayed with Williams as manager of the pressing plant operations until the proliferation of cassettes and the demise of the seven-inch forced them out of business. By that time, Williams had become attracted by a larger hustle, establishing himself as a major wildcatter in the oil business. He rigged a motor vehicle with multiple phone lines and rode throughout the South, checking on his sites and making deals. Oil remained his primary interest until his death in 1992. Buster Williams's Quonset hut stands today as a memorial to the era of vinyl records. Surrounded by the industrial decay of twenty years, much of the equipment remains at the ready, the same as it did on its last shift.

In 1949, RCA Records introduced the seven-inch 45-rpm record. It was meant to compete with the 33⅓ long player successfully marketed the previous year by Columbia. But the improved fidelity of the faster record was not enough to overcome the LP's advantage: symphonies only had to be flipped once, while the 45s spread them over several discs. RCA was ceding the race when they realized the smaller discs were perfect for the youth market's three-minute rock and roll song. The parent's disavowal of the format made it even more attractive. Here kids, identify with these—and collect them all.

The growth of seven-inch 45-rpm records was directly related to the era of the Saturday matinees, when sending kids to the movies was cheaper than hiring a baby-sitter and it occupied them all day. (TV was not yet firmly established, and owning a set was a luxury.) The serials, in which a story was continued week after week, established the rhythms of consumption that would later drive the rock and roll habit. Once the witnesses perceived that rock and roll 45s were going to keep coming out, it made it easier to part with that much silver. You had to get the next installment.

Saturdays at the cinema also produced the original rock and roll screen star. In 1953, the year before Elvis was unleashed, Marlon Brando's character in *The Wild One* summarized the philosophy of the burgeoning youth culture. He was asked, "What are you rebelling against?" He answered, "Whattaya got?" But Brando was spilling popcorn in the aisles when cowboy Lash LaRue premiered in 1945.

Unlike the clean and handsome cowboy stars Roy Rogers and Gene Autry, Lash LaRue was not so obviously a good guy. He brazenly wore black, and though he always performed the hero's duties, it was only after he was mistaken for the bad guy. Teen angst, western style! His cape further distinguished him, and this wild one of his day even had the equivalent of a motor-cycle: his bullwhip. Lash could shoot a gun with the best of them, but he achieved his individuality with the whip. His rebellious nature defined cool for the future rock and rollers. Writer Stanley Booth says, "I idolized Lash to the point I didn't just want to be like Lash, I became convinced I was Lash!" Mary Lindsay Dickinson, an early participant in the scene and Jim's wife, sums it up, "Roy Rogers was a wimp, Gene Autry could sing, but Lash LaRue was different. As children, millions of my generation looked up to Lash LaRue as a role model. We memorized his movies, never missed him on television, pored over his comic books, worshiped him at state fairs, and tried to be cool—like him."

The depth of his film character was evident in his first movie, *The Song of Old Wyoming,* in 1945. "They let me pick out my wardrobe," LaRue told me in 1993 while in Memphis for a western film convention, "and I selected a black outfit. I liked black. In the picture, I was the bad guy turned good. The picture closed on my gravestone and it said, 'In the worst of us, there is some good.' I think that sums it up."

Lash had a few interesting encounters during his visits to Memphis. When his movie career began winding down, he led an exhibition rodeo at touring fairs. His name was huge on the banners, and the show featured something for everyone: fancy riding, a comedy mule, pretty women, and the whip. (At one time, Sun's only female recording artist, Barbara Pittman, was a member of his troupe.) While performing in Memphis in 1956, the cowboy lived out a mod-ern interpretation of his films. The *Commercial Appeal*'s front-page headline read, "Lash LaRue Arrested at Fair—Charged with Buying Loot." The article begins, "Police cracked the whip on Lash LaRue last night. . . ." In his posses-sion was a stolen adding machine and three hot typewriters. His cohort Fuzzy St. John was also arrested, along with a showgirl who tried to strangle herself with a scarf during her night in jail.

"I was crushed when he got arrested," recalls Wayne Jackson, later a mem-ber of the Stax house band. "I couldn't believe he might steal. I didn't know why he wasn't just rich, why he and his guys were stealing typewriters." Jackson's sentiments are uniformly echoed by his peers. Elvis Presley, by then the world's highest-paid recording star, sent word to Lash that he could help. "I told him to let it go," LaRue says about Presley. "I didn't want anybody get-ting messed up in it because it was a stinking lousy thing."

At the arraignment, Lash followed his old movie scripts and pleaded inno-cent. He claimed he'd purchased the goods, valued at $1,200, from a salesman for $105. And, from the same script, a four-day trial commenced, at the end of which he was exonerated. But unlike in his old films, many of his fans forgot the hero's ending, for the shock of the headline still weighed heavily. Typically hip, he summed up the incident to me with a quote from Lord Buckley, the British hepster comedian of the 1950s: "The bad jazz a man blows wails long after he's cut out."

But his exploits over the years kept him endeared to the rock and rollers. In the 1960s, he was reportedly pulled over in Hollywood while driving a red convertible and wearing scuba gear. His car was searched and he went down as an early marijuana bust. When he was in Memphis with another convention in the mid-1970s, several local musicians introduced themselves, explained their longtime admiration of him, and invited him to a party. Intrigued by the company, Lash accepted. He drove from the downtown Peabody Hotel to rural East Memphis to pass an evening. Mary Lindsay Dickinson recounts, "Lash drove through the city, from the Mississippi River past Germantown at literally 110 miles per hour. He had just one finger on the steering wheel of the Red Sled, his Cadillac convertible. We passed many cars and several police cars who completely ignored us. It seemed we were invisible to the rest of the world." The party lasted all night, during which time Lash told of his visits to the planet Jupiter. He produced some pot, which he claimed was a gift from God himself. "Lash leaned back for a thoughtful moment," continues Mary Lindsay Dickinson. "We sorcerer's apprentices sat at the master's feet, hostages for the night to the world's most unique cosmic cowboy. When Lash opened his mouth again, he spoke quietly. 'I have no home in the universe. I am hunted by the police of Jupiter and the police of Earth. My great fear is that they will arrest me at the same moment in each place. That would be more pain than I could bear.'"

Lash LaRue had prepared the witnesses for Dewey Phillips, and although they thought they were just having fun, they unwittingly became students of Dewey's ideas on racial equality and social freedom. For years to come, they would realize the depth of his lessons. One of their earliest chances to test their education was at the wrestling matches, held every Monday night at Ellis Auditorium. In the mid-1950s, a new champion came to town and he had a gimmick unlike anyone else's.

Sputnik Monroe arrived in Memphis in 1957, "220 pounds of twisted steel and sex appeal." He had been garnering acclaim in Mobile, Alabama, and the Memphis promoter, whose receipts had been slipping, was looking for a new draw. Wrestling had been like the movies: either you stood for Good or for

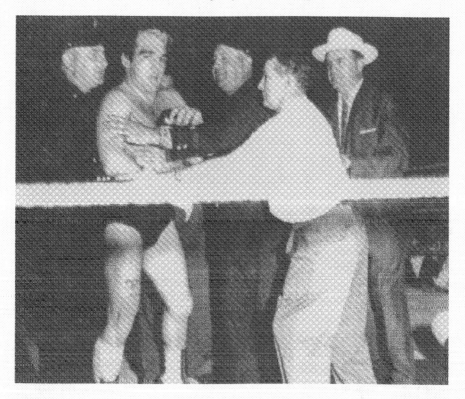

Sputnik Monroe: 220 pounds of twisted steel and sex appeal. Photo courtesy of Sputnik Monroe.

Bad. Monroe wrestled hard and played fair—unless he was losing, and then he cheated. He described himself as neither good nor bad, but "scientifically rough." His philosophy was, "Win if you can, lose if you must, always cheat, and if they take you out, leave tearing down the ring."

Sputnik Monroe, now in his sixties, lives in obscurity in Houston, where he works as a security guard. Although flesh has settled in places where there once was muscle, he is still a large man, powerful and agile. He used to boast, "I'll jump in the air and shit in your hair," and you wouldn't want to dare him today. His ears are cauliflowered, his face battered. As I pass a day with him in an anonymous Houston hotel room, he smokes cigarettes constantly, picking his ears with a toothpick he also chews, speaking in a voice that would carry easily to the cheap seats.

"I started in the carnival athletic show, meeting all comers," he explains. It was nearly half a century ago, when half a sawbuck and plenty of machismo could get you five minutes in the ring with the strong man and a chance at fifty bucks. "Whoever wants to do their thing, however they want to do it," he says. "I had shovel fights, rope fights, pickax-handle fights, wrestled, boxed, one hand tied down, whatever their specialty was. One time I had a guy turn his back to me and hook me by the head, and I realized he'd seen something on TV and wanted to flip me over his back. So I let him flying-mare me. I got up and staggered around, and let him do it to me again. The people cheered and he did it again. And he did it again and he did it again and then he puked and fell over. I never let anybody get out of there a winner."

In addition to brute strength and a consummate understanding of the sport, Monroe had an instinctual mastery of crowd psychology. He would damage or destroy his opponent and then, like the other wrestlers, turn to the audience for approbation and praise. But Sputnik Monroe did not turn to the box seats down front, not to the women in the audience, not to the first balcony, not the second or third balcony. After each triumphant trick, Sputnik Monroe would turn his back on the vanquished, strut like a barnyard rooster, and then fling his hands high above his head, asking for, and receiving, respect and adulation from the black audience, segregated and confined to the crow's nest, the small balcony at the very top of the hall.

"When I arrived in Memphis, I went straight to Beale Street where the blacks hung out and from there straight to jail and got Sugarmon, the black attorney, to defend me in court. They charged me with 'mopery and attempted gawk,' that's an old southern vagrancy thing they made up. I was on Beale Street every night for the first six months. I got arrested three or four times until that didn't work anymore and then the cops left me alone."

Ellis Auditorium, where the big musical acts played and the same site that Elvis had aspired to, began selling out for Monroe's matches. "There got to be a couple thousand blacks outside wanting to get in," he recalls. "So I told the management I'd be cutting out if they don't let my black friends in. I had power because I'm selling out the place, the first guy that ever did it, and they damn sure wanted the revenue."

"I remember one time Sputnik was wrassling in Louisville," says Johnny Dark, now a Memphis sportscaster but then the president and founder of the Sputnik Monroe Fan Club. "In the dressing room, this little black lady came up to Sputnik, she had tears in her eyes, she said, 'You don't remember me, you never met me, but I used to live in Memphis when they made us sit upstairs in those buzzard seats.' She said, 'You're the one who got them to change that.' That was the first time I saw Sputnik with tears in his eyes."

Jim Dickinson was another Sputnik Monroe worshiper. "The way they would cut off the black audience," he explains, "they had a guy counting the white door and a guy on the black door. And they knew how many blacks the section could hold. Sputnik paid the guy who counted the blacks to say a low number every time he was asked, so when the boss said, 'How many have you let in?' he would say 'Twenty-five,' or whatever, and there was five hundred people up there. Finally the audience got so big and so heavily black that they had to integrate the seating. That really is how integration in Memphis started. There's no other single event that integrated the audience other than the wrassling matches and Sputnik paying the guy to lie."

Jim Crow laws were outlawed in 1954, though little practical effect was felt until Lyndon Johnson pushed the Civil Rights Act through Congress in 1964. In Memphis, as in much of the nation, another decade would pass before there was any attempt at mass integration, usually in the form of busing. During the 1968 Memphis sanitation workers' strike, during which the Reverend Martin Luther King Jr. was assassinated, the placards carried by African-American workers had to convey the simplest of ideas to the noncomprehending white majority: "I Am a Man."

"You're talking about separate water fountains, you're talking about back of the bus," says Jim Blake, who managed wrestler Jerry Lawler in the 1970s, and whose Barbarian Records recorded several heroes of the ring. "I went through my whole twelve years at school having never been able to share an experience with a black, and I was starting to resent this, because I was also listening to radio and Dewey Phillips and hearing all these great black records and realizing that these were some talented artists, this was another culture. Where at first we'd gone to the matches hoping to see Sputnik get beat, we started to realize that he was pretty fucking cool. He had his audience and he never played down to 'em, never talked down to 'em. He became a role model."

Monroe had size, demeanor, sharp costumes, good looks, and certainly a boisterous attitude—even without a trademark he would have been conspicuous. Early in his career, however, he was beaned with a wooden chair. After a large splinter was removed from the top of his forehead, a patch of hair grew in white. Perusing Memphis high-school yearbooks from the late 1950s, it's easy to spot the members of his fan club: Johnny Dark is one among many who sported a white streak in his annual photograph. In an early promotional photo, Jerry Lawler, whose career began well after Sputnik's and continues today, also has a white streak.

"If you would have had some kind of election about who was the best-known face in Memphis at the time—Sputnik, Elvis, and the mayor—Sputnik would have been real close to Elvis," says Johnny Dark.

By bonding himself to the tension of the era, Sputnik Monroe became a hero to the rebellious white youth culture. Wrestling, like rock and roll, thrives on the energy of a crowd gone wild. By the end of the decade, Sputnik had become friendly with Sam Phillips, and a hero to Sam's children, Knox and Jerry. Jerry Phillips was an athletic twelve-year-old, short, and wanted to get into wrestling. Sputnik was a muscle of a man who could have flossed his teeth with Phillips, but the young lad's desire gave him an idea. It might not make a main event, but midget wrestling had its possibilities.

That Phillips wasn't a midget was no problem. For Sputnik, in fact, it was the heart of his scheme. Professional wrestling is about frustrating the audience. In a humid and smelly high-school gymnasium, there's a great potential for aggression, the thick smoke and bad lighting, the rage to be roused among a mob of tanked-up hicks—"Get him outta there! He ain't a midget!"—the frustration waiting to be vented by an audience who spent their days and weeks and years beating the earth, powerless against the elements—"That one don't belong! He ain't no midget!" A fan that felt a blue vein popping out of his neck would return week after week.

Sputnik was friendly with Fabulous Frankie Thumb, a midget proper, and he put both Jerry and Frankie in training. He enjoyed Jerry's attitude and soon was taking him to bars and nightclubs, sticking a cigar in Jerry's mouth and lifting him onto the bar. "The bartender would say, 'How old is that guy?'" says Phillips. "And Sputnik would say, 'He's twenty-one. He's with me.' Who's going to argue with Sputnik Monroe? Anywhere that he went, he was king."

They set up matches on the circuit all around Memphis. More midgets came forward and soon there were tag teams. Phillips remembers, "The announcer would say, 'He doesn't have short legs, his arms appear normal . . . ,' that sort of talk. If I had been twenty-five and the size of a midget, it might have been believable, but I was obviously a kid, twelve or thirteen. They'd have me walk through the crowd, chewing a big cigar, taunting the people. Sputnik had taught me pretty good how to pull my pants down and tell 'em to kiss my ass. The audience knew I wasn't real and I just made 'em madder."

The act's run came to a close after a couple short years in a small Arkansas town around 1962. An angry fan—a deranged wrestling zealot caught up in the believability of that which was so plainly not believable—pulled a knife and tried to stab Sputnik Monroe's most inspired idea. Phillips's parents said he could no longer continue the act: "DeLayne" Phillips, the World's Most Perfectly Formed Midget Wrestler, was officially retired.

While white parents hated Sputnik Monroe, the kids loved him. "There was a group of wealthy white kids that dug me because I was a rebel. I'm saying what they wanted to say, only they were too young or inexperienced or afraid to say it. You have a black maid raising your kids and she's talking about me all the time, so I may not be in the front living room, but I'm going in the back door of your goddamn house, feeding your kids on Monday morning and sending 'em to school. And meeting the bus when they come home. Pretty powerful thing."

He created a life of altruism built on self-promotion. After he integrated Ellis Auditorium, his power within the black community caused fear among the city fathers. While the black leaders were arguing about how to protest the segregation of an automobile show, Sputnik called the sponsoring dealership and threatened to open a car lot in a black neighborhood; that night's evening news announced the changed admission policy.

"Another time I give away a hundred watermelons—Sputnik melons; they had white stripes—and announced that I was gonna run for sheriff. People thought prostitution and incest would flourish, 'motherfucker' would be a household word. I could have run for mayor and made it. I could have black-mailed the city. I could have done any goddamn thing I wanted. I was general of a little black army."

By 1960, Monroe couldn't get any bigger in the mid-South. But wrestling has always been regional, and outside his region, his stature was not the same. He wanted to go national. "Before I left Memphis, I read in the paper where Gene Barry was coming to the Mid-South Fair and I went out there to hit him in the nose for copying the way I dress. I was born and raised in Dodge City, Kansas, which is the cowboy town of the world. Gene Barry was the star on 'Bat Masterson' and dressed like I dressed, with a homburg and a vest. I figured if I jerked him off a horse and hit him in the nose for dressing Dodge City –style, I'd get a national reputation."

Police protection kept Gene Barry's nose from its appointment with Sputnik's fist, though the wrestler did manage to pick a fight that night with a cowboy and make the front page of the local paper, his picture as large as President Eisenhower's. After that, Monroe tried becoming a national star by racing from territory to territory, but the lapses between appearances were too great; he couldn't rally the support.

Despite his popularity with the fans, Monroe had always frightened promoters; in wrestling, he was known as a "charger," someone who could lose control. He was not averse to hurting his opponent, nor to being hurt himself. This attitude gave promoters ulcers, because they usually had the same card booked the whole week in different cities and couldn't afford an injury.

The 1960s found Monroe traveling again, but his magic didn't click in other territories. He made occasional returns to Memphis to boost his morale. A bitter divorce led to a drinking binge that spilled from months to years. In the early 1970s, Sputnik wore the Junior Heavyweight Champion belt, and in 1972 he was back in Memphis and back on top.

Randy Haspel, whose band the Radiants was one of the first post-Beatles Memphis bands and one of the last recording acts on the original Sun Records, remembers an encounter with Sputnik in the early 1970s. "I was sitting around Phillips Studio with Skip Owsley, this black conga drummer from my band, and Sputnik came in. He wasn't as active in wrestling as he had been, and he was saying, 'I don't know what to do anymore. I used to be able to tell 'em their wimmin were trash, or I'd shake my ass and them broads would flip out and the guys would want to fight. I can't get these people to hate me like they used to!' This was during the hippie heyday, and we said, 'What people hate now are longhairs. If you talked about love, Sputnik, they'd probably hate you.' Skip, the black guy, said, 'You need to find you a black wrestler and tag team with him.' So two weeks later Sputnik appears on TV with Norvell Austin, and he's dyed a blond streak in *his* hair. They're beating up some designated opponents, and they tied up one guy's arms in the ropes. Sputnik goes over to the corner and gets a bucket and pours it over this guy's head. It's a bucket of black paint. And then Sputnik and Norvell go over to the announcer and Sputnik says, 'Black is beautiful!' and Norvell says, 'White is beautiful!' and Sputnik held up his arm with Norvell's and he said, 'Black and white together is beautiful.' Next time I saw Sputnik he's real excited and says, 'They hate me again!'"

The interracial tag team thrived in Memphis. After he cloned the white streak, the younger Norvell was rumored to be Sputnik's son. The partnership lasted three years, and Norvell, who had never traveled, celebrated his twenty-first birthday while on a Japanese tour. Monroe was left untethered when Austin decided to go solo. After a car wreck in 1978, he recuperated in a Texas beer joint, holding court from a recliner on stacked Coke crates. Since his heyday, he has owned bars and restaurants, sold turquoise jewelry, had a wrecker service, a transmission shop, and taught at wrestling schools. Recently, he has considered becoming a stand-up comedian. Monroe has not wrestled since 1991, but wouldn't decline a challenge. His son Bubba "The Brawler" Monroe, Texas All-Pro in Houston, has been under his father's tutelage for nearly a decade, slowly climbing professional wrestling's ranks.

Despite its popularity, the World Wrestling Federation gets little respect from Sputnik. "My business is dead," he says. "There are no tough guys left in wrestling." The sport of body manipulation has been replaced by acrobats on steroids. Tumbling makes for good television, but the science of the sport has been replaced by pantomime and buffoonery. "Wherever I put your head, your body's gonna follow. Wrestling amounts to one thing: A fulcrum and a lever. Long enough lever, big enough fulcrum, you can pick anything up."

Whatever else the WWF has done, it has finally made wrestling the popular means of expression it had the potential to be back in the 1950s. It may be bereft of the social value it toyed with then, but it is able to tour like rock bands, packing arenas and selling T-shirts and videos. Albums, even.

Sputnik was in the right place to be a societal influence, but his timing was a little late. American youth culture in the 1950s was a whitewall tire about to blow. Major cities were too self-reflexive for this explosion—it needed innocence. A place where racial tensions had been so deeply repressed that society was about to choke on its own sweetness, where urban civilization could obstruct all hopes but a short drive out of town declared the possibilities endless: It was Memphis and it was rock and roll. But had Sputnik Monroe come along a few years earlier, we might all be products of sex, drugs, and wrestling. He is the guy who did not become Elvis Presley.

Sputnik Monroe summed up the common attitude between wrestling and rock and roll one afternoon in a Memphis studio. This was 1972, at the Sam Phillips Recording Service. Jim Dickinson was just off the road from a tour, and he was showing off his recently purchased red, white, and blue leather boots, emblazoned with tricolored double eagles. These were boots that would turn heads, boots that would be the envy of any self-respecting biker and most corrupt sheriff's deputies. If you didn't speak the language in a foreign country, these boots could get you around.

Sputnik Monroe was singularly unimpressed. Perhaps because his feet were not breaking them in. Perhaps because the boots were the center of attention and not him. The reasoning only obscures the facts: These double eagle boots were so engrossing that none of the admirers noticed his eyes impatiently darting.

The compliments continued.

"Those goddamn boots ain't shit," Sputnik finally growled. And before anyone could beg to differ, he continued. "I know a place in Mexico where you can get boots with big dicks and balls on 'em."

The laughter in the room died like a suffocated fire as everyone became aware of Sputnik's smoldering anger. People got fidgety trying to think of what to say. The obvious dawned on someone: "What're you gonna do with boots that have big dicks and balls on 'em, Sputnik?"

Sputnik, like anyone whose work involves shouting over the din of an outraged crowd, has always had a gruff voice, but maybe he plucked a little extra coarseness for this answer. A real attitude is one you can feel. "You go into a bar with them on," he said, "You can get into a fight in fifteen minutes."

CHAPTER FOUR

Nothing Ever Happens But the Impossible

THIS WHITE KID WALKS OUT THE SIDE DOOR OF THE TALL BUILDING where his dad works. It's Saturday, a short day in the office, mostly knocking around. The sunlight is the bluish cool of the coming autumn, and it's not that you can feel winter in the breeze, but the oppression of summer is noticeably absent.

A band is playing, people are dancing. His dad stops and so does the kid. They're in an alleyway, Whiskey Chute, where jugheads used to roll barrels up to town from the riverboats below. Whiskey is in the air. Whiskey is in the white couple dancing, and whiskey is in the black people making the music. Oh it's definitely music, the guitar, the violin confirm that, even though the other instruments seem to be kitchen utensils. A laundry basin. A washboard. A comb. A jug.

The dad nudges the kid once, then a second time, a little harder. The boy nods without hearing. His father puts his big palm on the nine-year-old's shoulder, summoning a little more strength than he thought would be needed, urging his son along. The music follows them as they walk out of the alley into the brighter street. There's summer, felt it then. Dad starts to say something, but he sees the kid's mind is still back at the jug band. Oh well, let him chew on that anyway.

The kid looks over his shoulder when he knows it's too late to see the musicians. "Come on down to my house, honey, ain't nobody home but me." His nine-year-old mind tingles, something juicy in the way the man sang that line. The way the male dancer gestured to the woman every time that chorus came around, and what she did in response. And how often that chorus came around!

Blame it on the war. The increase in industrial jobs for the 1940s military effort drew country people to the city, and after the war, letters back home kept them coming. Escaping from the treadmill of sharecropping, out from the shadow of the Man and into the robotic grind of the factory, Delta residents came to Memphis, moved on to St. Louis, and finally to Chicago. They peeled off along the way, finding work, finding family, finding friends. Swept into the urban migration, musicians dotted the exodus. Woe to the bass fiddle player and his baggage. Better learn the violin, buddy.

The city had something that was less common in the country: electricity. And that made the city a louder place. In the rural juke joints, a lone acoustic guitarist or a band of all acoustic instruments could propel a crowd to madness, but in the city, the musicians adapted their style to eardrums attacked by the clanging of streetcars and the pounding of factories and warehouses. They plugged in. But the acoustic instrument retained its place. Instead of waiting for the audience to find the club, street musicians went outside and found a crowd. "Music for sale," they'd hawk between songs and watch their bucket or their hat fill with change. And if a cop came, they could quickly pack up and walk away. Or run.

The jug band, in its forced union of diverse instruments and in the absolute singularity of the jug's sound, is Memphis music incarnate. It creates a sound where there should be none, from instruments intended for other purposes. The kitchen may be for cooking, but if we rattle around it long enough, we'll surely have a hit. Or at least a good time. The handmade equipment—a guitar from a cigar box, a harmonica from a corncob—conveyed an egalitarianism that reached into the guts of their audience, making anyone who clapped along, danced, or even nodded a part of their act. The jug band repertoire was a combination of past and present, culling from the African heritage of the banjo and guitar, the European heritage of the violin, and the contemporary life built around the washboard and the jug. Their music was sophisticated. Just as Harry Fritzius created art from an ordinary mask, the jug blowers made keeping the beat into a touch of God. Their *whoomp whoomp* filled with character, the musicians themselves responding to the audience's disbelief of their capabilities, pushing their talents to new heights while their heads floated off their shoulders from hyperventilating.

Unlike its contents, the sound of a jug cannot be distilled. The joy created from such a household item is at the heart of Memphis music, the simplicity, the eccentricity, the soul. In that peculiar thump is heard the city's avowal to buck trends, to respond, Weird? Damn right it's weird, and if I keep at it a few minutes longer, it may get weirder still. With the Delta blues, Sun, and Stax,

Memphis's peculiar mix became not only popular but also permanent. Pop culture is a continuing shift of trends, disposing of the new with the newer, but *whoomp whoomp,* Memphis won't go away. Three times it hit, which is more than Detroit, more than Cleveland, more than New Orleans, and the music bookies are wagering it'll come from here again. Sometime. And when it does, this bettor says it'll be some variation of its roots.

For the Memphis kids in the 1950s who would witness the creation of rock and roll—unlike for, say, Mick Jagger—pure Delta blues wasn't necessarily a detached voice on a piece of black vinyl. Like the kid in Whiskey Chute—an epiphanic incident in Jim Dickinson's life—the mystery of that sound was not "Where?" but "How?" How do these people next to me on the street do something that I've never seen done by any of my parent's friends or anyone I know? Such cultural collisions are the foundation of Memphis's artistic contribution. "I was struck like it was lightning," Dickinson says of his jug band encounter. "I'd never heard anything like it. I'd heard some Dixieland music on the radio, a little boogie woogie, but that's all that was accessible to a white kid."

Jim Dickinson lives deep in the Mississippi woods today, where he smokes spider webs, eats rattlesnake meat, and fends off voodoo spirits with possum tails. Or so those who don't know him would have you believe. In the contemporary music industry, Dickinson is Memphis Whitey, the beast from underground who travels in the corporate world, the man with corporate connections who prefers the underworld. His head is attuned to the sounds of tomorrow, rooted in the ways of yesterday. He learned music and attitude from bluesmen who created the recorded genre, and that—the music *and* the attitude—scares lots of people. His career parallels rock and roll's evolution from a business to an industry. Like the members of another early Memphis band, the Mar-Keys, he learned the ropes as the ropes were being strung. He's seen every kind of deal. His resume includes playing piano with the Rolling Stones ("Wild Horses"), Arlo Guthrie ("City of New Orleans"), and bluesman Sleepy John Estes; he's produced several Ry Cooder albums and recorded ten soundtracks with him (*Paris, Texas* being one); he's produced the Replacements, Alex Chilton, Toots Hibbert, and pianist Grandma Dixie Davis; and he's written songs that have been sung by Bob Dylan, the Flying Burrito Brothers, and Albert King. While geniuses of the subbasement seek him out, record company executives cringe when his name is mentioned. He has a saying they abhor: "Hits are in baseball, singles are in bars, and your royalty lives in a castle in Europe."

Dickinson's Mississippi home is mostly surrounded by trees; the one clear-

ing reveals a model suburban house across the hill—exactly what he was trying
to escape. But paradox vibrates to his core. He's purchased a converted barn
that's even more remote, an old structure filled with ghosts. When it's out-
fitted with recording equipment, he'll have the ultimate treehouse, moving
further from people to attract people. Jim Dickinson oozes funkiness. His
beefy appearance carries a biker air, his clothes hail to hippiedom, and his
voice, rattling through Delta silt, says backwoods. Gentle by nature, he is a
family man. With his wife of thirty years he has raised two rock and roll kids;
his ma lives with them. Through fad, fashion, and fallow, Jim Dickinson has
plied his trade, taking the accolades with the admonishments. In a business
that thrives on the disposable, he continues to make lasting contributions.

In 1950s Memphis, the continuing Civil War was also a war of civility. In
the same arena where black and white cultures were roiling, there was a meeting of urban and rural. The city's old money had been established on the sweat
of the fieldhand's brow, and the conversion of farmland into suburbia created
a random mash between country and country club. There were few four-lane
roads in the city, none in suburbia. Pecan orchards were coming down as fast
as cotton fields were being paved, brick homes going up in their place. Restricted neighborhoods all—whites only, with the rural blacks being squeezed
into pockets close enough to work in the new neighborhoods' new homes.
But the hypocrisy of segregation was laid bare in the very houses where racism
was inculcated. The cook in the kitchen was a Sputnik Monroe fan; the man in
the yard was an R&B devotee.

"Everybody learned it from the yard man," says Dickinson. "Alex Tiel
taught me everything he thought was important to teach a nine-year-old
white boy. How to shoot craps, how to throw a knife underhanded—the important life lessons. When it came to something he didn't know, he would run
in an expert. He wasn't a musician, but he sang as he worked, unaccompanied,
and when he realized I was interested in the music, he brought in a man who
taught me this technique that I learned to play from.

"This unknown man told me all music is made up out of 'codes,' and I
thought he meant a secret code like Captain Midnight, which I was way off
into. But he meant 'chords.' And he says, 'This is how you make a code. You
take a note, any note on the piano, and you go three up and four down, like in
poker, and that's a code.' Now I know it's a major triad, and the thumb always
lands on the key signature note. It works anywhere on the keyboard. And
when he showed me that I thought, Alright, this is a system, I can do that.
And rock and roll came along soon enough that there was a reason it all started
to make sense."

Jim Dickinson with his first guitar, 1956. Photo by Mr. J. B. Dickinson.

Despite its growing presence, black music was still considered trash music by white society. But across town, the white engineer Sam Phillips had begun recording black artists in 1950. He had come to Memphis from the cotton fields of Alabama and was familiar with the sounds that the city slickers gawked at. When he got tired of recording the smooth big bands playing sophisticated music for sophisticated people, he set up a small recording studio and sought what invigorated him. His rural background gave him the insight to tell Howlin' Wolf to play what he played at home, not the more accessible style he'd adapted for the white folks. Phillips knew the audience could conform to the music. His peers asked him why he'd spend time with people who smelled like mules. But the recordings he made—Wolf, Ike Turner, B. B. King—found their way to younger white ears, whose failed attempts at imitating them created rock and roll. The scorn of their parents and friends could not keep them away from this music, and, as is evident in this excerpt of an argument between Sam Phillips and Jerry Lee Lewis right before they recorded "Great Balls of Fire," not even God could deter these men and women who were drawn to what mainstream society referred to as the music of the Devil.

"Jerry. Jerry," Sam Phillips says, calming a man who is haunted by the fire and brimstone of his childhood and the whiskey of his adulthood. "If you think that you can't, can't do good if you're a rock and roll exponent—"

"You can do good, Mr. Phillips, don't get me wrong—"

"Now wait, wait, listen. When I say do good—"

"You can have a kind heart!"

"I don't mean, I don't mean just—"

"You can help people!" Lewis is now chanting a refrain.

"You can save souls!" responds Phillips.

"No! No! No! No!"

"Yes!"

"How can the Devil save souls? What are you talking about?"

The rockabilly artists like Elvis and Jerry Lee brought the strange things that happened on WHBQ at night brazenly into the daylight. To the rest of the world, Elvis in 1954 was as alien as Dewey Phillips's skronk had been coming out of the night sky five years earlier. In his hometown, however, Elvis was not such a freak. Ducktails were becoming common, along with sideburns and a change in the style of dress. What had been latent in the relationship between black and white music was becoming overt; each was groping for the other.

Rock and roll's audience is now a huge chunk of society. But in the music's puberty, the kids and the sound were just becoming acquainted, seeking out each other. Don Nix, a member of the Mar-Keys, remembers, "Nobody had ever heard rock and roll. In Memphis, we were the first ones hearing it, but we didn't realize it. We thought everybody was doing this. Elvis Presley played at our high school, Messick, and it's the first time that I'd ever heard girls scream at anybody they weren't mad at. That was really new to us—screaming! Yeah, I'll have some of that. We formed a garage band, and the fun of it was trying to play whatever was the new record. You never expected to play it like that, but it was fun to try!"

"At our high-school talent show," says Dickinson, "my band and another played rock and roll. The song the other band played had three chords, and the guitarist only knew two, so whenever the third chord came along, he just stopped." The other group had a better drummer and two ducktailed, pretty-boy singers. By the end of the show, Dickinson's band had the singers and the drummer, and everyone else had day jobs.

They became the Regents ('Regency' was the telephone exchange in West Memphis). This was 1957. The core of the group was guitarist Rick Ireland, later an engineer at Memphis's Ardent Studios; a country guitarist named Stanley Neal who had only disdain for rock and roll, except when it paid; the drummer was "Steady" Eddie Tauber. The two singers later enjoyed careers at Stax; Ronnie Stoots toured as the vocalist with the Mar-Keys, and Charles Heinz recorded one of the label's first singles, which won him a career-making offer from ABC. Rejecting it, Heinz cleared the path for Stax's alliance with Atlantic, established with their next release, Rufus and Carla Thomas's "Cause I Love You."

"I didn't take music seriously in high school because the possibility didn't seem to be in the world," says Dickinson, now eligible for a thirty-year pin. "I graduated from high school in 1960, and my band played blues, and we played it like white boys, because that's what we were. And that doesn't seem like a very big deal now, but before the Rolling Stones did it, it wasn't a popular concept. It wasn't okay to play this black music, and it was constantly an issue.

"Other bands in Memphis played some Dixieland, some jazz, various types of more acceptable music, and they might touch one or two rock songs. I maintain that the Regents were the first East Memphis band that played all rock, exclusively rock. And in the whole city, the only other one was what became the Mar-Keys, with Packy Axton and Charlie Freeman. There was nothing acceptable about the music that we played, and there was certainly no way to make it into a career."

"I had developed quite a collection of Sun 45s," says Rick Ireland. "I had the Sonny Burgess stuff, the Warren Smith stuff. All of Billy Riley's stuff. Roland Janes, who played guitar on most of that, was my idol. Dickinson and I met at high school and were both listening to the same thing. First thing we ever learned as a band was 'My Bucket's Got a Hole in It,' Sonny Burgess's version. And we did 'Red Headed Woman' and all that stuff. Stanley, our other guitarist, didn't approve of that but he would play it. He was country-oriented but we made a nice pair, because he was aggressive and would play a lot of solos, and I had jazz tendencies and would lay back and comp things in the background.

"Stanley got me involved with Roy Cash, Johnny Cash's nephew. We played way out in the country and sometimes on this little radio station called KWAM. I had this real nice fifty-foot black extension cord and after we started playing the radio gigs, it disappeared. We used to say they were running KWAM off the extension cord. One day we went to somebody's house to rehearse and there were a couple other guys there who played in some country band. I had a Fender Esquire, a flat solid body guitar, and when one of them saw it, he drawled, 'He got one uh them there biscuit board guitars.' I thought, Ooh shit, what kind of company am I in now?"

The innocence in Memphis nurtured wild times. Adults saw a city of beautiful trees and churches on every corner. Kids saw everything else. They were dancing in the donut shops, kissing at the drive-ins, and fighting wherever they could. A well-tipped carhop could always produce a round of beers, which directly increased the chances of a rumble between preening teens in the parking lot. One particular gang of toughs were all related, the Tillers. In high school, they'd been football stars and always in the newspapers. Later, they made headlines with their criminal exploits. Jimmy Crosthwait, a puppeteer and the washboard player in Mud Boy and the Neutrons, "saw Mike Tiller carve his initials into a guy's chest, not deep, but with a broken bottle, and it was disgusting. It was then that I noticed that his initials were 'emp—ty.'" Another member of Mud Boy, Lee Baker, saw justice served at a teen hangout called Clearpool. "Some guys jumped Mike Tiller and he was wandering around the parking lot with his damn ear in his hand, trying to hold it on. 'Hey man, take me to the hospital.' We did, we took him up to the emergency room and dumped him. I said, 'I ain't going in there with you because I don't want to get involved in this shit.' That was the fighting days."

White adults wanted to believe that their kids' interest in black music was a passing phase. In their day, they had gone to many of the same clubs their children now frequented, enjoying the black big bands that played for white audiences. But when Dickinson's parents found a photograph taken at the Flamingo Room of their son standing between Ike and Tina Turner, they didn't have to know who they were to know what they meant.

West Memphis, Arkansas, is directly across the Mississippi River from Memphis, Tennessee. There is no natural bluff on the Arkansas side, so every spring the farmlands flood. Some springs, water spreads throughout the whole town. Farmers in Arkansas and Missouri conduct their trade there, where the tallest buildings are storage silos, while across the river, people in skyscrapers bet on their labor as commodities like gamblers at the track. Law was a whimsy in West Memphis. The drinking age had more to do with inches than years; if you were tall enough to hand your fifty cents to the bouncer, you were old enough to get in the club. My father moved to Memphis in 1955, and his uncle drove him around town to get a feel for the city. When they had crossed the Mississippi River and were in West Memphis, Uncle Meyer said, "Let me tell you about where you are. In West Memphis, with three hundred dollars, you could phone the sheriff at any time of the day or night and he would meet you, the mayor in tow. You could shoot the mayor dead in cold blood, and for another three hundred, the sheriff would dispose of the body." (When my mother moved to Memphis from New York later in the decade, she left the city's only Chinese restaurant in tears; the waiters weren't Asian and there was white bread on every table.)

Trumpeter Wayne Jackson, white, was born and raised in West Memphis, an unlikely candidate for house musician at Stax or sideman for Jimmy Buffet and Peter Gabriel. "West Memphis is where everybody came to party back then," he says. "I think they could serve liquor. Or they did, anyway. The sailors from Millington [Naval Base, outside Memphis] would all come across the bridge. And Eighth Street, in quote Colored Town unquote, was big gambling. So all the black people would come over there too, gambling along Eighth, Ninth and Tenth Streets in little old dives and honky tonks, drinking rotgut whiskey. West Memphis was wild. They had cockfights under the bridge. And they had a game called Coon on the Log. They would catch a raccoon and put it on a log in the river, just a few yards off the shore, and everybody brings their coon dogs. And they bet on the dogs to see how long it'll take to get that coon off that log. One dog at a time. A lot of times the coon'd win, stay on the log and just wear the dog out."

"I guess West Memphis had laxer cops or something," says Jimmy Crosthwait. "Everybody over there was drunk, and they had to get from there to here, and nobody ever seemed to stop 'em. West Memphis was where Memphians could get extra wild. They always had the girlie flicks over there, where you could see a little tits and ass, or something weird—nudist colony footage."

Everything was looser across the river. The thriving film scene there was the result of Memphis's puritanical Board of Censors. Dominated by Lloyd T. Binford from 1928 to 1955, its authority was so mighty and its parameters of decency so fastidious that the industry lingo adopted the term "Binfordized" when films were heavily censored or banned. As a child, Binford had witnessed a train robbery, and he seized the opportunity to ban all films on the topic; he forbade anything portraying blacks on a social level equal to whites. Charlie Chaplin was considered a communist sympathizer, his work "inimical to the public welfare"; *Rebel Without a Cause, The Wild One,* and, for its lack of biblical accuracy, Cecil B. DeMille's *King of Kings* were all banned.

But it was the music, especially in a trio of clubs, that drew most people across the bridge. In 1959, at the age of sixteen, guitarist Rick Ireland was asked by the owner of the Cotton Club to join the house band on weekends. That he was not legally of age concerned no one. "These were pretty rowdy crowds. Real heavy-duty, sure-enough, truck-driving rednecks—beer-drinking, truck-driving rednecks. Danny's Club was down the street, and they had chicken wire around the bandstand so the beer bottles wouldn't hit the musicians when the fights broke out. At the Cotton Club, they were a little more subtle. We were open to the flying bottles, but if any of the drunks wandered up to the bandstand, they were in for a little surprise. I was playing my guitar and I noticed this piece of bare copper wire that went all around the two-foot-high railing on the bandstand. I just followed this thing off to the dressing room by the stage, and the damn thing was plugged into the wall and in series with a hundred-watt lightbulb. If somebody ran into that, they were going to get quite a jolt."

The Plantation Inn (the PI) was the most popular club of the three. The other two featured country music by white bands, but this one had black bands playing for white audiences. The PI had been established a generation before and had catered to the parents of the teenagers who regularly puked in its parking lot. Throughout the 1950s, the house bands there had evolved from the big swing sound of the Phineas Newborn Sr. Family Band, featuring Phineas Jr. on piano and Calvin on guitar, to the smoother sounds of Willie Mitchell and the Four Kings, and later to an even smaller combo led by Ben Branch, who would become a prominent civil rights activist. Whatever happened in the audience, the bands never played less than world-class music. Patrons were allowed to bring in hard liquor, which was not officially sold on the premises; if one actually had to step outside for the transaction, it was never farther than the parking lot.

The Plantation Inn was a family place, in the way a swing joint run by the Addams Family might be. Morris Berger owned it with his son Louis Jack. There were many places a person could get wild and drunk, but with blacks and whites in the same room, even if separated by the proscenium, the PI provided a peek behind the wall erected by society. Its spirit was summed up on a neon sign hanging near the stage that bore the name of a radio show once hosted by the senior Berger and broadcast from the club: HAVING FUN WITH MORRIS.

"The Plantation Inn looked like a big two-story house," says Wayne Jackson. "There was a doorway about a quarter of the way down the building, and you went in there, and the bar part and the restaurant part was on the left and the bouncer—he was a boxer—you'd go past him and his little desk, and then you'd turn right into the main, big room. There was a sunken dance floor over about sixty percent of the area, and the tables were on the sides. The bandstand was on the far end, where Willie Mitchell and the Four Kings would do their thing. And at the back of the bandstand was a big fan that sucked out the smoke and hats and ladies' wigs. Before I began sneaking in there, I'd stand back behind that fan and listen to the band. So, Willie Mitchell always sounded like, '*Wwwuuhhhwuuuhhhhwuhhh*.'"

"The Plantation Inn was like a roadhouse out of a movie," says Jim Dickinson. "The bouncer's name was Raymond Vega, big ol' nasty guy. Wore a cast on his arm but his arm wasn't broken. It was for hitting people. Sometimes he'd have a cane, and I remember thinking, What's this crippled guy going to do?"

The Phineas Newborn Orchestra was the house band from 1948, the year Calvin began high school, through 1950, when Calvin and Phineas Jr. went on the road with Ike Turner and Jackie Brenston behind what is often considered the first rock and roll record, "Rocket 88."

"My brother had been in high school a year and I was a grade behind him," says Calvin Newborn, who became renowned for his showmanship. "It was pretty tough even for teenagers, going to school every day and playing from nine until two at night, but I enjoyed it because my pockets stayed full and I was able to buy nice clothes. I wore the best shoes. There was a shoe shop right on the corner where I lived, and every morning when I turned the corner going toward the railroad track that I crossed to get to school, I would get my stumps shined."

The Newborn Orchestra employed sophisticated, schooled musicians who could read charts. Phineas Sr. prided himself on his diversity, maintaining a repertoire that included pop hits and smooth jazz standards. His stage shows competed with those of other bands—and with regular Sunday church services—for the most exciting. "It was hard for me to stay still and play," Calvin says. "I was used to doing like them basketball stars, flying. I would get about six feet in the air playing the guitar. As a matter of fact, I used to think I could fly. I felt like I could make myself as light as I wanted to. Even today I dream that I'm walking down the street and spread my arms and just take off and fly." Mama Rose Newborn, Phineas Sr.'s wife, remembers, "They played 'Tennessee Waltz' at the Plantation Inn every night, and the Plantation Inn wife and husband would come out and dance to it." The band was allowed to dip into bebop but, according to Calvin, only late in the night. The generation that followed Phineas Newborn Sr.—Willie Mitchell, Gene "Bowlegs" Miller, Ben Branch—played with more of a bebop edge. Their bands were smaller, shifting to beat-heavy rhythm and blues. "When I was a kid, I loved to dance," says Charlie Miller, a painter. "At the PI, if there were several people on the dance floor that were really dancing well, the band would keep going. There were times when the bands and dancers were jamming. That was beautiful, it really was."

The peculiar spectrum of a Memphis audience created a challenge for the musicians. Fred Ford, a black saxophone player who toured with B. B. King and Johnny Otis, explains, "When I was coming up in the forties, you had to play everything. Even the radio stations played some of everything. You heard Goodman, you heard Basie, you heard Artie Shaw, you heard Lunceford,

Charlie Miller and date at the Plantation Inn. Photo courtesy of
Charlie Miller.

Ellington, Guy Lombardo. You heard country music. Different tastes from
different people. You couldn't go in and play blues all night or jazz all night or
ballads and love songs all night. You had to be very talented, and you had to
have an open mind."

The Stax sound grew out of the bands that played to white audiences at the
Plantation Inn and to black audiences in Memphis clubs. "Ben Branch was the
leader of the band when I started going," says Dickinson. "He eventually went
to Chicago and got into Operation Bread Basket. He was standing next to
King when he was assassinated. He recorded at Stax when it was still Satellite.
These guys played jazz and they sat down when they played. They had music
stands. I don't know what was on them—racing forms, maybe. But they were
the band that everybody copied—the two horns, the thin sound. As compared
to five horns. Or seven horns. Two horns isn't even a chord, it's just an inter-
val. Two horns takes the keyboard to make a chord. It's less sophisticated. The
horn parts by nature become more percussive and Memphis-y. Packy [Axton,
a saxophonist in the Mar-Keys] learned to play from Gilbert Caples. That's
where the whole Stax sound comes from. It's Ben Branch's band, pure and
simple. The idea of light horns is, I think, the Memphis sound phenomenon."

"If Ben Branch was an influence, Bowlegs Miller was too," says Stax saxman
Andrew Love, who was not allowed in the PI audience because of the color of
his skin. "The Stax sound was just a Memphis sound, and Ben and Bowlegs

were two of the most popular bandleaders in town." In Memphis proper, there were black clubs up and down Beale Street and scattered through the north and south sides of the city. When he was in the tenth grade, Love was tapped by Bowlegs Miller, and he had to regularly sneak out to make the gig; his father, a preacher, forbade this devil's music. Love remembers that his mother bought his horn when his father was out of town. They came out of the store and a big long car drove past, on the side of which was painted "B. B. King." Someone yelled out the car window, "You'll be sorry!"

"Memphis was a music town, and some of the best musicians in the country lived here and played here for five dollars a night, ten, twelve, fifteen dollars on up through the years," says Love. "Fred Ford would come by and borrow my saxophone and before he'd leave, he'd play some licks for me. 'Can you do this?' I learned from Fred Ford, I learned from Robert Talley—I had some of the best teachers around. When I was about fifteen, a big band asked me to try out. They told me I wasn't ready and to come back when I got a little more control of my horn. I was just happy to be there trying, high-school kid."

Underage Memphis teens both black and white were sneaking into clubs across town from each other to hear the same bands, who played differently—like different dialects of the same language—to each audience. That intensified the cultural divide the players had to cross when they finally met. The Stax sound is the result of a post-bebop generation coming together from semi-quarantined cultures to imitate different versions of the same bands.

The West Memphis scene careened along pleasantly for several years. "We thought we were sneaky for going to the other end of West Memphis," says Wayne Jackson, "which was really just down the street from where our parents lived. The deal was that Louis Jack knew all our parents—hell, West Memphis was five thousand people back then. Everybody knew everybody. And they knew where we were the whole time. Louis Jack would say, 'Well, I won't let 'em drink but a little, and I'll run 'em off before it gets too late.' We thought we was hiding. Mamma and Daddy'd say, 'Well, Louis Jack'll run them out about ten-thirty,' and sure enough, we'd be home about eleven."

"Hanging out in nightclubs really wasn't that big a deal," says Charlie Miller, the painter who loved to dance. "After the prom, you were expected to go to the PI. That was a tradition, everybody did it. Our parents knew we were drinking, but it wasn't that big a deal to them. When I was a kid, if you were drinking, it was uncool to look like you were drunk. Anybody that got out of hand was looked down on."

On the morning of February 20, 1960, one girl did not come home on time. One boy had gotten out of hand. "Memphis Girl Found Slain—Police

Say Boy Admits It" screamed the *Memphis Press Scimitar* headline. The sub-headline, "Stamp on Hand," rang the death knell for both fourteen-year-old Carol Feathers and the West Memphis club scene.

By her mother's account in the newspaper, the ninth-grader frequented the Cotton Club. "Carol was a wonderful dancer. Many times they'd clear the floor at the Cotton Club or wherever she was just to let her dance. She could just dance and dance, and she would always stay until the place closed at 4:30 in the morning, just dancing." On the night of the nineteenth, she ran into an old beau, former high-school basketball star Jerry Blankenship, seventeen, married, with a wife nine months pregnant. Blankenship drove her to an abandoned dog track in West Memphis that had become a lover's lane. She refused his advances, a fight ensued, and after hitting her with a tree branch, Blankenship, according to the newspaper, "left the dying girl, her life-blood dripping onto an old crime magazine in the dump."

Heavy emphasis was placed on the Cotton Club stamp still on Blankenship's hand at the time of his arrest. The papers reported that from behind the Crittenden County jail's bars, he shouted, "All this would never have happened if I hadn't been allowed to go in the Cotton Club and drink. They ought to padlock that place and burn it to the ground."

Blankenship got his wish. By the twenty-fourth of the month, the Cotton Club and Danny's were padlocked. The court order cited "public disturbances, unlawful drinking of beer by minors, quarrels, affrays and general breaches of the peace." The Plantation Inn was allowed to remain open. But the Bergers knew they had an image problem and soon built a new establishment, Pancho's, serving Mexican food. It included a club in the back, the El Toro, which became the hip spot in the mid-sixties. During the interim, the PI enacted a change and minors, as the sign had always declared, were not allowed in.

In consideration of their motto, "Having Fun with Morris," a large speaker was attached to the exterior of the building so the music could be heard in the parking lot. "I remember going over there," says Dickinson, "laying in the back of the car listening to the band through that metal horn, just drunk as a dog."

The venues for the young white bands in the late fifties were rental halls, churches, and YMCAs, with sponsors ranging from high-school fraternities to more stoic church groups. The bar scene was not open to them, nor was it appealing. Few of the older white bands were getting lost in the new music.

"We were playing with girl dancers and did the things that should have been impossible for a sixteen-, seventeen-year-old kid from East Memphis to do," says Dickinson. "The two other vocalists sang the slick pretty stuff, and I sang the ugly stuff. We played Muddy Waters and Howlin' Wolf and what I thought then was Chicago music, which was in reality all mid-South music. We used to save blues for the end of the night to run off the crowds, and I remember real well when they began staying, when they started requesting Jimmy Reed songs and stuff like that. I thought, Well obviously something is changing here."

"Jimmy Reed was somebody who had a bunch of harps and was real big and had a big old blue shiny suit and was insane," says Lee Baker, Mud Boy's guitarist. "He had a hit record, 'Baby, What You Want Me to Do?' on the white peoples' chart. They played dances and stuff here, like at Clearpool, and people would go out to hear Jimmy Reed. It was conducive to having a good time because you could hear that stuff, get drunk on your hidden bottle, and just go nuts. Which we did. Hank Ballard, Bo Diddley, Jimmy Reed—that was pop music. Not pop music as such, but talk about hit records and Jimmy Reed was right up there."

"The first records I ever bought were Jimmy Reed and Nat King Cole," says Don Nix of the Mar-Keys. "I thought that Jimmy Reed lived in New York in a penthouse. People that made records, especially records that I loved—I thought that everybody on the Jimmy Reed album was rich. I knew that Nat King Cole was on TV and he was a big star and real wealthy, so I just assumed that Jimmy Reed was, with a chauffeur and all that. And four years later I'm playing with Jimmy Reed! And he's bringing in the equipment out of an old Mercury station wagon, doesn't even have a roadie! It was a shock to me even then."

By the late 1950s, if your guitarist knew a Chuck Berry song, your band could get a gig. (Berry's first hit, "Maybelline," was released in July of 1955.) Most bands had incorporated rock and roll into their repertoire, but few had dispensed with the other, more acceptable styles. Only the Regents and the Mar-Keys devoted themselves to what was termed by others "nigger music," and the anger these two bands heard from those who used the term let them know they were reaching people. Jim King and the Crowns tried. King was a guitarist, and the few years he had on the Regents and the Mar-Keys put a showbiz taint to his act. His vocalist was Jerry McGill, who couldn't shake the full, almost operatic quality of his voice. McGill, however, was a wild man, and his devotion to the rock and roll life earned him a stint as Waylon Jennings's road manager and later a felony conviction for which he went on the lam. Sam Phillips recognized his talent and released one record on McGill and the Topcoats in 1959.

The fraternity parties that did not go to the wild white bands usually went

to an older black guitarist named Thomas Pinkston. He maintained a staid society gig at the Tennessee Club, where many of these kids' parents were members. His playing was lively and full of character. But he'd been raised on Beale
Street and was not easy to impress. His combos could perform on sandbars
and in barns, places where there was no electricity and the focus of the party
was a raging bonfire. Pinkston's business card read "World's Finest Negro
Hawaiian Guitarist."

While they were dabbling in studios trying to record something good
enough to release, the Regents, because nobody else would, began backing a
clean-cut local singer named Kimball Coburn. In his favor, he had a regional
hit with the apropos title "Cute," and he only joined them for two songs per
set. But when he'd lay on his back and wiggle his legs in the air, the Regents
didn't feel like the nasty rockers they knew themselves to be.

When Bill Black and Scotty Moore quit Elvis in 1958, their first gig back in
Memphis was the going-away party for Wink Martindale's move to California. On the bill were local stars Thomas "Tragedy" Wayne, Warren Smith,
and Kimball Coburn, the Regents' recompense. Bill Black was an extremely af-
fable, warm-hearted, and humorous guy who loved and appreciated the craziness in rock and roll, and who died from a brain tumor at thirty-nine in 1965.
In the small circle of Memphis rock, he'd previously admired Dickinson's
band, noting that they played without a bassist. That night, he volunteered to
join them onstage.

Each band did two sets. The Regents opened, with Dickinson singing
"Send Me Some Loving." "Warren Smith came up to me after the set and
complimented me on that song. It was the first time anybody heavy had said
something to me like that. Blew me away." Then Ronnie Angel did two
songs, then Kimball did his two. "Bill never asked what key we were in or
nothing, just fell right in," remembers Dickinson. "We got to 'Cute,' which
had four or five chords in it, which at the time was a hell of a lot of chords. Especially for one song. I was playing an upright piano and there was a microphone stuck up by the strings. Bill leaned down by me and says real loud over
the music, right into the microphone, 'What's the name of this song?' He's
playing along, and his question is broadcast over the P.A. I say, 'Cute.' He then
announces, 'Never heard it.'

"Second set, Bill came on the stage with us again and by that time we were
all reasonably lit. It was a little looser. Kimball's big song in the second set was
'Boo-Be-Ah-Be Pretty Baby,' which I can still barely bring myself to say. He
starts playing this song, and Bill starts shaking his head. He leans down to me,

he had to see the microphone there, and he yells, 'Dickinson! What are you doing playing with this fruit?'"

The Regents did make a few early recordings, though they were so dissatisfied with what would have been their first single that they had to threaten to sue to keep it from coming out. How bad could it have been that the band would have canceled their debut? "The session was something our vocalist Stoots put together, and it was humiliating. It was called 'Education Blues,' and the producer's girlfriend had written it. We recorded it because we were children doing what we were told." With no pause in his conversation, Dickinson begins to recite lyrics from three decades back: "Brand-new pair of blue jeans/brand-new white buck shoes/I'm ready for the school days/Got the education blues."

Before Dickinson went to Texas for theater school in 1960, breaking up the Regents, they were invited out to the nascent Stax studio, then called Satellite and located outside of Memphis in Brunswick, Tennessee. "That was the first night I ever met Packy Axton," says Dickinson. "He was cooking hamburgers in the ice cream stand out front and running back and trying to make the music stick to the tape. You could see the needle move but you couldn't hear anything. Boy, that was so primitive, it's hard to imagine how primitive that was. Ampex mono machines. Ricky [Ireland] got on the telephone and called one of the local equipment suppliers. He comes back and says it wasn't working because the tape wasn't lubricated. [Laughs.] And Packy, I thought, We're out here in Brunswick with this fucking teenage wino! That's one of the reasons that I always thought that Stax shit was funny. I know where it came from."

CHAPTER FIVE

Kicks and Spins and All the Flips

AS THE 1950S BECAME THE 1960S, MORE AND MORE WHITE KIDS WERE digging black music. Once Stax Records began moving in that direction, the route from a barn behind a burger stand in Brunswick, Tennessee, to the top of the pop charts with Otis Redding's "Dock of the Bay" proved astonishingly direct. However, soul music was not their original intention. The label began as a hobby for a banker, Jim Stewart, who also played fiddle in a country band. His sister, Estelle Axton, was a bank teller and thought her brother could carry a nice little tune. The combination of their last names gave the label its title, but its direction came from elsewhere.

Estelle Axton had a son, Packy, who was kind of big and a little bit clumsy. He had a goofy grin and he loved, positively *loved*, having a good time. While the story of Stax falls like dominoes, it was the oft-overlooked Packy who tipped the first one. Jim Stewart the fiddle player wasn't considering a career in black music, Estelle Axton the bank teller sure wasn't, and Steve Cropper, who was, would never have been around the place had it not been for Packy.

"As it turned out, Packy was a really, really good saxophone player and played on a lot of hit records and produced a lot of good records over at Stax," says Steve Cropper, revealing the happy ending to a story with dubious beginnings: "Charles Axton, we called him Packy, came to me one day in school, we were going to Messick, and he said, 'Hey, I hear you guys got a band and I'd like to be in your band.' And I go, 'Well, we're really not looking for anybody, we're pretty happy with what we've got.' And he said, 'Well, I play horn,' and I go, 'Well, I don't think we want horns.' It was two guitarists, bass, and drums, and we were perfectly happy with that. We'd been playing a lot of sock hops and dances and stuff like that. I asked Packy, 'How long have you been playing?' and he said, 'I've been taking lessons for about three months,' and I'm going, yeah, okay, great. Somewhere in the conversation he mentioned something about his mother or his uncle having a recording studio, and I went, 'Oh, really?' And it sort of ended with, 'Can you be at rehearsal this coming Saturday?'"

Cropper played with a band called the Royal Spades. Born of youthful exuberance, the name now seems offensive; they say they were named for the suit in cards, like other soul groups. They had a regular gig near the naval base, where the rowdiness of the sailors was second to theirs. The quartet included Donald "Duck" Dunn, who would join Cropper in Booker T. and the MGs, the Stax rhythm section; Charlie Freeman, the envy of most other guitarists in town; and Terry Johnson, the youngest member, playing drums. Before expanding their lineup and releasing their first record, "Last Night," which propelled them to national fame, they changed their name to the Marquis, then changing the spelling so there'd be no doubt about how to pronounce it: The Mar-Keys. They became one of the earliest, if not the first white band accepted on the black music circuit.

"In about 1957, I was taking lessons from the Memphis Symphony and playing in a jug band," says Johnson, the drummer. "What we played wasn't even music, but a shopping center hired us anyway. Steve Cropper lived near there, happened to walk by, and then asked me if I wanted to play with him and Charlie. They told Duck to buy a bass and taught him. We did Chuck Berry songs, Bo Diddley, that kind of stuff. People hired us to play for free beer—I was thirteen so free beer was great—but after we played seven or eight tunes, we'd quit because we didn't know any more."

With the addition of Packy, the band moved their rehearsals to the Brunswick storehouse that his uncle, Jim Stewart, was converting to a one-track studio. Soon they added countrified keyboardist Jerry Lee "Smoochy" Smith; vocalist Ronnie "Angel" Stoots, who'd begun his professional career with Dickinson in the Regents; and perhaps the most important addition, an expanded horn section with Don Nix on baritone sax and occasional vocals and Wayne Jackson on trumpet. Several of the musicians in this lineup had already garnered professional experience. Cropper had written an instrumental, "Flea Circus," when he was fifteen that Bill Justis recorded in 1958, and, concurrent with playing in Brunswick, Cropper was also doing some session work at the Sam Phillips Recording Service. Roland Janes remembers, "We worked three or four sessions there with Jerry Lee Lewis where we had Scotty [Moore] playing the rhythm guitar, Steve Cropper played baritone guitar, and I played lead."

Wayne Jackson, the last member to join the band, regularly sneaked out his bedroom window to establish himself as "the West Memphis Flash," playing trumpet with acts ranging from the Arkansas All State Symphony to "this guy who billed himself as 'Jim Climer, Ninety Pounds of Rock and Roll.'" Married in the eleventh grade, he played the Memphis Rodeo and was paid enough to cover the expenses for his daughter's birth that year. "It dawned on me, I had just made more money in ten days than I had made all year."

His first gig in a nightclub prepared him for the excitement that would later surround the Mar-Keys. "Beale Street wasn't a place I went, but on North Main Street in Memphis there was the Copacabana. I went there with a drummer who was deaf, and I know I was fifteen because I'd just bought my car. I knew 'Cherry Pink and Apple Blossom White,' 'Stardust,' a few songs. We sat in and on the first song a fight broke out. I'd parked that Plymouth near the club. I never will forget, man, the bottles were flying and people were fighting, and I got my trumpet in my case and me and the drummer were headed for the door—Errol Flynn escaping! We were hanging on the wall trying to get by and some pregnant woman was there on crutches. She stood up and said to some guy, 'You can't hit me, I'm pregnant.' And she lowered the boom on him and broke her crutches all to pieces."

Jackson met a couple members of the Royal Spades when they heard him rehearsing with another band. They were looking for a trumpet to finish their lineup, and since the gig came with a recording studio, Jackson accepted. While the kids practiced, Jim Stewart learned to operate the equipment he'd bought when his sister had mortgaged her house. She kept her job at the bank, and she opened the Satellite Dairy, an ice cream stand, to bring in spare change. With the same eye toward cash flow, she began retailing records, discovering that it was a quick way to judge market trends. When Stax was finally established in a former Memphis movie house, they sold records from the theater's old lobby.

In Brunswick, Stewart made several unremarkable attempts at country music and white pop. The first effort released, however, featured the Veltones, a black vocal group. The reason these country gentlemen got involved with soul stirrers is the reason Packy Axton is responsible for Stax's direction: He was taking saxophone lessons from the Veltones' Gilbert Caples, whom he'd admired from the floor of the Plantation Inn. He brought these black musicians to the studio. "Like Dewey Phillips, Packy saw race in a more enlightened way than was typical in Memphis in the late fifties and early sixties," says Jim Dickinson, who later worked with him. "The community aspect of Stax in the ghetto, I don't think any of that would have happened but for the influence of Packy Axton, and Packy's friendship with Bongo Johnny Keyes, his black conga-playing partner who worked at the lobby record store. I don't think there's any doubt about what Packy brought 'em. Jim Stewart was upstairs in the office behind the dragon door. Packy was in the street. And that's where the music is."

"The music was changing in those days," says Andrew Love, the black saxophone player with the Memphis Horns. "The big-band players were getting older and the music in the clubs was rhythm and blues, the kind of music rock and roll came from. They used to call me Andrew 'Honky Tonk' Love, because of how I could play that Bill Doggett tune. I loved jazz then, still do, but I got married at an early age, and jazz players didn't make that many gigs and didn't make as much money around here. I had a young family so I had to stick to the more commercial side, the money-making kind of music."

"The Mar-Keys were the first white band in Memphis to have horn players," says Don Nix, who now lives near Nashville but bypassed all those recording studios to return to Memphis in 1993 to make *Back to the Well*, his first album in over a decade. "We used to sneak over to West Memphis to the Plantation Inn and those places where all the black bands played. And all the black bands had horns. So while everybody else was playing Elvis Presley songs with two guitars and a bass or whatever, we had baritone, tenor, and trumpet, and we played all rhythm and blues music, which no other white band at that time was doing in Memphis. Or anywhere that I knew of. It was just there, and nobody was playing it."

"We were fourteen, fifteen, sixteen years old," says Terry Johnson, the Mar-Keys' drummer, "playing serious black music. Other bands would play 'Walk, Don't Run,' basic guitar rock and roll. We would be out there playing 'You Can't Sit Down' by Phil Upchurch. We'd go over to the Plantation Inn and buy liquor. And they'd let us in over at Currie's Tropicana [off Beale Street], or we'd spend all night sitting on the curb down on Beale Street by the old Handy Club and listen to Evelyn Young play saxophone, sitting there with beer that some black guy had gone around the corner and bought for us. Sometimes we'd encounter 'What are you doing here?' and 'Get out of our neighborhood,' but when we said, 'Hey, we play, we want to learn this stuff,' everybody was real congenial. Particularly because Charlie Freeman was always with us. Charlie was the guy who really had this vision of white guys playing black music. And he had a silver tongue and he was slick and he could talk us into anywhere and get us anything we wanted anywhere we wanted. Charlie could always pull it off."

Painter Charlie Miller was a student at Tech High when Don Nix was sent

there. Tech was the city school's safety net, where the delinquents were transferred and taught a trade before they flunked out completely. "I went out to
listen to the rehearsals in a garage behind somebody's house," says the soft-
spoken Miller. "That was funny, I knew they were pretty heavy back then.
That guy Charlie Freeman, he was a fantastic damn guitar player. When he
played, you knew that was world-class. You knew right away. The others in
the band all respected the hell out of him. They knew how good he was."

But back then, a great guitar player did not a popular band make. Don Nix
was the loaded gun, the one who could draw the crowds because he was so
completely entertaining to watch. "Nix had a hell of a personality," says Miller.
"He could do the same thing anyone else would do, but it would be entertaining. Back when all the guys wanted to be Marlon Brando, Don wasn't quite
like that. Don was a real skinny guy, and everybody had their shirt sleeves
pegged to show off their muscles. Don's would be pegged, and his arms looked
like string hanging out. I remember one time at one of those dances, he walked
up to some real big guy, tapped the guy on the shoulder like you do to cut in,
and when the guy turned around, Don grabbed *him* and started dancing. And
then he could convince the guy not to beat him up."

The Royal Spades continued to play sock hops and teen dances, while
Charlie Freeman's style was winning attention from other musicians in town.
Well-known white bands began hiring him. Between his talent and Duck
Dunn's amiability and eagerness, they wound up integrating the Memphis
club scene.

In 1960 or early 1961, shortly after the Feathers murder, the Penthouse was
an ailing Memphis nightspot. Its owners approached an enterprising young
man named Herbie O'Mell. A go-getter, O'Mell had struck up a friendship
with Dewey Phillips in the 1950s, so that when he sponsored dances at the
Chisca Hotel, the disc jockey would encourage all the kids to come down.
O'Mell was a dancing fiend. He'd won a local twist contest, gone on to Dallas
and then the Palladium in New York where he was declared the national twist
champion. The afternoon gigs were his favorite. "Every club had tea dances,"
he says. "Every day. Boy, you'd go out there at one or two o'clock in the afternoon and I mean every married woman in town would be there, and salesmen
from all over. At five o'clock you'd better be out of the way of the door or
you'd get trampled, those women trying to beat their husbands home."

O'Mell's face is still boyish. Beneath a full head of curly hair, his prominent
eyes shine blue. Several of his clubs have been integral in shaping Memphis
music, and he remains active in the entertainment business, most recently
sought by the casinos now proliferating in the Mississippi Delta. "First thing,

I went upstairs to the Penthouse and saw they had a band in white tux coats with music stands. I closed the place down. I went out to Thomas Street and raided Club Currie's where the Largos and Ben Branch were playing. Ben was the tenor player, Floyd Newman on bari sax, Mickey Collins, he's a great piano player, and Big Bell was playing drums. Then I got Duck Dunn and Charlie Freeman to come up there, and that became the first integrated band in Memphis. It wasn't that I ran out and got Duck and Charlie and said, 'Here are the two guys.' Ben was talking to 'em and I was talking to 'em and they wanted to play."

Isaac Hayes, who sang with Ben Branch for five dollars a night, confirms the event. "It was a big deal. Everybody was talking about it. 'Wow, man! They got a white dude playing with a black band!' That was something in those days."

O'Mell consciously remodeled the Penthouse after the black joints on Beale. He was older than the upcoming crop of musicians; he'd been in the same grade as Elvis, though he attended a different school. As an entrepreneur, he had established friendships with Sunbeam Mitchell and various other Beale Street club owners, gaining access where other whites would not or could not go. "I was really influenced by the black scene in the late fifties. They'd let me in the Hippodrome on Beale and make me stand behind the bar, but I got to watch those acts. I was seeing Joe Henderson and Faye Adams and Evelyn Young and Bill Harvey and the guys that passed through his band. I could get into Club Handy or the Flamingo Hotel, and there wouldn't be three white people in the whole place." O'Mell was taken to the Village Vanguard in North Memphis, a jazz bar; to a no-name place at Third and McLemore beneath the viaduct that promoted younger black bands—like the Impalas, featuring the Hodges brothers before they settled in at Hi Records; to the Rosewood, to Melvin Malunda's and Melvin Bonds's clubs.

Willie Mitchell and O'Mell had become fast friends early on, and the two would go out late nights for chorus girls. "Willie would play until four or five in the morning at the Manhattan Club, and we'd leave there and go over to a place called Tony's and order a plate of what was called 'chorus girls.' They'd take a can of sardines and line 'em up real pretty on a big oval platter, and we'd eat those while listening to Ironin' Board Sam play."

When the Penthouse reopened, it was rocking. It was the first place whites could go within the city limits for the West Memphis experience. "I'll never forget the first two weeks," says O'Mell. "Big Bell made Duck turn around backward to the audience and face him. He said, 'I'll show you how to play that.' I think Duck got a lot of influence there playing with them. It was really a great band." Little Willie John was a regular at the club, living at Herbie's house for a few months. Despite the excitement, the Penthouse lasted less than a year. Though the place stayed jammed, the cops, in an effort to discourage the interracial mixing, regularly stopped cars leaving the club, harassing the patrons. O'Mell says squarely, "The people stopped coming because they got worn out by the Memphis Police Department."

While gigging at the Penthouse, Freeman and Dunn were still rehearsing in the studio with the Royal Spades. Things were heating up there too. They'd moved from the country to an old movie theater that producer Chips Moman found. Mr. Stewart, in Wayne Jackson's words, "was trying to plug the walls into the walls and figure out what a microphone was," and the Mar-Keys were developing a basic riff into a basic song, one that would become a national hit they could call their own, even if no one can say with certainty who is playing what on the record. "'Last Night' was the biggest mistake that ever happened," says Terry Johnson, whose version of events turns magnetic tape to Scotch tape, but it conveys the aptitude—and attitude—of the people trying to plug the walls into the walls. "'Last Night' has eighty-six splices on it," says Johnson, "and probably twenty to twenty-five musicians. I would seriously doubt if any musician played through the whole tune. Probably the most famous person on that record was Steve Cropper, who is a real premier guitarist. People don't even realize there was no guitar on the song! Cropper's alternating keyboards with Smoochy. Some drummer named Curtis Green, I know for sure, did the final roll on it because he could never explain to any of the rest of us how in the hell he did it. And what it was was another mistake. He entered half a beat early, and somehow tripped himself up and caught himself, and it came out to this great, terrific roll. He got his money after the tune was cut and we never saw him again."

Like Ray Charles's "What'd I Say," released two years earlier, "Last Night" is so simple it's almost silly. But it's that very baseness that makes it transcend time, makes it as exciting today as when first released in 1961. "What'd I Say," with its sultry call and response, captured the crest of America's sexual freedom. "Last Night" is about ass-shaking. It's an instrumental with a bunch of horns and a cheesy organ. It says, We know we're not much, folks, but watch this. And then, like a jug band, from nothing they make something great. You can feel the fun in the song, the teenage freedom, the glee of kids achieving something they thought beyond their capabilities. The song takes us with them as they sneak out to West Memphis when they're supposed to be dreaming in the comfort of their parents' heated homes. It plays just behind the beat, most obviously when the musicians break, and suddenly we feel like we're fall-

The Mar-Keys, before and after the innocence.

On tour, August 1961. Left to right: Wayne Jackson, Packy Axton, Steve Cropper, Don Nix, Ronnie Stoots, Terry Johnson, Duck Dunn. Photo courtesy of Memphis Music Hall of Fame.

Mar-Keys promo shot taken in spring 1965 for a Ray Brown–organized European tour that didn't happen. Left to right: Don Nix, Duck Dunn, Terry Johnson, Wayne Jackson, Packy Axton, Steve Cropper. Photo courtesy of the Memphis Music and Blues Museum.

ing forward. The horns, just barely in time, come in and save us. That sort of tension was common in clubs in Memphis and across the river, but the way people outside responded was another hint to locals that things happened differently here. "Last Night" was not Ray Charles, not Motown, not slick, and people all over the country loved it.

And no one had any reason to suspect it was white kids.

The guys who had recently been trying to shoo Packy Axton in the high-school hall were suddenly national sensations. They'd found their voice in R&B, bypassing jazz. Dewey Phillips liked the song because the break gave him a natural place to talk. After the record got hot regionally, Atlantic gave it national distribution. The Memphis company learned of another Satellite label already established, and "Last Night" was reissued as the first release under the new Stax name. The record's staged growth allowed Terry Johnson to finish high school before touring. Between its recording and release, Charlie Freeman had taken a job with a "mickey" band, a road act that wore fancy clothes and played Mickey Mouse music; he was traveling when he heard the song on the radio and did not rejoin the Mar-Keys until Steve Cropper quit during the first tour. For the tour, the Mar-Keys brought Ronnie Stoots as vocalist, Carla Thomas came along to promote her hit, "Gee Whiz," and Mrs. Axton boarded the van as the watchful chaperone. The kids wasted no time in grossing out the women, who quickly fled. With the van to themselves, the road as their home, and stardom as their oyster, they toured for months at a stretch, returning to Memphis long enough to throw wild rock and roll parties, and then setting out for another string of one-nighters.

"We were making a hundred dollars a night in 1961!" remembers Jackson. "Plus royalties—in our teens! People were taking our pictures!"

"What you had was eight guys between the ages of eighteen and twenty who just wanted to get out on the road and play and party their butts off. And that's exactly what we did, and that's probably why the band was a one-hit wonder," says Johnson. "It's hard to be a two-hit wonder when you leave the Dick Clark show and he's waving at you and everybody in the band is shooting him the bird. Typically, they don't play your second record when you do that. It's hard to be more than a one-hit wonder when you've got a twenty-one-day tour of Texas booked and the whole band takes off to Mexico. Mexico was great. We'd come into this little town, all of us in a line like in the Westerns, and the Mexican kids in the street would start going, 'Ba-dup ba-dup,' imitating the horn riff from the song. After three weeks we phoned home and said, 'We've lost our bus because we sold it.' All we wanted to do was have fun, chase women, drink beer. We did it the storybook way. And I think everybody at the time knew we had to live this experience now, and the hell with the consequences. We wanted this memory burning in our brains when we're sitting in the old folks' home, incontinent."

"We were just dumb teenagers that had never been out of Memphis," says Don Nix, "and it's a wonder we're still alive. Ninety percent of the places we were booked were black clubs, and in 1961 it wasn't really cool for either the white side of town or the black side of town to have white teenage boys playing in a black club."

On the road, their gigs were divided between package shows, sometimes with R&B stars, sometimes with country acts, and roadside joints where the Mar-Keys were the evening's entertainment. On the package shows, segregation forced them to stay in separate hotels, eat in separate restaurants, and ride a separate bus. "We were booked at the Regal Theatre, which is in South Chicago, all black neighborhood, all black audience—all black," says Don Nix. "There were nine other acts on the show. LaVern Baker was the headline. Everybody else would go on and do their record at the time, one or two songs, and come off. But LaVern got to do thirty minutes. We came on before her because 'Last Night' was number one and the flip side, 'The Night Before,' was number two in Chicago. So we got to come on next to last.

"The announcer said, 'The Mar-Keys!' and there was a lot of applause as the curtain opened and then everybody in the audience just kind of set and looked. And you could hear throughout the audience: 'White boys!' Oh lord! But the Mar-Keys were a really good band at that time. And we destroyed that audience. So much so that LaVern Baker came out and they didn't really want to hear her. The next day we were the headliners and she was on before us. Which didn't sit very well with LaVern Baker and she cussed us the whole time. We did a whole week there. But on the last night they had a big party for everybody and she bought us a bottle of champagne."

"Don knew more about entertaining than we did," says Wayne Jackson. "He knew to be crazy and do really wild stuff. If the audience threw stuff at us for fun, he'd throw it back and start a riot. We didn't know to do that. So we thought he was nuts. But everybody liked Don, he's got a personality. He looks right and he's funny and he just would be there—that was his talent. Like Steve Cropper had a talent for being in the right place in the right circumstances, Don Nix had his own kind of talent."

Cropper remembers another kind of show. "We played up in Kentucky, a place called the Cherry Club. It was back in the woods, and we had to drive way down this dirt road, took us forever to find it. We got the van to the back door and started unloading these instruments, and there's not too many people around. It comes pretty close to about show time, and now these people are wondering what are all these white guys doing. And we had noticed, when we were setting up the bandstand, there were holes in the wall that looked like they could have been made by a shotgun or something. It turned out to be a pretty rowdy place. And of course they started drinking early. When we got up to play, they all but booed us off the stage. And I never will forget a big lady grabbed a butcher knife out of the kitchen, she had heard us warming up during the day, and she jumped up on stage and says, 'You're gonna listen to these guys!' because she knew that it was us who had the hit record. And so we started right off with 'Last Night' and the minute we hit it, six bars in, everybody's jumping, dancing, and at the end of the night they didn't want us to go.

"People always had doubts about us being the same guys who had 'Last Night,'" he continues. "We'd go out there and open up with Ray Charles's 'Sticks and Stones' or something like that and do all these steps and flips we'd learned from West Memphis, and people were just amazed. Duck and I would flank the horns so you had two guitar players with three horns in the middle—a five-man front—and we're doing kicks and spins and all the flips and all that, people couldn't believe it. We put on a pretty impressive show, and that kept us in big demand everywhere. We drew from what we'd seen in clubs as teenagers, and I think that's what made the Mar-Keys go over. We had to perform that, that service, do more than just play our instruments."

There was an ongoing power struggle in the band and that tension kept their gigs crisp and tight. Packy, drunk and whining, complained that since he'd brought the Mar-Keys into the studio, the band should be his. Cropper, unflappable, stern, the responsible one, wasn't about to yield the reigns to an alcoholic. He did finally quit, though Packy was not the victor. Cropper returned to the studio, his first love, and while touring one day in some indistinguishable city, Packy saw his band's second album for sale.

"Last Night" had made it clear that the Mar-Keys were never assured of playing on their own records. However, they had at least been there; they had even, by default, become the studio's first house band, backing William Bell ("You Don't Miss Your Water") and touring behind him regionally. But as the studio drew more players, and as the Mar-Keys kept to the road, they had less and less involvement with songs issued under that name. (By the mid-sixties, a Mar-Keys performance was simply Booker T. and the MGs with horns.) "The second album was on the market, and it sure as hell couldn't have been us," says Johnson, "because we were gone the whole time. But Floyd Newman and those guys put a nice one together."

"I don't know if Charlie Freeman ever got to play on the Mar-Keys records," says Wayne Jackson. "Terry wasn't a studio-quality drummer—at least that's what they said. And Packy could not get along with Jim Stewart, so he wasn't allowed. Don Nix can't play a lick and he would do strange things, so he was out. He eventually learned to play enough to keep his job. And Smoochy was such a redneck, he didn't fit in the studio scene, although he continued to bring in little songs and things. Duck, Steve, and I were the only ones who actually made it into the studio."

"I didn't play on any sessions after a certain point," says Nix. "Not after they got good musicians to play. I was the only thing they had for a while. I could do it on the road, but for records it was clear they'd rather use other guys. I understood that. Eventually, I was producing, and that's all I ever wanted to do. I wanted to write and to put records together in the studio."

The touring Mar-Keys milked "Last Night" for nearly two years. Stax continued to release follow-up songs ("Banana Juice" is one of my favorites), then a second album. In 1963, they played a cold three-week stint in St. Paul, Minnesota. They had no record on the charts, the gigs were paying less, Freeman and Packy were getting crazier, and it was starting to snow. "We all hated each other's guts from being cooped up on that damn bus for so long," says Johnson, adding that they all remain friends—those who survived. "We quit, and it looked like rats leaving a sinking ship. We'd run the bus into the ocean when we were in South Carolina so we were taking our own personal cars. It was eight guys saying, 'It's over, it's over.' And driving south at this incredible speed just to end it.

"Of the people in the band, the live ones ended up staying in music. When we used to say, 'What do you want to be when you grow up,' none of us ever thought you could make your living as a musician. Packy's ambition, he would tell us, 'Be an alcoholic, that's what I'm gonna be.' And he set out on that trail. And Charlie [Freeman] was set on that path very early. Packy died at age thirty with acute cirrhosis of the liver. And a drug overdose at thirty-one killed Charlie Freeman. They could have been plumbers or fishermen or God knows what, and they'd still be dead."

Theirs were two of the earliest rock and roll deaths, warning flags to others. Axton and Freeman had never suspected their destinies could really be so free. The life their talents brought them made every day an unreality, and indulgences had been part of the unreal game since they'd been invited to play. Two polar opposites taken down in their primes: Packy too big for his body, constantly pushing toward the front; Freeman introspective, a master of subtlety and taste.

Steve Cropper became an essential member of the Stax organization, writing songs, producing, and playing guitar. Don Nix would produce many albums for the company, working hard to bring a white hit to the label—Stax wanted what Sun had gotten—and in the 1970s he worked closely with Leon Russell and Joe Cocker. Terry Johnson became a clinical psychologist, and vocalist Ronnie Stoots a graphic artist; both keep a hand in music. Smoochy Smith has run several nightclubs and always remained a player, currently joining several Sun veterans playing rockabilly in the Sun Rhythm Section. Duck Dunn and Wayne Jackson were integral at Stax, and they also remained active in Memphis clubs until 1967, when they realized they could make a living without wearing themselves out every night. "It takes a long time, when you're good and people love to hear you play, to get the hard-on down," says Jackson. "To get where you don't want to play all the time. I still love it, and if it were fun music, I'd still be out there playing all the time. I moved back to West Memphis after the Mar-Keys, and on the way home from my gig, I'd pass the El Toro, which had been the Plantation Inn. Sitting in on someone's last set was just strictly to do it, to go play something different. Not for pay. A lot of times there would be just enough amphetamine left in me at two A.M. to want to stop in there and play until three, chase some leg around the room and drink enough booze to go home, try and get some sleep and do it again."

CHAPTER SIX

I Know You Can Play, But Can You Dance?

IF YOU BUMPED INTO MUD BOY'S GUITARIST LEE BAKER IN A DARK alley, you wouldn't know whether to run for safety or loan him a quarter. He is burly like a mountain man, bearded, a hippie's ponytail. There's a sense of Harley-Davidson all about him. The biker's road, in fact, is one he might have ridden. In high school, his attitude got him regularly kicked out of his parents' house. He ran with similar company, passing many teen nights with his childhood friend Mike Alexander, a bassist, talking themselves to sleep in their cars, home away from home, parked in the East High parking lot.

Instead of focusing his renegade spirit on a six-gun, Lee Baker chose six strings, developing his artistic side and creating a singular guitar style that he learned as the country blues masters' chosen one. Baker can hang a note like age, or gnarl his strings like a watch spring uncoiling, resurrecting Furry Lewis and Mississippi Fred McDowell every time he runs a bottleneck slide down the neck of his National steel guitar. He plays with a spaciousness and respect for silence that usually requires more decades than he's yet lived. Barely fifty, he was a malleable teenager when he met the people who created the blues, who invited him to accompany them because he didn't impose his style on theirs. "I can imitate Elmore James and stuff like everybody does," he drawls in his gentle Arkansas accent, "but that's not what Furry did. Furry taught me how to lay back—a whole lot. I think the reason that Furry tolerated me playing with him is that I didn't get in the way. I played with him, I played with Bukka White, Gus Cannon, Sleepy John. I'd just play rhythm and listen to what they were doing."

Furry Lewis could express the world with a single note. He taught Baker to respect the space that surrounds that note, before and after, using the silences to create three notes from one. Baker lives with his family in a hundred-year-old cabin on a lake in Arkansas, where the soil and the sky continue to teach his kids what Furry first showed them. From his screened-in porch in late summer, the cicadas may be nearly as loud as the urban noise half an hour away, but they're much more eloquent. He's got roosters, chickens, and dogs in his yard, a big blue tractor, rusting cars. Fields of cotton have become fields of soybeans, reflecting the steadiness of time, the unchanging nature of change.

A few years younger than Dickinson and the Mar-Keys, Baker was an early beneficiary to the small tears they made in society's fabric. When age differences would hold less importance than character, he became a peer. White pop attracted Baker not at all, and after he found a collection of regional blues recorded by folklorist Alan Lomax and released in 1960, he sought his way to the other side. (The series was repackaged in 1993 and rereleased by Atlantic as a four-CD box entitled *Sounds of the South*.) "I came to the blues through people like B. B. King, Freddie King, and Albert Collins," Baker says. "Wes Montgomery. I loved James Burton. I used to watch him on the 'Ricky Nelson Show,' and there was just something about the way he played, real lyrical, a country player. That solo that he does on 'Fools Rush In' is one of my all-time favorite rock and roll guitar solos. But when I first heard Fred McDowell, I said, 'My God, what is this guy doing? Just one guy and he's doing all this?' I said, 'It's only got one chord!' I didn't know how to do it, but I heard it and I started trying to play bottleneck a little bit, just sliding up and down the guitar."

Within a short time of hearing Fred McDowell on record, Baker would find himself at the bluesman's side, and invited to return. His training as an accompanist began when he and Mike Alexander, jamming on teenage ideas while the sun rose over their steering wheels, heard about a gig in the pit band at a talent show. The W. C. Handy Theater was in Memphis's first black subdivision, Orange Mound. They went together to audition. "The group was called the Ultrasonics, about six pieces," says Baker, "and me and Mike were the only white guys. Our job was to back anybody that came in. They wouldn't know what key they were in, they wouldn't know the name of the song, they didn't know nothing. We'd have to feel our way along, and it was cool for me, exactly what I wanted to do, exactly where I wanted to be.

"They had a tenor player named George, and George was nuts, certified crazy. He was a serious jazz player and had played with a bunch of people, but no telling what he took. He'd say he was playing the molecules; not the notes, but the molecules. Our band had a gig backing Rufus Thomas, and George wound up turning everybody out of the club, going crazy, had the band running, breaking bottles and saying, 'All rags must go.' He was so far out that I don't even know what to say about him. The piano player was named Tommy Lemmons. He'd been on the road with the Five Royales or somebody and he was good, but he was a juicehead, it was interfering with his thing. We rehearsed at the promoter's house, right next door to the theater. They called him Longheaded Joe, and he had a brother or something that was also crazy, and we'd go in there and this guy would come in, he had one weird eye, we'd play the old Mar-Keys song 'Bo Time,' and he'd start dancing, just going nuts. We'd be in this guy's living room rehearsing and he'd just yell, 'Hey, "Bo Time!"' and boy, he'd be dancing, it was great."

The pit band's job was not to play the song properly, but play it as the talent thought it went. By the time he met the bluesmen, Baker knew to shape his playing around theirs, to change chords when they changed, whether it was the twelfth bar, the tenth, or the fiftieth. The structure of the blues is the structure of a story being told, and everybody tells theirs differently. It's possible Baker could have enjoyed a career as a successful session guitarist. He has maintained a heartfelt devotion to the instrument and was developing a rare versatility while in his teens. But his music, his life, was irrevocably changed. Rather than generic excellence and commercial potential, he was transformed by the time these bluesmen accorded him. He made himself a willing disciple and, as if from outside his body, he watched everything he'd learned become bent out of shape, rearranged, until today he slips his bottleneck slide over his pinky, and his own parents wouldn't recognize him.

Country blues has always been another name for obscurity, the remarkable sales of the 1990 Robert Johnson box set notwithstanding. So instead of taking calls for session work, Baker spends his time on a tractor, every turn of the blade, every field cut adding a little more frustration for him to release the next time he plays for his small audience. When he tears loose live, he is the definition of rocking, pitching his upper body forth and back in a tight motion, his feet firmly planted to keep him from whirling away like the Tasmanian Devil. He cradles the guitar in his body, his head turned slightly away, safe in case of explosion, soloing, soloing, a spiral staircase with floor on top of floor. Baker has tasted the mass appeal of fame, and the flavor still lingers. In high school, his band was one of the busiest in the region; in the early seventies, he led Moloch, a pioneer blues-rock band, releasing an album on Stax and playing gigs with the MC5 and Iggy Pop. He reached a new audience later that decade through the Alex Chilton records *Big Star 3rd* and *Like Flies on Sherbert*. Baker's hands grip the tractor's steering wheel tighter, his knuckles turning white as some kid in France grooves to his sound on the Mud Boy album

Negro Streets at Dawn, as British kids try to imitate him in their gothic blues
creations, as he thinks about talking to people with his guitar. Whether two or
two hundred show up to see him play, he speaks the same language.

While training to become unknown at the Handy Theater, Baker was simultaneously playing in the local vacuum left by the Mar-Keys' move to national prominence. "The Blazers had four horns and three rhythm pieces and
a vocalist," he says of his high-school band. "Our setup with the horns and all
was probably due to the Mar-Keys. Our attitude was, we play the Booker T.
shit as good as Booker T. and the MGs. We knew we were bad. We played all
the Memphis stuff plus we did lots of James Brown, because we had the horns.
We worked up about half the *James Brown Live at the Apollo,* man, we did it
with all the kicks and everything. Plus, in those days, you had to play standards, 'Three Coins in the Fountain,' you had to be able to play a lead-out for
a prom and stuff like that. And we were playing real hard blues and rock and
roll. I respected the early R&B players because they were really jazz cats and
could play the funky stuff. I always wanted to be more than just somebody
that could play three chords. Shit, in high school, man, I never asked my parents for any money. We could have worked every night if we'd wanted to."

Until the arrival of the Beatles in 1964, the model for success throughout
the mid-South remained the West Memphis scene. A whole generation who
never experienced the PI spoke of it with reverence, emulating bands who, at
their best, were an imitation of the real thing. While a great number of bands
like the Blazers were drawing from the rowdiness across the river, clean-
cut Tommy Burk and the Counts drew from the slick vocal groups there.
They studied harmonies, tuned more to Dion and the Belmonts and other
"American Bandstand" acts. They packed their shows with loafer-wearing,
bow-headed clean-cut fans. Managers were afraid of the wilder bands, but an
entertainment attorney in Memphis named Seymour Rosenberg heard the
Counts at his daughter's dance, or maybe he just saw the crowd response, and
he offered them a recording contract.

Rosenberg played trumpet, managed Charlie Rich, and cofounded American Recording Studio with Chips Moman, which would later be home to the
Box Tops and attract Neil Diamond, Dionne Warwick, Wilson Pickett, and
Elvis. The Counts were one of the earliest acts to record there. Though their
debt was not to the Mar-Keys, it was to West Memphis. They hit with their
second single, copping the Spaniels' arrangement of "Stormy Weather" that
they heard at the PI. Area bands couldn't perform without people requesting
the Counts' version of "Stormy Weather."

Like the Blazers, the LeSabres were a horn band, and Randy Haspel, who watched from the audience until forming the Radiants, remembers the competition between the two types. "The rivalry between the LeSabres and the Counts was like the Mods and the Rockers in England," he says. "This was like the battle between the greasers and the Ivy Leaguers. The Counts dressed real sharp in blazers that had their own crest on the breast pocket. The LeSabres came straight out of the Elvis, Billy Lee Riley kind of thing. Where the Counts were very disciplined and did steps and had a lot of vocal harmony, the LeSabres were like leather boys with greasy hair, no discipline, smoking on stage and running around."

The Counts won the battles of the bands, but they lost the war in music. Their generic character offered nothing new or unusual, and they could never break beyond a regional following. After the demise of the LeSabres in 1962, their guitarist, Laddie Hutcherson, began touring the region with a racially mixed band, playing colleges. "I met a guy who took me to Beale Street," he says, "took me to see Bowlegs Miller at the Flamingo Room. I topped two flights of stairs and when I opened that door I thought I'd gone to heaven. I thought, This is where my heart is. I started going down regularly and never dreamed I'd get to sit in with the band. But soon enough, Bowlegs told me to bring my guitar and it would alternate between me and Teenie Hodges and Lee Baker."

Bowlegs Miller recorded for Hi Records, where Teenie Hodges and his brothers backed Willie Mitchell and, later, created a classic sound behind Al Green. Bowlegs Miller scouted talent for Hi, discovering Ann Peebles ("I Can't Stand the Rain") among others. Though he never achieved national fame, his patience with younger musicians assured his influence. "Bowlegs didn't try to tell me what to play," explains Hutcherson, "he just showed me when. Andrew Love had a lot to do with it too. I was on a riser behind the horn section, and I didn't know a lot of the songs. The first time Bowlegs counted a tune off, Spencer Wiggins was coming onstage to sing and I had an intro to play. Bowlegs said, 'Five flats,' and started counting. I didn't know five flats from one flat. I said, 'Andrew! What's this?' He said, 'D flat.' So I went into the intro, but when Spencer started singing, I kept on playing. Bowlegs turned around and it just took one look from him for me to learn not to ever, ever step on the singer."

A couple years earlier, it would have been impossible for Hutcherson or Baker to share the stage with black musicians. But two years before President Johnson would sign the Civil Rights Act in 1964, and two years after Charlie Freeman and Duck Dunn had joined Ben Branch's band, Memphis stages and audiences were casually breaking down barriers. Often, it was high schoolers who were blazing the way. If making music was still not something they could do with their lives, it was becoming apparent it might last past graduation. A local booking agency, National Artists Attractions, had a constant demand for talent. Established when the Sun Records explosion had settled and the artists were gigging to earn a living, it drew many clients from Stax. Walking through their office door was stepping from society's strictures into a musician's world. "You could go there and you weren't weird," says Lee Baker. The proprietor was an avuncular man named Ray Brown who'd been a prominent white disc jockey on WMPS, WHBQ's rival station. "Mother Brown's Round Mound of Sound." Brown and his partner were relaxed and friendly, running an office where blacks and whites were equals, and everyone could talk shop and tell Jerry Lee Lewis stories. National Artists Attractions needed its own neon sign: "Having Fun with Ray."

"I got my first gig with Charlie Rich because I was hanging out at Ray Brown's," Baker says. "I was a junior in high school and they needed a guitar player, so I went. Charlie hadn't heard me. Ray said, 'You need to be at this club in Waynesboro, Tennessee, by seven o'clock. Meet Charlie at the motel at five.' First time I ever shook hands with him, his manager gave me some pills. We played several gigs together. The principal would let me and Mike Alexander out at noon Friday so we could go to Columbus, Mississippi, or different places. There are so many opportunities to self-destruct in music, and when you're real young or if you're of an addictive personality or something like that, you can get really messed up. All the people that are still afloat have come through it. Charlie's one of them. One time they carried us offa this base somewhere, and we wound up at this country club in the middle of the night out in God knows where. Charlie's just drunk as a dog and he started playing all this jazz. Really good, intricate piano stuff, and he could hardly hold his drink in hand. I remember thinking, Well, I'm running in pretty fast company here."

Ray Brown's was like a day labor office, where the phone might ring and suddenly there would be a call for guitarists. Each weekend, various versions of the Mar-Keys were put together, two, three, four bands with the same name heading out to different locations. When Lee Baker played a Mar-Keys gig in Texarkana with no horns, the crowd got unruly. "Me and Charlie Freeman worked out the horn stuff on guitars," he says, "so they recognized 'Philly Dog' and all that. And after people had a few drinks, it didn't make any difference." Dickinson and Freeman, who would end up playing together behind Aretha Franklin in an Atlantic Records house band, first played together as Mar-Keys; Laddie Hutcherson's popular sixties group the Guilloteens met the same way. And when the Mar-Keys name wore out, Ray Brown would hurl a *Billboard* at the musicians on his sofa and say, "Who do you want to be this weekend?"

Laddie Hutcherson, late of the LeSabres, went out one weekend as Ronnie and the Daytonas, the Tennessee band that had a surf hit with "Little GTO." When the promoter asked why the van had Mar-Keys written all over it, they said their own vehicle broke down so they'd borrowed their friends'. The second day out, they stopped in a music store and were swarmed by kids. "We're signing autographs as the Daytonas, big-timing it," says Hutcherson. "One of my friends comes up to me, batting his nose, nervous, and says, 'C'mon! We've got to get out of here, right now!' I said, 'Hey man, sign some autographs.' He told me to turn around, and there was a row of records going all the way across the wall, Ronnie and the Daytonas, big photograph of them, and not any of us in the picture."

National Artists Attractions booked stars in distant cities and booked the funkiest places at the smallest crossroads. "There was a gig that was famous among musicians," says Baker. "I played it with Booker T. Jones, a honky-tonk in the middle of nowhere, the Big Apple in Birdsong, Arkansas. For fifty cents you could get a fucking barbecue as big as two hands. I mean it was good! The club had a wood stove and all the country people came, and they didn't want to hear nothing but blues and funky. No jazz, nothing cool, just down-home gut-bucket blues. Whites came in there too, because in the country there's not—there's a distinction but they still socialize. There was usually white men, and not usually white women. They had quarts of beer and they had gambling, people coming to listen to music and play cards."

Original Mar-Keys Wayne Jackson and Duck Dunn were getting studio work at Stax, but they continued to gig regularly in the Memphis area. "You have to remember that I had had a hit record immediately," says Jackson. "Before that, it was just Willie Mitchell through the fan in the parking lot. When I got back from touring, I had to learn showbiz. Club owners wouldn't let you stand still. They'd say, 'I know you can play, but can you dance?' And you better say, 'Yeah, I can dance. And tell jokes too.' You had to make people want to come back and pay that $2.50 again. There's an art to that and I learned it from Robert Talley, a black keyboard player and bandleader who was older than us. I worked with him for two and a half years. Every afternoon he'd come in and teach me a song to do that night. I probably knew three hundred old ballads with beautiful melodies before that was over. Robert taught Duck to hear outside of just R&B. He'd tell you what notes to play coming from that change to this change. And he played so well, it was easy to learn from him. He was a great teacher."

Robert Talley still performs in Memphis clubs, seventy-four years old, retired from the post office, and agile on the piano. He cowrote the Mar-Keys' follow-up hit, "The Morning After." His current groups don't share his breadth of knowledge, and his passion for the old days is almost tangible. "These guys today," he says, "I have to play their program. They don't know the stuff I know. At the Rebel Room, with Wayne and Duck Dunn, Terry Johnson on drums, they kicked my ass. Wayne could hear grass growing, he's a talented guy. We did all kinds of songs and kept that audience dancing. We had a versatile band. When they went to Stax, they were good, but even then it didn't have the fire, the innovation, like we had on that bandstand."

On the folk scene, there was growing personal interaction between the artists, white and black, young and old. By the mid-1960s, these encounters were popular enough to be called a national blues revival. Experiences such as Charlie Miller's were not uncommon for a mid-1950s afternoon. "There was a black guy who had a little shack in one of the alleys in a white neighborhood. My school friends and I would go there, he'd buy wine for us, we'd buy him a bottle too, and he'd sit around and play blues. I can still see that in my mind, the wood-burning stove with this guy sitting there playing, little kids taking a drink of that white port wine and getting just sick as a dog."

No longer schoolkids by the early 1960s, the witnesses discovered languishing Delta greats not only alive, but living around the corner. "Having seen the jug band in Whiskey Chute, I knew these men were out there somewhere," says Dickinson. "Until the Samuel Charters book [*Country Blues*, 1959], there didn't seem any possibility of contacting them. In the summer of 1960, a friend and I followed the trail that Charters left to Gus Cannon, who was the first one I actually met. He was the yardman for an anthropology professor. Gus had told this family that he used to make records and he had been on RCA and they'd say, 'Yeah Gus, sure, cut the grass.' When we met him, he was bending down over the lawnmower, he had this big Russian rabbit hat on, like Davy Crockett. He lived on the property, back over a garage, and he took us up into his room, and on the wall he had a certificate for sales from 'Walk Right In,' for which of course he didn't get any money. And he had a copy of the record that Charters had made for Folkways, but he had no record player. That was a real good introduction to the blues."

In this first encounter with an original bluesman, Dickinson and his cohort were anxious to learn about Cannon's roots. They were taken aback when, after asking where he learned his material, he answered, "From the radio." "It really surprised me," recalls Dickinson. "That's where I had learned stuff. These guys had learned it exactly the way we had. What else were they exposed to except each other?"

By the early 1960s, rock and roll had become formulaic enough to send Jimmy Crosthwait, washboardist in Mud Boy and the Neutrons, searching for new directions. "I was playing in rock and roll bands but I was listening more to jazz. Mose Allison, Charlie Mingus. And by the time of 'Last Night,' I'm just about to be caught up in the folk thing. Dylan comes along around sixty-two and makes folk really kind of fun and not so college preppy as Peter, Paul and Mary or the Kingston Trio and all that creepy shit. There were also all of the Alan Lomax folk albums. Around 1961, when I was about sixteen, I found a little black joint downtown that served greasy hamburgers called the Cotton Row Inn. It had a great jukebox with Art Blakey and the Jazz Messengers, Coltrane, some really good stuff. I loved the atmosphere and I was a beatnik going into the only place I could find where there was jazz on the jukebox. All of this blurs for me with the sit-ins that were happening, black people going into white joints. That's a real confrontational thing, and so I would feel a little leery going into the Cotton Row, but I did, and it worked."

There was a record store on Beale Street called Home of the Blues that attracted blacks and whites. A peculiar white man named Ruben Cherry ran the place. "Lots of people didn't like Ruben," recalls Milton Pond, who frequented every record counter in the city when he wasn't behind the one at Poplar Tunes. "They thought he was pushy and obnoxious. If two people were in there, he made it feel like a crowd. The main thing I remember about him, up by the cash register, he had a nickel glued on the glass counter. He'd wait and wait for somebody to try to pick it up, and when it wouldn't move he'd get the biggest kick out of that."

"I went into Ruben's once with Stanley Booth," says Dickinson. "Ruben kept this rubber rattlesnake behind the counter which he used to scare off would-be stickup men. It was rubber and when he held it, it really looked real. Stanley says, 'Hey Ruben, where's your rubber snake?' As an answer, not as telling a story but just answering the question, Ruben says, 'That goddamn Elvis Presley, he came in here and stole my rubber snake and ran down Beale Street shaking it.' The thing that tickled me so much was that his anger at Elvis was real. He'd known Elvis before he'd started recording. Elvis bought records from Ruben Cherry same as everyone else."

Established in 1949, Home of the Blues had the flavor of old Beale. Wood floors, worn counters, old record racks. Cherry had been president of the local Variety Club, an entertainers organization, and on the walls were casual shots, enlarged, of him and Jackie Wilson, Marilyn Monroe, and James Brown. He made a living off the records Poplar Tunes stopped carrying, buying one of everything released, figuring eventually somebody would come looking for what didn't sell right away.

Cherry's Beale Street location made him accessible to the numerous musicians who wandered by, and eventually he started his own label. He recorded black artists like the Five Royales and Willie Mitchell, and white artists like Billy Lee Riley, as well as lesser-known talents he encountered. Through store talk, Cherry heard about the Regents' blues numbers and Dickinson's own scraggly solo renderings. Home from his first year of college during the summer of 1961, Dickinson brought him a tape he'd recorded with his old band, and Cherry signed him to his label. He called Dickinson "Little Muddy," after Muddy Waters, and brought in Bowlegs Miller to produce him at Scotty Moore's Fernwood studio. Cherry liked to play the tape for his black customers and have them guess who was singing; Dickinson thought he sounded like Ricky Nelson. A popular disc jockey named Hunky Dory became his manager. "One of my early career problems," says Dickinson, "was calling WLOK and not knowing whether to ask for Hunky or Mr. Dory." In 1962, Cherry sold his masters to Vee-Jay, which never issued the tape and went bankrupt in 1965. Ruben Cherry died at fifty-three in 1976, after twenty-seven years in the business.

The folk scene introduced the beatnik coffeehouse, which became the venue for the return of Furry Lewis, Bukka White, Joe Callicott, Nathan Beauregard, and the other blues pioneers who had been neglected since the Depression. Initially, coffeehouses in Memphis were stuffy affairs with a forced seriousness and no tingle whatsoever. The Cottage was the first to explore the territory, opening sometime in 1960, closing the next year. The house band, a trio from Wisconsin, was so unhip that even the leader's goatee looked square. When the Pastime opened the next year, it managed to last a little longer, but its atmosphere never got past encouraging people to quietly sip their coffee and stare at the piano. The coffeehouse scene was slow in finding an audience. "The Cottage barely attracted anyone because everybody was afraid of it," says Mary Lindsay Dickinson. "They were afraid weirdos would get them. But I already knew I was a weirdo and I was ready to go and be and have some fun. I was a little young for it but I found it nonetheless." One of her earliest memories of the place is Jimmy Crosthwait sitting in the corner beating bongo drums and reading poetry up on the stage. "I met Jimmy through our involvement in the bohemian circles in Memphis," says Lee Baker. "Crosthwait was real intense, and he would do things like go sit under the piano at a crowded party. Good-looking women would bring him drinks."

A bit too devilish to be the brooding artiste, Jimmy Crosthwait has always scouted the future, returning to coax others along. He embraced the coffee-houses precisely because their intention was not defined. Undermining pre-conceptions is his specialty, a part of his being. Slight of frame, he has always worn his hair long, easily mistaken for a hippie. But even a brief conversation with Crosthwait reveals the trickster just below the surface, his eye for the chaos at the core of truth. In a crowded diner known for the electric train that runs around its wall, he'll call you over and say, "Watch this," slipping a melted butter pat onto the tracks. Crosthwait rejected society's conventions before he was of driving age, driving to the Arkansas side of the river and rent-ing a sharecropper's shack. Surrounded by driftwood and river oddities, he shifted from painting to collage, stepping into puppetry through a rejection of kinetic art: "All those people are making one statement that says, 'Here we are in a big mechanical world, see how the big machines work.'" Puppets, instead, are sculptures that happen to move: "Humans provide the movement. The flesh against the spirit is pretty much my entire theme. Finite mortals oppos-ing infinite space, all the mystery is right there in how those two things can exist together and how at one point they become one thing in God."

Crosthwait was entering high school when he first met Dickinson, who was finishing. Their friendship and collaboration broadened in the summer of 1962, when Dickinson returned to Memphis after two years in the drama pro-gram at Baylor College in Texas. Still not considering a career in music, Dickinson enrolled in theater at Memphis State, picking up gigs as a Mar-Key. A small private women's college asked him to direct *The Glass Menagerie*. The night before the show, as he and a cohort were building the set, they discov-ered a shared desire for an alternative performance space. With a third friend they founded the Market Theater in the fall of 1963. "We were leaving the Market Theater one day," remembers Mary Lindsay Dickinson, "when we en-countered Jimmy driving by. He couldn't have been a legal driver. He waved to Jim, we pulled over, and he came up talking about building a guitar out of wood. Shortly after that Crosthwait worked up his act playing garbage cans, and he became a great presence at all the hootenannies."

The Market Theater was an ambitious name for a room in a farmer's mar-ket with holes in the wall. They built a small stage at one end and bought used theater seats from a church. The size of the venue made microphones moot. Jimmy Crosthwait painted the men's bathroom and the women's room was given to Joe McConico, who as Hilton McConico became an acclaimed fashion designer and set designer (*Diva, Confidentially Yours*). "The mayor had de-creed Market Theater Day and he was coming, we had Miss Memphis in a swimsuit, we had champagne for celebrities," remembers Dickinson. "A cou-ple days before the opening, this fireman guy with a clipboard shows up, says the city has a hundred-something codes to meet and this place doesn't meet any of 'em. Whenever we had a problem, my partner Phil had an uncle. The phone rings the next day and a voice says, 'How many chairs you got?' We said fifty. He said, 'Take one out and it's not a theater,' and he hung up. So we seated forty-nine, and he told us to charge a dollar or less at the door to avoid entertainment tax. We were on our way."

Their way was brilliantly lit for two and a half months. They performed plays six nights a week, with folk music Sunday afternoons and, because of its popularity, sometimes on weekends. But the space became claustrophobic, with one show rehearsing afternoons while another was staged evenings. As the chilly weather moved in, the charming breaches in the wall became fore-boding. Perhaps the most significant contribution of the Market Theater was the new folk audience it revealed. The Hammer Singers at the Pastime wal-lowed in the commercially appealing style of the Kingston Trio, eviscerating the social significance of the music that the Market Theater hailed—work songs, scruffy blues covers, and obscure Lomax finds. Dylan had released his first album the previous year, and though sappy versions of his material quickly made national hits, the witnesses were reverberating with his renegade spirit, finding in folk and blues more than just a source for pop music.

Sid Selvidge established himself as a folk presence around Memphis in the early 1960s. With Dickinson, Baker, and Crosthwait, he rounds out the core of Mud Boy and the Neutrons. Selvidge brings to the group a voice as pure and sweet as a Delta songbird, with as much range as the expansive sky. It's been said he can perform in a stampede of elephants, which I take to mean that his voice can accompany the marauding beasts, or it could still them. His trade-mark is a falsetto, which he leaps into for emphasis, not unlike Little Richard's whoops, but less manic. Selvidge only plays acoustic guitar; his piano burned down in a 1970s bar fire and he took it as an omen. Back then, when I began seeing him regularly, he was a folk punk of sorts. The Sex Pistols and the Ramones had just come out, and Selvidge's Peabody label was preparing to record Alex Chilton's *Like Flies on Sherbert*. Sid was playing every weekend at a downtown bar, the business district like civic tooth decay. There'd be a single chair onstage, a single light. He'd appear out of the darkness, walk down the aisle, sit at either the guitar or the piano and not bother to remove his leather jacket. Then, without the slightest acknowledgment to the audience, he'd begin forty-five minutes of beautiful playing. Sometimes when he sipped his water, he'd sneak a look, but usually he furrowed his eyebrows to block us out. When the minute hand made three quarters of a circle, he was up, disappearing again into the darkness.

In 1961, Selvidge came from the Delta to Memphis for college. "I was down in Greenville listening to WLAC [a powerful radio station out of Nashville], disc jockeys like John R., the Hossman, Gene Nobles, and they were playing Muddy Waters and Little Walter and Jimmy Reed. Visiting Memphis, we were driving right up through the Delta, and I didn't know that was where the music came from. I was playing guitar at the time, and my grandfather would come in and say, 'I saw some guy out on a place and he would put a knife between his little finger and this finger. Can you do that?' But that didn't make any sense to me—why would somebody want to play a guitar like that? I would try and the knife would fall between my fingers and the strings were in standard key and it sounded terrible. And being a little dumb white boy I didn't have sense enough to go ten miles away from the house and say, 'Show me how to do that.' My mother hired a guy to teach me how to play a guitar, and he had grown up in the same waifs home as Louis Armstrong in New Orleans. So he played a syncopated thing that didn't have anything to do with what Muddy and them were playing. When I said I wanted to learn folk music, he taught me 'Old Spinning Wheel in the Parlor' and I thought I was getting somewhere."

Once in the city, Selvidge befriended Horace Hull and was "catapulted out of the dorm scene." Hull, like Selvidge, had a beautiful voice, and in addition to playing a gut-stringed guitar, he also played banjo. They wore blue work shirts and sang "Cumberland Gap" and other excerpts from the Lomax songbook. Like Selvidge, Hull had incredible vocal range; because of his classical background, his harmonies were Bachian, based on counterpoint. Hull came from a monied family, and he was never able to resolve the conflict of being a folkie from a privileged background. Despite his obvious talent, he'd been taught that folk was not serious music. Hull sometimes snuck to a church pipe organ where he could play Bach fugues in solitude. He and Selvidge were hired by Dickinson in 1963, along with several other young white folk singers, for what was billed as the First Annual Memphis Folk Festival, which was really a concert to help pay off the debts left by the Market Theater. Held at the Overton Park Band Shell—a comfortable outdoor amphitheater built with a utilitarian grace by the WPA in 1936, nestled amongst trees in the open air, lined with rows of wood-backed benches—the show laid a cornerstone for the four Memphis Country Blues Festivals that were to come later in the decade, events that brought the Delta bluesmen and the Memphis hippies into the international spotlight.

Though he'd been unable to meet bluesmen in the Delta, in Memphis Selvidge began sharing the stage with them. Folklorists like Sam Charters and Paul Oliver had begun rediscovering the first recorded blues artists in the late fifties, the witnesses had begun meeting them by the early sixties, but nobody thought to hire them until 1963, when the gregarious Charlie Brown was managing a coffeehouse called the Oso. Brown was born Charles Elmore in Sardis, Mississippi, but his head was round and his face flat, so that he actually looked like the comic strip character. He realized it wouldn't kill the bluesmen to give them gigs; playing, in fact, was their thing. Their rediscovery by a new generation was still draped in awe, academia, and anthropology. Brown simply removed them from the display shelves. Gus Cannon and Furry Lewis became regular performers alongside Selvidge at the Oso, joined by lesser-known artists like the moaning jug band vocalist Van Zula Hunt. They didn't fool with no "Puff the Magic Dragon."

It was 1966 before the ideas of hiring the bluesmen to play and of renting the Overton Park Band Shell would merge, creating the first of the Country Blues Festivals. Memphis's proximity to the Delta meant a concentration of talent in a native setting that was beyond the ken of places up North. The Newport Folk Festival was hosted by Theodore Bikel, and *Newsweek* termed the audience "Milk Drinkers." The games were as different as wiffle ball and pro baseball.

Nashville, where ideas are imported for fun and profit, decided to capitalize on the folk movement in the early 1960s. Former Sun Records horn man and producer Bill Justis, who had achieved national fame in 1957 with the saxophone-based "Raunchy," had moved to Nashville and was cranking out easy instrumental remakes of pop hits for Smash Records. Middle America, housewives, drunk drivers—everybody was scooping them up, which amused Justis greatly. He was a most unusual character. His disdain for rock and roll was only slightly weaker than his desire to profit by it, a fact he did not hide. Sun historian Colin Escott writes in his *Good Rockin' Tonight* (1991) that on session reels Justis can be heard saying, "Let's get real bad now so we can sell some records. Instant crapsville, girls. Here we go. . . ." In his band was a former schoolmate of Dickinson's whose mother had sent him newspaper clippings about the First Annual Memphis Folk Festival. One afternoon in 1963, Dickinson's phone rang and it was his friend saying hold for Bill Justis, who came on the line and offered him a major label recording contract. With it came a priceless music biz lesson.

The very name of the record they made is meaningless: *Dixieland Folkstyle*. The first word implies New Orleans, the second implies Appalachia, vocal harmonies, and an entirely different kind of banjo playing. The studio was filled with entirely too many musicians to replicate any sort of folkiness. And the only hint of the Crescent City, buried among schmaltz like "Green Green" and "Michael Row the Boat Ashore," is the New Orleans standard "St. James Infirmary." But Justis lumped the two buzzwords together, assuring those not in the know that this record was in the know—and then he smiled as sales racked up.

The lesson came on the middle of the third day of sessions. "We're working real tight Nashville union sessions, three hours by the clock, when these big loading doors that had never been touched come flying open in the middle of a cut and in comes this big fat redneck all dressed in black. He had a long, greasy ducktail and mirror sunglasses, and he's talking real fast and loud. I thought, Boy this guy is history. They're gonna throw his ass outta here.

"But everybody stops. He walks up to one of the women who's singing with the Anita Kerr singers and he's saying, 'Baby, I'm sorry, but I just couldn't make up my mind, so I bought both of 'em.' The whole session goes out to the parking lot to look at these two new Jaguars. He was handing out these Sherman Cheroots, brown cigarettes, and from one end of the cigarette to the other, every little microspace occupied, he had his name in gold letters: Shelby S. Singleton. Finally I see my buddy the trumpet player, who had written all the arrangements (not that I could read 'em). I said, 'Who *is* this guy, man?' And he says, 'He's the producer.' And I said, 'The producer! Well what is Justis?' 'Justis is the arranger.' 'Then what are you?' And he says, 'Oh, I'm the copyist.' It was like lightning again. I thought, Somewhere in this is a place for me."

Not long after returning home, Dickinson opened his mail and found a contract. He thought it seemed a little after the fact, so he phoned Justis. "He said, 'Don't you want to make a record?' and I said, 'Didn't we just make a record?' and he said, 'No. You. Don't *you* want to make a record?' I said yeah, sure and he says sign the contract and send it back."

Justis had Sun beams dancing in his head. The lack of polish in Dickinson's voice fit perfectly his notion of rock and roll. Hitsville. Promptly, he sent Dickinson a tape of a Shel Silverstein song, "The Unicorn," and booked time at the Sam Phillips Recording Service, the studio built after Elvis's contract was sold to RCA. Justis produced this session as Shelby Singleton had done the last, *in absentia*. Dickinson noted the pattern. (Actually, the idea of producing *in absentia* is not terribly far-fetched. Consider: The producer is the one who determines the recording's direction. That is, the band performs *for* the producer, playing to satisfy him or her. Some producers are such a presence that they need not even be in attendance for the artist to direct their performance toward them.)

"The Unicorn" was a Nashville folk song, as opposed to a folk song by the folks. Dickinson presumed that the folks might be ready for the folks and pretended he didn't receive Justis's tape. He reached back to his Whiskey Chute encounter, to the abandon of the players whose instruments were portable enough to run from the cops. "Come on down to my house, honey," the singer had encouraged, "there ain't nobody home but me." He formed a jug band, the New Beale Street Sheiks. Crosthwait, a drummer, was dispatched to buy a washboard. They had a guitar-playing friend smart enough to figure out the tub bass. Dickinson pulled the harmonica from his neck rack and replaced it with a kazoo. "We got one gig the night before the recording session and people loved it," Dickinson recalls. "So we went to Phillips the next day. Crosthwait had real long hair, and this was pre-Beatles. He had a rag around his neck and we all looked wretched and they didn't want to let us in. Bill Black and Scotty Moore were there. Scotty Moore never did trust me. But Bill Black thought it was funny. He said, 'No, that's Dickinson, that's his thing, let 'em in.'

"My whole deal was just not to cut 'The Unicorn.' Bill started calling people, telling them to come down. I would see him at the window, talking on the phone and pointing at us. He really thought it was funny. Crosthwait was playing the washboard for the second day in his life. We may have had two microphones on the session, but I think it was one. We cut four songs as a demo. When we were done, Scotty Moore wouldn't even let me have the tape. He said, 'I'm going to Nashville tomorrow and I'm going to take this to Justis.'

"I didn't hear anything for a couple weeks so I finally called Justis and I said, 'What'd you think of the tape?' and he says 'The tape! The tape is great! But what's making that noise on there?' I says, 'It's a zinc tub bass, it's just a tub and a rope.' He shouts, 'It's a rope! A rope! I went all over Nashville trying to e.q. [sonically adjust] a rope!'

"Then he says, 'The record will be out Thursday.' I said, 'But that's the demo, Bill,' and he says, 'No, no man, you could never do it that bad again.' We were talking on the same level and I paused, because I wanted him to hear me. 'Bill,' I said, 'you have no concept of how bad I could do it.'"

"You'll Do It All the Time" backed with "Down and Out," by the New Beale Street Sheiks, was released on Thursday, February 6, 1964. *Billboard* called it "a contagious, hard-driving, pulsating, folk-blueser . . . , appealing,

The New Beale Street Sheiks. Left to right: Sid Selvidge, Jim Dickinson, Bill Newport, Jim Vinson, Jimmy Crosthwait. Photo by Steve Jensen.

nostalgic." The powerful John R. on WLAC, whose R&B radio shows had influenced all these musicians when they were kids, played it. Chet Atkins called Justis, tried to buy the record. Then three days later, on Sunday, February 9, 1964, the Beatles appeared for the first time on "The Ed Sullivan Show." And the American record industry ground to a halt.

CHAPTER SEVEN

What's What

WHEN THE BEATLES HIT, KIDS IN MEMPHIS WERE CAUGHT IN THE dueling forces of the new pop sound and the continuing success of Memphis R&B. The first single on Stax in January of 1964 was Rufus Thomas's "Can Your Monkey Do the Dog." Otis Redding was beginning his ascent, Booker T. and the MGs were preparing to release "Soul Dressing," and the upstart Goldwax label would introduce James Carr that year and begin competing with Hi Records for Memphis soul's second notch. Rockabilly still cast its shadow: Elvis was deep into Hollywood schlock, but 1964 would see the release of one of his best movie singles, "Viva Las Vegas." Charlie Rich moved to Smash that year and would soon enjoy "Mohair Sam."

"The first night I ever heard 'I Want to Hold Your Hand,' I heard it on the radio coming home from a Blazers gig at Ole Miss," says Lee Baker. "I said, 'Goddamn, that's it. You watch.' I'd been hearing about it and I said, 'That's the future knocking at our door, we're gonna have to change,' and we did. Horn bands bit the dust. And everybody had horns. The Beatles were replacing the Mar-Keys, rhythm and blues. The LeSabres had horns, the Blazers, even Mississippi bands—everybody, because it was more versatile. And all that changed."

While the Beatles brought a new excitement to pop music, some people saw them as a distraction. Dan Penn, an Alabama songwriter who would come to Memphis in 1966 and produce the Box Tops, sums up the feelings of those who entered the Memphis coffeehouse era with their mind more on black music than British white. "Tommy Roe was working at Fame studios in Muscle Shoals, and he'd been going to England. He came in one night and he had this test pressing in his hand, and he said, 'Boys, I've got something right here that's going to change the world.' And we said, 'Put it on, put it on!' He puts it on and here it comes, 'I Want to Hold Your Hand.' 'Wha'd y'all think?' Everybody in that room cared for nothing but R&B and nobody said much. And he said, 'What do you think?' And I said, 'Man, if that's gon' change the world, I don't know whether I want to live in it or not.'"

Once the Beatles were in the world and every kid everywhere wanted to be a rock star, guitar manufacturers were in heaven. The trend had begun with Elvis, but by the time of the Fab Four, music stores were increasing exponentially. The 1967 "Report on Amateur Instrumental Music in the United States," a survey of the American Music Conference, indicated that between 1956 and 1966, the number of guitar players rose from 2.6 million to 10 million. Memphis musicians from the witnesses on through bands like Randy and the Radiants and the Box Tops had followed the same pattern when purchasing their instruments. They started with the pawnshops on Beale, which sold equipment cheap.

There were up to fourteen pawnshops within two blocks on Beale, but Lou Rafael at Nathan Novick's Sales Store dominated the music trade. The child of European immigrants, Rafael was born in Brooklyn in 1910 and came to Memphis during World War II. He retired in 1983 after forty-one years on Beale. When we spoke at his home, he was wearing brownish plaid pants, brightly striped suspenders, a peach-colored shirt, a powder-blue baseball cap, and had on terry-cloth house shoes. His face is long, his features large, and a cigar is a permanent fixture beneath his pencil-thin mustache. When I greeted him, my stomach dropped as it had the day in the early 1970s when I'd entered Novick's and asked the cost of a harmonica; he'd pulled the cigar out of his mouth to answer and the sight of that mangled, sopped butt has never left my mind.

You married? You're not? What do you do for aggravation?

When tour buses stopped on Beale in the 1970s and all that was left in the crumbling remains was a few pawnshops, the guides would direct their patrons into Novick's, introducing them to Lou Rafael. "They tell me I sold Elvis his first guitar," he says in a husky voice that still has a trace of a Brooklyn accent. "Whether it's true or not, I don't remember. They've talked me into it. People from all over the world have taken their pictures with me because they were so happy I sold Elvis his first guitar." In the old days, it'd never have happened. Lou would have charged them for the privilege. "I remember one time a man stepped out of a taxicab, he was looking for a pawnshop. What did he have? He wanted to pawn his artificial leg. Sometimes people wanted to pawn their teeth, but I wouldn't take teeth unless there was gold in it."

Lou used to brag that he bought his instruments by the boxcar load, but some kids swore he was buying the trade-ins from other stores around the city. Novick's was dark and filled with whirligigs, but musical instruments and band gear were prominently displayed in the window. An elderly, yellowish man sat in a chair by the door. He wore a hat and usually had his hands folded atop his cane, a place for his chin to rest. When a kid would stop to admire the bait, the shill would laugh softly, wisely, and tell the kid to go on in, look around, gots lots more inside, purrrty ones. The mark entered innocently, and like a scene from the Marx Brothers, Lou pounced. "Ya got any money!" he demanded. "How much! Don't look around, com'ere, whaddaya want!" The shill's soft laugh was distant, like the rattling of a jailer's keychain.

Ever hear about the man who went in the restaurant and ordered a hot bowl of soup? It sits on the table for fifteen minutes. The waiter comes by and says, "I see you're not eating the soup, is anything wrong?" The customer says, "You taste it." The waiter says, "Okay," looks around, then says, "Where's the spoon?"

"My father was a salesman's salesman," says Jim Dickinson, "and he took me to every pawnshop on Beale before we bought my first guitar at Novick's. It was pressed masonite covered in wallpaper. The other guys couldn't sell my father. Lou could." Dickinson went with a friend to buy his second guitar from Lou. His third he bought alone. "We're haggling about it and it's getting very tense. We get it down to seventy-five cents between us, and neither one of us is going to give it up. I walk out the store, down Mulberry to where my car is parked, Lou is chasing me out the door with a cigar in his mouth. 'Come back here you motherfucker,' he's screaming, and I'm cussing him out. Finally he said something that made me turn around, and he had me. He said, 'I wouldn't fuck you.' I turned and said, 'You fucked me twice.' Quick as a flash he said, 'I wouldn't fuck you three times.' We walked back to the store and he agreed to take the seventy-five cents off the price. But when he's writing out the bill, I see that he adds seventy-five cents on the bottom. 'What's that, Lou?' 'I'll itemize,' he says. He writes, 'Fifty cents, Tennessee State guitar tax.' 'What's the quarter?' 'My cigar.'

"I had traded in my beat-up old Gibson, got twenty bucks credit for it. When we were done, I asked him what he was going to do with it. He said, 'I wouldn't sell it for less than a hundred fifty.' I said he'd never get that much money for a beat-up guitar like that. He smiled confidently, said he was going to cover it in shoe polish."

A boy is working for his father. Says, "Pop, I want to go to college and become a lawyer or doctor. I don't want to work in the factory anymore." His father says, "Do you know what's what?" "No." "Go back to work." Six months later the kid comes back and says he wants to go to college. The father is fed up, figures he'll fix him up on a date with his secretary. They go out dining and dancing, have a good time, and they wind up at her apartment. She says, "Sit down, make yourself comfortable." She returns in a negligee and he takes a look at her and says, "What's that?" She says, "What's what?" He says, "If I knew what's what, I'd be in college."

From the pawnshops, most kids went to Boyden's Melody Music, where Jack Boyden would usually forget that he had extended credit to the kids, but his mother would remember. "After you bought your first set from Lou on Beale, you bought better stuff from Jack Boyden," says David Fleischman, the "Flash" in Flash and the Board of Directors. "My organist got his B3 at Melody Music. Everybody bought equipment there. The guy extended credit —to kids! Most kids paid him back, I guess. We did, we were fortunate, we always worked."

Sid Selvidge remembers that Melody Music became a place to meet other musicians because the Boydens would let anybody play any instrument in the store. "People were just hanging out over there and playing guitars. Any new guitar that came in, you could test it out, so you were always gonna run into somebody over there. I'd see Baker, Dickinson, Charlie Freeman, Sid Manker —any guitar player or aspiring guitar player in there."

"I probably met Dickinson at Melody Music," says Lee Baker. "The store was right across the street from a coffeehouse called the Bitter Lemon and we were all running around there."

"Jack's mother made that store a success," continues Selvidge. "If you needed strings and they cost fifteen cents and you didn't have it, he'd put it on account. But come the first of the month, you'd get a call, 'Hello, this is Miss Boyden, you need to bring that fifteen cents in.' Mrs. Boyden died and Jack kept going out on the golf course, and the business went out the window."

As guitars proliferated, so did the demand for music lessons. But these kids didn't want to learn theory; they didn't want notes or scales. They wanted to rock and roll. There weren't as many places to take lessons as there were to buy instruments, but a surprising number of successful artists went to the same teacher: Lynn Vernon, Memphis's secret guitar hero. A jazz player, Vernon led a three-piece combo for twenty years on a morning TV show. He also had a studio where he gave lessons.

Roland Janes, in whose hands a guitar was defenseless, describes Lynn Vernon as a great. Though he was already well established, Janes asked Vernon to give him lessons. "He asked me, 'What do you want me to teach you?' I said basically to read chord charts and maybe read music. After my first lesson, I got real busy and never was able to come back. I always kind of regretted that. He could play a lot of styles, but he was more big band–oriented. Chords, lotta chords. And kind of a jazzy feel." Rick Ireland, the guitarist for the Regents, purchased his guitar from Boyden's and took lessons at the store from a preacher. Later, a singing cop taught him. But when he got proficient and could read music, he asked Lynn Vernon to take him to the next level. "He said, 'Show me what you know,'" says Ireland. "I played him something and he says, 'Well, I'll tell ya, I'm kind of jammed up right now, why don't you start teaching for me?' I was still in my teens, and I had his overflow and some students of my own.

"Unlike most jazz players, Lynn played a Stratocaster. He loved that Stratocaster. I started hanging out with Sid Manker as a result of my association with Lynn. Sid was one of the heavier jazz guitar players around here. He played with Justis, and I used to go with them down to the Press Club. It was a jazz place, heavy duty, across the street from the newspaper, upstairs. Every Saturday night, if there were touring bands, those musicians would come down there. The bands were black and white. This was heavy bebop. I saw my first heroin withdrawal there, a bass player. I was hearing all this really heavy jazz when I was still a teenager, still playing with the Regents.

"I met Charlie Freeman through Lynn because he was one of Lynn's students. Lynn got us a job backing this gal that used to sing on the WREC morning show, Dolly Holiday. Charlie and I were supposed to play for her, and we drove somewhere down in South Memphis to her home and sat out there in the dark waiting for her. The rehearsal never came off but Charlie and I got real friendly." After his lessons, Freeman would share what he'd learned from Vernon with the other guitarist in his band, Steve Cropper.

"Mr. Vernon's studio was upstairs from a girls' ballet studio," says Randy Haspel. "You had a guitar case as big as you were and you had to walk through fifty little girls in tutus to get to the stairs. And when I was walking down, Larry Raspberry [later of the Gentrys and then the Highsteppers] was walking up. Mr. Vernon taught me, he taught Raspberry, he taught Bob Simon [The Radiants], he taught Bobby Manuel [Stax session man; "Disco Duck" cowriter]. We all ended up playing the same style Fender Stratocaster because Mr. Vernon had one. You'd say, 'Mr. Vernon, please can I play your guitar?' He'd make you wash your hands and only after that would he let you play his guitar."

When the Beatles turned the world upside down in February 1964, older bands like Tommy Burk and the Counts and Lee Baker's Blazers were already in college, somewhat set in their ways. "I graduated from East High in 1963," says Lee Baker. "The Blazers stayed together because all of us went to Memphis State. And when the Beatles came in, we kept the band together but nobody wanted to hear horns anymore. The sax player started playing electric piano, and one of the other horn players picked up guitar, and the rest got percussion instruments and harmonicas and stuff like that. We were able to keep that big band together, but we had to revamp and start doing more rhythm section stuff."

For a younger band like Randy and the Radiants, adapting to the Beatles was easy. "The British Invasion made us popular because we were just coming into our own," says Haspel. "I was about sixteen years old. My partner, Bob Simon, had been writing songs since we were kids. When the Beatles hit, we already had a band that was up and working. The next time we had rehearsal, people started to assume their roles. Mike Gardner loosened his trap cymbals and started making those kinda slashing motions that Ringo would make. I learned how to rock back and forth like John Lennon. And we started to get really popular. We had been strictly rhythm and blues until the British Invasion, and then we became sort of a hybrid rhythm and blues/Memphis/British pop. It affected the Gentrys in the same way."

The changing of the guard became apparent at the battles of the bands. Even after the Beatles, when most rules changed, these showdowns remained an indefatigable defense of one's honor. Bands set up at either end of the venue—gym, social hall, hotel ballroom, someone's basement—a box before them. Each ticket buyer would vote by placing their torn stub in one of the boxes. The winning band returned the following week to take on new competition.

Haspel remembers that, until the Beatles, everything his band did was because of the Counts. "They did the Five Royales song list, and when we were little kids coming along, we did the same list. We had heard about the West Memphis scene and we knew we were doing their songs, but we were too young to have experienced it. The Counts began booking themselves with this black band called the Avantis that had sung at the Plantation Inn. When they did that, I figured I should do the same. But this is when high schools were still segregated. I was at Christian Brothers High, and Christian Brothers College was integrated. I was a sophomore and Eddie Harrison was a sophomore in college. He had a vocal group called the Premieres—Eddie, his sister, and three other guys. We started booking out with them. For seventy bucks, you could get the Radiants, for a hundred twenty you could get the Radiants with the Premieres. Eddie said he'd never been to East Memphis before he came to my house to rehearse." Integrating the teen bands was the work of Sputnik

Monroe's shadow; the kids achieved nonchalantly what society seemed unable to forcefully wrestle.

Haspel continues: "The Radiants had beat the Devilles [who later became the Box Tops], the Scepters, the Gentrys—everybody. We'd keep winning and be asked back, and that was how we started getting popular. So the final week they brought in Tommy Burk and the Counts. And I mean we went into rehearsals like this was the biggest show of our life. A gymnasium in East Memphis in the middle of summer, must have been a hundred-six degrees in there, packed out with six hundred kids to watch this battle between us and the Counts.

"And we whupped 'em."

By then, the Radiants also had demographics in their favor. While the Counts were at Memphis State, each of the six Radiants attended a different high school, making them eligible for six times as many gigs. As well, two of the members were Baptists, two were Catholics, and two were Jewish. They had entrance to every venue in town. "Music was everywhere," says one person on the scene. "It had become accepted. By then, department stores would have a promotion of English-looking Beatle clothes and they would hire a band to play."

The success of Randy and the Radiants came to the attention of Sam Phillips. By the time of their showdown with the Counts, several disc jockeys had appeared wanting to manage them. The Radiants selected Johnny Dark, a founding member of the Sputnik Monroe Fan Club. "He was even-tempered and good-humored and closer to our age than the other disc jockeys," says Randy Haspel. "At the time, we didn't know that he was friends with Knox and Jerry Phillips. Knox was going to Southwestern, a local college, where he was a Sigma Chi, so we started playing for Knox's frat parties and they loved us. Between Johnny and Knox, they agreed to have us audition for Mr. Phillips. I think Mr. Phillips had an eye for this new thing that was happening with the teens and he saw that with Bob Simon we had original material. And he was also looking to get Knox into producing. We were the first band that Knox produced. We cut our teeth on each other."

Though they were being courted by the label that inaugurated rock and roll, the Radiants had mixed feelings. "I think the only person left on Sun by 1964 was Jerry Lee, and he was just as dead as dead could get. We knew the label had seen its better days. Still and all, to be ushered in by Mr. Phillips, it was something. First time we met him, he'd just come in off the lake somewhere, he had on a yachtsman's hat, and sat in there and he was just as charming as he could be. After that it was, 'We'll do anything for you, Mr. Phillips.'

But our initial response had been much more hesitant. We had big plans, and we didn't know if Sun would be right for us.

"Our first sessions were produced by Mr. Phillips. We had a handful of original songs but we were warming up with songs from our set list. We started 'Mountain High' by Dick and Deedee and all of a sudden Mr. Phillips comes out of the studio and goes, 'What're ya doin'?' We'd grown up on the Elvis legend, you know, and we said, 'Well, we're just warming up, Mr. Phillips.' 'Keep playing it, I like this.' And we're looking at each other like, What's he trying to pull? And I said, 'Mr. Phillips, this was a hit record just a year or two ago. He said, 'I like it, I want you to do it.' So that became our first record."

Through Johnny Dark, the Radiants became close with Sputnik Monroe. "We were playing a dance at Clearpool, a Memphis teen hangout, and the owner and his two bad-boy bouncers flicked on the lights kind of early and chased everybody out," remembers Haspel. "They were drinking and wanted to get out of there. We were taking our time packing up, and words were exchanged. I got beat up and my drummer did too. It went to court and they were all fined for assault and battery, disorderly conduct. When it came time for us to play Clearpool again—we were the most popular band in town so they couldn't keep us out—we had a security guard go with us. He had a gun. These bouncers had been arrested and they wanted revenge. And made no real secret about that fact.

"The stage was set up right across from the concession stand, and the owner with his two greaser bouncers are standing directly across the room from us, and I mean they're staring daggers. They didn't look like they were too afraid of our security guard. Right in the middle of the set, the Clearpool door swings open and our manager Johnny Dark walks in, and right behind him, here comes Sputnik, and he's doing that strut. The whole party just went crazy. 'SPUTNIK! YAY!!!!!' and that kind of stuff. I was just dumbfounded and I said, 'Well folks, Sputnik Monroe is here at our gig. Sputnik, would you like to say a few words?' He got up there and everybody was clapping and cheering for him and he was flexing his muscles and everything. He waited for the applause to die down, then he pointed his finger across at the concession stand and he says, 'I want everybody to know one thing,' and he paused and pointed his thumb back at us, 'These boys are Sputnik's boys, and if you mess with them, you're messing with Sputnik!' And he left.

"The next morning, like Sunday at nine A.M., I get a call from the owner of Clearpool telling me he's apologizing, he's so sorry that the incident ever happened, he fired those guys that punched me out and he hoped that it would never happen again, we were welcome back at his club anytime we wanted to come. We kind of became Sputnik's boys after that."

A year later, in November 1965, Sun released a Radiants follow-up. "We had a Bob Simon song called 'Truth from My Eyes.' Bob was a year younger than I was, and I'd talked him into letting me sing lead. I think he might regret that to this day. We begged Mr. Phillips to make 'Truth' the A-side. He had a song called 'My Way of Thinking,' written by Donna Weiss, a Memphian who later wrote 'Bette Davis Eyes.' Her song was an absolute rip-off of the Kinks, opening with the same guitar as 'You Really Got Me,' and we thought it was embarrassing. Soon 'Truth from My Eyes' was number one on WMPS every night and we kept getting in the papers, sixteen years old, seventeen years old. But WHBQ wouldn't play it. So I went down there and talked to the program director, and he said, 'We won't play a Sun record.' I was incensed. 'Wha'da'ya mean you won't play a Sun record? What are you talking about!' So I told Knox, who fired off an angry letter to WHBQ." As "Truth" was winding down its two-month crest on WMPS, the song got a whole new life on WHBQ.

In the half-decade since Cropper, the Mar-Keys, Dickinson, and the other witnesses had finished high school, the music world had turned upside down. As teenagers, a *career* in music had been something they didn't even dream about. But for the next generation, the horizon was boundless. The difference is illustrated by Haspel's conclusion of the Radiants' story: "Sam put Jud [Phillips] Sr. on the road for us, a tentative tour of the South was planned, and we were riding high. Somehow it seemed at the last minute things collapsed and the plans fell through. I tell you what, it's tough to think you peaked when you were seventeen years old. I don't think I've ever had a more thrilling time in my life. It seemed like everything was possible, anything could happen, and it was all gonna come true."

Roland Janes, whose patience and wisdom make him the answer to a Zen koan, produced a song in 1964 that merged the city's traditional roots with the new musical energy of the Beatles. "Scratchy" was a collaboration between Janes and Travis Wammack, a teenage hotshot guitarist he'd found in a Memphis redneck suburb. Mostly instrumental and full of youthful energy, the song has a vocal break that sets it apart, epitomizing the Memphis philosophy of bucking trends: It's played backward. The music is built around a ticking of the drumsticks, with the guitar sounding like Wile E. Coyote escaping the Roadrunner. They come to a natural break where the ear expects a vocal refrain—and this incredibly maniacal-sounding backward voice comes out.

Nothing anyone could say forward could be as rebellious or as much fun. The song was a direct result of Janes's studio philosophy: "When I had Rita Records with Billy Riley, we were spending quite a bit of money on studio time. Your best time in the studio is your experimental time, and when you're renting studios, experimental time gets kind of expensive. So I finally got myself together and opened Sonic in 1961. My main purpose was to use it as an experimental laboratory, so to speak. To work with young groups and talented singers and writers. And I got into custom recording for other people to support the studio."

The abundance of music in the city had resulted in the proliferation of recording studios. And of music industry wanna-bes. The success of Sun in the latter 1950s and Stax throughout the 1960s encouraged barbers, auto mechanics, hardware salesmen, and just about anyone else to try their hand at some aspect of the music business. They all could have learned something from Roland Janes. Janes maintained his one-man operation through 1974, refusing lucrative tour offers from Jerry Lee Lewis (for whom he'd played guitar), and turning down other studios and artists interested in his services. He stayed busy, attracting young bands who thought they might be the next Mar-Keys, or the next Beatles. Or the next Travis Wammack. Sonic was a tight little space with a great sounding control room. Janes recorded mono and mixed as the band played, "defensive mixing—try to keep the bad stuff out and the good stuff in." He was limited to seven microphones. "I learned an awful lot watching the master, Sam Phillips," says Janes. "He was a great, great engineer."

Janes remembers his first encounter with the long arm of the Beatles. "I was recording a group at Sonic one day, and a kid came in that had just been to England and he had this weird-looking little hairdo. The musicians were sitting in the control room with me, peeking around at him and laughing and making little remarks about that weird hair. Well, turned out that he had a Beatle hairdo and we just hadn't seen one yet."

Janes's background may have been country and rockabilly, and the Beatles may have been the contemporary rage, and Stax was surely happening across town—but in all recording studios, the game was the same. "I didn't really envision anything other than trying to get a hit, and I really didn't care if it was rockabilly or pure country or rock and roll or what have you. And with the other studios, it was the same. In the early years, nobody could beat my rates. Then they started doing spec sessions and their rates were lower than mine. Basically, you had Sonic and then you had all the four-track studios. Ardent was starting up, Phillips was here. Fernwood, Hi, Satellite. But we all kind of had our own thing going, and we really didn't look at it as a competitive thing. In a way, I guess I was the alternative music of the day."

American Sound Studio began on a scale similar to Sonic but would become a major force in pop music. Between November 1967 and January 1971, American landed 120 records on the *Billboard* charts. One week, over a quarter of *Billboard*'s top 100 not only came from the same studio but featured the same core band backing a variety of artists—black, white, male, female. While the soul labels produced soul hit upon soul hit, American recorded an astonishing diversity of styles: spare soul, funky white stuff, lush pop orchestrations.

American was established by producer Chips Moman on a quiet corner in a black part of North Memphis. The building had a barbershop on one side and a restaurant on the other; when the barbers didn't like the music, they'd stick a loud radio in the common ceiling, making recording impossible. The Phillips family had their record distribution warehouse nearby, and Buster Williams's Plastic Products pressing plant was down the road. Music attorney Seymour Rosenberg had his office around the corner in his family's auto parts shop, and directly across the street from American was Lynn-Lou, a smaller studio run by Bill Black. This corner, by the latter 1970s, would devolve into shells of burned-out buildings, and the studio was bulldozed. But the impact of what happened inside the building affected late 1960s and early 1970s pop radio as much as, if not more than, any other studio in America, including Stax across town and Motown in Detroit.

The secret of American's success was the Memphis air. Or the river. Or the barbecue sauce. In other words: Dewey Phillips. In other words: There was no secret—there is nothing anyone could do to make it happen again. But it happened. It was the happening. Chips Moman was the pivotal figure, producing most of the sessions and responsible for assembling the house band. He'd been around the Memphis scene since Stax's gestation, giving direction to "Last Night" and many of the label's early hits. In late 1961, a dispute at Stax arose over production credit, over influence, over restitution and seniority—a rumble among the egos—and Steve Cropper came to the fore, Packy Axton was pushed to the rear, and Moman stomped out the door. He ultimately got a $3,000 settlement, negotiated by a trumpet-playing attorney who also did work for the defendant. Moman moved into the building, wired a rickety mono recorder, and began creating the machine that would soon dominate pop music. His house rhythm section, unlike the cultural collision at Stax, was a group of musicians raised together and familiar with each other's charms and idiosyncrasies. They simply did what they could do and watched the nation and the world applaud.

The first few years of American are a bit cloudy. Moman was out on a wet one, and though he still had his touch, he'd sold his ownership in the studio for an amount he could calculate in cases of whiskey. Tommy Burk remembers cutting there with his Counts as early as 1962; it was 1964 when Moman regained control, solidifying ownership with a bean farmer from Arkansas named Don Crews. That year, after cutting several hot records, goes a story in Peter Guralnick's *Sweet Soul Music* (1986), a singer friend of Moman's was contacted by a small label in Memphis and told, "We got this producer, man, all we ever have to do is give him a bottle of whiskey and a couple of pills, man, and he'll cut you a fucking record." For the label's next session, Moman charged five thousand dollars, up from his previous rate of twenty. They gladly paid.

At the time, Moman was making spare change shooting pool and painting gas stations. He didn't look much like a record producer when he encountered the group of pretty boys that would change his fortunes. Brandishing the blades of his double-edged life at Berretta's Drive-Inn one night in late 1964, he approached these young men who were dressed like a band. Moman is said to have drawled, "Yew boys got a band? Yew wanner make a record?"

"We had played a free show that night at the Veterans Hospital and were still in our gig clothes," remembers Larry Raspberry of the Gentrys. "Chips didn't look like anything we thought was our genre of music, and frankly we didn't take him seriously. We exchanged phone numbers but I don't think we called him back." Moman, however, pursued them. "We needed to make a tape for 'Talent Party,'" continues Raspberry, "and he told us to come in and do it with him." The Gentrys had been the Gents before the Beatles convinced the septet to add a British flavor to their name. They were a popular group in the city, but not overwhelmingly so. In the talent competition at the Mid-South Fair, they came in third. On the nationally televised "Ted Mack Amateur Hour" (where Memphis's Johnny Burnette and the Rock and Roll Trio had gotten their break a generation before) they won two out of their three appearances.

In 1965 the West Memphis scene was only an afterglow. The Avantis, a black Memphis vocal group that had regularly performed at the PI and followed the scene across the river to Memphis, were performing at venues like Clearpool and various YMCAs, enjoying some small success from their record "Keep on Dancing." The Gentrys had heard the song on the radio and had seen the band perform it live. At the end of a session, at Moman's behest, they cut their own version; Moman shared publishing rights to the song.

Later that year, the Gentrys' version was in the top five on the national charts. Sounding like the senior in high school that he and the others were, Larry Raspberry told a journalist during the band's peak, "Ours is a fast, peppy kind of sound, one that makes you feel good to play. The old slow stuff kind of depresses you. Ours has more drive and makes you want to get out and dance." Raspberry and Randy Haspel had begun a friendly rivalry even before each passed the other on the stairs at Lynn Vernon's guitar lessons. Both had R&B bands before the Beatles, and both rolled with the rock. The Radiants had a hit single first, but when the Gentrys got their turn, they reached new heights.

"Keep on Dancing" was originally a B-side. The band's version was brief, so Moman looped the parts that worked—all twenty-five words—and made it long enough to qualify as a song: two minutes, eight seconds. It sold a million copies. Fan clubs were established across the country. Their national head-quarters in Memphis hired two staff members to answer mail. The Gentrys performed a few times on "American Bandstand," appeared on "Hullabaloo" and "Shindig," appeared in the MGM film *The Girl in Daddy's Bikini,* and recorded a national radio commercial for Juicy Fruit gum. "Keep on Dancing" also reconstituted Moman. He traded half his interest in the song to farmer Crews, who had recently bought out the other partners. Moman had half his studio back and was working toward a house band, a concept he'd admired at Stax.

"Mary Lindsay and I were married, and I was living at Memphis State," says Jim Dickinson, talking like 1965 was yesterday. "I was playing an occa-sional Mar-Key gig, not doing a whole lot. Raspberry called me up, ten o'clock one night, and 'Keep on Dancing' was a hit. He says, 'Dickinson, my record is number fifteen with a bullet.' And I says, 'Good, Larry,' and he says, 'Half my band just quit, both the keyboard players and the girl saxophone player.' I says, 'That's pretty bad, Larry,' and he says, 'Yeah. I gotta go on the road and I can't go on the road without a band. I've gotta turn in an album, and Chips won't start because the band has quit. Will you go on the road with the Gentrys?' I says, 'No, Larry.' He says, 'Will you go to American and tell Chips you will?' I understood exactly where he was and I said, 'Yeah, sure, Larry.' So Mary Lindsay and I went down to the studio, middle of the night. I'd seen Chips around and knew who he was. He says, 'Yew go on the road with the Gentrys?' and I said, 'Yeah, sure.'

"While we were standing around talking, Chips locks the door and doesn't open it 'til noon the next day, at which time we'd made the whole first album and half of the second. Chips says to me, 'Yew too good to go on the road with the Gentrys,' and I says, 'That's what I think!' Suddenly I was back in the music business, Chips paying me $92.50 every other week, maybe. And maybe was part of the deal. My first payment was a counter check on mimeograph paper from Lepanto, Arkansas. It didn't look like it was worth $92.50 but it cashed alright. I stayed for about six months, from the fall of 1965 to the spring of 1966, playing on everything after 'Keep on Dancing' and before Sandy Posey's 'Born a Woman.' When I went to work for John Fry at Ardent, all he did was erase the maybe."

One of the Gentrys who didn't quit was Jimmy Hart. During the band's later days, they backed the king of local wrestling, Jerry Lawler, before the regular—and hallowed—Monday Night Wrestling in Memphis. While Lawler was singing, his then-nemesis Handsome Jimmy Valiant—whose own name had tarnished several pieces of vinyl—broke a guitar over Lawler's head. The incident apparently lit a bulb over Hart's. As of this writing, he is ring manager for wrestling magnate Hulk Hogan; stores sell little plastic dolls in his image.

The Beatles also transformed the LeSabres, the band that Haspel describes as "leather boys with greasy hair, smoking onstage and running around." Their lead singer, Laddie Hutcherson, formed the Guilloteens, a trio with a drummer named Joe Davis and guitarist and vocalist Louis Paul, later a solo artist on Stax. Hutcherson met Davis through Ray Brown's agency, when he sent them out together as Mar-Keys. "We let our hair grow long and we started dressing in English-looking clothes," Hutcherson has said. "We chose a name that sounded European since we were trying to cash in on the Beatles." The Guilloteens got a job as house band at a Memphis teen club, the Roaring Sixties, and soon were drawing a crowd. Despite a lack of original material, their manager, Jerry Williams (later a partner with Steve Cropper in the Trans-Maximus studio and label and also the manager for Paul Revere and the Raiders and, for a time, Neil Diamond), took them to Los Angeles hoping to get a break on the TV show "Shindig." "We bought some Hollywood clothes and auditioned for a gig at the Red Velvet Club," recalls Hutcherson. "We were nervous, but our manager was tight with Elvis, and the club owner thought Jerry could get his daughter a date with him. With those connections, I guess we sounded good."

They shared the Red Velvet stage with bands like the Byrds and the Turtles, also unsigned at the time. "The Righteous Brothers loved Louis's voice and took us under their wing, helped us develop our presentation," says Hutcherson. "They brought Phil Spector in to hear us one night, he was producing them, and Spector asked if we had any original music. We played him 'I Don't Believe,' which was barely a song then. The very next day we were in Spector's living room, which was big as a hotel lobby, and he came down this huge flight of stairs, and I remember he was wearing house shoes that were gorilla's feet." After overhauling the song, he produced a demo in the studio. "It had that wall of sound, Spector sound," says Hutcherson. "It was unbelievable." Williams was in Memphis when the Spector session transpired, and when he found out about it, his ego popped a wheelie. "He worked out a deal with Hanna-Barbera—the cartoon company!" Hutcherson continues. "We had to sign the contract or go home, and we signed. In the back of my mind I'm thinking, Spector's going to be pissed!"

Despite more experience in promoting cartoons than rock and roll records, the company made a minor hit of the recut version in 1966. Part of its distinct sound was Louis Paul playing the electric twelve-string guitar. In Randy Haspel's perception, perhaps because their success began so far from home, they were bigger even than the Gentrys. "This was teenage pop success like no one had ever seen. They were the dream. Los Angeles, long hair, a hit record, 'Shindig.' It was our world." They did a couple tours with Paul Revere and the Raiders, but none of their songs took off after the first one. Hutcherson remains active on the Memphis stage, part of the Funn Brothers duo.

Unlike most of Memphis's other studios, Ardent Recording has survived the bulldozer and the other confrontations from the city and the industry. Ardent was begun by three tenth-graders in 1960, established in John Fry's grandmother's sewing room when she wasn't using it. It's now a multimillion-dollar business and remains among the South's premier studios. Its walls are lined with hit records recorded there—ZZ Top, R.E.M., Leon Russell, the Bar-Kays, Travis Tritt, and its halls are haunted by the spirits of the musicians who've passed through—Big Star, Packy Axton, Isaac Hayes, the Replacements. Ardent's reputation has always been grounded in its equipment; it is a studio that understands new recording products and stays on the crest of technological advances while maintaining an atmosphere of ease and earthiness. It is an approachable place with great sound.

Ardent was initially a response to the only recording studio John Fry had ever been in. He'd begun tinkering with electronics in the late 1950s, especially interested in radio. While a sophomore in high school, he and two friends decided to establish a record label; John King would remain in the music business, but their other friend got out when he went to college. His name was Fred Smith, and he later founded a delivery company called Federal Express.

The Ardent label's first release was on an artist from Jacksonville, Florida. "His name was Freddie Cadell, and he was an acquaintance of the folks who lived across the street from my parents," says Fry. "We didn't know any of the bands around town. Subsequently we found plenty, but in 1960 it was not as common. He was recorded in some strange studio in Jacksonville, very primitive."

"At the Rock House," backed with "Big Fat Mama," didn't leap onto charts anywhere, but it walked the teens through the production and manufacturing process. "The norm at that time," says Fry, "was if somebody could render a fairly complete performance without serious errors in it, and if there was no technical mishap, then you considered the recording completed. And you know," he adds wryly, "maybe we knew more than we realized then. That may have been to the benefit of the music." When technology moved from sixteen tracks to twenty-four, Fry, who recorded and mixed the first two Big Star albums, quit producing records; the process had become too tedious.

Ardent created recording equipment from materials built for radio stations, modified by the young electronics whizzes. The first incarnation of the Ardent label released five singles, achieving some success with a popular band from the nearby University of Mississippi, and establishing themselves with the Shades, a band that included a former member of the Counts, Charlie Hull, and Lee Baker's talent show partner, Mike Alexander. Baker began hanging around the studio with Alexander. "Ardent was all white, but everyone was digging black stuff, really committed," says Baker. "People around town were going, 'Yeah, there's this guy that's got a studio in his house.' It was a big deal."

Then John Fry retired from the recording business. He was seventeen. "My interest was as much in radio as a medium as in the records. I think one of the reasons that we started recording was that we were just a bunch of kids and we sure couldn't get a radio station, so we'd do the next best thing. A little bit after I graduated high school in 1962, a friend of my family's got a grant to build a radio station in Pine Bluff, Arkansas. We thought, Well it's not exactly a major market, but this guy'll let us mess with it some."

"When I came along about 1964, I just talked Fry into reviving the label," says Jim Dickinson. Ardent was still in the sewing room, an enclosed garage across the patio in the back; the control room, along with an office, was in the main house. The talkback between the two was a covered walkway. Fry was cutting radio announcements for Pine Bluff when a friend named Bob Fisher came to him with Lawson and Four More, a group he'd met through the music store where he worked. This group piqued Fry's interest. Fry remembers, "Fisher needed help with Lawson's band and brought in Dickinson. Dickinson had recorded with Bill Justis for a Mercury-affiliated label. He was known to have ideas."

"Fisher calls me up," remembers Dickinson, "and says he's found this band of teenagers, fourteen and fifteen—he was lying because they were a little bit older—and he said they played great. He was lying about that too. He said, 'I need some songs.' I said, 'Sure Fisher, what kind of songs?' He said, 'I want a Kinks song.' 'When do you want it?' 'What about tonight?' I said, 'Come by and pick it up.' So I went in the bedroom and I wrote 'Back for More,' put it down on tape.

"It was done when Fisher came by, but I was already angling to get in at Ardent so I said to Fisher that I wanted to play it for them myself, make sure they understood it. We go over to Fry's house, there's Fry and Lawson and Four More. Little babies. Fisher was going to produce the record, and I just took over. It was the first record I produced. By the time it was done, I had also written and cut the A-side, 'If You Want Me You Can Find Me.' Fry appreciated a cocktail back then and he sat there, stewed, his feet up on the console listening to the playback. 'What do you think of that, John?' He says, 'Best damn sound that ever came over these speakers.' I thought, Yeah, this guy's got something going here."

One of the "little babies" in the band was particularly drawn to the studio experience. He played organ with Lawson's group, but was equally comfortable on guitar and, soon, a variety of instruments. Off the stage he was kind of quiet, but in performance he was as excitable as James Brown and as active as Tarzan. His name was Terry Manning, and he's since coproduced or engineered most every ZZ Top album, several George Thorogood hits, the Staple Singers' "I'll Take You There," was involved in mixing Led Zeppelin's second and third albums, and recorded Furry Lewis playing guitar in his bed with his leg off.

Manning was from El Paso and had played in the Bobby Fuller Four before they had a hit with "I Fought the Law." When he heard "Last Night" on the radio, he made his parents drive him to the nearest department store, where he bought his 45 on the Satellite label and began wearing it out. His father was a preacher who moved frequently, and Terry remembers nagging his parents about Memphis until they consented. A week after he arrived in town, he went to Stax, knocked on the door and said, or thought, "Here I am."

After gaining entrance to Ardent as an artist in the mid-1960s, Manning remained for twenty years. At first he answered the phone a lot, but he was watching everything that had anything to do with running the board and soon was producing. By the late 1960s, Manning was involved in many Stax hits, including albums from the Staple Singers, Booker T. and the MGs, and Isaac

Hayes's breakthrough. By then he was John Fry's main man, and Ardent was Stax's B-studio.

Lawson and Four More—Lost in the Morgue, as one local deejay mispronounced it—didn't do much, but because everyone had had a good time recording it, they got to cut another single. Fry's family was moving from their residence, so in 1966, he moved his business. Once on National Street, Ardent became an alternative rental space in town, featuring high-tech equipment and an open mind, a willingness to work with whatever sort of material was brought in. Black Oak Arkansas cut there when every other studio in town thought they were too loud. Leon Russell, Sam the Sham, and many Stax artists recorded there, too.

"In our early days," says Fry, "Dickinson was the guy who'd had some experience. And he knew some players and had industry connections. As well, he had a healthy skepticism toward the business which probably provided some good guidance for a lot of people. He had an experimental spirit, too, not afraid to try doing stuff a different way. That's a great catalyst to have. He encouraged others not to worry too much in advance about whether it's gonna work out, that will become obvious. Just do it and see what happens.

"Our facility coincided with the rapid upswing of the technology. In 1966, if you had four-track equipment, you had as many tracks as anybody had and more than most. Between 1966 and about 1970, you've gone from four to sixteen tracks and consoles much larger, and gone from almost no outboard equipment to at least some, and to using Dolby noise reduction and equipment that required a fair amount of alignment and attention in order to work right. We wound up mixing a lot of stuff that other people would record because we could apply some technological efforts that seemed to enhance it a little bit. Also, our console was the same make as Stax's, so that somebody from there could feel at home with what we had. We stayed busy."

At the local dances when the bands took a break, a disc jockey kept the music going with records. Dewey Phillips was enjoying a minor comeback, broadcasting from a tiny Millington station, and he began to work the dances. "Dewey's Millington show became very popular with a generation of young people who were just kids when he was making musical history at WHBQ," says Haspel. "This was evidenced by the hundreds of teenagers who would flock to the station-sponsored dances every Saturday night at T. Walker Lewis YMCA in East Memphis. Phillips would play 45s and assault the audiences with his nonstop verbiage. The kids would gather around to hear his jokes and get his autograph."

Radio in the early 1960s was beginning its move toward narrowcasting (epitomized by the strict playlists of today), away from the free-form shows by pioneer tastemakers like Phillips and Rufus Thomas, John R. and Wolfman Jack. Disc jockeys still had some influence on the music they played, and on WHBQ and WMPS, the AM stations catering to the white rock and roll audience, local bands releasing local records were not discounted. The concept of playing a record on TV had advanced a little, but not much. The "American Bandstand" method—a bunch of honkies moving whitely while a band lip-synched—had won out over Dewey and Harry doing whatever crazy things the music inspired them to do. (That same trend, unfortunately, dominates current music videos.) The Wink Martindale Saturday show, "Dance Party," had passed through the hands of a couple other deejays before settling into the twelve-year reign of Dewey's protégé, George Klein, beginning in 1964.

At Humes High, Klein had been class president, and Elvis had been his classmate. His break into radio came in the early fifties when WHBQ hired him to "baby-sit" Dewey Phillips, buffering him from his fans. When Klein began as host, "Dance Party" was still reeling from the station's decree banning the dancers, a move they chose over integrating them. So there was no dancing and it wasn't much of a party. He changed the name to "Talent Party" and put the emphasis on the bands. Touring acts stopped by the station and videotaped interviews and performances; when the show was broadcast on Saturday, Klein made all the acts appear to be live and in the studio. After a couple months, he shanghaied the "Shindig" concept and added a chorus of six dancing girls, the WHBQ-ties; within a couple years, he integrated them.

"Television gave a visibility to pop music that it didn't have before," says John Fry. "All of a sudden you were seeing people interviewed and seeing them perform. It sort of opened up the horizons." Everything about "Talent Party" rode the fine line between amateurism and inspired genius. The sets were models of innovation. One band was surrounded by a few dozen paper plates spray-painted in various colors; the next band performed against a psychedelic backdrop that, on closer inspection, was revealed as the board on which the plates had been painted. Klein's radio popularity brought an audience to the TV show. He also had connections in the business, which assured him the bands' cooperation. His patter was rapid, he favored goofy rhymes, and in the interviews he conducted his nervousness sometimes won out. He once asked B. J. Thomas, "You were fatally stabbed in New York, right?"

But—there was B. J. Thomas, a top star, standing right next to George Klein, and it was live from a studio in the heart of Memphis. With the recording studios in town amassing local talent and attracting international stars, Klein was ideally situated to draw major acts on his local show. Except that so many stars were black and all the guests were white. "We were doing the show for a while," remembers Klein, "and I said to the program director, 'Here we are right in the heart of what's happening—Stax, Hi, American, Sun, all the studios—yet we've never had a black act on the show.' And they saw what was coming, and they said, 'You're exactly right, George, but to open the door can you get a big star?' It just so happened that Fats Domino was coming to town so I went down to Ellis Auditorium, it was about ten-thirty, eleven at night, after Fats's show. And I had told my crew to stay in the studio after the news if possible because I was hoping to get Fats to come down and videotape some songs for 'Talent Party.'

"Fats was a little apprehensive. Black acts hadn't done much TV in the South. After talking about some of his records and talking about Felton Jarvis, a producer of his that I knew, and then the Elvis stories came up—finally when we started communicating really nice I said, 'Fats, you said you don't do local TV, but you'll be the first black guy to ever do the show and it would really open the door for other black entertainers.' He said, 'I'd be the first black guy? C'mon, let's go.' He got in my car, we stopped at a liquor store on the way, got him a little nip. He did four songs and an interview, and in the mid-sixties that just opened the door for integrating the show."

"Talent Party" remained faithful to local talent. Every show featured at least one local act, no matter whether they had a recording contract. If they hadn't recorded, they were directed to Roland Janes's Sonic Studio or, later, to John Fry's Ardent to get their lip-synch tape made. "I charged ten dollars an hour and three dollars for the tape," says Janes. "For thirteen bucks you could come in, set up, and cut four songs and be on television. I got kidded about it a lot. Some of the bands didn't sound so good, but some of 'em sounded really, really good. And for any number of bands, that was their first recording experience. I used to tell them if they didn't behave theirselves I'd spank 'em."

Klein says, "I had acts that couldn't get their records played on local radio, yet I was blowing 'em hard and heavy, breaking 'em on TV like Dick Clark used to break acts on 'American Bandstand.' Sam the Sham with 'Wooly Bully' and the Gentrys with 'Keep on Dancing.' A band could come on 'Talent Party' and reach the entire mid-South area—Tennessee, Arkansas, Mississippi, and some parts of Missouri. It was great exposure for local bands and national acts. After many of these bands got big, they told me they appreciated being able to do a local show before they had to go on the road and do bigger shows. We showed them how the lip-synch situation worked and that when the red light came on they were supposed to sing and the floor directors would point at the camera they were supposed to look at. When they got to Cleveland or Detroit or New York or Los Angeles, they had an idea about what they were doing."

Felton Pilate, now the producer for rap and pop star Hammer, credits "Talent Party" with his start. His band, the Soul Children, formed in California, and after backing up Stax acts during the 1972 WattStax concert in Los Angeles, came to Memphis and changed their name to Con Funk Shun. "'Talent Party' got us a lot of local gigs," he said during the 1992 world tour with Hammer. "But the tape we made at a local recording studio for the television show got us signed to our production company deal, which got us signed to Polygram." Cybill Shepherd is another success story. During the annual Miss Teenage Memphis Pageant, the "Talent Party" fashion coordinator spotted Cybill and said she'd like to send some photos to someone she knew at a modeling agency in New York. "Cybill didn't want to do it," says George, "but we sent 'em up there, the agency accepted her, she became model of the year, and Hollywood came calling."

In 1965, Sam Phillips's younger son Jerry, formerly the World's Most Perfectly Formed Midget Wrestler, was in a band that owed more to his father's earlier work than to the Beatles. Jerry played rhythm guitar in the Jesters and had found a punkish kid with lots of attitude to write songs and play lead. His name was Teddy Paige, though he was born Edward Lapaglio. His values were different than those of the other East Memphis white kids. Dickinson, who recorded with him, remembers that from the stage, he would introduce songs with lines like, "Well, here's another little song you're not gonna like," or, "Something else you've never heard." Randy Haspel remembers Paige's burning electric guitar style as unlike anything he'd yet seen; others cite Paige as the first in the area to say that the Beatles ruined music.

Teddy Paige wrote a song called "Cadillac Man," and it was the last Sun release that had the power of the earlier material. "Cadillac Man" was produced by Jerry's older brother Knox in late 1965, after the Radiants had been through the studio. Like all the Sun sessions from 1958 on—everything after the handclaps and saxophone on "Lonely Weekends"—this one was done at the Phillips studio on Madison. The previous year, Stan Kesler had cut "Wooly Bully" with Sam the Sham there. Knox had not been much interested in music then.

He wore V-neck sweaters with button-down shirts. He married young, he taught Sunday school, he worked hard to keep the madness beneath the surface. Once his divorce transpired, he took more interest in the family heirlooms—music, the studio, mayhem. "I wasn't even in the band," says Dickinson, who played piano and sang the song. "I was under contract to Bill Justis at the time. The Jesters had another singer that Sam hated. The session was supposed to be a demo for Teddy's song, and I was hired to play piano. And then the singer didn't show up, so I read the lyrics off notebook paper while we cut it."

Sam Phillips heard "Cadillac Man" and decided he'd like to release it. Another session was booked, what's called a "smoker," to be filed with the union to explain how the song was recorded. "I really thought we would sit around and smoke," says Dickinson. "But we got there and Sam had a suit and tie on and he was walking around with a clipboard in his hand, writing down microphones and stuff and I got real excited. I'd been around him, but I'd never really met him. That session was the first time I felt the hands of the master. I looked into the black pools of madness in Sam's eyes and I saw the same thing Elvis and Howlin' Wolf saw."

Sam Phillips called Dickinson before the record was pressed, reaching him at Ardent when it was still in Granny's sewing room. "Sam put [his brother] Jud on the phone and Jud was an even more dynamic speaker than Sam is. Jud says to me in this booming voice, 'Boy, you gotta cast your lot.' And I told Jud that my lot was already cast, that I was under contract to Bill Justis. And he said, 'Aw hell, boy, Bill won't mind.' So they put the record out."

CHAPTER EIGHT

The Catfish That Ate Memphis

❧

THE PROBLEM WITH THE BEATLES WAS THEIR MUSIC. AND THEIR FANS. Though their hair was radical for the time, that sort of statement paled next to drinking whiskey with someone who'd invented the blues, the very root of the Beatles' music. Their press conferences were entertaining, and in a few short years they would establish hippie fashion and philosophy, but the Beatles' early career indicates they would have leapt at the opportunity to pass a day or a year in Memphis, keeping the company the witnesses enjoyed. By the time they hit the states in 1964, they were slowly finding their way to the source.

For their first American tour, of all the bands available to open for them, the Beatles selected the Bill Black Combo, a Memphis instrumental group founded by Elvis's former bassist. They'd scored an early hit with the instrumental "Smokie (Part 2)" and had made a career appealing to the same audience that enjoyed Bill Justis albums. The Beatles must have known that Black had retired from the band two years earlier, yet the selection remains puzzling. "*They* requested *us*," remembers guitarist Reggie Young, still sounding amazed. He was the sole original member in the group. In his mid-twenties during the tour, Young was already a studio veteran, playing on Eddie Bond's late-fifties hit "Rockin' Daddy" before joining Black and helping define the Hi Records sound. The Combo traveled with the Beatles, and there is an oft-repeated story about the young George Harrison staring rapt while Young noodled on his guitar, having fun bending strings; Harrison's own sound would develop from the bent-string style. "We all hung out together for the whole thirty days," Young remembers. "We swapped stories and stuff, you know, talking shop. I remember we had some time off in Key West and we got in a little cafe and jammed for two days."

The Bill Black Combo may have been roots music to the Beatles, but the radical route for Memphis witnesses was folk music. Dylan had popularized the tradition, maintaining the elements of social commentary that were the music's guts and that had been diluted by the folk-pop that preceded him. Integration and rejection of the Vietnam war provided two mighty subjects. Folk fans found that the next step forward was two steps back, reaching for their roots and finding the witnesses already there. Greenwich Village contributed the venue—the coffeehouse—and kept the music in the national spotlight. In Memphis, where the attempts of previous coffeehouses had proven arch, the Bitter Lemon, yet more arty than its predecessors, proved innocent enough to work. An accidental sort of place, it was imbued with the character of its owner, John McIntire.

On an otherwise ordinary afternoon in Wellsville, Ohio, in the 1930s, a small propeller plane landed in a cornfield. The kids from town ran to see the contraption. From the cockpit stepped a Chicago millionaire, and he began tinkering with the engine. A lanky high-school senior moved forward. John McIntire watched, along with the other kids, as his eldest brother repaired the plane. John was six. This brother—there were ten siblings—was a gifted artist who had accepted an animator's contract from Disney and was to begin employment upon his high-school graduation, one month away.

Once the engine was working, the millionaire led the kids into town and bought them a meal. He swilled several drinks himself. Like the pied piper, he paraded the entourage back to the cornfield, where he rewarded the eldest McIntire with a ride. The plane took off and all the kids watched as it looped the loop. Then it looped again. Then it came very close to the ground and was out of control. McIntire's brother leapt out. The plane crashed, and both men were killed.

Before that time, John McIntire had dreams of playing professional baseball. Upon his brother's death, he was seized with an artistic drive. He was quickly drawing landscapes, exhibiting an acute understanding of perspective. When he finished high school, he worked two years in a steel mill, attending art classes in Steubenville, Ohio. He was awarded a four-year scholarship to the Cleveland Institute of Art, after which came a scholarship to the prestigious Cranbrook Institute. When the Memphis Academy of Arts solicited a teacher, the other students were busy creating resumes, their eyes on big cities. To McIntire, having a job didn't seem like a bad idea, and creating a resume did.

Within four days of his arrival in Memphis in 1961, he had experienced the city's great social chasm. The Academy, located in the beautifully wooded

Overton Park, lodged him for three nights nearby at the posh Park View hotel. He had room service and amenities he'd never experienced. But those quarters were temporary. He found a small place of his own behind Pappy's restaurant, and his first morning there, he awoke to a child standing over his mattress on the floor, filthy, diapered, sucking his thumb. On his windowsill there was a rooster.

"They used to call me the Warlock at Cranbrook because I had these visions of things that happened," he says. "One time in Memphis I saw a murder. I called the police and they said nothing like that happened. But they hadn't got the news yet. The guy called me back and said, 'How did you know about this?' I said, 'I saw it in my sleep when I lay down, middle of the afternoon.' It just flashed on me, I saw this guy shoot another guy and his girlfriend. It scared me to death."

McIntire had two suitcases when he moved to Memphis, tools and photographs of his work in one, and clothes in the other. But he'd had a dream about coming here and opening a coffeehouse. "I even saw people I was going to know. And when I'd later run into them, we were already friends. Carl Orr, I saw him a long time before I met him. Told people about him. When he came into my class, I stared at this kid. I knew he was different. Carl knows when I'm sick. Randall Lyon's the same way. Randall called me the other day, said, 'What the hell's wrong with you?' I'd been in the hospital and the message was on my machine when I got home. He just felt it."

Sitting with "John Mac" is like sitting with the wind. Part of his presence is his absence. Ideas and thoughts hang all around him, and if they can't be seen, they are definitely felt. His home is not unlike his long-gone coffee shop, every nook and shelf filled with paintings, drawings, and sculptures, or with yard sale remnants and oddities which he collects, ponders, then resells for a small profit or a small loss. Seated in a rocking chair, this virtuoso of chaos remains serene, if forever slightly distracted. He is tall and lanky, his longish hair and bushy mustache making him appear younger than his mid-fifties. He moves with an odd jerkiness, not unlike Charlie Chaplin; watching him sculpt is as pleasing as contemplating his artistic result. His rational side intended to stay just a year in Memphis, but McIntire's visionary side predominates. Twenty-four years of students credit him as a major influence. His imagination has not dimmed with age. He embraces everything and puts his art first.

Overwhelmingly shy, he communicated with his first classes only through the chalkboard. His withdrawn nature was interpreted as an air of mysticism. Combined with his commitment to his sculpting, evident not only in his devotion to his work but in the unusual objects with which he surrounded himself, McIntire became an artistic guru in Memphis. He held yard sales that people attended like church.

The Bitter Lemon Coffee Shop and Gallery was an extension of McIntire's personal life. The scene had begun gathering around him when he moved into an old, big house in semi-disrepair. He'd been in town long enough to recognize a group of artists trying to find each other, and this place at 2166 Madison, near Cooper, had room enough for everybody. There was something magnetic about that corner. It's not a major thoroughfare, though it stays busy, the heart of the large neighborhood known as Midtown. Long before McIntire settled there, a physician named Doc McQueen held musical jams in his home near the corner. Roland Janes met Jack Clement through Doc McQueen in 1955. Chips Moman made contacts there, the rockabilly Burnette Brothers. The corner would draw Crosthwait to stage one of Memphis's first art happenings there, a guerrilla event involving a toilet bowl placed in the intersection and set on fire. The dumbfounded look on the faces of the police and the neighbors indicated its success.

McIntire's house became known as Beatnik Manor. The vision taking shape. At one time, there were fourteen people and fourteen cats living there. Rarely did he have it to himself; he met many of his housemates only after they'd moved in. Bands that played the coffeehouse slept there. Kids who ran away from home stayed there. Allen Ginsberg came through, Marcel Marceau. "I bought an old VW van and everybody used it. Sometimes I wouldn't see it for weeks at a time. Guys would borrow it and leave it, they'd be stoned and wouldn't remember where. We'd have to ride around the streets of Memphis looking for it."

Unlike those around him, McIntire held a regular job. His teaching position came with a studio and materials, and since his art was his life, much of his income was disposable. There was never any shortage of people to help spend it. "I always made sure the refrigerator was full of food," he says. "Randall Lyon would be the head chef, the madam of the house. Madam Randall. He never wore clothes, except a big robe and half the time he didn't wear that. He'd go to the door buck naked. He didn't care."

Randall Lyon, stage center, entrance. A shock of wiry hair, a hulking figure, a walrus mustache. He is the (butter and) eggman. Goo goo goo joob. Coming to Memphis because he outgrew Little Rock, Lyon cavorted with writers and musicians, theatrical talents and film technicians, amalgamating them all into an art of himself, at the fringe of the fringe, articulating the maelstrom while increasing the chaos. A self-described obscurantist, he reaches his widest audience through influencing others, keeping himself in the shadows.

"The Bitter Lemon was the place that drew us together," he says. "If it wasn't for McIntire being in touch with artists, poets, musicians, there wouldn't have been a center for the situation, and he was it. The Bitter Lemon was a good place to play. Fred McDowell was playing there, Furry was playing there, the Allman Joys played there, Lee [Baker] played there, Don Nix, Charlie Freeman, Dickinson—that was the hub. And you could eat there too. John had a place to work, a place to crash, a place for food."

"It's hard to describe what kind of figure John was," says Robert Palmer, an aggressive clarinetist who began regularly trekking from Little Rock to Memphis in 1965; also a writer, he would become the chief pop music critic at the *New York Times* from 1976 to 1986, publishing his book *Deep Blues* in 1981. He and Lyon are lifelong friends. "McIntire was like a nonguru. He was a bit older than everybody else, he had this great visual eye and this unlimited tolerance for weirdness. I think of his place over there on Madison, Beatnik Manor, as having been like a salon for artists. There was always somebody doing something interesting around there. Always. And there were always interesting and very weird people staying there. From night to night it was hard to tell who lived there and who didn't. The epicenter of the Memphis beatnik scene was for sure with McIntire. And it wasn't really anything he said or did, although he could be incredibly charming and funny. His attitude was like, I'm doing art, here's my house, you know, rock on."

Once in the Manor, McIntire met an older art student who shared his desire to open a coffeehouse and was grounded enough to handle the business affairs. During the summer of 1964, they found a place at a perfect distance from the house: far enough to keep crowds from spilling into the Manor at closing, but near enough that residents too drunk or high could walk from one to the other—and arrive feeling refreshed. The aura of the coffeehouse came from McIntire's predilection for secondhand merchandise and old junk. "The Bitter Lemon looked like a beatnik place," says Sid Selvidge, "where the Oso had been kind of a hootenanny place." "The Bitter Lemon was the personification of the sixties in Memphis," says Lee Baker. "During the folk times, it was folkie, and when the psychedelic thing began, McIntire painted the whole inside psychedelic."

"The setup was simple," says McIntire. "If you drank coffee it was okay, but the other drinks were horrible, sweet and syrupy. We had an ice machine, and a stupid little pizza oven. We'd buy these commercial pizza crusts and put ketchup on 'em. It was making lots of money in the beginning, and people tried to buy that place from me. Everybody said not to sell it. We only had fifteen hundred dollars or so in it, that was everything. And we were offered

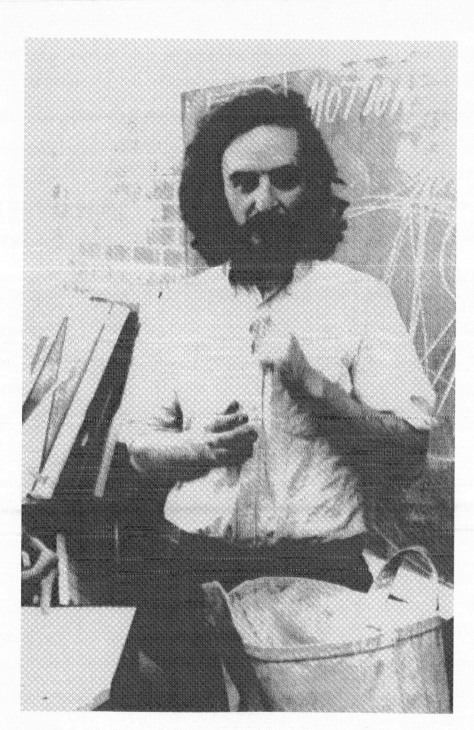

John McIntire. "It's hard to describe what kind of figure John was." Photo courtesy of John McIntire.

ten thousand. People who owned other coffeehouses were calling us from around the country. They wanted to franchise us. We went to Little Rock to look at places to open. Bitter Lemons across the United States."

"The Bitter Lemon was an innocent place that seemed to have all kinds of dark foreboding about it," says Jimmy Crosthwait, an early champion of the scene. "Coffeehouses at the time were dens of something or other. But looking back at it, it was like an ice cream parlor. It had ice cream parlor chairs and little ice cream parlor tables and it really tried to sell different kinds of espresso and shit. But there were poetry readings a little bit and maybe every now and then somebody would want to play chess."

"The rich kids would come and spend money in there," says Marcia Hare, who collected their tips as an underage waitress. "They'd get drinks with names like Passion Fruit and they were real expensive—today it would be a five-dollar drink—and it was nothing but orange juice with an umbrella in it. We'd wait on the customers before the band played, but once they began, you didn't want to interrupt. So we'd just dig the music and then go out in the parking lot and get high with the band. We were real into drugs. I guess the crowd inside was spiking their drinks."

Marcia Hare speaks with a purr in her voice, her coquettishness deflecting her commanding presence. Though she has experienced a very full forty-something years, she looks much younger. "Are you going to put me in your book?" she asks. "Ah'm a tittie dancer." I know who you are, I tell Marcia, and tell her the first time I saw her was when the plug was pulled on Mud Boy at the downtown festival. She has since retired from the stage, invested her earnings in a modest house. She came to Memphis in 1964 at the age of fifteen, moving from Maryland. Her sister and she hated the dullness of the city when they first arrived, but by the following year, when Marcia was in the eleventh grade, she found herself in the midst of a unique experience. "My dad was an English professor, and when we moved down here, first thing he did was take us to the civil rights marches and demonstrations. That didn't make us real popular at school. We were Yankees and nigger lovers too." At her father's instruction, Marcia and her sister volunteered their after-school time at a local theater, helping build sets. "He wanted us to do something educational, to keep us out of trouble," she says with a laugh. "But that's where we got into acid."

Theaters, at the time, were Memphis's bastions of alternative culture, and a couple of older hippies were soon taking these girls around the scene. Daughters of a French mother who was working in a New Orleans strip joint, they were wise without study. "We were desperate for a nightclub," Hare says. "In

D.C., we'd been going to Georgetown, and here there wasn't a thing to do. The Bitter Lemon was somewhere to go to hear music. My older sister got a job there right away, because we always thought if you liked to be somewhere, it's better to work there than pay to go in. Through the theater, we met Bill Barth, and Barth was the big hash dealer and that's how I finally got to meet some blues artists. Blues was the one thing we liked about Memphis when we first moved here." The sisters alternated nights waiting tables.

Marcia's sister began dating a playwright, and Marcia ran with a lighting tech who had come from San Francisco. His California roommate had been a man named Kenneth Owsley, aka Oz, aka the Bear. Owsley was a chemist, then brewing huge batches of LSD, which was not yet illegal. The hallucinogen had been invented in 1938 by the Swiss scientist Albert Hoffman, and was, by the 1960s, being manufactured for behavior-modification programs such as the treatment of alcoholism. Scientists and medical students in San Francisco were using it, as Randall Lyon says, "to figure out a way, through equations, to describe a thunderstorm." Owsley had impressed Hoffman with his knowledge of organic chemistry and become the premier brewmeister. When his roommate moved to Memphis, he found, of course, Beatnik Manor. The LSD connection between Memphis and San Francisco could not have been more direct.

"Little Rock and Memphis had LSD in sixty-five," says Lyon. "Really radical, unmeasured LSD was coming here way before other places. We were a very aggressive bohemian community, and there was this very direct connection between San Francisco and Memphis. We took enormous amounts. Huge doses. Well over five thousand micrograms. Major doses. Everyone was transformed by that experience. That happened before the blues festivals, though they were one of the next things to happen. The LSD gave us the inspiration, the understanding that we could do that. We had no fear."

In San Francisco, the acid scene was still a year away from going public, and two from going national. The three-day "acid test" at the Longshoreman's Hall featuring Ken Kesey's Merry Pranksters was in January 1966. The Fillmore would be opening in a few months. *Surrealistic Pillow*, the first Jefferson Airplane record with Grace Slick, came out in 1967. In Memphis in 1965, acid became an underpinning of the scene. "You could take the stuff and go out and run around and not be paranoid because it wasn't illegal," says Robert Palmer. "I remember in 1965 and 1966 we occasionally used to trip with a few people and go out marching through the streets wearing things like oriental rugs and banging cymbals and playing flutes and chanting and yelling, and cops would drive by and say, 'Oh it's a bunch of drunk college kids, ha ha.'"

The acid arrived in Memphis on powdered chalk. A teaspoon of it made forty gelatin caps of 250 micrograms per dose. One shipment got mixed up, and the dosages were much higher. Marcia Hare remembers they were going to meet for a big trip in Little Rock at a friend of Randall's. "We'd gotten this Owsley package and divvied it up in Memphis, licking our fingers all the while. We were already kind of rubbery when we left and halfway down there, everybody was losing it. Carl Orr had a death grip on the steering wheel and was driving real fast. He wiped out four or five markers on the side of the road. When we got to Little Rock, we realized we didn't have an address and we had no idea where we were going. Little Rock was a tiny town then, and it was about midnight. We could hear Bob Dylan music, and I swear we followed the Bob Dylan music and it led us to the right apartment."

Though some were getting heavily into substances, and surely there was abuse, debauchery was not the goal. The heavier doses of the drug did not send one, like today, out into nightclubs to party, but rather on inward, contemplative trips. "It was exceedingly peaceful," says Lyon. "Peaceful contemplation is what it was about. And McIntire and his coffeehouse provided this surrealistic world, removed from the world because it was all secondhand. He had eighteenth-century actors' robes in there, mannequin heads and weird models and strange glass bead curtains and oriental rugs from Goodwill. We got oriental rugs from the fucking Goodwill! McIntire set the imaginal criteria, helped give a certain visual language. John still does that. But when we were all tripping, the high end of the LSD experience was focused on that world of his."

"I only tried it several times, but it'd put you out for three days," says McIntire. "It was real pure. You'd have a fantastic trip and didn't worry about going crazy. Sometimes I'd ride a bicycle all over Memphis, take photographs. Later on, people started putting speed into it. I never did that anymore. I had goals, I wanted to be an artist and I didn't want to let that get in my road. A lot of these kids were younger, had no goals and went looking for heavier stuff and killed themselves. We lost a lot of friends. Blew their brains out. Usually they had money, and their families abandoned 'em. It was terrible when somebody would be missing and you'd find out they were dead."

While the acid community was relatively small and tight, more and more people from the mainstream began sharing their other interests—folk music, artistic inquiry, and the bluesmen. The Beatles had shaken the moss from society, and when the sun shone in, people began seeing beyond the four square walls that defined them. The Bitter Lemon became a hub for persons involved in a process that consumes society today: deculturalization. Beatniks in the

1950s got out of society's box, recognizing black culture as an alternative to their own. They revered the jazzmen, bop, music made by breaking the rules, and they tried to create a society from the same concept. Their inroads paved the way for the early sixties, when integration began taking hold, and in 1962, when Bob Dylan burst on the scene, the glint of marginalia available to the baby boomers kaleidoscoped, telescoped, landed in their lap and began to touch the mainstream populace.

As an impetus for deculturalization, the Vietnam war cannot be underestimated. Though full-scale rebellion against it was still several years away, by the middle of the decade soldiers were returning from their mandatory service, exposed to new lifestyles. Between 1962 and 1964, Randall Lyon had served two years in intelligence. His clearance was so high that he is nervous talking about it today. "Information was my job. I learned how to do propaganda, psychological warfare, and I went overseas and it changed my whole scene. What can you do when you find out that the government is your enemy? Don't worry about the Vietnamese, worry about your government." Goo goo goo joob.

Segregation remained the law of the land, right down to separate water fountains, but youth culture began embracing the dignity and elegance of those not like themselves. The friendships that the witnesses in Memphis developed with blues artists—older men and women, often rural, always poor, ostracized and rejected by "society"—became living proof that there was life beyond what they'd been raised to see.

The attention given the blues artists was an indication that the walls fortifying "high" art were crumbling. Through the Second World War, photography had been dominated by grandiose drama, Ansel Adams lugging his camera to extreme mountaintops to get shots of what the average person would not ordinarily see. But by the 1950s, artists like Lee Friedlander and Robert Frank were expanding ideas tendered by Henri Cartier-Bresson and his candid photographs capturing Parisian daily life. The Delta-born and raised William Eggleston began making strides in photography at the same time the blues renaissance was happening around him. Moved by the images of Cartier-Bresson, Walker Evans, and Friedlander, he turned his eye toward the details of the world about him—the South at first, but place was not integral to his idea. Eggleston discovered life, passion and color—glorious color—in what others dismissed as mundane. "I got serious about being a photographer in the late fifties," Eggleston says. "During the sixties I had an intense period of development, and by the late sixties I had formed a way of working that was thought out, that is still continuing. It's evolved, but it's identifiable as the same person's work.

"I was interested in taking pictures to make photographs more than to record social things or events. I wanted to make a picture that could stand on its own, regardless of what it was a picture of. I was interested in the photograph and still am. I personally don't have much use for pictures of things that are not images with integrity to them. I have never been a bit interested in the fact that this was a picture of a blues musician or a street corner or something." The public's warming to Eggleston's approach was nearly simultaneous with the realization that the yardman could be a major American artist. It would be the mid-1970s before Eggleston achieved his breakthrough, for the first time elevating color photography from the pages of advertising to the walls of the Museum of Modern Art in New York. In the meantime, he found welcome company among his musician friends, and no lack of challenging work near his Memphis home.

"I can see it in the 1965 sunlight," says Lyon. "Bill and his wife Rosa pulling up to Beatnik Manor in the Lincoln. Bill would step out, always wearing a real severe suit, it was like he was the fucking count. Voluptuous and corrupt, a striking image. It was unreal, what an aura. He stopped traffic. It was absolutely fucking Tennessee Williams beautiful."

"I knew everyone around Beatnik Manor," says Eggleston, "was close friends, but that was not a place I spent much time. For one thing, I had my own house, with a laboratory, with music, with lots of things I needed that were not at Beatnik Manor. I was less of a strolling minstrel than some of those people." Eggleston was older than these beatniks, and in the earlier 1960s he'd been part of a different artists group. "Sidney and Mary Chilton, Alex's parents, were some of my closest friends. They were two of the most important people in Memphis from that time, the Kennedy era. Mary held what you might call a salon, and things happened in the house. People would come there, it was an art gallery. They had a piano and Sidney would play, I would play, different people would come in. He was very good at analyzing how jazz things were constructed. I don't know who else would have fostered what they did. That's the kind of environment Alex grew up in. A different generation than Beatnik Manor, but just as intense."

The sixties brought the issues of racism, sexism, and class inequities to the fore of America's political agenda. A faction of contemporary society believes that change in focus destroyed cultural standards. The disintegration of public schools and the lack of "cultural literacy," the importance now accorded popular culture, even rampant violence, are attributed to the social movements of the sixties. This belief ignores or denies the value of non-European contributions. For our purposes, it denigrates the blues artists and the expression in their music. But since they began recording in the early years of the twentieth century, society has refused to let go of their work. From swing bands to the Rolling Stones to the rhythms of machine-influenced music, the bluesmen's ideas are continually reexamined. The Next Big Thing has always been a re-working of the union between the African tradition and the Western folk tra-dition. The sixties did not deny the beauties of our classical heritage but elevated other formative influences.

"Furry and Bukka White and Freddy McDowell and Joe Callicott and Nathan Beauregard, those people are really the groundwork of it all," says Lyon. "They were this combination of entertainer, performer, and Magus— they had full Magus status. What they were doing and what they were talking about and dealing with in their music—it was compelling. You had to respond to it."

"We would go out in the country and to joints and stuff and run around with those people," says Robert Palmer. "Randall and I used to ride the hour out to Como, Mississippi, and pick up Fred McDowell at the Stuckeys where he pumped gas. It's something none of us ever got over. It was really interest-ing to hear those people doing their individual stuff and not really changing, not giving a shit about trends or fashion or anything like that. And we were very, very devoted to those people."

The fact that blacks and whites of any age were at each other's homes was a new experience. The whites had attended their twelve years of school during a time when blacks, even if they lived next to the schoolyard, were not allowed to attend the same facilities. "You could go visit Memphis Minnie," continues Lyon. "Across from her bed, she had this picture of her in a white dress with the guitar and it was in a silver frame. She'd had a stroke. You would say, 'Minnie! I really love your music,' and she would start crying. It was heavy. Sleepy John was a saint. He used to have all these little jokes. If he thought there were people around who didn't know him, he would tell them to go turn the light on. Because he was blind. Somebody would go turn the light on and he would have a fit, just howl! He'd need a ride somewhere and we'd drive out to Brownsville to pick him up. He would call up at three o'clock in the morning, ask us questions about his social security, stuff like that. He felt pretty chipper. To his family, he was a meal ticket, which was normal. He was real old then and probably a real hassle, and we only saw the good part."

"First time I went to visit Furry," says Marcia Hare, "Ve. 'ene, Furry's girl-friend, was so nice. She said, 'Come in all you children, make yourself com-fortable.' You'd sit down and she would go, 'No, make yourself comfortable!' And she'd make you lie down on the couch until she felt that you were comfortable. One day she called me in the kitchen because something I couldn't see was going on in the living room. I found out later Furry was putting his leg on and didn't want anybody to see him do that.

"Furry was a big ham. One time we were over there and Gus Cannon was there. 'Walk Right In' was a big hit where I was from, so for me it was like meeting a star. I really wanted to hear Gus play the song. Furry did not want him to share the limelight. So they sat there like two little children fighting to see who was going to play. Furry literally snatched the guitar out of Gus's hands to prevent it from happening."

Once communication between the cultures had been established, a last confusion had to be overcome. "They had no idea why we were there," says Lyon, "because we weren't much about money or anything. We just wanted to know 'em, they were fascinating people. Finally, they accepted us. Furry became highly socialized, he could work the white folks. He could send the best of 'em to the pawnshop for that guitar." The pawnshop scheme was a way the bluesmen could be sure they got paid to perform. It was obvious that money didn't stick to the scenesters, yet they could also see how anxiously their own company and performance were desired. To perform, they gots to have they axe, and if they pawned it for eighty-five dollars before a gig and had it re-deemed by whomever was hiring them, they were assured some minimum payment.

"To go see Bukka White on a gray afternoon like this," says Lyon, and he leans back in the sofa and shuts his eyes, "and you walk in and there's his wife in the kitchen with a little girl, she's heating up curling irons, holding these things on the gas stove for fifteen minutes till they get really hot, and then putting them in her little girl's hair, and this blue smoke would come up, the little girl would twist around and her mamma would say, 'Stop it,' and Bukka would growl, 'I'm gonna put a screw in your eye.'" Lyon is recalling this story from a sprawling loft on Main Street in tiny North Little Rock, surrounded by compact discs. The sound of traffic drifts in the window, mixed with voices conducting business at the post office across the street. The phone has been turned off, the answering machine operating silently if at all, while Randall re-treats to a time and place that may be gone but that continues to move him and that still lies at the heart of modern social issues. He is in the company of dead friends, and his being radiates such an energy that I flash on how the sub-ject of this book became such an interest to me, why I was moved to give my-self over to the writing of it. As Lyon describes the scene at Bukka White's home, I am transported to gray afternoons at 811 Mosby, where Furry Lewis lived for the years that I knew him. I was an abashed white kid, high school, a

product of the last perimeter before urban sprawl. My suburbia still had a lo-
cale, and I had a sense of Memphis as a town, of the river as lifeblood.

I was changed by being in the presence of Furry, in a tiny duplex on a
crumbling street that was only a block from Poplar Avenue, Memphis's major
traffic corridor, but seemed a giant world away. A room that was always real
hot, even in winter, with a girlfriend or two attending Furry, with a picture of
Muhammad Ali on the wall, and later one of Burt Reynolds. There was a
string rigged from the TV to the bed so Furry could turn it on and off without
having to attach his wooden leg and get out of bed. My work is a response to
the impression made on an impressionable me when, while sipping Ten High
bourbon, I asked Furry why he kept a jar lid on his shot glass, and turning his
boney body like a ballet, he answered, "My eyes is bad and I can't see well.
Don't want a spider to get in it and bite me when I takes a sip."

We had never had that problem at my home.

Deculturalization.

You had to respond to it.

A mutual interest between a few individuals was becoming a community, with
the Bitter Lemon at its core. Although Dylan had opened a new world to the
mainstream in 1962, and though the Beatles had rocked that new world in
1964, the dominance of the old world remained clear. Society changes slowly.
It would be the 1970s before the 1960s rattled mainstream politics, deposing a
president and ending a war. Indicative of how far removed this culture remained in the mid-sixties—the extent of their deculturalization—the painter
Charlie Miller remembers walking through Overton Park wearing leather sandals and people stopping their cars to accost him, to yell and ask him if he
thought he was Jesus. "I remember teachers getting kicked out of Memphis
State for wearing Bermuda shorts and sandals," adds McIntire. "Got fired.
And growing a mustache. These guys attacked me one night and were going
to beat the hell out of me because I had a mustache."

The Bitter Lemon narrowly escaped immediate failure. Upon opening, a
contract was signed with a miasmic local girl to sing "from Saturday to Saturday." "Her big song was 'Mariah.' She could bellow it out real loud," says
McIntire. "When people realized she was there every night, they stopped
coming in. I was sitting there going, Oh man, we're going to close before we
even started. Her mother was smiling at us. She was a lawyer and she had this
contract. These two guys were sitting in the audience, I didn't know who they
were. They were writing and talking to each other real loud, they didn't pay
any attention to her. They were going, Yech. But it was the only coffeehouse

at the time. One of 'em picks up a guitar I had lying around and starts strumming it. I said, 'You guys can play?' He said, 'You want us to play something for you?'

"They started playing and nobody could believe it. They played this open-tuned blues guitar, and they went into their act. John Fahey was Blind Joe Death. He wore dark glasses and Bill Barth would lead him up onstage and they would play together. When he was done, he took his glasses off and sat back in the audience. This girl got real jealous because they were stealing her show. They looked at the contract, it said 'from Saturday to Saturday' on there. We said to her mom, 'Okay, we'll just let her sing on Saturday.'

"She quit."

Bill Barth had moved to Memphis from Queens, New York, in search of old bluesmen. John Fahey, who had written his doctoral thesis on the late Charlie Patton, one of the most popular Delta songsters, joined him in the hunt. Both were accomplished musicians, annually releasing recordings on Fahey's label, Takoma. Fahey's style drew from the acoustic bluesmen whom he admired, employing a percussive finger-picking. Barth began applying Fahey's style to the electric guitar, drawing out the moods like a raga. "Barth sat around and played guitar a lot," says Lyon, "which was real nice, it was exceptional. He hates my guts now, but I spent many an afternoon on the front porch with him playing for six hours." Barth and Fahey made national news when they located Skip James, a singular Delta artist.

They came from the Northeast, where the Delta blues was shrouded in mystery and novelty, and was still rare, making it a valuable commodity. The idea of Furry Lewis or Gus Cannon regularly playing a coffeehouse gave them palpitations. Nick Perls, their friend at home, had established the Yazoo label and was reissuing country blues from the 1920s and 1930s. Fahey and Barth had a sense of what blues, bluesmen, old 78 rpm discs, and such related affairs were commercially worth. "Nick's reissues sometimes didn't have the words right," says Lyon, "because they didn't know what a jack and a doney was, for instance [male and female donkey, literally; slang for a man and woman]. So when Charlie Patton sang that song, they didn't know what he was talking about. We were southerners and had been around the rural scene, so at least we could understand them when they sang. Here's Nick, his father was Alexander Calder's agent and he'd grown up in the whole 1950s Abstract Expressionist movement, and he still couldn't understand this shit." Conversely, while this group of locals understood not to take the blues players and their culture for granted, they needed the outsiders to indicate that careers beyond the Bitter Lemon were possible. Though their goals were compatible, their styles were different. The northerners thought the southerners lazy; the southerners thought the northerners pushy and coarse.

"Barth was about business all day long," says William Eggleston. "The local people had a resentment against those we called carpetbaggers. I think that's just human nature, though. To most southerners, and it's not founded on any kind of logic, people like them come off as sleazy. But that's been going on for ages down here because unlike, say, New York, the South is not an international place. In New York you're accustomed to seeing foreigners, and you're just not in this part of the country.

"I didn't go out of my way to spend time with Barth, probably because we were from such different backgrounds. I kept hearing people like him going on and on about how fantastic this or that discovery was, and it wasn't a bit unusual to me. When I was growing up in the Delta, the places you would hear this music were 'juk' houses out in the country, which were all black. I had known about these people always, had always heard them, thought they were great."

A tenuous trust developed. "Barth would have been able to discuss modal tuning or whatever with any of these musicians," says Lyon, "but he was a Yankee from Flushing Meadows, and there wasn't any language between them except the music. Barth and Fahey didn't dig that southern thing, they didn't know the ropes. I always thought Barth hated that part the most. He needed some southerners along to mitigate some of that stuff. The old guys didn't know who we were, but they understood we were from around there. But they *really* didn't know who he was."

Rediscovering blues players, as the successes continued to mount, became quite the thing to do. People from all over the country converged on Memphis, heading south with a sense of conquest: Come! There are more figures to liberate! It was a different outlook than what seemed appropriate to the young local whites, who were aware that despite their proximity, they too were invading a culture. Their attitude was more about getting to know the players as humans and not statistics, "feel" and not trophies; the locals were interested in who they were, not what they were. Nonetheless, these people were accomplishing things that the locals had not done; Barth, for example, did not *have* to be here helping blues artists get work. Fahey's Takoma Records documented and released albums by them. (One of their cohorts, David Evans, remained in Memphis and continues to actively record obscure local blues for the High Water label.)

"When Barth and Fahey came down, they would try to go to the black parts of Mississippi and get the black people to talk to 'em," remembers Lyon.

"And that's difficult, because you don't know what order you are impinging on down there. At that time, black people were very suspicious of white people going far enough into the scene to find someone like Fred McDowell or Bukka White. They were protected, they were special resources that the people needed. They didn't like that invasion and the white folks just hated that feeling, so you had to forget all that and grin and bear it and go down there and confront it. It was really something. And Barth and Fahey were the first people I knew that were interested in getting next to that and had the courage to do it. But they sure as fuck brought us along. They were living in our house and we went with them, because we were interested too."

As recently as 1994, I have been eyewitness to intelligent film crews who come down from the Northeast to Memphis and the Mississippi Delta and ask for the crown jewels in exchange for nothing. I have heard forethinking people devoted to breaking down cultural barriers say, We are PBS, we are the taxpayers' dollars, we are going into the homes of sixty million people and this is the kind of publicity that you cannot buy. For more than thirty-five years, for almost four decades, the most and the least well-intentioned carpetbaggers have come to Memphis musicians and asked them for the one thing that over the years of plunder and abuse they have retained as exclusively their own: their presence. In exchange for the one thing that Sleepy John Estes had that put food on his table, the one thing that Gus Cannon could do that would make anyone think of Gus Cannon, the one thing that the Center for Southern Folklore has got when they can't even get a lease on their building—they offer an intangible. I have sat at a table with an internationally respected and admired filmmaker whose work has affected the social conscience of America and heard him say, not with braggadocio in his voice but certainly with a sense of pride, In my twenty-five years of filmmaking, pause, in which I have interviewed—and here there was a long pause, some sort of calculation—ten thousand people—ten thousand interviews, he says—in my twenty-five years of filmmaking in which I have interviewed ten thousand people, I have never paid for an interview.

It's not that he's expecting me to admire this. We've previously agreed on our difference of opinion. But he is exasperated, truly exasperated that he would come to Memphis from New York to earn his living, giving the people of America and the people of the world a documentary in which his interviewees' statements might get a minute of air time, might get two separate forty-five-second bites, and though his documentary won't be what he wants it to be unless these artists give him their presence, these people won't give away to him the only thing they have.

He's shocked—in *Nashville* he didn't have to pay those even more famous artists—but after tiring negotiations, professing still not to understand, he relents. They will pay these people in fifty-dollar lumps for the only thing they have. And then the filmmaker, the producer (who will reneg on the payments after shooting), and the crew get up from the table where they've eaten on the taxpayers' money and I watch them go to one of the three most expensive hotels in the city. On the taxpayers' money.

In 1964. In 1994.

In 1965, while canvassing for old 78s, Bill Barth encountered a family who said, "We ain't got no 78s, but would you want to buy this chere guitar?" Barth strummed the instrument, sat down and played a few songs, thanked the family, and left without the guitar. When he returned a few days later, Nathan Beauregard, born a century earlier into a world as different as another planet, was strumming and singing in the living room. Beauregard had played all his life till he no longer felt like it, had never recorded. When Barth helped inaugurate the Memphis Country Blues Festivals the next year, Beauregard became a featured performer.

Born blind, Beauregard was led around by his nephew, a man in his seventies. His withered skin hugged his high cheekbones, the lids over his sunken eyes always shut so that he resembled a mummy. He'd begun developing his repertoire when Lincoln was still president. He was booked on the blues festival not for what he'd known and lived through but for what he still did; that is, the show was about the music, and he could still play. He'd have his amp set up slightly in front of him and to the left so he could lean over and work feedback into his sound. "Nathan Beauregard was cosmic, like some Tibetan monk." Randall's eyes are once again closed. "He lived behind the B'nai B'rith home in Midtown, in a row of shack houses for maids. Barth discovered him in one of those houses. To be walking past somewhere and hear someone moaning, 'Bumble bee, bumble bee, got a stinger long as my right arm.' And the guy's a hundred and something years old. . . ." And alive and well in an old friend's mind.

These musicians were not just artists but spiritual leaders, spiritual beings whose very presence was an education to people raised during segregation. "I'd had my washboard since recording with Dickinson," says Crosthwait, "and now I was getting to see from whence it all came. By 1968, there's Nathan Beauregard, Reverend Robert Wilkins, Bukka [White]—and I got to play with all these guys. In a way, we have become the white boys that inherited this thing, like it or not. Lee [Baker] is definitely the best blues guitarist from

Nathan Beauregard's nephew Marvin: Communication between the cultures is established.
Photo courtesy of John McIntire.

that school. Hell, he played with Furry for so many years, he has inherited that mantle. I don't know of any blues guitar player in the world, from Eric Clapton on, who can say they came by it as honestly as Baker."

"I played in standard tuning and Furry taught me to tune the guitar to the chords," says Baker. "That's how they were making it sound so good with the slide, because it didn't sound good to me just to play the open string. Then I read more about the style off the records. Some of the first electric slide I played was at the Bitter Lemon. Me and Dickinson would do 'Little Red Rooster' there, the Stones had a thing on it and so I would play that. It was all happening at the same time, I got it from Brian Jones, I was getting it from Furry and everywhere."

"The Lemon was the first place where we could play on equal footing with the bluesmen," says Dickinson. "There was a sense of community. We were all there doing the same thing. Some of the stuff that happened there was so cosmically disorganized, it wouldn't have happened anywhere else, even in Memphis, which is typical of the city. There must have been places in Cambridge where the entertainers were on an equal footing, but how could it have been the same? We were all home. On nights when Furry played a third or fourth set, he did it because he wanted to. If there ever was a white place that was like a honky-tonk, it was the Lemon."

The Lemon continued to book Baker, Crosthwait, Dickinson, Selvidge, Don Nix, and a variety of local and out-of-town folk and blues talent from the coffeehouse circuit. "I thought my music career, such as it was, was over when I finished high school," says Dickinson. "But then the blues artists were coming out, and once I heard Dylan there was no doubt. This guy's voice was worse than mine. Doing folk, there was no band to hassle with, you didn't have to carry a bunch of amps, didn't have to worry if the bass player was drunk, and you could keep all the money. I saw folk as an opportunity to mix cowboy songs and Rambling Jack Elliot stuff and gospel. Mixing it all up was what I liked. Then when rock and roll came back around, it was easy to me because I'd already done it."

"When Sid would play, it would pack the place," says McIntire. "I'd make big banners to put across the front of the building, TONIGHT FURRY LEWIS AND SID SELVIDGE. The people would line up outside. One show, then you had to get out. If you wanted to stay again, you'd have to pay another two dollars."

"Our rent was $37.50 including utilities, and we ate for ten dollars a week," says Mary Lindsay Dickinson, "and Husband could go down there and make fifty dollars on a weekend night. We were rich!"

The ages and background of the Bitter Lemon's clientele grew more varied. As the occasional "older" person became interested in youth culture, they went to the Lemon for a firsthand look. Kids from affluent East Memphis would have to sneak there. Certain ages were not allowed in; even though they weren't serving alcohol, the club was hassled by the police over curfews and other blue laws.

McIntire did his best to extend a welcome to minorities, both onstage and in the audience, though he often found circumstances beyond his control. A black friend of his named Ford moved down from New York and into Beatnik Manor. While walking in front of the house one day with fellow lodger Lydia Saltzman, white, Ford was promptly accosted by a Memphis cop for the crime of being black. When he responded to the officer's interrogation in his northern accent, the cops pounded him. "Next time I saw him, he was in the hospital," says McIntire. "He didn't know what happened. He developed a black accent, yassuh, yassuh. He had a job here driving a laundry truck and they followed him around one afternoon and gave him six or eight tickets. Run him off because they didn't like his accent."

Teenie Hodges was already accustomed to crossing over when he played the Bitter Lemon. As a young teen, he'd joined his brother Leroy in the Impalas, where their popularity at black dances began attracting the attention of some whites. Willie Mitchell, the popular black bandleader who was a favorite at the Plantation Inn, soon enlisted Teenie, Leroy, and their brother Charles to accompany him. As Mitchell began moving Hi Records toward soul music, he would make the Hodges Brothers his house band; with his direction and their sound, it was no wonder Al Green enjoyed such crossover success. (The Hi Rhythm drummer, Howard Grimes, had integrated the popular white band Flash and the Board of Directors.) When the Bitter Lemon was hot, Teenie formed a group known as JAMF—Jive Ass Mother Fuckers. "After the Flamingo Room, the Handy Club, the Elks Club, and those other [black] places closed, the Bitter Lemon was one of the first places they started back to playing blues," Teenie says. "We were a little funkier than blues, but we had the blues taste to it. We played four or five hours each night, and the audience danced the whole time."

The Manor remained ever happening. It spilled over into the two apartments next door, and then to three more apartments on the corner. The neighbors complained about a nude man sitting on the porch of Beatnik Manor. It was a sculpture made by one of McIntire's students, who had moved in after he grew a beard and his family kicked him out. Since the manor had become a beatnik haven, the cops always lingered near Madison and Cooper, spying and trying to act tough. "The police used to park behind our hedges and watch the house," says McIntire. "This girl in the house, Jo Lynn, felt sorry for them and used to take them coffee. They'd get real mad at her. They'd split and we'd see them down the street watching from another angle with binoculars, so obvious. It was crazy."

From midnight to three, the house would be awash in music. All the radios in all the rooms were tuned to WDIA, where Rufus Thomas would be broadcasting "Hoot and Holler," a show of lowdown blues, playing it real because he knew the music for real, announcing after each solid sender, "And I ain't just clacking my falsies." Carl Orr was a writer and filmmaker who was awake when others slept, pounding the keys on his typewriters, which he regularly smashed or threw into the river. He usually had a 16 mm movie camera on his arm and a vague idea for a film that would solidify once the processing was done, but if you wouldn't mind standing over there and wearing this sculpture on your head, and sashaying into this room—don't look at the camera—it might be just the scene needed. Regular visits from Marcia Hare's mother never ceased to amaze McIntire. La Paulette was a hostess in a Bourbon Street strip bar and would entertain her daughter's friends in the kitchen with lessons on the seduction of married men.

The presence of bands like JAMF and the coterie of blues artists at the Bitter Lemon was the result of Charlie Brown. The early days of "Mariah" and tame folk passed with the entrance of the new manager. "When Charlie Brown moved into the house, it got notorious," McIntire continues. Brown was the former manager of the Oso who, even when his wildness had him banned from the Bitter Lemon, claimed he ran the place. "He stayed for a long time. He and his friends, they'd sit up all night and drink beer, play poker. All night long. I had to go down the street sometimes and call the police on my own house. They wouldn't listen to me. One night, they piled all the furniture in the front yard, lit it and danced around it. They were shooting out the street light with a .22 rifle and that woke me up. The flames were coming up by my window, and I was on the second floor. A couple of them were buck naked. They wanted to make a ritual. I said, "Charlie, get these people out of here." The cops came and ran everybody off, and in about half an hour they were back again.

"I remember one time, I didn't know what marijuana was. I was cutting a big stone in the backyard, in the shade of all these bushes that Charlie had planted. The police heard me, and came down the alley and through the bushes and asked me what I was doing. We talked for a while. I kept seeing Charlie at the house, peeking around the door, up the steps, across the backyard. After they left, he came down and said, 'Are they gone? I thought we'd had it.' I said, 'Why?' He said, 'You don't know what these are?' It was marijuana plants, like twelve feet high. It was a nice shady place to work. I said, 'Gyad Charlie, isn't it illegal?'"

When his own house got too wild for him, McIntire retreated to his studio at the Academy, or to a completely unpretentious restaurant across the street. Burkle's Bakery was run by an elderly couple, employed elderly waitresses, and featured a sixty-five-cent vegetable plate with rolls and corn bread. "We'd hang out there a lot," says Marcia Hare. "But even that got overrun. McIntire lived across the street, and because John was there all the time, people from the art school were there all the time. It got to be the center for the so-called artists and hippies to hang out. They thought that was the place to be because John was there."

"Charlie Brown had a lot of charisma," says Lyon. "People just met back then. You could tell walking down the street if someone was hip or not. If you met 'em and it was cool, it was like you knew them for all their lives. Charlie was one of those people. He ran the Bitter Lemon. He was going wild of course, like everybody else. We were all totally out of control, no grip on reality whatsoever. The Lemon was packed all the time but it never seemed to make any money. Charlie never paid any of the bills and always took all the cash. Poor McIntire. The thing became an albatross. It was open season on fun. Back then shit was cheap. There was always enough cash around for Charlie to have a ball."

"I never saw any cash," says McIntire. "Most of it went to keeping the place alive, and my salary from the Art Academy paid off the rest. I'd go there, that place would be packed, a waiting line outside, and not a penny in the cash register. It might cost a dollar and a half or two dollars cover charge. I'd go, 'C'mon guys, the place is packed, where's the money?' 'I dunno.' They were buying drugs, it went up in smoke. We were robbed a few times, the sound system, the pizza oven, the supplies. We had a cigarette machine in there, a pay phone, I never saw any of that money. But everybody was doing good. Nobody really had a salary, except the singers mostly. They were on a circuit and demanded their money." One time McIntire's mother got sick and he left town for a week. When he returned, all the posters he'd put up on the walls were gone, many of the musical instruments hanging had disappeared, and so had the Tiffany lamps. "The people who worked there stripped my coffeehouse of everything except some of the chairs and tables. They took a great big bronze statue. Don Nix had the lamps in his apartment. About four or five years ago he came by and said he felt he ought to pay me back. I said, Forget it. It was a good experience. I don't miss that stuff now." Some of McIntire's friends may have been abusing his openness, but the relationship was essentially symbiotic. People lived off of him, but he needed them around, collecting their characters the way he collected secondhand miscellany. The clamoring throng fired his vision.

Many of the traveling bands on the coffeehouse circuit were impressed when they got to Memphis and found themselves sharing a stage with an artist they'd assumed either mythical or dead. One trio from New York, the Solip Singers, was so impressed that they stayed. "We were working our way across the country, with the idea of going to San Francisco," says Solip vocalist Nancy Jeffries, now a senior vice president of A&R at Elektra Records. "We didn't have much money and we'd just go to each town, find the coffeehouse, audition for the owner, sleep on someone's floor. Our trek ended in Memphis because all that stuff was happening, the scene with the young people and the older blues artists. They were so accessible. You didn't realize how important it would be to meet them, and once it happened, it's all I wanted to do."

The Solips were considered a radical band at the time, playing a set made up almost entirely of Bob Dylan songs, supplemented by material from Richard and Mimi Farina, Joan Baez, and the like. Though a folk band, they used electric instruments. Their twelve-string acoustic was amplified, and Nancy played the electric bass. "When Dylan plugged in," she says, "we were for it." In 1966 they got a three-month gig shuttling between Little Rock, where they met Bob Palmer, and Fayetteville, where Randall Lyon was hanging out with John Clellon Holmes, the beat writer (*Go* [1952], *The Horn* [1958]). When the work ended, Jeffries returned to Memphis. The Solips evolved to include Palmer as a regular guest and Barth as a regular member. They would all become instrumental in planning the Country Blues Festivals, and their band would evolve into one of the decade's most experimental amalgamations, the Insect Trust.

In the early spring of 1966, Dylan played Ellis Auditorium, previewing his *Blonde on Blonde* material with the Hawks. The Hawks had been around the same roadhouse circuit that the Solips played, that Dickinson and Baker and everyone who'd been out of town had played. The show was an inspiration, not only because it was the loudest thing anyone had yet heard, but because the band was dressed like the audience, had come from the same place, and was not only getting over nationally, but doing it with something original. Everyone in the audience had hope, a sense of a greater community out there, a sense of the power they would wield in the next decade's battle to depose the president and end the Vietnam war.

"We had what you would call in rhetoric *eroico furore*, poetic furor," says Randall Lyon. "We were inspired, we were in a frenzy. We had heroic passion. I always figured that was the best thing that could happen to you, to be caught up with a group of people with heroic enthusiasm for what they're doing. And how it's received was beyond our consideration."

CHAPTER NINE

Smile on the Outlaw Dreamer's Face

A WEEK BEFORE THE FIRST MEMPHIS BLUES FESTIVAL, THE KU KLUX Klan held a rally at the event site, the Overton Park Band Shell. Racial tension was high all over the country in the midsummer of 1966. Riots erupted in several cities. A hundred miles from Memphis, in Grenada, Mississippi, blacks marched silently around the county courthouse, jeered at by a crowd of whites; highway patrolmen stood guard with shotguns, gas masks swinging from their hips. This was a time when the black student union at Memphis State University was commonly referred to as the "coal bin." At the Shell, segregated rest rooms for the employees were still enforced. "It wouldn't do any good to take the signs down," a black civic employee told the *Tri-State Defender,* "because the white folks would still give you those nasty looks and try to take it out on you in some way." At the Klan rally, the imperial wizard of the United Klans of America spoke to 400 masked followers.

More than double that number showed up at the same location a week later to see the stage shared by black and white, united in music, new social mores trimmed and burning. That the first Memphis Country Blues Festival even happened seems a minor miracle, organized as it was by a group of beatnik blues fans—social outcasts, experimenters in hard chemical substances. However great the differences between them and the bluesmen, their social ostracism was a common bond. An informal organization formed, the Memphis Country Blues Society, that put together a sound system and made sure the bluesmen were paid from the gate receipts. For advertising, Charlie Brown hawking the event at the Bitter Lemon was all they needed.

The only expense in putting on the show was the deposit required on the venue. Charlie Brown raised that, convincing Dickinson to sign over the sixty-

134

five-dollar check that he'd been paid by Sam Phillips for his Jesters session. Barth put up a softball of hash for barter.

The media attention made this first festival a grand coming out, both for the country blues performers, who had been largely ignored by the city since the 1920s, and for the hippie scene, which the city had tried not to notice. As well, it was a positive result of the mix of locals and northerners. Such festivals had begun defining youth culture since the latter 1950s, notably the Newport, Rhode Island, events. The success in Memphis created a community that traveled regularly from here to New York, a community built upon the respect the hippies (née beatniks) and bluesmen had for each other.

Over a thousand people paid the price of admission on July 30, 1966, for the first festival. Honors for kicking off the event went to Lee Baker, who introduced the blues and the hippies with a screaming electric band described in a newspaper review as "near cacophony." His set was the brass blast that precedes the entrance of royalty: Memphis, meet your past, meet your future. Someone was wise enough to invite the black disc jockey and community spokesman Nat D. Williams to speak. He'd been the first black voice on WDIA, was a syndicated columnist for black newspapers across the country, and an influential teacher at Booker T. Washington High School (whence came many of the Stax artists). His recitation of Mr. Handy's "Beale Street Blues" was renowned by then, and he did not disappoint the hippie crowd. Others performing were Mississippi John Hurt, Bukka White, Furry Lewis, Nathan Beauregard, Reverend Robert Wilkins, Fred McDowell, Sid Selvidge, Jim Dickinson and band, and the Solip Singers. The show went off without any unusual hitches, the review in the newspaper somehow validated it, and the bluesmen and the hippies were suddenly a presence.

The corporeal spirituality of the blues musicians was as gripping as their music. What they played was unencumbered by progress, as relevant in 1966 as in 1926. They cut through the urban soundtrack, transporting listeners back in time with them. At their feet, confronted by them, one could not help but be moved. They physically embodied the music: leathery and worn, dusty, dry. The repetition in what they played, the hypnotism, was the sonic equivalent of a plowed field, row upon row. This music is the distinct product of an African musical tradition, an American landscape, and an unjust social system; all blues has to be traced through these Delta artists.

Some newcomer fans had yet to learn the nuances of the styles. One wanted to give Furry Lewis a National steel guitar like Bukka White's. Furry was a subtle player who controlled his instrument like a puppet. Wearing a bottleneck slide, he could make a string coo like a loving cup, then make it

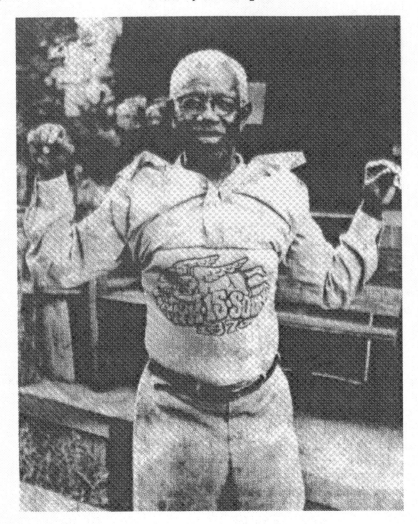

Furry Lewis entertaining a crowd, circa 1970. ("Memphis Sound" T-shirt designed by John McIntire.) Photo by Jimmy Godown.

whine for more. He wound his voice and slide around each other, calling up God from the pit of his soul and hoarsely asking for mercy. He picked where Bukka hammered, and when Furry did strum, it was often just to keep a rhythm on open strings while he told a story. Furry came from a medicine show tradition, and a large part of his performance was shenanigans, entertaining the crowd with stories, playing guitar with his elbow, or some other musical clowning. Bukka White played guitar like John Henry drove steel. A burly man, his voice was gruff, his steel guitar percussive and loud. Both Bukka and Furry could plumb uncharted depths of your soul. Bukka's style was immediate; Furry's required a little more attention.

The kindhearted visitor who gave Furry the steel guitar could probably discourse profoundly on the difference between a Petrarchan and a Shakespearean sonnet. But he was unable to comprehend that Furry and Bukka were writing different poems; the force of Bukka's style had captured him, and he thought the power was in the instrument and not the musician. The way others lumped together verse, he lumped blues. In that sense, it's easy to understand the bewilderment on his face when Furry politely refused his gift.

"Furry played at the Lemon, and I could back him up there," says Lee Baker. "But I still played with a pick when we started those Memphis Country Blues Festivals. I'd have an electric band on the show, and Furry would be there and he'd ask me to come up and play with him. Soon enough, I was also playing with Bukka White, Gus Cannon, Sleepy John—anybody that was there that wanted me to play with 'em, I would. By the last festival, *I was* the backup band."

Baker understands the role of accompanist. He knows that less can be much, much more, that he doesn't have to run through his bag o' tricks every time he's on the stage. "Furry could say more in a couple notes than Stevie Ray Vaughan could say in twenty-four bars. One or two little notes, the way he could do the things he could do, that's becoming a lost art. Everybody, myself included, plays a million notes all the time. But it's the nuances, the inside stuff, that I admire in Furry's playing."

Sid Selvidge got his comeuppance at the blues festival, well after he'd come to know many Delta bluesmen. "Furry had to go on and his guitar was out of tune and I said, 'Oh my God, I'm gon' get this thing in tune because Furry's gonna embarrass himself.' And I went over and meticulously tuned Furry's guitar and gave it to him and he got on stage and strummed it and went *wang-a-wang-a-wang* and got it back like he wanted it. I realized, Oh, this is African music we're listening to! It doesn't have anything to do with Mozart!"

The first festival spawned four more, ultimately creating a struggle for ownership of the event between the hippies and the city government. In 1966, however, the future was bright and full of color and long hair, racial and class respect. "I can't even imagine how our friendship happened," says Randall Lyon, who began his long association with Bill Eggleston when he asked to borrow his 16 mm movie camera to document the first blues festival. "I was the kind of person Bill despised the most. He hated hippies and there I was, the arch-hippie. But the first time I met him, borrowing the camera, we got into this long discussion about the piano. Bill had this Steinway Grand and he was very interested in how it was tuned. He was experimenting with tuning. He and Rosa [his wife] had just been to Guatemala and Kathmandu. In the early sixties, he hung out with international jet set bohemians like Charles Henri Ford and Ruth Roman and all those people. He had come home to roost about sixty-four, sixty-five, and I had no idea who he was. We just got to be really good friends. Bill and Rosa were deculturalized by wealth and power, and we were deculturalized by putting ourselves in harm's way, so there was a possible meeting." Eggleston, along with Buster Williams's son Robert, made field recordings of the first festival.

Another result of the first blues fest was the emancipation of the Solip Singers from their folk life. "I had been playing professionally since I was about fourteen and I thought I could get through a blues progression pretty good," says Robert Palmer. "But boy, that first time I tried to play with Bukka, I thought, Oh! This is a whole other thing! Barth and I got to jamming with those guys a lot, with Furry and Bukka and so forth, and then later after we moved to New York, Barth and me and Alan Wilson of Canned Heat used to jam together a lot on country blues stuff. And from all that Memphis experience we were into rocking out jams on country blues tunes, playing the structures of the country blues, thirteen and a half bars, the funny modal tunings, the whole bit. The Insect Trust's version of Elmore James's 'Special Rider' grows out of that."

The Insect Trust was the second incarnation of the Solip Singers, solidifying in New York in 1967. The name comes from William S. Burroughs's *Naked Lunch;* though Palmer couldn't have imagined it at the time, in four years he would travel to Morocco with Burroughs; the two maintain a working relationship. The Solip Singers recorded an album for Chips Moman at American Studios; only a single was released. ("Comeback Baby," an Elmore James-ish blues is on one side, and the folk ballad "He Was a Friend of Mine," with recorder solo, is on the other.) "Privately amongst ourselves," says Palmer, "we referred to the American house band as rednecks. Certainly compared to us they were rednecks. Compared to rednecks they were probably somewhat different. They used to tease us about smoking pot."

Palmer talked his way into a job around American, saving a couple hundred dollars with which he made his first trek to the northeast, 1966. "I was a jazz fanatic, and Barth set me up for the most singular introduction to New York. I drove up there with this girl that I knew from Little Rock who knew a piano teacher there. We drove past Manhattan to Stoney Point, and got to this guy's house and I crashed out on the couch. About twelve hours later I woke up and I looked across this big room, it was a pretty house in the woods, and sitting across from me is John Cage. And what's even weirder about it is I knew exactly who he was and had read his stuff. We proceeded to spend the entire day together, walking around, listening to some of his music that hadn't been commercially issued. We speculated on the future of music in really interesting ways, and that was my first day in New York. Then I went down to Manhattan and I had one contact that Barth had given me, Peter Stampfel of the Holy Modal Rounders. I went over to Stampfel's apartment and it's a block from Bleecker and MacDougal, which was like the center of the universe. I'm not there five minutes and the Blues Magoos come in to score speed and then we all go over to the Kettle of Fish and Bob Dylan was in there and Eric Anderson, Dave Van Ronk, all those guys. That was my second day in New York. Not bad! I also went to see this great Cecil Taylor concert at Town Hall, which was the music for *Unit Structures*, probably the best Cecil Taylor album ever. And I was thinking, Wow, I thought it would be really difficult to get anywhere in New York but this is great. So with some reluctance I went back to Little Rock and finished my last year of college."

The Memphis weave in New York was drawn ever tighter the summer of 1967 with the arrival of Jimmy Crosthwait, his wife Linda, and Chris Wimmer. Crosthwait was working toward merging his artistic handiwork with his natural theatricality; the problem with sculptures, he'd come to realize, was that they didn't move. In 1965, he and Linda were trained in Florida as puppeteers and spent a year touring the Southeast, as far north as Virginia, performing mostly in school assemblies. The next year they did the same for a man in Chicago. "We worked for him during the 1966 and 1967 school year and I was getting tired of doing kid shit," says Crosthwait. "I began conceiving this play with immolating monks and melting-face clowns and was steady building it. A friend from Memphis, Chris Wimmer, who I knew from the Market Theater, came up to Chicago and helped me make the puppets and props. I had been thinking I could book this far-out, hip sort of puppet show in coffeehouses, and just when I was realizing I ain't gonna book this damn thing anywhere, his ex-girlfriend calls from New York and says there's an ad in the *Village Voice*, 'Hippie puppet show wanted.'"

Hippie puppet show they got. Crosthwait's work evolved from his affection for the Bauhaus movement's concept of total theater. In the late 1920s, as the Weimar Republic was dismantling this integration of art and science, the Bauhaus proponents were working with the technological advances created during the First World War—the total war—and conceiving of total theater.

"They wanted to artistically integrate the production of artificial arms and legs that came out of that war," says Crosthwait. "They were conceiving of giant robot actors, plastic stages that you watched from below, things that weren't executed until Disneyland came along. It was carnival, ballet, and sporting event." Of the many things Jimmy Crosthwait has undoubtedly been accused of, being athletic is surely not one. However, ballet, music, and carnival atmosphere are integral to his character.

Crosthwait, twenty-two, a New York virgin, and Wimmer, twenty-one, a minimalist in both figure and theory, were looking for St. Mark's Place as the Six-Day War was coming to a close. At the Electric Circus they met the idea man, Michael Gruener, the son of a successful advertising executive in Los Angeles, and the two people running the show, Jerry Brandt and Stan Freedman, who had caused a splash when they threw green cash money from the balcony onto the floor of the New York Stock Exchange. In the city less than a day, Wimmer was standing at the upstairs window of the club in progress, gawking at the passersby on the street below, when he suddenly bellowed to Crosthwait, "Hey! There's Warren Gardener."

Gardener was a beatnik from Maryland who had lived the bohemian life in Paris, running with William Burroughs and Brion Gysin before heeding the boho call from Memphis in the mid-sixties. In Paris, he had appeared in a Burroughs play, *Junk Is No Good Baby,* in which his character shot up onstage. Let's say Gardener was a method actor. Once in Memphis, he quickly established himself as a live wire and became known as Electricity Man; he referred to himself as Chang, The Unavoidable. "It was almost bad to bring up his name," Crosthwait says, "because then he would show up at your door and live with you until you were out of food and nerves and everything else." One surmises he was more fun to watch than encounter. The last Crosthwait had known of him, Gardener had been busted in Memphis and was doing time in the Shelby County Penal Farm. He'd been at an all-night Memphis diner, laying his jive on another patron, trying to sign him to a recording contract. Gardener boasted of a song called "Smile on the Outlaw Dreamer's Face." This particular diner was near one of the few theaters in Memphis, so the clientele tended toward the artsy. With the guy showing interest, Gardener dug into his bag for a contract. Rooting through, he nonchalantly pulled out his pot and set it on the counter. His future Willie Nelson nonchalantly stopped being an undercover cop and arrested him.

Marcia Hare met Gardener when she was volunteering at the theater after school, knew he was trouble, and followed him everywhere. She reads from a newspaper clipping she's saved: "Gardener pretended he was blind and begged for a living. Gardener's address was termed 'at large' by police. He told police he found the marijuana growing wild in a field in Arkansas. The bearded bicycle rider said his latest musical composition was 'Smile on the Outlaw Dreamer's Face.'" Hare doesn't miss a beat as she puts down the clipping and recites from memory: "It's been down to hell and back again/Been up to heaven once or twice/the Devil and the Lord it seems/both hear and heed the same advice. And that's that/though this life's a whitewashed blackboard baby/don't you know it ain't ever gonna erase/the smile of the blues on the outlaw dreamer's face."

Wimmer yelled to the Manhattan street below. "Warren looks up and sure enough it's him," says Crosthwait. "He beats it up the steps, and when he learns what my puppet show is about, he goes, 'God, that's far out.' And Warren went right up to the executive offices of *Time* magazine, barefoot, talking about, 'Hey man, there's this guy's puppet show and you have got to put a melting clown face on the cover.' And they listened to him."

They didn't put Crosthwait on the cover of *Time,* but it was 1967, it was New York, and everybody was listening to anybody about anything. Things were changing very rapidly, and no one knew what strange idea today would be tomorrow's rage. Which must be how the American Coffee Growers Association agreed to put up a large sum of money to sponsor the Electric Circus. The snack area sold only coffee and coffee-based products, no alcohol.

The Electric Circus became the voice of the psychedelic times. It was mixed media, culling from bands and solo performances, from audio recordings and film, from pantomime to small theater, and the show was not restricted to the stage. Many of the staff were out in the audience, and many of the audience became part of the show. Like a multiring circus, "happenings" would occur simultaneously. "Chris Wimmer was very much a body caricature," says Crosthwait. "He was the guy who would do nothing in the midst of everything. When people were dancing he would come into the middle of the room wearing a kind of white popcorn vendor's uniform, he'd take a white sheet and flip it a few times, lie down and lay the sheet over him. Four or five minutes later he'd get up and walk away."

Wimmer remembers, "I was standing along the wall at the opening night of the Electric Circus and when Crosthwait walked past, Allen Ginsberg turned to Timothy Leary and says, 'Keep your eye on that guy, he's nuts.'"

Who do we listen to?

There were three lighting booths projecting liquid formations, film loops, and slides. Someone had purchased a bulk supply of the sheeny material from which ladies' underwear is made, and the walls and ceiling were scalloped with it. Crosthwait was working a light booth one night when Greta Garbo walked in. "She was being shown around and wanted to see how the booth worked. She was probably sixty and seemed more beautiful than when she was young. Her hair was solid white and she had a lot of curiosity and enthusiasm, a radiant beauty." Before the doors opened one evening, Wimmer tossed a Frisbee with a kindly, slightly older gentleman for fifteen minutes before realizing it was the film director Michelangelo Antonioni, who'd recently made *Blow-Up*. Bill Barth traced Fred Astaire's shoe on a piece of paper and got it autographed. "The Rolling Stones walked into my puppet room at one point, wearing their big furry coats. Jerry Brandt says, 'Rolling Stones, puppeteers . . . puppeteers, Rolling Stones.' "

Security at the club was culled from Black Power activists and the local president of Hell's Angels. "This biker would come to the Circus every night," Crosthwait says, "take off his colors and his gun and his dope, put them in his locker and then transform himself into an Emmett Kelly, a clown with a frown, and he'd walk around with a little stuffed dog and go, 'Ruff ruff! Woof woof woof!' "

Crosthwait's puppet show was held in a little room off the balcony, seating about forty people on the astroturf floor. The show was titled *Iom Dod*, was mostly marionettes, and it ran for half an hour. His immolating monk was the first scene, and the finale was a clown's face melting into a puddle. "The name was a combination of diode and debt-owed and ion dode. It was kind of theater of the absurd, a surrealistic black comedy. I had a Viet clown in his little black pajamas and sanpan hat and he's confronted by the elf plane, which was this military presence. For another scene I reproduced the image on a Camel pack and had an artist pushing his cart at the bazaar."

Crosthwait was responsible for two shows a night, but the second was iffy. While his stage was being reset, he played Tinkerbell in the main hall, donning a clown suit and sliding down a wire from the back of the room to the stage, whipping off his hat and showering confetti. His ride stopped just short of a pedestal upon which he was supposed to dismount, and he made a show of inching and slinking ever closer. Just when it seemed he would make it, he'd fall to the floor and the tall and lanky Chris Wimmer would appear, pick up the scraggly elf, and carry him out. When Jimi Hendrix returned to England after establishing himself in America that summer of 1967, he was asked how things were in the States. His reply was that the only thing really happening was a little guy in a yellow coat hanging on a wire at the Electric Circus.

Upon graduating from college in 1967, Robert Palmer did indeed return to New York. It was the Summer of Love and San Francisco was attracting lots of people and even more media attention, but Palmer knew that New York was jazz, and promptly found himself writing about music for *Go* magazine, employed by Robin "Lifestyles of the Rich and Famous" Leech. (Randall Lyon says of Palmer's writing, "Even as a teenager he had the most finely tuned acoustical sensibility and a way of explaining shit to you. When we were listening to early Coltrane, *Ascension*, for example, it was culturally and musically way beyond my accomplishments, but Bob could make me hear that. And when he told you about it, it was so fucking interesting you just wanted to die. By the time he finished it was, oh my God, the most important thing you ever heard.")

"I was reading the *East Village Other* one night about eleven," says Palmer, "and I see an article on the Electric Circus and I see that Crosthwait, Chris Wimmer, and Lydia Saltzman are there. It's nearly midnight and I go running up to the Electric Circus on St. Mark's Place and talk my way in. We have a little reunion and soon Barth and Nancy [Jeffries] show up, having decided to bail out of Memphis—they'd been traveling back and forth for a while, sometimes with Randall. We start playing together again and get a gig at the Electric Circus, where for most of the summer we opened for Sly and the Family Stone—pre–recording contract. Just awesome music." Lydia Saltzman had been a stalwart at Beatnik Manor. At the Circus, she had a side room where she would do body painting. Palmer played a twenty-five-dollar recorder through a fifty-thousand-dollar state-of-the-art sound system while the lights danced ballet with Wimmer. "There were banks of reverb and echo on my little recorder and it was really loud. I would get all these trills going and then I could just play over 'em and it was like it went on and on and on."

The Memphians whipped up enthusiasm amongst the New Yorkers, and when they returned to Memphis midsummer for the Second Annual Country Blues Festival, Gruener, who'd conceived of the Circus, was among those who joined them. His sophisticated bicoastal mind was blown. He began making arrangements to bring regional country blues artists to Manhattan. Bukka White, Furry Lewis, even Muddy Waters. (When Muddy Waters was asked what he thought of the Electric Circus, his response was reported to be, "Blinking blinking jiving jiving shit.")

For the second festival, even though the Shell is an aesthetically pleasing and stimulating environment, the Country Blues Society wanted to make their own imprint on the environment. That job, naturally, was left to McIntire. "I bought all this crepe paper and gigantic bamboo poles, and I put streamers all the way around the Shell. And bags and bags of balloons." The 1967 festival was also distinguished by the stage props someone had found in an old theater.

A seated golden Buddha towered into the open air, shining over Furry Lewis, over centenarian Nathan Beauregard, and over everyone who took to the stage. Placed beneath his countenance were stage prop trees and stage prop bushes and center stage there was even a stage prop outhouse.

Baker once again opened the festival, this time with a band he dubbed Funky Down Home and the Electric Blue Watermelon. It was a mishmash of blacks and whites and styles, blues-based but free enough for Palmer and New Orleans saxophonist Trevor Koehler to have their reedy way. The Watermelon took the stage and kicked up a solid blues racket, full of guitar but with no sign of the guitarist, Mr. Funky. Suddenly the outhouse door kicked open and there's Baker, wearing a mortarboard hat with a springing plastic flower. To wild applause, he mounted a waiting Harley-Davidson, playing guitar, the picture of rock and roll. "People thought our scene was a bunch of folkies," says Baker. "But we played good, over and above all the theatrics."

At the blues festivals, perhaps because they weren't under his own auspices, McIntire was capable of organizational skills he lacked at his own club. "These two girls were supposed to take the money at the gate," he says, "and they were so stoned that people were just walking in, pretending to put money in the box. So I got under the table, and every time money went in the box, I took it out. I had a shoebox and I was stuffing dollars in it, because I knew they lost money at these things all the time. Nobody could pay anybody and it caused a big fight. After everybody was in, I counted $2,200 in there. That was more money than anybody'd ever seen in their life. I sat in the audience, in the middle, with the box in my lap. When it was all over, Barth was running around, 'Who's got the money?!' I opened the box, and he was so surprised! After it was all done, I ended up making twenty bucks. Twenty dollars off feeding all these damn people. They were sleeping at my damn house, on the floors, I had to keep food in the refrigerators, driving 'em around. But I never got mad. I was too crazy. I'd get mad on the spur of the moment and forget about it. The next day I couldn't remember what I was mad about."

The Memphis Country Blues Festival was becoming a workshop, of sorts, for the younger white musicians. They were able to test the fusion of their diverse influences—culling from the distinguished bluesmen as well as the protonihilism of the Velvet Underground and the Fugs. Solid doses of horns were culled from free jazz as much as R&B. "There was a lot of experimentation that went on at the blues festivals," says Palmer, "a lot of cross-fertilization. Charlie Freeman played with us several times, and we did some free jazz jamming at the blues festival one year. And Dickinson was always real open to all these different kinds of music. Not everybody was. I remember Charlie

Charlie Freeman (middle) with Bill Barth (left) and Joe Grey, performing for Buddha at the 1967 Memphis Country Blues Festival. "There was a lot of experimentation that went on at the blues festivals." Photo by Randall Lyon.

Freeman coming up after the Insect Trust was in New York, doing a session for someone and afterward he came out and jammed with us all day, really stretching out. It was just spectacular. And Dickinson told me at one point that his solo album, *Dixie Fried,* with all those different kinds of music on it, was very much influenced by what the Insect Trust was trying to do. I remember when I came back from Morocco the first time with all these recordings of Moroccan music, Dickinson totally got into it, immediately. He and Charlie could always be counted on for that."

The Insect Trust relocated to New York, joined shortly by saxman Koehler and then rounded out by folk guitar guru Luke Faust. Now a five-piece, they were creating country blues–inspired free jazz. Barth was a serious blues guitarist, Luke was fluent in sea chanties and Appalachian banjo, guitar, and fiddle. Trevor was a postbop jazz musician who had toured with Anita O'Day among others, and Nancy had folk roots. Palmer's role was to tie it together by mashing it up.

Word about the hip Memphis scene spread. Many of the expatriates took over an apartment building in Hoboken. Barth referred to it as the Hoboken Power and Light Company. "There were ten apartments, five floors, in this place on 39 Second Street in Hoboken," says Crosthwait. "On the bottom floor was an alcoholic lady with cigarette burns all on her arms. She made me nervous. I kept waiting for her to nod out with a cigarette on her bunk, and we'd all be gone! I'd think, Just keep dropping 'em on your arm, lady, and wake yourself up."

The landlord was a mafioso who protected the motley crew because they actually tried to pay rent. They learned the power of his connections one day after sax great Pharoah Sanders came by to jam. "We just played at peak intensity for hours and hours and hours," says Palmer, "and I'm sure it could be heard for miles. Three screaming saxophones, electric guitars, and drums. It was really loud and we felt like it got real cosmic, transported us." When they picked up the morning paper the next day, a front-page story told about the noise disturbance and a slew of complaints, and then about the resulting bust of the perpetrators. "The bust never happened," says Palmer. "The story was planted. It was one of those neighborhoods full of candy stores that didn't have any candy but had fifteen telephones, and our landlord fit right in."

Randall Lyon lived in the building for a time. "Rambling Jack Elliot used to pay homage to Luke Faust. Luke's father was the Gloucester fisherman. He knew all these New England shanties and stuff. That was a great building in Hoboken. Sam Shepard was the drummer in the Insect Trust for a brief moment. Sam had this performance art troupe called the Group Image Sucks. He came over to Hoboken to rehearse a few times with the band and I think he freaked out when he realized the potential madness. We were way out of control. Dylan was around but everybody was pissed at him because they figured he ripped off Rambling Jack and Luke. There were fistfights over that, people got hurt in that discussion. That's what was so cool about those people: they didn't accept any authority about anything. They questioned every manifestation of authority. Even if one of their friends became hugely successful, it was still like, Wellll."

Joe Callicott was one of the first bluesmen that Gruener brought to New York, booking him at the swanky 150th anniversary of a large museum. "I was at McIntire's house, had been going to Memphis State for about a month, and these two friends came by and asked if anybody wanted to go to New York," remembers Marcia Hare. "I said, 'Yeah, I do.' I got my coat and my purse and I went to New York. So much for that semester of college. We drove the whole way with Joe in the backseat and the three of us up front. My friends would stop at these gas stations and go in the rest room together, and Joe Callicott would say to me, 'They're fucking.' But they were really shooting Desoxyn. By the time we got to New York, they were in a big fight and Joe was uncomfortable being so far from home. I bumped into Warren Gardener and went off with him." The museum party featured a 1920s orchestra on the main floor, playing in tuxes beneath potted palms. There was a disco on another floor, and then there was Joe Callicott, accompanied by Barth, Luke Faust, and Palmer. Callicott had never been far from his Hernando, Mississippi, home and wore his farm clothes and work boots. In the elevator, he was introduced to Mayor John Lindsay. They stayed in New York less than a week, but Joe Callicott couldn't get home fast enough. Driving back, when they stopped in Nashville to rest for the night, he snuck off. "In the morning," says Hare, "people said they'd seen an old black man hitchhiking on the highway."

Later that summer at a *Go* magazine party, the Insect Trust met Steve Duboff, who became their producer/manager. Without telling them he'd written a couple of Cowsills hits, he asked the band what they thought of the songs. Palmer remembers, "We told him that we thought they were shit, absolute shit. He liked that because he thought they were shit too. He had been involved in bubblegum, and now he was ready for some weirdness, and we gave it to him." They released two albums, one on Capitol in early 1968 and the other on Atco in 1970. Their material included songs learned from Joe Callicott and writings by Thomas Pynchon set to music; they sent a tape of the latter to the author in Mexico for permission. Duboff arranged for their live bookings to be handled by Bill Graham, which resulted in this very strange quintet opening shows for Santana, Frank Zappa, Pink Floyd, and, in Baltimore, the Doors in front of 50,000 people.

Barth was showing signs of strain and left the band during their arena days. Ed Finney, a Memphis jazz guitarist who'd studied with the Regents' Rick Ireland, replaced him. After several more incarnations, including a funk rhythm section, the fabric holding together the Insect Trust became too sheer. Their final dates were a response to the growing slickness of the arena rock around them, with the band abandoning all structure. Palmer went on to collaborate with Lenny Kaye in an early noise band. "Through that last Insect Trust noise thing, then through doing it with Lenny Kaye," muses Palmer, "I feel like our influence filters into a certain wing of the New York punk scene. Lenny took a lot of our thing with him to Patti Smith. When they were first living together in New York, they used to call me all the time and they'd be listening to our tapes. She said that 'Radio Ethiopia' was especially inspired by that music." Joe Callicott probably never heard Patti Smith, but if she was driving to Memphis, he'd have gladly caught a ride.

After seven months, spanning the summer of 1967, Crosthwait had had enough of New York City. What had been "tweed and tennis shoes psychedelia" with the Jefferson Airplane became, he says, "a Quicksilver Messenger Service Methadone nightmare—black and crystal and sharp-edged and New York brittle." Sly Stone had helped launch the Circus, but when he came back six months later, he was "a completely different arrogant son of a bitch."

The Bitter Lemon rode the artistic crest until 1968, when the sublime turned to the loud. When "happenings" were in, McIntire had no qualms about accommodating such events. "We'd close up to get the place fixed up. They were freaky things. One time you had to get on your hands and knees and crawl through boxes to come in the door. Inside, you'd come into a plastic box, and the seats were all pushed together, touching. You could only get twenty-five or thirty people in this plastic box. They had to sit on their haunches, grown people. And the box got real hot. The stage had a guy and a girl sitting on it, staring at each other, with an alarm clock between them, and a spotlight overhead. The alarm would go off and they would do something, stand up or maybe say two words, and then reset the clock and set it down. The people in the box were going nuts, they got to where they couldn't handle it any longer, screaming. They tore the box apart and ripped the whole interior to pieces and ran out the door. It was a real good happening, worked just like it was planned."

The demise and ultimate death of the Bitter Lemon was neither a great ball of fire nor an anguished last gasp. It seemed to mark the changing waves of fashion, the point where one trend was retreating as another came crashing on, and in the collision it simply sank. "The very same people who put me down for being a Yankee and a nigger lover and for the way that I looked were coming out looking exactly like I looked," says Marcia Hare. "I remember Randall and I freaking out that these people who didn't have any sensitivity or any culture or any artistic sense, that they could grow their hair long. It didn't work though, because the fat rednecks still had the goofy look on their face. But we didn't want to get busted for looking weird when everybody suddenly knew what pot was, so we started trying to look straight and let the rednecks wear their hair long."

At the Lemon, bookings became infrequent for traditional blues, for Memphis jazz artists like Fred Ford and Phineas Newborn Jr. The audience was no longer into listening, but rather being loud, a post-Beatles syndrome of yelling and screaming. Roland Robinson, a black bass player in Eddie Floyd's band, remembers stopping by the club because he'd always seen a line going out the door. "I was back from a tour, living at Willie Mitchell's house," he says. "Me and Hubbie, Willie's son, would just get in a convertible and drive around and find a good time. We walked in that place, looked at each other and said, 'Wrong!' And got back in our car and left." It seemed like a long time back when Harry Belafonte had stopped by, or when McIntire had lunched with Marcel Marceau. McIntire became less interested in his own club. And more frightened. The new patrons, attracted by the dissonance that had become hip, did not encourage the tortoise from his shell.

Manager Charlie Brown got more and more crazed. Herpetology, for example. Though it scared most others, it thrilled him. Bluesmen, tending toward frailty, found no pleasure when he excitedly entered the club, piqued everyone's curiosity with a burlap bag, then emptied it on the floor, producing a mass of rattlesnakes untangling themselves. The last to get anywhere safe was Furry Lewis, or Gus Cannon, or whichever elder bluesman was nearby.

Drugs got out of the hands of artists and into the audience. People were milling peyote buttons in the supermarket coffee grinder. Police began raiding the Bitter Lemon so often that McIntire would return to his home and find them there, searching with intimidation instead of a warrant. The vice squad finally chased Charlie Brown to Miami. "It had been a lot of fun but at the end it was scary. I'd sneak in late at night after I knew it was closed, I'd scrub the tables and sweep the floors, wash it all up. I finally just gave the coffeehouse to Herman, the cook. Sign these papers, it's all yours. We went to a lawyer, Herman agreed to pay the $239 in back taxes. But he never reopened it and I ended up having to pay the $239. The government took my paycheck from school. We all sort of left, went to our different places, like an Indian thing, very religious."

On April 4, 1968, Dr. Martin Luther King Jr. was assassinated in Memphis at the culmination of the sanitation worker's strike. Musicians had achieved a racial unity at the start of the decade, but as the strife before the rioting laid bare for the world to see, the Memphis government was not interested in treating all human beings like human beings: full-time pay still left the sanitation workers qualified for welfare. Rioting after the assassination was intense. King's death left Isaac Hayes creatively blocked for a year. Stax saxman Andrew Love remembers, "There was a helicopter flying overhead when the riots were going on, and I actually had thoughts of getting my gun and shooting at it. It *actually* crossed my mind."

"It certainly wasn't any intention of anyone at Stax for all the civil rights implication that came out of soul music," says Terry Johnson, another original Mar-Key. "The music made that happen because people who had never known each other, who had never gone to lunch together, who had never eaten a barbecue together, who had never done the things that typically people do—all of a sudden were doing those things." Stax music appealed to blacks and whites because it came from blacks and whites.

Don Nix, the former Mar-Key who became a songwriter and producer for Stax, remembers going to the studio even when he didn't have work. "You could go and there was Johnnie Taylor and Rufus Thomas and Eddie Floyd—just hanging out! I went there every day not to do anything but hang out with everybody. It was a big family kind of deal. I was at Stax Records the night Martin Luther King was assassinated. When they came to the door and told us he'd been shot, Duck Dunn and I started to go out to our cars. Isaac Hayes came and said, 'No, I'll drive you out,' because it was doubtful whether we would have made it. When I got home and turned on the TV, I found out he had died. It never was the same after that. Maybe for another year I would go over there and hang out, but I think for the black people in that neighborhood, that was the final straw. I knew it was never going to be the same when they were burning everything down and Stax hired a bunch of guys to go up on the roof with machine guns. I saw that and I said, 'Boy! This is it. This is it, folks, it's never going to go back to the way it was.'"

It took the crack of a rifle shot and the silence of Dr. Martin Luther King's last breath for the city fathers to hear the call of their fellow men, but for the blues festivals to get their attention, it only took the ringing of the cash register. The 1968 show was recorded by Seymour Stein—now president of Sire Records—and released as an album by London Records. That outside affirmation of the event's importance was all the city needed to begin interfering, and by the following year, they had just about rurnt it. The city sponsored an indoor stage simultaneous with the 1969 event. Their featured Memphis country blues performer was Johnny Winter, not from Memphis, not a country blues player. In their list of preferred artists, he was behind, as Stanley Booth has written, "such noted blues artists as Louis Armstrong and Marguerite Piazza."

At the Shell, downtown had interfered with down-home. The 1969 festival was expanded from one day to three. Friday afternoon was given over to a rehearsal for the benefit of a public television documentary crew. They were from the "Sounds of the Summer" series, hosted by Steve Allen, who would edit himself in later. Another documentary crew came down from Maryland, their multicamera shoot documenting the multi-cameras present. The album from that year was made in a recording studio. Perhaps the festival's encapsulation is the Bar-Kays' performance. All but two members of the band had been killed in the December 1967 plane crash with Otis Redding. Reformed around the survivors, they came out in full funk garb, and despite the sweat that ran into their eyes, they got down. It was not country blues, but it was part of the extended family. Then Rufus Thomas came out, the funkiest man alive, and the Bar-Kays backed him. And when it was all over and all the water in the Mississippi didn't seem like enough to quench their thirst nor cool them down, a meekish representative from the educational network explained that there had been a mishap in the filming and asked if they would mind performing their sets again. "They did the whole thing over in that fucking heat," says Palmer. "I don't know how they did it, but I remember being real impressed by the fact that they could get through it, and that it was as good as the first one."

The blues show regulars were there: Sleepy John Estes, Mississippi Fred McDowell, Bukka White, Furry Lewis. Johnny Woods made his Memphis debut, playing harmonica like he was from a part of Mississippi not yet discovered. "Johnny Woods had gone from the tractor to the stage," says Marcia Hare. "I was a teenager checking on their dressing rooms, getting 'em what they needed, a bottle of whiskey, pack of cigarettes, trying to make 'em feel comfortable. I asked Johnny Woods if he needed something, and oh boy, did he ever. He took my hand and put it right on his crotch. I went running out of there. I knew then to stick with Furry because he would never do anything like that." Lee Baker's band Moloch performed, and the Insect Trust played. Dickinson, Freeman, and a rhythm section had recently backed Albert Collins for

Steve Holt, of the Bar-Kays, at the Memphis Country Blues Festival, circa 1969. Seated in the background (second from left) is Charlie Freeman; seated on right (in hat) is Jim Dickinson. Photo by Marcia Hare.

his album *Trash Talkin'*; that grouping was to become the Dixie Flyers, and they performed at the festival as the Soldiers of the Cross. Yet and still, when the Fourth Annual Country Blues Festival is discussed, one need not be very astute or familiar with the artists to hear the disgust that quickly creeps into the conversation, and invariably the first thing mentioned is that Johnny Winter played. Real loud.

The city won, and lost. Their bad vibe, combined with Barth's unfortunate bust (headline: "Drugs Trip Up Blues Promoter") left the Memphis Country Blues Society crippled. A group of Memphis hippies tried to rescue the tradition the following year, but it proved to be a blues festival coda. New nonprofit organizations began to appear, along with degreed academics. Those who had done the work but not graduated from the proper institution found themselves ostracized. "Like twenty years' worth of work wasn't enough, you had to be at Yale or something," spits Randall Lyon. "They had the meeting of the National Endowment for the Arts Folklore Panel in Memphis. Bess

Furry Lewis and Marcia Hare at the corner of Madison and Cooper. Photo courtesy of Marcia Hare.

Lomax Hawes was there, a lot of bigwigs. They were setting themselves up to adjudicate who the folk was and what folk wisdom was, circumscribing these artists with this academic folderol, this ethno babble. Several of us stood up and said, 'Folklore is a racist concept and it should not be used.' It was objectionable to everyone present. They disbanded the panel. I videotaped it. I mean, you listen to Skip James and have someone tell you about the folklore of his songs. It was very obnoxious. We figured there was not enough known about class and gender and racism in general for any comment to be made about the aesthetics or the meaning of the music. Other than participating in it and enjoying it as a human fucking being. It was an obscure moment, but still, there ain't no fucking Folklore Panel no more."

CHAPTER TEN
Magic Time

⟊⟊

WHEN THE BOX TOPS' "THE LETTER" BECAME THE HIT OF THE SUMMER of 1967, no one was more surprised than the two band members who had quit the group before its release. They would have laughed aloud if told that their average Memphis teen band was going to have such an impact. "The Letter" became one of the biggest-selling records of 1967. Truly, everything was possible, anything could happen, and it all did come true.

"The Letter" introduced a sixteen-year-old vocalist who remains a presence on the pop music scene to this day, a presence so strong that his absences are influential. That session marked the first time that singer Alex Chilton had ever worked in a recording studio, though he'd been surrounded by music all his life. Dan Penn, the song's producer, had also surrounded himself with music, but "The Letter" was his first time in charge of a serious session. And, judging by the other two numbers on the demo tape submitted by Wayne Carson Thompson, the song's young writer, he'd gotten lucky while still learning his craft.

Such left-field success proves there's no formula for a hit, and it keeps the music industry ticking. It's a gambler's business, a game of numbers and chance, and when the long shot wins, it reminds everyone that the fix is never 100 percent. The bread and butter of the industry is the little guy who gambles on being the big guy. All the unheard records are necessary to support those few that actually find their audience. And the occasional jackpot keeps the gifted and the giving returning for one more try.

The only element of "The Letter" with any experience behind it was the American Sound Studio, and one member of the house band describes it as "pretty primitive, one set of earphones, and they were army surplus." Another says it was "really a barely rigged situation." Dan Penn came along while they were still trying to plug the walls into the walls. A singer, songwriter, and future producer, Penn had led several popular white R&B bands around the Muscle Shoals area. "The night Chips invited me to come up and check out his operation," Penn recalls, "his whole studio consisted of an A7 and an RCA board that wasn't very big. They were recording the Gentrys. Rick [Hall] had better equipment [at Fame in Muscle Shoals] than Chips had, but I was hearing something in that record Chips was making. That old studio was really moaning. Chips had done everything wrong, seemed like, to have made it all come out right."

Dan Penn speaks in the softest of southern drawls. His manner today is sagelike, a fine whiskey that's mellowed in a fine oak barrel. The wiry speed demon of yore has been replaced by a ruminator with a trucker's gut. The fire still crackles when his poker face breaks and the corners of a grin creep around the toothpick he chews. Once the wildest of them all, or perhaps the most driven, Penn today spends time in his garden and working on vintage cars. "Me and Moman had tried to produce some records together, but I was having a pretty hard time getting my ideas across," he continues. "So I told him, 'I want to produce a record and I want to do it my way and I want to do it by myself.' It didn't make no difference to me who it was, I would have cut anybody. I was twenty-six years old, I was ready to cut a hit. Chips was big friends with this disc jockey, Roy Mack, and Chips had him bring this band in. Their little singer was acting kind of smart-aleck, so I told Roy to bring me another singer and I'd cut 'em. I handed them a tape with some Wayne Carson songs on there, and told them to pick anything they wanted from this tape, but make sure that we do 'The Letter.' They came Saturday morning about ten o'clock and they had Alex Chilton with them, who I'd never seen. We started running 'The Letter' down, and he sounded pretty good. I coached him a little, not much, told him to say 'aer-o-plane,' told him to get a little gruff, and I didn't have to say anything else to him, he was hooking 'em, a natural singer."

This natural singer, at sixteen, had come up a natural artist. His father's day gig was commercial lighting, but in the glow of the moon he was a well-respected jazz pianist. His mother ran an art gallery out of their expansive home, and the couple's fondness for hospitality created a salon atmosphere in the early 1960s, attracting artists like William Eggleston and Burton Callicott. In a time when hi-fi was rare and record collections more so, Sidney Chilton, Alex's father, had both. From his bedroom at night, Alex heard the sounds of blues and jazz, Chet Baker, Ray Charles, Dave Brubeck, Mingus wafting up the stairs and into his bedroom.

"Taking it all the way back," Chilton says, "the first record that I really became aware of was 'Youngblood' by the Coasters, backed with 'Searchin'.' My oldest brother had a copy of that, and I remember really well him hanging around the house with his girlfriend one night while my parents were out, playing that record over and over again. I was maybe five or six. My dad was into jazz, and I got into his Glenn Miller records first. I became a big fan of Chet Baker singing in about 1957 or 1958, and that was when I first really wanted to sing. He first inspired me. When I got to be eleven or twelve, the start of the sixties, I began listening to the radio. 'Johnny Angel,' the Ronettes' 'Be My Baby,' the Orlons' 'Don't Hang Up.' George Klein was playing a lot of great stuff. I was aware of Elvis and Jerry Lee, I was given a copy of 'Great Balls of Fire' for my seventh or eighth birthday, but I really wasn't much of a fan of all that. And by 1959, Elvis was syrup and Jerry Lee was pretty much gone, and the rockabilly thing was sort of over. I didn't get really caught up in the rock scene until the Beatles came along.

"A lot of times I'd come home from school and my dad and some of his friends would be jamming out. In the 1930s, he'd been traveling around as a musician and when he got married and they started having kids, he blew off music. But I was the youngest kid, and he started playing more music as I was growing up. By the time I was ten, man! It was party time around my parents' house. We moved from the suburbs into the city and I remember countless nights of going to sleep with, like, sixteen jazz musicians playing downstairs."

In 1966, when Alex entered the tenth grade at Central High in Memphis, blacks and whites in the same school district were finally being allowed to attend school together. (Anticipating the possibility of mixed dancing, the school had not held a prom since 1964.) A band of recently graduated Central High students was going through a personnel change and enlisted John Evans, who could double on guitar and organ and who owned his own equipment. "They asked me if I knew anybody who could quote unquote sing like a nigger," Evans recalls in 1994. "In private conversation at the time, that was the word that was used. I was talking to another friend and he told me that at the Central High talent show, there was a kid who sang 'Sunny' by Bobby Hebb, and all the girls really loved him.

"Alex showed up at our practice and he was—" Evans pauses, groping for the right word, "—different. For one, he was a good bit younger than us. We were all about nineteen years old, Alex had just turned sixteen. He had come from a different background. He was wearing—and we would never have worn this, you've got to understand—blue jeans with holes in the knees. We'd have thrown them away if they had holes in the knees. He was wearing a black

T-shirt. I'd never *seen* a black T-shirt, I thought they only came in white. He was wearing a woolen dress scarf like you wear with an overcoat, wrapped around his neck like Bob Dylan, and a blue jean jacket. To all of us, sitting there in our MacGregor and Gant shirts and permanent press cuff trousers with penny loafers, Alex was unusual looking. But he could sing, and sing soulfully."

That was January. In March, Roy Mack, the influential disc jockey who was the band's manager, suggested they return to Moman's studio. At that time, disc jockeys were the interface between the public and the recording industry. If you wanted to book a band but didn't know where to turn, or if you were a band but didn't know where to record, you'd phone the guy who played the hip tunes. Disc jockeys and studios necessarily had friendly relationships: One made records, the other made hits.

The Box Tops' John Evans remembers picking up the Wayne Carson demo tape the night before the session. "We were going to rehearse and we played the tape. I think there were three songs. I've forgotten one altogether. There was one called either 'White Velvet Cat' or 'Pink Velvet Cat' that was unbelievably bad. Imagine a small-town, country-influenced songwriter growing up on fifties rock and roll and trying to write a sophisticated slightly jazzy song based on his experiences at a local bar seeing a beautiful woman. On the other hand, imagine him trying to do something like the Everly Brothers, and that's 'The Letter.'" The band played the demo at their rehearsal on Friday night. Everyone laughed at the cat song and agreed that "The Letter" was the one to cut. While Evans began mapping out the chord changes, one member went off to meet his girlfriend, Alex and another went to get some beer; rehearsal never really happened.

They showed up at the studio promptly at ten A.M. on Saturday. Evans describes Dan Penn's arrival, shortly behind them: "He was wearing this polyester narrow-brimmed fishing hat thing on the back of his head, a white T-shirt with a pack of Lucky Strikes rolled up in his sleeve. We didn't see Lucky Strikes much back then, so that put him on another planet. Also, we came from schools where you had to wear the right brands of the right clothing. One thing you would never do was wear false copies of madras handwoven cloth from India. But he was wearing madras that looked like it came from Kmart. He was wearing Bermuda shorts down to his kneecaps, and sports socks with different colored stripes. And hi-top tennis shoes. He walked in, drawling his talk, and Danny, our drummer, in his white button-down-collar Gant shirt, said, 'Where's Chips?' Dan said, 'Chips won't be in today, I'll be cutting you.' We get introduced all around, and Danny, who'd cut with Chips before, is behind this guy's back, rolling his eyes like, What's wrong with this weirdo and why did Chips do this to us?"

John Evans says "The Letter" took over thirty takes. Penn was twisting knobs and making studio adjustments for about half of them. The rest were working up the song, getting a single take all the way through, the lead vocals becoming slightly more gruff each time. The studio was still moaning: Penn had to get on his knees to change the routing of cords through a patch bay; Chilton remembers that the recording console had big dials for faders, like a radio station board. There was no Leslie speaker for the Hammond organ; instead it was miked from the little built-in cone near the player's feet, giving it a funeral parlor sound. By three o'clock, the band was done.

Penn: "And we cut 'The Letter.' One Saturday morning. Put some strings and horns on it with Mike Leach and then me and this black fellow that used to hang around the studio, we took the jet sound off a record in the office next to the control room. He put the needle on the acetate for me, and I went inside and I was working to get it in the right spot. We got lucky and I mixed it down, and I thought it was okay. 'I'm a Believer' was happening then, little organ going *chink chink chink*. You'll hear a little of that in 'The Letter.' I thought I got my licks in on a little rock and roll record. I didn't think, 'This is a million seller.' But it was."

"I had been playing with a garage group of my friends," says Chilton. "We never had gigs too much, but a few. I was the singer. My father had bought me a guitar, but playing all those notes at once—it seemed impossible to me. One of the guys that we were fooling around with wanted to be in the talent show at school, so I went along with that. Then this band called me up to audition. They had made some records with Moman before, a vocal version of Floyd Cramer's 'Last Date,' and another version of Thomas Wayne's 'Tragedy,' just horrible stuff. But okay, I'll go to the studio and give it a try. We recorded 'The Letter,' and that was how I fell into doing this."

"This" for Chilton has differed from the "this" of most of his musical peers. His career has been long and fragmented, disjointed by explorations into various facets of music, various facets of his background. It is the exploring that sets him apart. Where other musicians have tried to follow the flow, he has ignored it, charting a personal course. In the Box Tops, he may have been the producer's puppet—"The Box Tops are only marginally my records, I listen to them and I hear Dan Penn, I don't hear me"—but through the experience he learned the workings of the recording studio, he learned to play the guitar and write songs, to tour, to survive: Offered the rape stick by the industry as a kid, he succeeded in dismounting and is no longer its fuck-ee. Chilton's artistic horizons broadened in early 1970 when he departed the Box Tops. After attempting a solo career, he found a venue for some of his new ideas in the band Big Star, a group whose influence and popularity has steadily increased since its demise in 1974. He made soul-searching records in the 1970s, soul music in the 1980s, and in 1994 has gone back to the music etched on his childhood soul when his jazzy parents entertained downstairs. The joy, pride, and pleasure he has found in his vocal control is at the heart of his 1994 solo recording, *Clichés*.

Disc jockey and manager Roy Mack had been waiting for the right product to throw his weight behind. He knew that a hit song is never inherent in the music, that it takes promotion, which takes connections, which takes years. All of which he had invested and accumulated. Once "The Letter" broke in Memphis, Mack called on a deejay friend in Birmingham who made the record a hit there. The band was flown down as stars, all expenses paid, and they headlined a big dance in the armory. The teens swarmed, the girls screamed. The deejay made the dance money, Roy Mack proved the record's worth, and the band got to feel good. They were not paid for their appearance. Shortly after the Second Annual Memphis Country Blues Festival, the Box Tops, almost defunct half a year earlier, had a number-one record and more attention coming. "At that time," says John Evans, "the way distribution and promotion were, hits were often not number one nationwide at the same time. Like the whole time we were on the road, we heard the Doors' 'Light My Fire' in different areas of the country at different times." The Mar-Keys had chased their hit all around the country for years, and that honor now belonged to the Box Tops.

The Box Tops were then playing several Rascals covers, "I've Been Lonely Too Long," an assortment of Stax material, and the odd obscure number, like the Wildweeds' "No Good to Cry." As their popularity rose, the technology was unable to keep up. They played arena-sized venues without benefit of stage monitors, without a sound engineer; the audio, in fact, often went out through the sports announcing equipment. But Roy Mack's push got the label's attention. "Our label, Bell, was later home to the Fifth Dimension and Barry Manilow," says Evans, "but at the time we were on it, it was a black label, which meant connections at black radio stations. As a result, not only did 'The Letter' make number one on the pop charts, we got to number three on the R&B charts. We'd go places they couldn't believe we were white."

Even before their record was released to the public, the Box Tops were introduced to the veneer of pop music. Penn had hooked Larry Uttal of Bell Records when Uttal came to American Studio to hear another of his label's acts, James and Bobby Purify. Uttal ordered a Box Tops B-side, but when the band came to record it, they found it was already in the can. Wearing one of its many guises, the American house band, playing behind Alex Chilton, was now the Box Tops, thank you. "We played on 'The Letter' and later on 'Break My Mind,' that's the only other thing," says Evans. "The American house band backed Alex on everything else. I think Dan had it in his mind that if these guys played on something that became a hit, maybe we should give them another chance. He tried, but when we went in to American to cut, Chips had booked the studio on top of us. Dan got pissed off, wanted to do what he wanted to do, so he went to the nearest phone and called Rick Hall at Fame in Muscle Shoals and we drove down there. We'd met at American at seven P.M., so we got to Muscle Shoals really late at night and recorded till the wee hours. To show you how innocent I was, I remember that was the first night I ever drank coffee to stay up. We recorded a few songs, but 'Break My Mind' was the only thing out of that session to ever appear on an album.

"I felt ripped off not playing on our records. Put yourself in my place. A nineteen-year-old kid, you finally get a chance to do something you've wanted to do for years, it ends up being number one in the country for an entire year. Does it even seem reasonable, much less fair that we can't play on our records? By that time, Roy had us under a contract which we signed, being stupid. Our lawyers didn't know the business. I stayed with the Box Tops for a year, and after touring twenty-five days out of each month, my royalties came to $4,000 and I left the band. It's like someone saw those golden eggs come out of that goose and said, Let's cut that sucker open."

"I was coming back through Memphis around 1990, been down in Alabama, and I thought I'd slip over to the old American and see where we'd made all the records." Dan Penn is speaking. "I drove up there and I couldn't find it. The building was nowhere to be seen. I pulled my car up there and sat for a little bit and said, Yeah, there was the control room and here's where we was when we were putting the jet plane on 'The Letter.' Here's where it all happened. It was real strange to see that place gone—as much as had gone down over there. I felt kind of empty, useless, kind of sad. And glad, too, like, this is where we done it, thank God for this little place. But that's Memphis. I'm sure the Stax people, when they pull up over where their building used to be, they must feel the same way. Memphis scraped them away."

Dan Penn's drawl is soft as cotton, slow and thick as mud. Where he's from in Vernon, Alabama, there must be plenty of people who sound just like him, but somehow the forces of life cloverleafed around Dan Penn, creativity intersecting with calculation, poetry getting tangled up in daily language, the passions of black and white culture twining themselves around a country boy, allowing him to effortlessly capture human emotions. His songs sound as truthful today as they did two and three decades ago: "Do Right Woman," "At the Dark End of the Street," "Cry Like a Baby." He began on the fraternity circuit with the soulful Mark V and later with the grittier Pallbearers, who carried him onto the stage in a casket. His vocals, gruff like Chilton's Box Tops era, can be heard on his 1972 debut album, *Nobody's Fool.* His second album, with the working title *Emmett the Singing Ranger Live in the Woods,* was produced by Jim Dickinson, mixed by Penn, and is now languishing in an unknown corner of the Arista vaults (probably near the same forgotten crevice where the Goldwax masters lay). In 1982, he released a gospel album about which he says, "I wouldn't call it great." In late 1993 I was present while Penn recorded a new album in Muscle Shoals for Sire Records, released in 1994 as *Do Right Man.*

The Alabama musical environment was even more insulated from national trends than Memphis's. The story is told of one musician accidentally walking in on a prominent Muscle Shoals producer while he was using the toilet. This producer, involved in bringing the world many hits of the 1960s and 1970s which remain staples of oldies radio—this producer was discovered not to be seated on the toilet bowl, but rather crouching on it, his feet on the rim and his knees around his chin, the technique acquired in the outhouses of his youth which kept his toes from being nibbled on.

Radio was their link with the outer world. "When I first heard Presley I was as enthralled as anybody," Penn says. "Sun was knockout. But it didn't last all that long, because as soon as he started making those slick movies and those funny little teenybopper records, well I slid away real fast and I never did go back. Here comes Ray Charles and then I don't have to worry about it no more because I know which way I'm going." Ray Charles led to Bobby Bland, whose singing was so gutsy that Penn puts him in a pantheon high and separate. In 1993, when Penn was recording his Sire album, he insisted that the photographer shoot him in front of the Muscle Shoals Sound Studio, where he posed in a hat and sunglasses, a coat thrown over his shoulder in direct imitation of and adulation for Bobby Bland's *Two Steps from the Blues.*

Rock and roll didn't get it for Dan Penn, two steps from Bobby Bland. "Chuck Berry didn't register on my little funk meter. He was cute and he was smart, but he never went to church. I never heard that in his voice. And if I can't hear that in your voice, I don't want to listen very long. It's gotta have that soul. Bobby Bland, Ray Charles, Aretha Franklin—Chuck Berry's over there, '*chinkalinkaching*,' and these guys are *serious*." Penn got serious early on, selling a country song to Conway Twitty, "Is a Bluebird Blue." (Not a man of means, Penn was spotted shortly thereafter eating a large steak. "Man with a Conway Twitty song," he said, "can eat what he wants.") When he was interviewed on the radio, the disc jockey said, "Tell us something about yourself, Dan," and teenaged Dan gave his height and weight. And that was it. He'd told 'em something. He's always stood out as someone who knows a little more, shows a little less, and probably has a really good idea if it can be drawn out of him.

In 1967, in the aftermath of the British Invasion, Penn turned out "At the Dark End of the Street," a collaboration with his friend Chips Moman. Pilled up at a music convention in Nashville, they took a break from a poker game, went to a piano, and hammered out the song in less than an hour, returning to play another hand. "We were always wanting to come up with the best cheatin' song. Ever. Me and Rick Hall began looking for the *best* cheatin' song years before 'Steal Away.' I don't know why 'Dark End' is so great. I guess it's the word 'street.' Everybody's interested in that word. The sounds that we were getting back then was the sounds of the street. And streets change. Now we've got *boomboompa boom chichichi*, and that's what the street is now, but in 1967, 'At the Dark End of the Street,' that had the street. I like to collaborate because two heads are better than one. It's easier to perform the miracle. And the miracle is, Can we jerk it out of the air or can't we. There are all kind of ideas always floating around. Other than Spooner Oldham, I guess Moman would be the closest person I ever come to breathing together with. All writers, music people, they can be playing poker, they can be swimming, whatever they're doing, and all they really want is another great song."

Spooner Oldham is a boyhood friend of Penn's who followed shortly behind him to American Sound from Muscle Shoals. Oldham joined the studio staff as a songwriter and also played keyboards on some sessions; this was when two keyboardists were as common as two guitarists. "Dan was living in Vernon, Alabama, when I met him," says the gentle Oldham, one of the few who speak slower than Penn, whose voice is even thicker and softer. "He'd come up to Muscle Shoals occasionally, to a little piano room over the drugstore. I'd written a couple of songs that I'd never showed anybody. I didn't really know any songwriters and there was no market here at the time. So we decided to get together one night and we wrote three or four songs. I can't attest to the quality or integrity, but we did realize that we could sit down and sing and play our instruments and write together. And we've just continued."

I learned all about Spooner Oldham's keyboard playing while watching him smoke a cigarette. After years of admiring his keyboard playing—on soul records, on Bob Dylan records, Ry Cooder, Neil Young, the Box Tops—I spent a few days with him in Muscle Shoals at Penn's recent recording sessions. Pictures of Spooner show a man impossibly thin. Even when you look right at him, you almost can't see him. He's never at the center of a crowd, nor is he far enough outside the edge to draw attention. He's like a distant star made visible only by looking away; if you look too closely at him—or listen too closely to what he's playing—he vanishes. His visage is beautiful, all lines and texture. When he smiles, it involves his whole face.

Spooner keeps a pack of filter cigarettes along with his nonfilters, for variety. He is always smoking, which does not mean that he always has a lit cigarette. The process is such a part of him that when he is empty-handed, he has just finished one or is preparing to light another. He rubs his hand across some pocket and like magic, a cigarette appears between his fingers. Once there, plenty of time will pass before it meets a match. Spooner coddles his cigarette, holds it now by the filter, now by the tip. If he were to do something as direct as point, he might use it for emphasis. But emphasis from "ol' Spoon," as Penn refers to his lifelong friend, comes not directly but indirectly.

On the final day of Dan Penn's 1993 sessions, they were scheduled to record three songs. The album was a mix of old material and new, and while some of the best had already been cut, Penn had saved three doozies for the end: "Dark End of the Street," "You Left the Water Running," and "Do Right Woman." When the Hammond B3 broke down at the start of the day, everybody poured more coffee and continued to schmooze. The delay may have postponed the actual recording, but rehearsal began when the coffee was brewed, when one player entered the studio and encountered another. The way that southern musicians play together is just an extension of the way they interact; their style is evident when they lace their shoes, when they play ping-pong, when they smoke a cigarette.

That last day, they got "Dark End" after five takes but recorded a dozen of the upbeat "You Left the Water Running." They didn't need that many, but playing the song was fun. Each take told the story differently. It was after ten P.M. when they began running down "Do Right Woman," the song that Aretha Franklin and William Bell and Gram Parsons have made a fundamental part of life. Players wandered on and off the studio floor, greeting old friends who dropped by to say hello, who stuck around once ensnared in the magic. Penn grabbed an acoustic guitar and began trying to remember the song's changes. Bassist David Hood was across the room, apparently in a world of his own though he was actually encoding on paper the chord sequence that

Penn was remembering. Spooner was at the organ, following Dan's lead, playing his part slow and full like blood from a deep wound.

No one told the others when to join in, and in the control room, they didn't need to be told when to roll tape. It all happened as naturally as sunset. Suddenly the first take was done, and there was discussion about what to do differently, and by the third take, they had it. "Should we go listen?" someone asked, and Penn paused, because he knew he had a take he could use, but he knew that if they got up, they'd never come back—magic time would be gone—so he said, "Let's do one more," and they did, and it was as if they had turned the first line of the song into credo, dogma, religion: "Take me to heart/and I'll always love you." No one said it but everyone felt that if they walked outside at that moment, the world would have been a different place; what they'd done in this little room a few feet from the Tennessee River seemed to have affected the course of mankind. And when they finished, drained by the intensity, Penn said, "One more."

There were three guitarists on the floor, three keyboardists, bass, and drums. But the space in the song was so wide that a history, a human, a life could get lost in it. From my seat on the sofa in the control room, I looked out at the dimmed room where the musicians' souls were naked as God and they were no longer breathing air but breathing this song, no longer humans but entirely musicians, part of a tribe whose numbers were no greater than those within earshot at that moment. Dan was singing, Reggie Young was strumming, Jimmy Johnson played guitar with his shoulders. My eyes rested on Spooner, an amp partially blocking my vision. His eyes were closed and his head swayed slightly and it would be obvious to a dead person that he was playing his guts out. I leaned to the right to see him better, and I saw his feet dangling from his stool, not touching the floor, not touching the foot pedals. I followed his legs up to his hands, aware I'm witnessing a master at work, a ballet of the greatest depth and dimension: His hands were neatly folded in his lap. His eyes were still closed, his feet still dangled, his palms were together and fingers interlocked: For Spooner, the notes he plays are so big that the space between them can extend for a whole verse. Another chorus passed before he moved, and when he did, David Briggs at the electric piano with his back to Spooner suddenly laid out. No words were exchanged. Spooner stepped into the song like a ghost, as forceful as when he was sitting out, summoning spirits from the vastness.

Oh, you should see him smoke a cigarette.

Spoon was in his late twenties when he came to Memphis, and he stayed for about three years. He and Penn were side by side when the Box Tops took off. "Weeks and months had rolled past since 'The Letter,' and the record company from New York is calling Dan regularly," remembers Oldham. "They keep asking, 'Where's the follow-up? We need a record yesterday.' After this went on for a while, Dan approached me and said, 'Spooner, people have sent me songs, but I really don't like any. All I know to do is you and I just try to write them a song.' So we went to American one evening and each pulled out our list of dozens of titles and ideas and spent ten minutes on each one and there was nothing, really."

Penn: "So me and Spooner stayed up a couple of nights lookin' for a song for the Box Tops' session. I had already booked the band for Saturday, which was like day after tomorrow, at ten o'clock in the morning. I need the song and I don't have a clue. Spooner don't either, and we're just working ourself into nowheres. So then it comes to tomorrow! And about dawn Saturday, we ended up over at Porky's, a restaurant right across from 827 [American's address]."

Oldham: "So daybreak, we go to this little cafe to eat breakfast and consider what to do next because Dan had booked all the musicians for a ten o'clock session to do our song. And we didn't have one yet. We were really getting tired, and considering the possibility of canceling everything."

Penn: "We were just settin' there with the comin' downs. We'd ordered our little bite to eat and figured we'll just mosey on home and crash, because it's been a long two days and we didn't get nothing. I'm looking at Spooner and he's looking at me, big old empty looks. And finally ol' Spooner just laid his head on the table and said, 'I could cry like a baby.'

"I set there a minute and I said, 'What'd you say, Spooner?' He still had his head down, he said, 'I could just cry like a baby.' And it hit me. I said, 'That's it, Spooner!' Ha! He said, 'That's it?' And it hit him 'bout between the booth and the cash register. Magic time had just got here and it was one hundred percent on. Suddenly the air had changed! Just that fast."

Oldham: "I guess we paid our tab and walking across the street, just shoulder to shoulder talking, we had the first verse of that song written before we got to the door. And we got the instruments, piano and guitar, and I think about an hour and a half later we had finished the song, put it on a little demo tape."

Penn: "Spooner's on the way to the organ, I'm on the way to the board to turn it on, throwin' on a piece of tape, he's got the Hammond whirling. We had been ready to give up, there had been no doubt in my mind that the session would not occur that morning, but it did. We stayed in the studio—from that moment I would not leave for nothing. When the band got there, we were fresh as a daisy. The song actually gave us eight hours of sleep and I never felt better in my life."

Oldham: "Alex Chilton came walking in at nine A.M., heard the song and I didn't know what we had at that point. We were just exasperated. Alex listened and he just reached his hand out to me and said, 'Thank you.' That was the first glimpse I had that maybe we'd done something right. And then at ten we recorded it."

Penn: "And it was a hit record."

By the time of the Box Tops, Moman's house band had solidified, about to embark on the legion of hits that keeps them in demand as session players to this day. Their chameleon-like capabilities are evident not only in the variety of artists they backed, but also in the different producers under whom they worked and the changes they could make in their sound from day to day. "That hot rhythm section drew a lot of work to that studio at one time," says guitarist Reggie Young. "We were all from Memphis, everybody'd come up on Dewey Phillips. We knew a lot of different kinds of music."

"It was bizarre," says Tom Dowd, whose credits as engineer and producer, and whose long association with Atlantic Records, make him a walking history of pop. "Jerry Wexler, Arif Mardin, myself, we might show up one day with a Lulu or a Dusty Springfield and a week later come in with Herbie Mann or Wilson Pickett—it didn't matter what artist we came in with. We knew we had an accumulation of musicians who were masters of their instruments, who were gracious and took our bizarre direction easily, who didn't rebel, and we enjoyed their company. They were punctual, they were prompt, and it was a pleasure making records. You'd go in and work five, six, seven hours and come back the next day, first thing you know, you had eight or nine songs done and gee, one more day, and ha ha, the album is done."

During the time his teen band was working with Moman, David "Flash" Fleischman remembers, "I walked in one day and Tom Dowd is talking to Dusty Springfield, who is musically educated. He's talking pianissimo and forte and obbligato, and the next day I walk in and he's in there passing a bucket of chicken around with Joe Tex." Working in Memphis seemed to free the producers from the strictures they felt in New York and Los Angeles, surrounded by the industry. The looseness of Memphis kept them from producing a song to death.

"In terms of the races, the sixties was the culmination of the forties and fifties," says Penn. "There were a lot of white people and black people who had tried to bring the R&B and the white side together. It became a white/

black situation, you had white players and black players together. The mixture, who knows what that does to us, but it does something. There was so much respect. Now we get all these white people in the studios. Everybody respects each other but it's like you ain't bringing anything different to 'em. We're trying to make a painting here, what color did *you* bring? You're orange and he's orange and we need some red, we need something different, and back then black people brought so much to the whole thing. I always related a record to painting a picture. Your speakers, or one speaker back then, you stretch this big old canvas—I see it, I try to physically see it. That cross-color respect was a wonderful thing. It carried a lot of power. We don't seem to have much of that now. Hope we get some more of it."

The Box Tops. King Curtis. The Gentrys. Sandy Posey. Lulu (the Brit with the Flip). Elvis. Joe Tex. Neil Diamond. Bobby Womack. Marilee Rush. Herbie Mann. James and Bobby Purify. Dusty Springfield. The Sweet Inspirations. Wilson Pickett.

Atlantic Records. RCA. Uni. Warner Brothers. Decca. Dial. Scepter. MGM. And the list goes on and on and on, ignoring genres, defying categorization, unified not by a sound but by the solid musicianship of the American house band.

House rhythm sections were not unique to Memphis, just successful there. At Sun, Billy Riley, Roland Janes, and J. M. Van Eaton—the Little Green Men—served as a backing unit. At Stax, the Mar-Keys evolved into Booker T. and the MGs—Booker T. Jones, Steve Cropper, Duck Dunn, and Al Jackson Jr.—who had hits on their own and backed countless sessions for others. When Willie Mitchell took the reins at Hi Records, he formed a house band that pooled not only talents but also genes. Three brothers—Teenie, Charles, and Leroy Hodges—locked into a single silky groove behind Al Green, Ann Peebles, and other R&B stars that Mitchell fanned into fires of smoldering sex.

For years the story about the evolution of the American rhythm section, the 827 Thomas Street Band (the studio's address), has been the easy version: They were formed by Stan Kesler and stolen by Moman. According to both Kesler and Young, that's a simplification. "It wasn't like we had never seen each other," says Young. "We intermingled and we played clubs together. But as a group, we were the merger of the Phillips studio section, formed by Stan, and the Hi rhythm section, sort of the Bill Black Combo, which was me and Bobby Emmons and a bass player named Bobby Stewart, who was later replaced by Mike Leach."

"I worked with all of them before they ever went to American," says Kesler, "though not as a group all together. Gene Chrisman, the first session he ever did he probably did for me. Same with Mike Leach and I know it's true with Bobby Wood. I hired Reggie for sessions, and Bobby Emmons was over there at Hi with him. Tommy Cogbill, I used him a lot. I probably could say that I trained them, played a part in getting them studio-wise. When Chips started recording, he had a bunch of success on the front end and that's where the work was. I didn't feel like that band was stolen."

"Some of the early records that Moman was doing, like the Gentrys, he kind of put us together," continues Reggie Young. "I remember we used to go out of town, me and Cogbill and Moman, like to New York and work for Wexler on different projects and go to Nashville, and then we decided to see if we couldn't get some people to come here and us not travel anymore. And it solidified with Gene Chrisman, me, Bobby Emmons, and Tommy Cogbill. We cut a lot of records with Chips producing. They'd have to come to town to get us, and the Atlantic account was one of them. The band bound ourselves together, and then eventually Bobby Wood came in, and then Mike Leach after Tommy started producing a lot and playing less. After we made a commitment to do that, we didn't work out of that studio. And Moman was a drawing card. He was a good writer and a good producer. And other producers would come in and use us. I guess at one point, my amp stayed in one place—I set in front of the control room window for years. I wouldn't take a million dollars for the experience, but it's like if you've been in the service, you don't ever want to do it again. The education was priceless but the job didn't pay that good."

Sharing in the excitement and success formed a natural bond among the members of the American rhythm section, and between them and Moman. One staff songwriter remembers that whatever toys Chips got into, the whole American group would follow. "They went through radios, motorcycles, ham radios, model airplanes, horse racing a little bit when Chips built a race track. Gene Chrisman's motorcycle fell over on him once and he couldn't get it off him. They had to help. Motorcycles didn't last very long." Like the strongest of such bonds, there was a tension to it too, not surprisingly about money. But the band was on a salary, and so to some extent relieved of the worry that comes with the natural ebb and flow of the music business. Moman bore that burden, which meant that the others also felt it.

"I worked all those years thinking every day I was going to lose my job, thinking this can't last forever," Moman says. "A musician ain't supposed to make money, that was what Daddy told us. He said that's nothing but just a waste of your life. That was a real fear. That's how I picked up the name 'the Front Money Kid.'"

(The friendship and the tension between Moman and the band kept each in check for years. And years. They all got fed up with Memphis before they got fed up with each other, and as a group they moved, yanking their kids out of school, packing their homes, and eventually settling in Nashville, where they wrote and cut "Luckenbach, Texas" for Waylon Jennings, creating country music's outlaw movement and making *Ol' Waylon* the second-ever platinum country album.)

Playing for a house rhythm section allows a musician a better shot at surviving in the music industry without the road-weariness or burnout that comes from playing gig after gig, night upon night, anonymous venue after anonymous hotel room. One gets all the thrills, chills, and spills of being a working musician without having to go on the road, although studio burnout remains a reality. However irregular the hours, you have a chance to see your family. You can have a life. So while they were cutting all those hit records, the stars they backed would get off the airplane and into the hotel room and into the limo and into the studio and back in the hotel room and back on the airplane, nodding hiply at the next star disembarking—while the rhythm section poured coffee at home from the same coffee pot (maybe having awakened in the middle of the afternoon), drove across town by the usual route, and went to work making another hit record in the recording studio.

Like the MGs, the American rhythm section worked up head charts on songs as they learned them, and their interpretations were hits. Unlike the MGs, the American music was not distinctly Memphis music. Artists were flying in from around the globe to get chameleonesque, solid backing on *their* music; had Neil Diamond cut at Stax, the resulting album would have stood out in his oeuvre much more than his *Brother Love's Traveling Salvation Show,* which was cut at American. "Memphis is a groove town. Musicians there don't even know they can play together. To them, it's second nature," says Don Nix. "In Nashville, there's a lot of good players. I have a couple of friends who are drummers from Chicago, and you can get that person to play real well on a session. But you can't get anybody to play with him. You've got to get somebody he doesn't know from Alabama to play guitar and a guy from Oklahoma to play bass, and the day they get in the studio they have nothing to do with each other. Although they play real well, it just don't click in the studio."

"Booker T. and the MGs was a perfect example of racial collision—four men who under normal circumstances would not have known each other, much less worked together in ensemble like they did," says Jim Dickinson. "The American rhythm section are guys who play golf together."

But they played golf together in the right town. "If I go to work now in Nashville, if I'm supposed to be there at ten o'clock, I can figure that at 10:01, we're going to be playing," says guitarist Reggie Young. "They've got three hours, and I get paid for three hours, so there's no messing around. At American, we weren't on a schedule, which means nobody really had to get in a hurry, till whoever was producing was in a mood to do that. We didn't have any really set time that we would come in every day. But when we did, most of the time we didn't know when we was gonna be leaving. It could last all day, all night, and all the next day—whatever. There wasn't a clock running. We'd go in a lot of times, set around, talking, talking, talking, which is cool too, building up to the point where, Okay, let's get serious."

Serious meant different things to different people. During one particularly crazy session, well into several days of amphetamines, they were trying to find the right keyboard sound to go with a song. Spooner, so the story went around Memphis shortly after it happened, finally spoke up: "I know the exact sound we need for this," and he walked out the door. The band waited a little while—they were in the middle of a session—and when Spooner didn't come back, they went ahead without him. It was days later, some say two weeks, when he came walking back in the studio door and he had in his hands a toy xylophone. His fellow players said, "Spooner, man, where've you been?" And he said, "Well, we were cutting that session and I knew just the right sound. I'd seen this in a store window in L.A. somewhere, and I went back out there and walked all over the place till I found it."

The late 1960s was the age of amphetamine. There was a lot happening, and people didn't like to sleep for fear they might miss something. "I guess speed was cheap and easy to buy and it was the drug of choice, although a lot of people were going the other direction with downers," Spooner Oldham says. "Myself, I saw more of everything during that period than I have the rest of my life, combined. There were a lot of days when a lot of work was done without anything, but there was a lot of writing done on amphetamines. Especially when one chose to write in the evening after working all day. Stay up all night, that seemed to be the thing to do at the time."

"People wanted to stay up," says Herbie O'Mell. "I was managing Dan Penn, and he and Wayne Carson Thompson, who'd written 'The Letter,' were over at our studio and had been there for about four days. I was coming and going. I would look in and say 'How y'all doing?' And they would go 'Fine,' and that was it. On the fourth day, I looked in and asked how they were, and Wayne fell off his chair. Dan said, 'Oh no, man, you ain't quitting on me now.' And I mean Wayne was out. Dan picked him up and took Wayne's belt off him and tied him to the back of the chair and he said, 'You're finishing this song with me.'"

O'Mell, who had begun the decade running the Penthouse, where Ben Branch integrated the stage with Duck Dunn and Charlie Freeman, ran the hangout for people with shrunken pupils. It was called TJ's. O'Mell and Chips Moman were longtime friends. They'd done bid'ness together. One of American's clients was the Scepter label. Dionne Warwick and B. J. Thomas were from that roster and had scored hits at the studio. When Scepter sent a struggling pop musician named Ronnie Milsap to American, the jigsaw puzzle that was occupying O'Mell fell into place. He'd been eyeing a failed club in Memphis on property owned by some friends; he and Moman were looking for a project to combine their efforts. With Milsap, they had the missing piece.

TJ's had been established by two out-of-towners from a Vegas-style touring show who played Memphis and liked it. T and J returned, and the club was their attempt to bring Vegas to the locals. "They went bankrupt," says O'Mell. "Everything stayed intact and the property owners said if I wanted to open up, pay a month's rent and go ahead. Everything was there, including the sign." Milsap had been in Georgia and was not happy with the direction his career was taking. "I guaranteed that he would make sixty thousand dollars a year," says O'Mell. "At that time he and his band were making about six hundred dollars a week and were living in Georgia playing the Playboy Club in Atlanta and different places. So he moved here, I became his manager, and I got TJ's going because I needed a place to base Ronnie. Moman signed him to a production agreement and we cut records on him over there. I got him gigs all over the South."

The combination worked all around. TJ's became a success. The inside of the club was nice—it had been built for customers expecting a touch of Vegas —and salesmen became steady clientele, buying dinner for clients without having to spring for the fanciest place in town. The weird musician shit happened after they left, or in a separate area of the club, or too subtly for them to notice—except when their attention was caught by flying bottles or a fistfight. O'Mell's years in the Memphis music world—he'd begun promoting dances during Dewey Phillips's glory days—made musicians feel at ease in his company. Moman and his entourage—Dan and Spooner, and whoever else happened to be in town working with them—they could hang out in TJ's without feeling too public. Stax soon moved its corporate offices upstairs, enhancing the insiderness of the club. People from all the studios—and there seemed to be more every day—caught up with each other there. Songwriters coming down off three days of work could nuzzle a bottle of whiskey while eating a steak. TJ's was the kind of place where Dan Penn could turn around at his table and see a stranger removing a handful of pills from his pocket, reach over and take some. "You don't have any idea what you just took," said the stranger. "Don't matter," said Penn, "I just want to ride along with you."

"I must say I frequented TJ's quite often," says Spooner Oldham. "Dan [Penn] and I would sometimes go there and, when we were gonna be in the songwriting mode, have our pencils and write on napkins, tidbits and ideas, and leave and try to finish 'em. TJ's was quite an environment for creativity, not to actually write a song there, but get information out of the air. It was people talking and listening to music. A lot of times we had been working in the studio the day before or maybe that day and it was like a relaxing chatter kind of environment."

TJ's was established before Memphis sold liquor by the drink. With beer and setups, they were supposed to close at three A.M. But when the music was going good and everybody was having a good time—that is to say, regularly—O'Mell would lock the door at the closing hour and not let people in or out until it was over. "We'd stay until five, six, or seven o'clock in the morning, just listening to the music," says O'Mell. "It got to be the place in town. You just never knew."

O'Mell remembers one night when Charlie Freeman came into TJ's and a guest band, "somebody like Creedence Clearwater," was onstage. "Charlie said, 'I'm gonna play.' I said, 'Charlie, you're too messed up, you can't go up there and play.' He said, 'I'm gonna play.' He went out to his car and he got that blue guitar of his, I'll never forget it. I said, 'No, no.' And he said, 'I'm gonna play!' So he walked over to the stage and he sat on the steps but he didn't bring his cord. He must have played for forty-five minutes, sitting on the steps, not plugged in, just doing everything on every song. He came back and he sat down and he said to me, 'I told you I'd burn 'em.'"

Arena bands knew to come to TJ's after their shows. "I had Three Dog Night and Dionne Warwick and Steve Alaimo and Roy Hamilton and Creedence Clearwater—you never knew," says O'Mell. "Musicians worked late, and whatever time we were open till, we served food. We didn't have a big menu, but you could get a good steak on the grill, a baked potato, a vegetable, whatever we were cooking. We had frozen lobster tails and roast beef, too. Chips would send his people over and the band'd be playing and it was one of those things. Oh yeah, well I'll get up and sing a song. That's how Dionne got up. And Steve Alaimo was there and got up with her. You just never knew. I had everybody in there from Elvis Presley to the Bar-Kays and Brother Dave Gardner."

"The bartender was a guy named J.," says Danny Graflund, who frequented the place, "and he had a connection with all these pharmaceutical salesmen. Back then it was loose. We were buying sealed bottles, thirty to a bottle, of Ambar twos, Desoxyn, ups, downs, whatever you wanted. Thirty bucks a hundred. J. bought a grocery store, bought his parents a farm, he was making more money than Herbie. And Herbie was cooking. J. collected empty half-pint bottles, and he would pour rotgut whiskey in 'em, squirt a little simple syrup on top, and guys would drift in from the Naval base outside town, ask, 'Know where I can buy a bottle?' J. would say, 'Well, liquor store's closed but I can sell you one. Taste it.' He'd act like he was breaking the seal, and the guys would go, 'Oh yeah, that's good.' He'd get five bucks for a dollar thirty cents' worth of hooch."

Ronnie Milsap had everything to do with the success of TJ's. He became a club phenomenon, playing an interpretation of popular hits that continues to awe people today. His full and rich voice was outstanding and nothing like what one expected to hear in a club. Though he later became famous as a country artist, his repertoire then was varied, drawing from contemporary hits in all the genres. The audience shared in his excitement as he mixed diverse sounds, working out his act in public. "Ronnie thought that he was the white Ray Charles," says O'Mell. "He could do anything. Anytime a new song came out and he would do it, you'd swear it was the artist singing. It took me a good while to get him to find his own voice. Way I did it, they were rehearsing one day at the club and I walked in and said, 'I want you to put these three songs in the act,' and I gave him three singles. He said okay and I went home. About an hour later he called me and he said, 'About these three songs?' And I said, 'Yeah, they're not hard songs, you can learn 'em can't you?' And he said, 'But they're girl songs.' I'd given him voices he couldn't copy. I said, 'So sing 'em,' and that was the start of getting him into being Ronnie Milsap."

I am familiar with Milsap's Nashville success, and with his 1971 rock and roll album. It's hard for me to imagine what he sounded like in the clubs, but from the impression he left on everyone who saw him at that time, it's obvious he was powerful. Almost to a person, they mention "MacArthur Park" as part of his set. He apparently packed a punch with the cake left out in the rain. "Windmills of My Mind," "Why Don't We Do It in the Road," "Roll Over Beethoven," he lacked nothing for diversity. His show was taped one night, and a few years later, the recordist played it for him. His drummer said that Milsap, by then a country star, never got over how good he sounded and was willing to pay six figures for a copy of that tape.

When Milsap's guitarist at TJ's was off for two weeks, one of the substitutes was Laddie Hutcherson, from the LeSabres and the Guilloteens. "I'd heard Ronnie and I idolized the guy," says Hutcherson. "I went down there and I said, 'Ronnie, I've heard you a bunch of times but I don't know a lot of the stuff you do.' He said, 'What kind of music do you do?' I said, 'Blues and R&B,' and he just made me feel comfortable and played blues and R&B all night long. Real magic night. He sang 'MacArthur Park,' 'Lay Lady Lay,' whatever he did, he made it his. I heard a Dodge commercial that Ronnie cut in Memphis once. It should have been a hit."

In a time and place where anything could happen, where the impossible seemed always occurring, a new rock star emerged. He didn't sing or play an instrument, he never released an album, but he achieved the stature and renown reserved for youth culture icons. The Rolling Stones' bad boy without the music and with triple the attitude, ruffian Campbell Kensinger was a landmark figure at TJ's and later worked for Chips Moman as a bodyguard. "I'll tell you exactly how I met Campbell," says Herbie O'Mell. "A fight broke out in TJ's one night and some guy was coming at me. This other guy that turned out to be Campbell went and grabbed him and physically restrained him. The guy was struggling with Campbell about a yard from me. Campbell says, 'I need a job, do you need a bouncer?' I looked at him and I looked at the guy he was holding. I said, 'You're hired.' He turned the guy around and threw him out. Campbell was a smart fellow, just a little nuts."

CHAPTER ELEVEN

Extreme
Realizations

⚜

IN THE BRIEF AND TROUBLED LIFE OF CAMPBELL KENSINGER, VIETNAM was not the source of his rage. The military just gave it shape. Taking note of Campbell's skill in hand-to-hand combat, the U.S. government transferred him to Hawaii, where he trained Marines to kill human beings with their hands. Later, in Memphis, he would revive the classes for his biker gang.

Campbell's fury began at the age of four and ended in a midtown Memphis apartment in 1975 when he was thirty-two, crawling across the floor toward a shotgun, seven holes in his body from a nine millimeter Luger—five in the torso, one in the neck, one in the head. When the police arrived, long after another human would have expired, Campbell realized he would not live to reach the shotgun, would not live to exact revenge on his killer. But within his reach was a telephone, a chance to make a last statement, and he hurled it at the cop standing in the doorway. He growled, then he died.

This from a man on barbiturates.

In the last years of his life, Campbell Kensinger embodied rock and roll, its darker side. He did not play an instrument, he did not sing, he did not have a band. But the lifestyle that radio had hinted at late in the 1949 night found its most extreme realization in the person of Campbell Kensinger. His theatrics extended the proscenium to the edge of death, and then further yet into the darkness. He was completely unfit for society and somehow at the center of it.

The seething ember of Kensinger's character was his size. He was big and strong, but not stocky enough for professional football. Playing pro had been his father's dream, and he wanted his son to realize it for him. Instead of forcing piano lessons on his four-year-old, the senior Kensinger gave the tot a weight-lifting regimen. In contrast, Campbell's mother maintained a large walk-in dollhouse in the backyard.

Campbell grew up in rural East Memphis. Among his neighbors were Jim Dickinson, Jimmy Crosthwait, and Danny Graflund. "First time I met Campbell," says Graflund, who was tough like his friend, "I was at Jump for Joy, this trampoline place near our neighborhood. One night a guy pulled up on a moped, and in his hand he carried a bullwhip. He had a buzzard tattooed on his right forearm that his dad had taken him to get when he was twelve. All the elements were right there. That was Campbell."

In high school, he became a touted athlete, written up in the newspaper. Headlines: "Kensinger Does It Again." Though he was hardy and strong, he did not have the bulk for college ball, for the pros. The Marines was a way of escaping his father's grip. In Hawaii, Campbell married and had a child. His wife wanted their son to have a Christmas tree and Campbell said no. She bought a little decorative tree and put it on top of the TV. When he came home and saw it, he whipped her with it. Three nights later she came back to him, woke him to say she was home. He said, "I told you never to wake me at night." He pulled a .45 from beneath his pillow, put the clip in it, and she ran out the door. "I was standing in the kitchen door," he told Graflund, "popping sand around her feet as she ran."

The Marines discarded Campbell, found him too far gone to be reconditioned for society. Figuring he'd soon effectuate his own demise, they turned him loose, section eight, mental. His first night back in Memphis, he went to his parents' new house in a posh section of East Memphis. He'd had no recent contact with them. It was snowing. He knocked on the door, his father answered in his pajamas. "Hi, I'm home." His father said, "What do you want here?" Campbell kicked his way in, broke open his father's gun cabinet and then the liquor cabinet. His parents ran next door to a neighbor's house and called the sheriff. Campbell told Danny, "I was sitting there in that entry hall in a chair with a bottle of whiskey and a shotgun across my lap. These two sheriff deputies come walking up the driveway and rang the doorbell. I let the action go on that .12 gauge. *Keewanggg*. All I saw was assholes and elbows."

He held them at bay until morning. Graflund: "That's the kind of thing that hurts. That's Campbell saying, 'This isn't fair. I've done nothing wrong except I didn't play for the Green Bay Packers.'" Campbell remained in Memphis but had no more contact with that family. He would name the biker gang he formed around 1972 the Family Nomads. The Family for short.

"By the time everybody in Memphis got to know him and he was like a rock star, head of what was like the Hell's Angels in Memphis," says Graflund,

"I really think he had been hurt so much in his life that he would not take friends, and he would be violent to keep people away. He wanted people at an actual distance. He didn't fear physical violence, but he thought, If I don't ever let you close to me, you can't know me, you can't hurt me. He had been mentally hurt to the point where he put a shell up. You'd have to have grown up with him to know what kind of warm person he really was."

Campbell began working for Herb O'Mell at TJ's in 1967. After the incident with the angry patron, Campbell and Herbie learned they shared several mutual friends. Herbie needed Campbell's help at the club, and Kensinger was impressed by Herbie's range of acquaintances and by his influence; O'Mell seemed on a first-name basis with every person in the Delta triangle. He was — and remains — a man who makes things happen.

There was a waitress at TJ's whom Campbell, divorced from his first wife, wanted to marry. She had been a Vegas showgirl. Graflund went in one night, they were sitting at a table, and Campbell was showing off. He had given her an engagement ring that had a tiny diamond in it. "He was proud. He was a whole new person. He was shaking peoples' hands. He was happy." Graflund continues, "I was also with Campbell the night she threw the ring down and said, 'That little piece of shit you gave me, motherfucker, I wouldn't marry you.' And she left with another girl to go to another club. We went outside and they were driving off in a little yellow Volkswagen bug. The first thing his fist hit was the windshield. In my mind I flashed, Not the windshield — that's the hard part. But the windshield went smash, and he kept hitting it till it broke through. He beat all the windows out, was beating on the car, screaming, hollering, crying, enraged, hurt. 'How can you do this to me!' He wasn't trying to hurt her, because he could have if he wanted to, he was just beating on the car. It seemed like hours, it may have been seconds. Someone got Herbie, Herbie came out, he hovered behind him, says, 'Campbell. Campbell.' Even Herbie wouldn't try to grab him."

Although Campbell shared a longtime trust with Graflund, and had a tight running buddy in another former serviceman, Frank Strausser, his relationship with Herbie was unique. "We were in TJ's one night and a guy walked in whose ass he'd been wanting to whip," says O'Mell, a man you would not mistake for a fighter. "It was just at closing time and Campbell said to the guy, 'I'm gonna whip your ass.' I said, 'Campbell, you can't do it. He's a customer in my place, and you just can't do it.' He said, 'I'm gonna whip his ass,' and I said, 'I tell you what you gotta do. You gotta whip mine first, you gotta go through me to get to him.' He swelled up and he got mad and he picked up a chair and threw it through my front glass door, turned around and said, 'Fuck you,' and walked out. I went after him and said, 'Campbell, come here!' I said, 'You son of a bitch, you broke this glass. Let me tell you something, I ain't got no glassmaker, you gotta stay here all night until I get a glassmaker. You gotta protect this place for me.' Campbell goes, 'Oh, okay.' And when I put a new glass in, I made him pay me five dollars a week."

Campbell was at another club one night when he saw another person who needed a taste of justice. As if psyching himself up for the pounding, he swelled his chest and raised one arm high, then the other, announcing, "In this hand I have life and in this hand I have death." Then he paused. "I am the awesome anaconda." O'Mell had seen him do this prelude before, but this night he bent down and bit a piece of the vinyl upholstery from off the edge of the bar. "I said, 'Aw man, Campbell,' but it was too late. He bit through the guy's shoe, and the guy started screaming. Campbell got up and whipped this guy unmercifully. When he was laid out, Campbell went up with the heel of his boot and stomped him right in his face. I saw it. Campbell was that way. He just would go off, but not on his friends."

Campbell's crank wound a little tighter when he began running with Frank Strausser. One afternoon in an East Memphis bar, Graflund was drinking beer when two of his pals burst in the door, knowing they'd find him there. He had to come right away if not sooner to a Midtown bar called the Toast because there was a guy just back from Nam who claimed he could beat anybody arm wrestling. Danny was comfortable inside and it was hot outside and he was in no mind just then to tangle with the heat. It took a few more beers to loosen him from his roost, which made it time anyway to move to the part of town where the general population was thinking about getting tight.

The upstart arm wrestler was Frank Strausser, fear incarnate. Strausser got wired on his own adrenaline in the Vietnam jungle, and the chill rush of danger in his lower backbone had become as necessary to him as air in and out of his lungs. Upon his return to Memphis, he'd become a cop, the paramilitary uniform and the weapon a sort of methadone. He was yanked from the dangerous Beale Street assignment after the pimps complained that he'd muscled in on their business. East Memphis responded poorly to his being assigned there, and ultimately he left the force. Unable to depart from the streets, he continues stalking the night as a cab driver. "When I get in that cab at three A.M. and I hit the road and I see the lights, I almost get wet," says Strausser. "I've had little punks in my cab who try to beat me out of a fare. I pull over and I face them in the back, say, 'You're giving me a choice. Either I eat the tab, or I shoot you as you're running away, take twenty bucks from my wallet, and put it in your hands and say you robbed me.'"

The tattooed Strausser may have been a grenade with a loose key, but Graflund had the bulk and pinned his arm that afternoon at the Toast. Three days later they were coming down from a run, bonded for life. Strausser and Kensinger become the pair thereafter, but Danny's place was respected. Drinking at TJ's, the two would rise and Campbell would growl at Danny, "You don't want to come with us, we're going to do a man's drug," and they would stroll off to inject amphetamine into the backs of their hands. "Strausser gets this thing when he's speeding," says Danny. "He grits his teeth and you can hear it across the room. When that would start, everybody knew he's about to flip. He'd be getting to a level where he focused on one thing: Punishment would be meted."

"They weren't the type that'd say, 'Let's go out tonight and whip somebody's ass,'" says O'Mell, "but they'd always find somebody. They would go to these places where all the boosters and criminals would show up at one or two in the morning. Thieves out robbing, stealing, breaking in houses. It'd be funny. You'd see one of Campbell's friends, and you'd be saying, 'Oh man, I saw the greatest-looking pair of shoes or gun or bowling ball,' and I remember one of these guys turned around and said, 'Well, I could get one of those for you. Could you just tell me where that item is stocked?'"

"Campbell and Frank got where they were popping that speed hard," Graflund continues. "They would go out to a place on Jackson, the old Broken Wheel, real late-night bar—off-duty policemen, waitresses, whatever. They would go out there and clean that place out, tear it up. They'd get in a fight, get back-to-back, and just fight their way out. Campbell said to me, 'That Strausser, that Strausser, he's alright. We took care of that place. One guy, I had my finger in his eyeball and I was swinging him around the room, threw him over against the wall. I'd have two of 'em and be backing up a little bit, Frank would finish one, turn around, and help me out.' And that's the way it was—'He's alright.' Each was a nice second to the other. Frank ended up marrying a girl I used to live with who was a waitress. They had a fight, got mad, so she fucked Campbell. Then she told Frank, 'Well your best friend came over here and screwed me.' So Frank went to TJ's and wanted to know if that was true. Campbell said, 'Hell yes it's true. If I was you, I'd beat her ass.'"

The American Studio crowd got to know Campbell through TJ's. Imagining a room that could contain a presence so delicate as that of Spooner Oldham's—a spirit—and also contain Campbell may seem scientifically impossible, but that is the kind of place TJ's was. Things at American had taken their own peculiar twists. After Martin Luther King's assassination, guns became common among many of the studio personnel. "Little handguns, something that could fit in a briefcase," remembers one staff person. "I had a little old pistol, something you'd buy over the counter at the 7-Eleven at the time. It wasn't nothing, but it gave me something sort of secure to have. Really, I didn't think it was that bad then. Today it would be a whole 'nother story." Like the radios and motorcycles that American got into, the guns became something to outdo. "I was at American one night when Chips took everyone outside and opened the trunk of his car," remembers a songwriter at the studio. "It was full of weapons. He was showing everybody, 'Hey, look.' I was like, Get me out of here."

Moman eventually hired Campbell as his de facto bodyguard. His duties were varied; it was his presence that counted. He might drop off the laundry for Chips's wife or pick up burgers for the kids; anytime a star was arriving at the airport, Campbell would be dispatched to pick them up in the Rolls Royce. Though he had a beastly side to him, his graces were such that female stars often succumbed to his charms. When Ronnie Milsap went to Muscle Shoals to record his Dan Penn–produced debut album, Campbell was dispatched with the entourage. Unsure how the locals might react to the hippies, he accompanied the wives to the laundromat. Several of the women began passing the time by embroidering, and Campbell asked for his own needle and thread, neatly sewing a row of tombstones around the bottom of his jeans.

Jim Blake, a former marine whose head shops, underground newspapers, and independent record labels made him the scene's impresario, had a reasonable relationship with Kensinger. "Campbell always told me, 'I'm in my world, you're in your world. I can come into your world and visit, and you can take me around, and you can come into my world and visit and I'll take you around. But don't ever try and be a part of my world because then you're playing by my rules—not yours and not anybody else's.'"

"Campbell and I were very close, sort of like opposites attract," says the wispish Bill Eggleston, photographer. "I don't think many people know, he had exquisitely beautiful handwriting. I first heard of him around the time of *A Clockwork Orange* [1971] and I had a mental picture that proved entirely wrong once I got to know him. We practically didn't even have to talk to each other, we got along perfectly. Sometimes he helped me photograph. He would be aware that I was after some kind of new strange bizarre picture, and it was as if he would impresario it and suddenly the event would fall into place. For both stills and video, he was a great help."

"He understood his dilemma," says Marcia Hare, who came to know him well in the last years of his life. She was running with Eggleston in the early 1970s, indulging in downs, and Campbell was employed to drive them around and keep them from getting rolled when rolling around was all they could do. "We'd all be sitting around somebody's house and Campbell would say, 'Excuse me,' and go out the back door. The guys in the living room would explain that he was going out there to get rid of it. He'd come back in and say, 'Sorry man, I tore the doors off your garage. I just didn't want to hurt anybody here.'" Eggleston says, "He kept saying, 'I'm trying to quit.' He meant killing people."

"He had been in the service and been trained to be bad and mean," continues Hare. "I don't think he had any skills other than killing people, and anything you get in the habit of doing is real hard to quit. I learned that from being a tittie dancer all those years. Hustling customers wasn't what I loved, but I'll still sit here, retired, and imagine myself hustling customers because I got in the habit of doing it. Campbell was good at killing people. It was something he did the best and you miss doing things you do well."

"Campbell was a watershed experience," says Randall Lyon, the scene's arch-hippie. "One day he came to my house. I was strung out, really high on narcotics, and Campbell shows up. Real scary guy. He sits on my bed, opens up a briefcase. On one side there's a .38, on the other side there were some Vietnam poems, and he wanted to read them to me because he said I looked like the Canterville Ghost. From then on, Campbell and I had this wonderful relationship. You could go into a place and sit down with Campbell, or if he came and sat with you, you were not going to be fucked with by anyone. Magnificent guy. Brilliant guy. Violent person. You could never tell what he was going to do. He was totally unpredictable."

"When Campbell entered a room," says scrawny Jimmy Crosthwait, "it quickened your spirit. Everything got a little more immediate. If he was sitting at a booth with me, there was always in the back of my mind the possibility that somebody was going to come in to waste his ass with a shotgun and take the booth with him."

Campbell attended parties that were not for the soft-hearted, not for the humane, and really not for human beings. "The group of people around Campbell had parties," says one acquaintance. "Hellbent for leather. They would show me Polaroids of the violence. It was intense. Way over the edge. It was like confessions of a serial killer." At the same time, he had become such a figure around town that knowing him was considered insiderly and hip. "People he didn't know were always inviting him to their parties," says Graflund, "because knowing him became cool. When he'd show up and be Campbell, they'd go, 'Oh no, I didn't think it was going to be this.'"

Reconciling Campbell the beast with Campbell the poet may be impossible for those of us who never knew him. But insight into his character can be gleaned from his friends, people who have a taste for the grit that produces pearls. They saw a reflection of themselves in Campbell, the balance of good and evil distorted by the indiscriminate flux of society. One can only wonder at how resplendent his beautiful side was—however small—that it could counter the monster.

Moman moved his studio to Atlanta in 1972. Campbell stayed in Memphis. O'Mell was running a beer joint where Rita Coolidge was a waitress and Campbell worked there and in a few other bars before ending up at a hot spot called Trader Dick's that featured Tony Joe White, Larry Raspberry, Keith Sykes, and several other soon-to-be national talents. Liquor by the drink had arrived in Memphis in 1969, and the city was still giddy. "The tops came down, the skirts flew up," says Sid Selvidge. "God, I can remember Jimmy Crosthwait out bouncing around on one leg in the middle of the street telling a policeman he hadn't had too much to drink. It was a nuts time."

"Three guys were hassling me in Trader Dick's one night," remembers Crosthwait, "and one said he had a brother who was a policeman in Dallas. I said, 'As far as I can tell, you guys could be fucking cops.' He turned to me and said, 'We could be.' One guy whipped out a little gun he was carrying, a five-shot .22. I suddenly had a real intuitive glimpse of the connection between the Memphis and the Dallas police departments. It's no small coincidence that Kennedy and King were killed in these two cities and there was sort of police help in both of them."

Quaaludes, a horse pill of a downer, had become the rage in the early 1970s. Hardcore partiers in Memphis were into rubberlegging, getting so fucked up they couldn't walk. Many times in Trader Dick's, more of the clientele was moving about on its hands and knees than on its feet. "Campbell was the bouncer there and expected ladies to be ladies," remembers Marcia Hare. "If there was ever some little chick drunk and showing her ass in Trader's, he'd slap her. I always asked Campbell for permission to get wild in there. I'd say, 'Campbell, can we throw all the ketchup bottles out the window?' He'd say, 'Sure, do anything you want.' And we'd do real juvenile stuff. But with Campbell's permission."

Trader Dick's became more and more like a private party. Campbell wrote a song while working there, and when the mood hit, nightly, he'd jump on stage, take the singer's mike and begin: "I am Trader Dick/I will make you sick/I'll beat you with my stick/You dirty little prick." (He and Jim Dickinson intended to cut the song in the studio as a jingle.) Working the door, he would refuse entrance to those he didn't know, and beat up anyone who

Jimmy Crosthwait. "It was a nuts time." Photo by William Eggleston.

didn't like it. "He might let in a couple suckers," Marcia remembers. "They didn't know the honor of being let in was only temporary. He would beat them up later. It got to be where other big guys would come to Trader's to challenge him. Everybody was getting hurt pretty bad out front. If he'd kept that job, he might have gone to jail a couple times but he might have had a chance to adapt to America. When he quit, he got into the biker stuff."

As leader of a biker gang, he no longer had time for jobs. He converted his home into a military-style bunker, the windows covered with chicken wire to keep out grenades. He told his gang, "Carrying a gun isn't going to do you any good unless you know how to use it," and he acquired a bazooka, anti-tank guns, automatic weaponry, and other heavy arms, organizing field trips to the country where he could militarize the bikers. President Nixon visited Memphis in 1973 and the FBI called Campbell and told him their planned route—different from that which had been publicized—and asked for his word that none of his gang would be in the vicinity. He said, "Fine, I got no problem with Nixon."

"That's where he had gotten to," says Graflund, "on the level of, Are you bad?"

Danny Graflund was with Campbell a couple days before he got killed. They went to the apartment where he would soon meet his fate. Campbell threatened the occupants, also bikers, forcing them to give him a handful of pills. When he had eaten all those, he returned, demanding more. It was three in the morning and James Townsend, thirty-three, told reporters that he awoke with Campbell sitting on his bed and was promptly beaten with brass knuckles. Mack McCollum, twenty-six, heard his roommate's cries, knew it was Campbell, and armed himself in his bedroom. When the door opened, he fired. Campbell was hit in the stomach but he did not fall. He took four more bullets in the torso, one in the neck, and one in the head and, though looped on pills, he still crawled across the floor toward that shotgun, still threw the telephone at the Man, still growled. Then he died.

Shortly thereafter, Mack McCollum was gunned down in the parking lot of Peanuts Pub, where Furry Lewis played every Sunday night. The weapon was a nine millimeter Luger. McCollum took five bullets in the torso, one bullet in the neck, one in the head.

The realization of youth power was in the early 1970s air, newfound dimensions, possibilities. Everybody was pushing their own envelope. The Memphis band Moloch, gripped by the blues, worked toward making the music they loved attractive to fans of Hendrix, of Marshall amps, and of outrageousness.

Named for the Babylonian god of chaos, one appeased by the parental sacrifice of children, Moloch was even more difficult to appease, grappling as they were with a musical form that was half a decade away from being acceptable.

"We formed Moloch before heavy metal and stuff like that," says Lee Baker, whose Blazers had faded with pop music's innocence. "We wanted to be loud, rockin' rock and roll, and offensive—grab peoples' attention. Now we'd probably be called heavy metal, but then we really didn't have anything to go by. There was the Yardbirds, but they were peers of ours. It was all happening at the same time, the growth of hard-edged rock and roll. It had been rhythm and blues and blues, and the Stones and the Beatles, and then it got a little harder and a little faster. A deejay gave us that name and we tried to have, not a real bad-guy image because nobody was bad guys, but we had a lot of fun with it. It was sarcastic. 'Yeah, we eat babies. That's what we do.' And people would actually be shocked when they understood the Biblical connotations of the name. It would gross them out. So that was good."

Baker met the charming Eugene Wilkins at a party at Jimmy Crosthwait's house in 1968. Wilkins had a theater background and had returned to Memphis wanting to merge those leanings with the burgeoning eccentricities in rock and roll. He had a good, strong voice. Baker introduced him to a band he'd been jamming with, led by Tarp Tarrant, who'd been Jerry Lee Lewis's wildman drummer. They were stone hippies. They became the band that ate babies. Moloch maintained a house that was a den of escape, where there was always room to sleep one more. Danny Graflund found refuge there and became the band's roadie. He hauled equipment and threatened shady club owners, his presence intensifying the band's bad-boy image. Moloch's other roadie was Randall Lyon. Though he was also built large, muscle was not his strength. Lyon was a junkie, a cook, and very entertaining. Michael "Busta" Jones, who became Moloch's bassist and lived in the house, describes Lyon as "the band's personal guru." Randall did not hide his homosexuality, which made some of his peers uncomfortable. Lee Baker, however, always made Randall feel welcome. "Lee was another person that would sit around and play guitar a lot," says Lyon. "He had some really cool Fender guitars and that was the most excellent thing, to hear somebody who could really play. When I was the roadie, I came on to Fred Nicholson, the organ player. He was born with this talent and while he was really good, he was just coasting on his natural ability. He did model airplanes. I said to him one night, 'Hey, you're here, I'm here,' and Fred came into existence for about twenty seconds and he fainted. Uh oh. Bam."

"Randall would have been a killer songwriter if he ever wanted to work in

Randall Lyon. "You had to respond to it." Photo by John McIntire.

that sort of frame," says Baker, "but he wouldn't be disciplined enough to make the verses come out like they should." His prowess in the kitchen had been established in the early days of Beatnik Manor, and when he didn't spend the food money on smack, he fed the band well. (When Leon Russell was spending a lot of time in Memphis, a battle of the bands was discussed between him and Moloch. An alternative was devised, though never carried out. Leon's entourage included a black cook named Miss Emily, and plans were made for a bake-off, Miss Emily versus Randall.)

Lyon remembers that he had no idea who Isaac Tigrett was when he woke up one day and found him living in the house. Tigrett, whose father's company invented the Slinky and the Happy Drinking Bird, later reaped his own when he founded a restaurant chain called the Hard Rock Cafe. "I have no idea how he ended up in the house," says Lyon. "It was a really weird mix of people, and we were all trying to do the boogie. One day Tigrett said, 'I want to take everybody out for lunch.' I look out the window and there's a 1935 Rolls Royce. We get in the Rolls and drive to his family's country home in Jackson, Tennessee. Goddamn! I mean I was sleeping in a closet."

(The success of the Hard Rock Cafes puts Tigrett in the ranks of Memphis's finest entrepreneurs. The future's celebrity, he is a rock star businessman, a good old-fashioned dealmaker who has taken the business out of conservative suits and dressed it in collarless Indian shirts, sharkskin, sunglasses, and a beard. His capacity for marketing has reached new heights with his latest venture, the House of Blues. A committed blues fan, he is erecting mock country juke joints in urban environments, promoting blues and blues-influenced music. With its extensive merchandising, the House of Blues offers itself as an image, and urbanites from Los Angeles to Tokyo can buy into the authenticity of Mississippi tarpaper shacks without ever riding on a dirt road. It's clean, it's easy, and it's elite. And it's so ingenious that Harvard University is one of his backers. Tied in to the promotion is an educational program entitled Blues in the Schools, attempting to rescue the blues from the junk heap of overlooked Americana. What Furry Lewis taught remains applicable today, even if someone else is to profit by it.)

Moloch's popularity was increasing at the same time as Don Nix's influence at Stax's Enterprise label. The band was signed by Don, and they recorded at Ardent on National. *Moloch* is a beastly-sounding blues-based swirl, the musicians trying to forge new ground with an old formula cranked up to the biggest and the baddest. The album holds a minor place in blues-rock history as the first recording of what's become a standard, "Going Down," since recorded by Joe Walsh, Freddie King, Jeff Beck, and a number of others. Lee Baker calls Moloch's album "a pretty fair representation of what Nix wanted us to do." Graflund refers to it as "the Don Nix Don Nix Don Nix album." On the back of the jacket and on both sides of the album's label is written, "Producer: Don Nix. Arranger: Don Nix. Engineer: Don Nix."

"We went in the studio with no tunes, not even a whole band," says Baker. The process was begun with drummer Phillip Dale Durham, Fred Nicholson on organ, and Baker. "We'd run the tracks down, I'd go back and play bass, put more guitars on 'em, fool with 'em. And we made up these songs. None of us knew then that publishing was where the money was, so we didn't care whose name went on 'em. 'Going Down' was put together in the studio. Nix had a line, we worked the rest out. All the stuff was done like that. The album was pretty much a blues album but it was heavier. We were influenced by Hendrix, like any player who heard him at the time."

Don Nix tells the story of the album's most famous song: "I didn't write 'Going Down,' I got drunk and made it up. I was living in an old apartment on Poplar Avenue in Memphis, sitting with my foot propped up in an open window in the summertime with no air conditioning. I fell asleep and fell two stories out this window into a garbage bin with paper and things. It didn't kill me, but that's when I wrote the song: 'Got my big feets in the window, got my mind down on the ground.'"

Proud of its musical debts, and hoping to give a break to a friend and influence, Moloch brought harmonica player Johnny Woods into the studio. "Gone Too Long" opens side two with Woods talking in his thick Mississippi accent, something about selling his cows, something about maybe needing to move in with his step-daughter, and then the band pounds out its pre-metal blues. Woods's harp fits in like he'd been born and raised in the band house.

By the time they were recording the album for its 1970 release, Baker had been a professional musician for a decade, and several other members had been through the music industry mill. Where management might have helped, they refused to let an outsider shape them. "I figured I knew as good as anybody else what was good for us," says Baker, "and I wasn't going to march to some other person's thing. We considered ourselves players and we weren't going to do anything to cheapen it." Their 1969 pre-album release tour of the Northeast exemplified that attitude. They were booked outdoors at the New York State Pavilion, built during the World's Fair, on a bill with the MC5 and the Stooges featuring Iggy Pop. The gig had come from a well-connected manager who wanted to sign them.

"There were some groupies hanging around backstage," says Baker, "and this manager wanted us to screw these girls onstage. He said, 'If you screw these girls'—and they weren't even good looking—'If you screw these girls onstage, you'll have it made. The world will be at your feet.' I said, 'I'm sorry, they're already at my feet because I'm up onstage. Fuck it, I ain't screwing that whore.' I was looking at Eugene, and we're going, Wow man. What we wanted to do was to burn the fucking show, and we did. We got three standing ovations in our set. We got respect and that's what we wanted.

"Phillip Dale would do this drum solo where he would walk around the drums playing 'em, play the floor, play the fucking mike stands. And he would testify. He'd hug himself, be moaning the blues, singing and playing the drums, sing to the drum solos. We did that shit up in New York and they didn't believe it. They'd never seen anything like us. I was playing a guitar solo and someone threw a cherry bomb that blew up in my face. I never missed a note, and when I got done with my solo I walked to the microphone and said, 'You're going to have to throw some fucking dynamite up here to fool with my playing.' And they went wild cheering. It was great.

"Then the MCs came out and they blew up amps. And the Stooges, Iggy jumped into the crowd and they beat the shit out of him! Shoved cigarettes in his mouth and he couldn't breathe. The band never quit playing, just grinding away, feedback, awful. It was a cool show, real powerful-sounding stuff, but it wasn't musical. And we were into playing music."

"I was always interested in crossover music," says black bassist Michael "Busta" Jones, who joined the band after the album was recorded. "There were definite black bands and definite white bands in Memphis. And the Shell was a place where both could play. That's probably where I first saw Moloch. There was the Bar-Kays of course, but there was also groups like the Brothers Unlimited, a Sly Stone kind of thing with nine pieces. I had a trio with Willie Mitchell's son Hubbie, we were called Black Rock, and we were trying to do that crossover thing, going for a white audience. I was real interested in English music and British rock bands, and I thought Moloch was the closest to something like that. That's what made me attracted to 'em. Eugene Wilkins always had this Jagger-like attitude about him, and the whole band had a Stonesy thing.

"There was one time I was over at Lee's house, we'd just finished rehearsing and we were sitting around. Don Nix called and said he was going to bring this dude by. All of a sudden [Rolling Stones bassist] Bill Wyman turned up at the door with Don. Everybody always tried to keep Lee abreast of anybody who was coming to town. Anybody asking about music, Lee's name always came up. Still to this day."

In the game of racial Red Rover, by 1970 each side stood just about where the other once had. There were white kids attentive to the old bluesmen and black kids grooving on rocked-out blues progressions. "Lee had more in common with the Delta blues musicians than I did," says Busta Jones. "I'd sit around with them and get the feel of it, but there wasn't really a bass guitar involved, it was mostly acoustic. He was really trying to pick the vibe, get the feelings from them. I was more into the electric power of the whole thing. I went on from Moloch to play with Albert King, and later Stevie Wonder, Brian Eno, and the Talking Heads. No one ever heard of Moloch, but I always credited it as my background."

Midtown, with its grand old homes, wide streets, and beautiful trees has always been a haven for the hip. It's where the action is in Memphis today, though compared to the 1970s, it's like living on the penal farm. "I'll tell you," says Lee Baker, leaning forward in his chair, "during the seventies, Midtown was loose. You'd be playing—acoustic even, like with Sid—and these girls would come up, start dancing, and they'd take their tops off. Just like that. Regular old everyday girls just going nuts. But it happened, it happened a lot."

The last of the original blues festivals had taken place in 1970. While that event was being planned, those who had conceived of the blues festivals were creating the first Dream Carnival, held in July of that year, exactly when their blues show would have been happening. The visionaries behind these new events were Jimmy Crosthwait and Randall Lyon, though every participant brought their own color. "There wasn't anything going on after the blues festivals," says Lee Baker, "so we invented these things called Dream Carnivals. Basically they were just gigs, but with a light show and lots of craziness." Moloch had released their one and only album in February of 1970. They were stone hippies playing loud, electric blues bent way out of shape and bent way, way back. For the first few Dream Carnivals, Moloch drew the sacrificial audience.

Dream Carnivals were the culmination of Crosthwait's affection for Bauhaus and their concept of total theater. He contributed his Electric Circus experience, and the literary background that had led him to puppetry. Lyon brought the enthusiasm, imagination, and, even, organization. "The Dream Carnivals started because we needed something to do," says Lyon. "Basically, they were happenings in the classic sense. I was exercising my full Jean Genet theatrical privileges. We had a Dance of Death with drag queens, bringing gays into straight venues for the first time. We broke a lot of rules. There would be a music section, then a reading might be acted out. Tav Falco might perform or a concept artist named Dixie Ashley, or I would sing Memphis

Minnie—the different parts making it like a carnival. We knew people would want to see us, we knew they'd want to look."

The economic and social risks involved made close friendship a prerequisite for the organizers, though they were not without dissension. Gays were subject to exactly what the civil rights movement had spent decades trying to eradicate. "Our circle wasn't homophobic, but they didn't understand," says Lyon. "They didn't quite get it. I was in on a lot of conceptual stuff, but because I was the hip queer, I did not enjoy total confidant status. Here we were on the heels of having the blues shows stolen from us. I said, 'Hey, we've been putting on these shows, why don't we do a Dream Carnival?' We had a meeting at Crosthwait's and decided we'd do one, even though we'd have to scam everything. It worked, and we always had enough money to pay for the next one. So as long as I was able to make stuff happen, I was allowed around. But I was always out front about my shit, and their problem was they didn't know what to do with a hip queer. It says a lot about the whole period."

Their ability to create a circus out of nothing was respected by a range of people, many of whom encouraged them by supplying materials. Seventy-year-old Cora Wooten, whose family had helped start Memphis's first TV station, waited on Randall or Eggleston whenever they came into her electrical supply shop. "Every time we asked for something, she gave it to us whether we had the money or not, and sometimes we asked for a lot. We might need a hundred feet of coaxial cable with obscure plugs on the end. Then a camera cable. Then a case of videotapes. She would make it no problem. She really inspired us too, encouraging us from her level."

When Lyon took the first Dream Carnival poster to Diamond Printing, he was angling on the best way to ask for a break. "Stefan Diamond looked up and saw me and this crazy poster and he said, 'Anarchists! My man!' One look, 'Anarchists! My man!' He was ready to print our shit in a second. He had those numbers on his arm [a Holocaust survivor], he was up for anything that would fuck things up." Radio commercials were created at John Fry's Ardent studio, where most of the musicians worked. They were able to indulge themselves, designing bizarre audio spots that would stand out even on the free-form, maturing FM radio band. Later carnivals held in a venue near the studio were actually broadcast live on one of the city's most powerful stations, dead air and all.

Although Jim Dickinson was in Florida with the Dixie Flyers, the Memphis house band exported to Miami by Atlantic Records, and was not a part of the first one, there is an anecdote he tells that captures the Dream Carnival spirit. It's about the French writer Alfred Jarry, who wrote the play *Ubu Roi*.

"It's all where you draw the line between the audience and the performer," Dickinson says. "Jarry went to the opera one night and he was wearing a suit that was actually paper on which he'd drawn a suit. They wouldn't let him take his seat in the loge, and he said, 'I don't think it's fair that they won't seat me, yet they've allowed the first five rows to come in carrying musical instruments.'"

"Dream Carnivals were an event," says Crosthwait. "The city woke up and went *bing bing bing* for a little while." The first carnival drew creatures of the night from the cracks in the sidewalk, but the human sacrifice was the high society who had come to rub shoulders with the underground culture. The audience was packed into a warehouse behind a drug-laced strip of blue jeans stores near Memphis State University, and the summer humidity had seeped deep into everyone's cranium. "The first one was like we'd been discovered," says Danny Graflund. "This warehouse was packed full of people, society matrons alongside the hippies. And I remember seeing Marcia Hare and Bill Barth bump into each other, start talking, and suddenly Marcia slaps Bill. 'You son of a bitch!' she shouts. Bill had a giant drink with crushed ice in his hand and he threw it all over her, spraying everywhere, and these rich people who had come to slum go, 'My God, we must get back to the country club immediately.'"

Music was the core of each event, but films, light shows, and theatricality were essential. Randall Lyon might wear a dress and sing, "In My Girlish Days," or carry a spear and pontificate, perhaps adding interpretive dance. "Some of his routines were really wonderful," remembers Crosthwait. "He would go into the Guru Biloxi: 'Yessir, the Guru Biloxi, that southern swami, the Mississippi mystic, get the Guru Biloxi holy dome and trailer park in Biloxi, Mississippi. I am the Guru Biloxi and for five hunnert dollahs I'll heal yawl and straighten yer entiyuh fambly and get you steel-belted radial tires for life. You can get the poster, book, the painting, and the record.'"

Gustavus Nelson (later transformed into Tav Falco) created various personae, including Tube Man. While Mud Boy scraped the guts out of Buffy St. Marie's "Codine," Tav wrapped himself in clear plastic tubing, writhing on the floor in a bondage scene. When he was the Three-Legged Man, he wore a fez on his head and had an artificial leg coming out of his fly. "He could manipulate that third leg, dancing," says Dickinson, "and with all of the other shit going on on the stage, it really looked like the guy had three legs."

Mary Lindsay Dickinson watched that performance from the audience. "He looked like the man on the wedding cake, only he had three legs. The two men in front of me were seriously discussing it. I heard them say, 'Do you think?' And the other one said, 'No, it can't be. But I don't know.' I had just taken my first Quaalude and I was going, Wow, I'm not believing this."

The Mud Boy dancers declared themselves at the Dream Carnivals. Chris Wimmer had returned from the Electric Circus and New York and made his regular disappearances. A performance troupe called the Big Dixie Brick Company formed. And the events were perfect venues for Campbell Kensinger. "After a while, he got to be a show himself," says Graflund. "He didn't have to do anything, because he was there. Since he didn't play guitar and he didn't sing, he didn't go out of style. He was what he was and he was the only one like him around." Other sites for these events included the Skyway of the Peabody Hotel, a grand room once reserved for the highest society. The hotel had become dilapidated; when they went to see the space and were told the guests would have to ride the service elevator to reach the roof, the room was quickly booked. One was held at Clearpool, the site of so many drunken high-school nights, and later, when John McIntire moved into what had been the Jewish Community Center, the building's gymnasium became a favorite site. That was a circle of sorts, because the old JCC was near the illustrious corner of Madison and Cooper, where Beatnik Manor had been.

With the blues festivals and Dream Carnivals under his belt, Randall Lyon was feeling semiconfident and semicompetent as as a promoter. Sojourning in Fayetteville, Arkansas, he schemed to make a little cash and invited Moloch to play the small town. Marcia Hare and one of her friends were part of the band's touring entourage. "We dropped a bunch of acid the night before," says Marcia, "and we were really ragged when it was show time. Randall gave us a hit of morphine to try to straighten us out for the show. We got just fucked up. We didn't know that Fayetteville didn't have an age restriction, and we were too messed up to notice that the house was packed with a bunch of twelve-year-olds. We had been in New Orleans stripping, so when the band started, we got up dancing, got carried away on the morphine, ended up laying on the floor and doing all that sexual stuff, taking our clothes all the way off, G-string, everything. About that time the parents were coming to pick up the kids, and they freaked all the way out. They seriously wanted us arrested. We had to hide out, sneak off before the sun came up and get back across the state line. Randall couldn't go back to Fayetteville for a long time. They didn't know who we were, but they knew his name." By 1972 Moloch had pushed blues-rock to an edge that was still years ahead of its audience, and the satisfaction they'd felt was now outweighed by the feeling of futility. After several changes in band personnel, Baker quit. Wilkins folded the group shortly thereafter.

The idea of two guitars, of three guitars, or of a guitar army is not foreign, but the band that applies that concept to keyboards is the exception. (The Band comes to mind.) This, despite the fact that organ and piano are much more distinct sounds than lead and rhythm guitars. At Stax, Isaac Hayes often sat in on sessions, playing piano when Booker T. was on the organ. Cropper was often the sole guitarist. At American, Bobby Emmons played organ, Bobby Woods played piano, and Reggie Young was usually the lone axeman. The Dixie Flyers, the Memphis house band hired by Atlantic Records to relocate to their new studio in Miami, also used the formula.

Stan Kesler pieced the Dixie Flyers together during his tenure at the Sounds of Memphis studio. Kesler had produced several hits and was looking for a house band that could help him attract major artists and produce several more. "I got them to where they could cut a good session," says Kesler, "and first thing you know Atlantic comes along and, I won't say 'steals' them, but offers them a deal and they left. I don't blame Atlantic for it, I don't blame anybody really. I think the musicians could have been a little more loyal. But people do what they think they have to do."

It was during Moloch's tenure that Dickinson was contacted by Jerry Wexler about moving a Memphis rhythm section to Miami. Dickinson had begun playing with guitarist Charlie Freeman when they would gig as fake Mar-Keys and they had recorded together in 1965 as the Katmandu Quartet. Kesler had been recording Charlie Freeman together with bassist Tommy McClure and drummer Sammy Creason since 1967; Dickinson had recently joined them on several sessions playing piano, notably with Albert Collins for the *Trash Talkin'* album, which was nominated for a Grammy. That was the record that had caught Wexler's ear. (Tarp Tarrant had subbed for Creason on that recording; with Tarp, the four performed as the Soldiers of the Cross at the 1969 blues festival.) Organist Mike Utley was hired when producer Lelan Rogers, Kenny's brother, used the group and wanted two keyboardists. In 1966 in his native Texas, Rogers cut the debut of Roky Erickson's first band, *The Psychedelic Sounds of: The 13th Floor Elevators*. He was in Memphis to record Hank Ballard updating his old hit with "Thrill on the Hill '69" on the King label and Betty Lavette doing "The Man Who Made a Woman Out of Me." Hiring two keyboardists was nothing to him. And that was what defined the section.

Freeman had recently become unwelcome at Sounds of Memphis, the studio where they were getting the most work. "He'd come in there drunk one morning, been out squirrel hunting," says Dickinson. "He wanted this producer to interrupt his session and play this fifteen-minute thing for his hunting friend that he'd been working on. The producer says they're busy and Charlie goes and gets his gun out of his car, blows a hole in the control room ceiling. Fortunately, the call from Wexler came just about then. I didn't care who he wanted, he could have hired Andr'es Segovia, I had to play with Charlie, that's what was working for me."

They signed with Atlantic for a year. The Dixie Flyers were never a touring band or a live band, only a recording band. The difference is that a recording unit does not have to maintain a consistent performance but rather record a series of peak performances. Peaking was what the Dixie Flyers did best. Their first big session was with Aretha Franklin, whose career with Atlantic had sunk into the doldrums. "She hadn't recorded in almost two years when they got her down there, and they weren't sure she was going to show up but they booked time," says Dickinson. "Wexler and I were out on his boat and we got the call on the radio that Aretha was in. Sammy was off fishing and they had to dredge him up from somewhere. We were a bunch of white boys and she didn't know whether she was going to stay. And after we did the first song, she moved in. She drank Orange Tommys, a prepackaged gin drink. She'd get a whole tray of 'em and line 'em up on the piano. And eat pig's feet.

"It was boogie at its highest level. She had an entourage that was three deep all around her. At the time it was very hip to know a Sam Cooke brother, and she had two who stayed throughout the whole session. She could make fourteen notes, seven notes with each hand. 'Don't Play That Song for Me' won her a Grammy, but 'The Thrill Is Gone (From Yesterday's Kiss)' is the best, because of Charlie. We had just done the track and they were envisioning some kind of Claptonesque guitar solo. Charlie went out and played his little Wes Montgomery stuff and I thought Wexler was gonna die. He said 'Baby, baby, I've had great guitar players before but Charlie Freeman is the only one who can take a real solo.'"

In Miami they recorded fourteen albums in six months, with artists as diverse as Carmen McCrae, Delaney and Bonnie, Jerry Jeff Walker, Sam and Dave, Sam the Sham, Lulu, and Ronnie Hawkins. But the work wasn't steady, coming in exhausting chunks followed by irritating lulls. The band was out of their element in Miami, and tried to mentally, and chemically, take themselves back to Memphis as often as possible. "For a while," Wexler writes in his autobiography, *Rhythm and the Blues* (1993), "the Dixie Flyers were flying high. I didn't know that they were doing everything in the drugstore, but I did know they were some wild motherfuckers. . . . I should've known there never were enough projects to keep a house rhythm section working steadily. My conception—to import and keep a cohesive group—was naive."

When things got slow, Atlantic asked the group to record an album of their own, which they would send them on tour to promote. Nobody wanted to tour. Creason and Utley had done long stints, Mar-Keys style, as the Bill Black Combo and had grown unaccustomed to the chore. Dickinson, throughout all his music biz, would not tour until 1972 with Arlo Guthrie and Ry Cooder. The tension got higher when there was disagreement over the album's direction. Dickinson cut a deal with Wexler converting the remaining six months of his contract to a production agreement for a solo album. It began in Miami and ended in Memphis, and is today a sought-after and hard-to-find rocking giant. "I titled the record *Dixie Fried* as a comment on my physical condition," he says. "I'm still satisfied with 'Wild Bill Jones' and 'Casey Jones' and sort of 'Louise.' 'O How She Dances' works real well on the record, but me and Crosthwait used to do that better in our coffeehouse act on any given night. The actual cut of 'Dixie Fried' is maybe the last thing I did. It's all me and Baker.

"I have John Fry totally to thank for the way that record sounds," Dickinson continues. "It was produced by Tom Dowd, and at one point I took it over myself and overdubbed crazy things on it, as I am wont to do. The final mix sounded terrible. I played it on an acetate for Fry and Fry says, 'Waal, Jim, I think that's the worst tape to disc transfer I've ever heard!' And I was out of budget, had nothing left to count on but my fingers. I went back to Fry, and this was long after I had been associated with Ardent, and I begged for help. I got on my knees and begged, which is something I think is very helpful in the music business. A grown man who'll get on his knees in a restaurant—they might give you a budget. Fry's remix is what exists today, which I think is why it has endured to the extent that it has." "*Dixie Fried* is a record I love," says Jerry Wexler, "a masterpiece. My hopes for it upon release were exiguous, to say the least."

The remaining Dixie Flyers worked on an instrumental album of their own. Atlantic rejected the product and the tapes are apparently lost. Most of the band stayed together, accepting a job backing Rita Coolidge and then Kris Kristofferson. Mike Utley went on to play with Jimmy Buffet, producing several hits and employing old friends and bandmates.

Finishing his record in Memphis, Dickinson was able to get back into the local scene. He sat in at the Dream Carnivals, jamming with Lee Baker. He and Dan Penn had become solid running buddies, and he was producing Penn's second album, *Emmett the Singing Ranger Live in the Woods*. CBS Records sent him to Hollywood to produce Brenda Patterson, a Memphis chanteuse who had achieved notoriety singing with Bob Dylan on "Knocking on Heaven's Door." For those sessions, Dickinson hired noted guitarist Ry Cooder and they struck up a quick friendship; Dickinson was cutting the traditional sort of material that Cooder cherished, and in a tradition-friendly manner. "Cooder had just fired Van Dyke Parks as producer of his second album and was in the middle of record company hell," says Dickinson. "After the first day with Brenda, he asked me to go to lunch. It was a very corny Hollywood thing. I thought he was going to ask me to tour with him. It was my first Hollywood session as a producer, I was green as grass. He was asking me to produce him. I said, 'Shit, of course.' I had heard his first album."

He shared production of Cooder's *Into the Purple Valley* with Lenny Waronker, now president of Warner Brothers Records. Los Angeles was dazzled by the southerner's independence, his dedication to roots, his . . . his . . . good God—*authenticity*. Waronker, then head of A&R, called Jim into his office and presented him with the Warner Brothers artist roster. Pick a name you would like to produce, Dickinson was told. "I looked at this list and I asked, 'Don't these people have producers?' 'Just look at the list,' they said. Dionne Warwick was on there, Little Feat. I told them I wanted to produce Bobby Ray Watson. Bobby Ray was from Mississippi and he wasn't on their list, but he was on mine. When Bobby Ray recorded a demo version of this great song of his, 'Fool for a Cigarette,' Cooder played on it, and then stole it, put it on his own album. I figured if they were giving away money, it should go to Bobby Ray. That's what I call regional morality."

CHAPTER TWELVE

That's Mister Boy to You

MUD BOY AND THE NEUTRONS WAS MORE THAN A REUNION OF SEVERAL core players from the Bitter Lemon. Lee Baker, Jimmy Crosthwait, Jim Dickinson, and Sid Selvidge had all felt their lives change after coming under the influence of the bluesmen. Mud Boy was a way for them to continue that discussion in public, sharing what they'd learned with their friends and fans. Though each musician was also a songwriter, the band preferred to reinterpret classics, because the language was universal and also because none figured they could write a better song than "Ubangi Stomp."

Selvidge and Dickinson had been involved in enough music deals gone sour that they were determined to play for themselves and not for the industry. Each was raising a family, and Selvidge also had an academic career; the rock and roll road looked most unattractive and, fortunately, unnecessary. A band that damned the recording business titillated Crosthwait, but Baker— Baker was caught in the crossed desires of artistic expression and commercial success. "I'd have gone on the road," he says. "Hell, I'd go now, playing to people that would like to hear you."

Baker had defected from Moloch in the spring of 1972, and on Halloween of that year, after a summer of rehearsing, Mud Boy made its debut. This Dream Carnival took its name from a line Dracula murmurs when he hears wolves howling: "Behold the Children of the Night." The band name came, indirectly, from Ry Cooder. Dickinson was with him when Cooder's record company asked, completely inappropriately, if he would open a tour for the horrific showman and teen-anthem star Alice Cooper. Cooder turned to Dickinson and exclaimed, "They've got to know I'm not going on the road with no Mud Boy and the Neutrons!" The name had come out of thin air and

Dickinson asked if he had any intentions for it. "One of the reasons we liked the name," he says, "was when people would ask us who was Mud Boy, our reply was going to be, 'That's Mister Boy to you.'"

The Children of the Night show was broadcast in its entirety on the city's most powerful FM station. The site was the former Jewish Community Center, which was only a block from Ardent's new location. Crosthwait says, "Me and Baker got some funny looks taking the wire from Ardent past people's apartment windows and out in their yards, but we just told 'em it was no big deal, not to worry." The show included Johnny Woods and his wife Verlina, he with painted white circles around his eyes and a pink satin shirt, she with a hat that looked like a shoe, bulbous sunglasses, a cape, and a tallboy beer. Furry was in grand form that night, playing to such a large and lively crowd. He thoroughly enjoyed costumes and way-out events, modern-day equivalents of the medicine show atmosphere. He donned a wig and an old smoking jacket worn inside out, the lining showing tigers and psychedelic imagery. "Furry took me and Bobby Ray Watson and Lee Baker aside," remembers Dickinson, "and he said, 'You know that stuff y'all smoke?' And we said, 'Yeah, Furry, you want a joint?' And he says, 'No, no, no, look at this.' And he opened up his coat and he had a lid of pot in each one of the pockets, just showing us he was hip." When Furry performed, he got deep into his playing and refused to quit. Baker sent Connie and Marcia onto the stage in their full regalia—wearing lots and covering little—and they threw a psychedelic net over Furry, dragging him to a cage that was serving as a jail for the evening.

To announce Mud Boy's debut, Crosthwait re-created his sliding wire act from the Electric Circus, running from the rear roof of the gym to a mud-filled raft on the floor in front of the stage. When the pixie hit the raft, the band was born. They had transformed themselves inside and out, way stoned and fully costumed. Each was dressed like something other than who and what he was. Selvidge painted his face blue-black and red like the mandril baboons he studied. Baker was all black hair and beard, his face painted black, a smear in the night, Negative Man. Dickinson wore a flowing orange cape, pink feathered headdress, a jumpsuit with skeleton bones painted on it, and a goat skull for a codpiece. Crosthwait was the most frightening thing he could imagine, a clown at midnight, after the tent is down and the spotlight out. With the dancing girls joined by Big Dixie, the show spilled off the stage. "It was incendiary," says Dickinson. "It made shit happen. The idea was if we put enough of this in front of people, maybe some of it will rub off on them. Memphis is about making chaos out of seeming order."

Itching to have another go at success, Baker urged them toward a recording contract. Dickinson secured a demo deal with Warner Brothers, and the band entered Ardent with McClure, Jerry Lee's former drummer Tarp Tarrant, and Moloch's second guitarist Jimmy Segerson. "It was the most uptight session I have ever been on in my life," says Selvidge. "It got to be like fingernails against the blackboard. Dickinson says that there's some salvageable material, but if there is, someone's going to have to put the happy vibe on it."

"I got one of the best vocals ever on Selvidge at those sessions," says Dickinson. "Most of the stuff was too arranged, and we weren't about arrangements. But even the stuff that didn't work, we at least got some good rhythm tracks."

The months of rehearsal had eroded the group's essence: Mud Boy makes good music because in the core of its conglomerated soul, none of the players is a musician. Each has been able to eke out a living of some sort from his talent, but it's their dimension that makes them what they are: Selvidge may be able to sing high notes of beauty like fields of autumn cotton, but he's an anthropologist. Dickinson is a musical chemist balancing order and chaos, with the approach of an historian. Baker can unleash heroic guitar riffs because he spends all summer atop a tractor cutting grass. Crosthwait may be the world's best white washboard player, but he plays with the hands of a puppeteer. It's the character and personality of each, the wit and response, that propels them. There are ways they play together that they could not train another person to do. They harmonize in their knowledge of each other. It's not a question of being loose or tight, it's a matter of intimacy, performing that intimacy onstage.

Mud Boy only gigs a few times a year, or every other year. Mostly for benefits, rarely out of Shelby County. Gigging infrequently, they maintain their spontaneity. One could say that Mud Boy is the inheritor of the Memphis Country Blues Festivals. Inheritor, yes, but also the inheritance. They played alongside the old bluesmen, they helped them to their chairs, sat behind them and not beside them. They didn't teach the old bluesmen anything and the old bluesmen didn't teach them much—it was osmosis and not a lecture. The medium was a glass of whiskey. The language was the jelly lid over Furry's shot glass.

> Had a little pig and I fed him lots of cheese
> Got so fat that he couldn't see his knees.
> Best ol' pig that we had on the farm
> Who's gonna buy some more bourbon when all this is gone?

Warner Brothers never heard the demos. The band began its self-reparation through live gigs, and fourteen years after their Halloween debut, they finally felt ready to return to the studio, releasing *Known Felons in Drag* in 1986. Their second release, *Negro Streets at Dawn* (a line from Allen Ginsberg's poem "Howl"), would follow seven years later. Mud Boy is the random element, the universal unknown. There are people in small rooms all over the world, in impersonal cubicles in large offices, in malls, in ghettos, and behind fenced mansions—who thrive on a little chaos, enjoy the occasional taste of 220 volts, live for the beauty of the flaw in the grain.

The Mud Boy shows were a continuation of the Dream Carnivals. Even after they stopped wearing costumes, theatricality remained a part of their show, making room for the dancers, for Randall Lyon, for any other appropriately theatrical event to occur. "Husband is smart," says Mary Lindsay Dickinson. (She says people all over the world may address Jim many different ways, but she's the only one who can refer to him as "husband.") "Mick Jagger has to knock himself out and stay skinny as a rail when he could just hire dancing girls. And Mud Boy never even had to hire them. They just wanted to be part of the show."

"The last costume gig we played was the night before Charlie Freeman's funeral," says Dickinson. "And then we just never did the costumes again. Never even talked about it. Baker was just a smear of black and fuzz by then. He had this kind of wooly vest, and his hair was real long and it would be down in his face when he played. He would pull his hair up and put his finger in his ear and sing 'Laundromat Blues' like a twelve-year-old black girl: really really good."

Guitarist Charlie Freeman's death on January 31, 1973, jolted the Memphis scene. Since declaring his subtlety in a garage in the late 1950s, he had never ceased to astound any who'd heard him, achieving in his short life things which compose the dreams or regrets of most thirty-one-year-olds. His legacy included the Mar-Keys, the integration of Memphis stages, and the Dixie Flyers; he'd also laid the groundwork for Phineas Newborn Jr.'s comeback. Freeman was enormously respected in the industry, though stardom had remained elusive; or he had eluded it. These are people skeptical of fame and its reported benefits, forsaking the financial security for the privacy of a normal life. They've watched too many great talents compromise the quality in their playing that makes it special and become just another name for a fast-food hamburger.

Charlie Freeman died of neglect, say some of his friends, and they hold themselves responsible. It seems more likely that he was his own victim: He'd ignored the asthma that had plagued him since he was a child. At the time of his death, he was in Texas, auditioning for a road gig beside Tommy McClure, trying to earn enough money to pay off old doctor's bills so they would examine his fluid-filled lungs. When he passed out from too much dope, his party acquaintances thought they were helping him by moving him from a chair to a bed. But Charlie always slept face down, and his acquaintances did not know that. When he choked on his own vomit, there was no question that he'd died accidentally. As accidentally as his lifestyle allowed. Did he fall from life or slowly jump? Herb O'Mell remembers a session in California. "This was after the Dixie Flyers, and Charlie was out there with Tommy McClure, Sammy Creason, and Spooner, recording with Rita Coolidge. Someone walked in and began passing a magazine with some [cocaine] lines on it. When it got to Spooner, he took the magazine, said, 'Oh,' and he opened it up to read. I saw Charlie go down on that carpet man, just laid on the floor going after that coke."

Freeman loved to party, but he was also a gentleman. "Even though I was a female and real young, Charlie treated me like a human being, not like a piece of ass," says Marcia Hare. "Charlie was the first southerner to accept me. I can say that Charlie Freeman gave me an early start on self-esteem by treating me like I had something important to say, and he would let me say it."

"Charlie and I were fishing buddies," says Jimmy Crosthwait. "Whenever we went fishing he would always, always, lock his keys in his trunk. After a dozen times I thought it might be a joke. He would open his trunk, put the keys in there, look for tackle boxes, and shut the trunk with the keys in it. Every time! And he'd say, 'It's no problem, it's a GM car,' and any GM car that comes by would have a key that would work his trunk. Charlie was drunk a lot of the time and he was part Indian, had a good sense of humor and just a great touch with the guitar. His death was a shame. He probably would have played with Mud Boy but he had to go on the road to make a living. When Charlie died, my next fishing buddy turned into Lee Baker."

The respect that Freeman had shown to Marcia Hare was also felt by Randall Lyon. The simplicity of going together to the cinema meant as much as the wild times they shared. "He radiated this power," says Lyon. "You could just look at Charlie and go, I'm gonna do something wrong and it's going to be great! He was really funny, very hip, and he knew what was going on. Some people on the scene were way far advanced, like angels. They lived in this alternative universe and every once in a while they would touch down. Charlie was working on something really deep. It was magnificent."

"The one gospel song that I'll never forget was at Charlie Freeman's funeral," says Jimmy Crosthwait. "There's Charlie's casket and the piano is back behind this latticework and flowers, you can hear it but you can't see it. I knew it was Jim [Dickinson] playing. An instrumental. And then another instrumental. And then, just out of nowhere, he sang. The third song was 'When the Lord Gets Ready You Gotta Move.' Man, I mean that was a heartbreaker. It was probably one of the best send-offs one musician has ever been able to give to another. It was completely invisible, just the sound. It was really nice. Really nice. 'When the Lord Gets Ready You Gotta Move.'"

"The last time I saw Charlie," says Dickinson, "he gave me Fred Ford's phone number. And it was a big deal because nobody white had Fred Ford's phone number." Fred Ford had played saxophone with Bill Harvey on Beale Street when the young B. B. King was plucked from amateur night and put in front of Harvey's band. Ford used to say he was the first Black Muslim in Memphis. Whether that's literally true, it exemplifies his militancy, an emotion underscored with bitterness. "Thirty years ago they used to call me Sweet Daddy Goodlow," Ford still says, "but I'm Bitter Father Badlow now." Then he sometimes pauses and sometimes he doesn't, but the conviction in his tone is obvious, and extremely unsettling, as he adds, "I have a right to be bitter." It's not that success eluded him—he chose to dedicate himself to the care of Phineas Newborn Jr., remaining in Memphis, and there established his prominence. And there, perhaps thinking of his career that could have been, he's felt the cold touch of exploitation. Among other shadows he's been in, he was with Johnny Otis's band when they backed Big Mama Thornton on "Hound Dog." That, of course, was before Elvis redid it. But even when his anger was fueled by youth, Ford got along with Charlie Freeman. Together, they were able to initiate the comeback of Newborn, one of Memphis's finest musical statements. Freeman had the record label connections and Ford had the artist's trust. Charlie didn't live to see it, but *Solo Piano*, the comeback album by jazz pianist Phineas Newborn Jr., was nominated for a Grammy Award in 1975.

Ours is not an age of genius. Eccentricities are shunned, blemishes quickly covered. But Newborn was a musical maverick. In 1956, at the age of twenty-four, he startled the world with his debut, *The Piano Artistry of Phineas Newborn, Jr.* His greatest achievement, perhaps, was his dexterity, making his left hand as important to the melody as his right. He sounded like more than one person playing. Memphis had long been aware of the boy prodigy. Not only was he born into a musical family—his father was one of the city's most respected bandleaders through the 1950s—but he was also born into a musical

Phineas Newborn Jr., circa 1945. In the collection of photos through which Mama Rose Newborn seems to be constantly browsing, she finds one of a young Junior in a bathing suit at the swimming pool. Phineas looks awkward, like maybe the sunlight and the outdoors are foreign to him, too many people around. "Yeah," she says, "they stole his clothes that day. He came home with some pants on big enough for that dresser. I said what, and he said, 'Well, I went swimming and I come out and I didn't have no clothes and I just went in the junk room at the swimming pool and put on something.' I say, 'Oh man!'" Photo courtesy of Calvin Newborn.

era. "My dad told Lionel Hampton about my brother," says Calvin Newborn, an accomplished guitarist who recorded with Phineas and with Charles Mingus, among others. "Lionel met Phineas on Beale Street and they played 'How High the Moon' for almost two hours, fast as you could play it. Phineas on one end of the keyboard, Lionel on the other. Count Basie gets the credit for discovering Phineas, but it was Lionel Hampton who put his name out there."

In the early 1960s, living in California, Newborn suffered a mental breakdown, was misdiagnosed, and never fully recovered. A decade later, he was in Memphis, still receiving treatment at the Veterans Hospital, looked after by Fred Ford. It took two people to fill Freeman's role in the comeback project. Both the writer Stanley Booth and Jim Dickinson were acquainted with Ford, and each had a long relationship with Atlantic; Dickinson could manage studio time in Memphis. The two approached Ford and discussed the project. He was leery but listened. Before parting, Booth pulled a ticket stub from his pocket to write his phone number on the back. Ford took the piece of paper, turned it over, and quickly said, "What do you know about this?" The stub was from a benefit to help Ford's former associate Bill Harvey get a new leg. The bonds were sealed.

"It was a hard deal to put together," says Dickinson. "Fred was existing very much on the borderline of society, and Junior was in the Veterans Hospital, psychiatric. I was cutting Bobby Ray Watson at Ardent and we would slip Junior in whenever Fred could get him out of the hospital. The first two sessions he didn't talk. He would come in wearing his overcoat and his hat and walk straight to the piano. His hands would be outstretched and he would begin playing before he even sat down. Then his foot would move to the pedals and then he would sit. He would take off his hat but not his overcoat. Just shaking hands with Phineas altered the way I play the piano."

Once at the studio's piano, Newborn seemed a recovered man. At one point, there was a baritone sax lying near the piano. Fred picked it up. "Whoa! The two of them playing together again, it was just unbelievable," says Dickinson. "They played 'Cherokee' and it became a game. Phineas was trying to play it faster than Fred, and Fred is playing it faster than you could think it." Newborn conceived music without boundaries, as *Solo Piano*'s medleys make evident; one blends a John Coltrane song, a selection from a Joan Crawford movie, and the pop hit "Where Is the Love." Another of *Solo Piano*'s highlights is the rendition of W. C. Handy's "Memphis Blues." "Fred was talking to Junior," continues Dickinson, "and he says, 'Ain't you got something country you could play?' Phineas broke into 'Memphis Blues.' That's his idea of country."

After that album, Ford and Dickinson worked together on a project for Cybill Shepherd. Phineas, then living with his mother, was to play piano and Fred insisted it be Jim who picked him up. Though Jim's expertise may have been better utilized in the studio, Ford has his own way of imparting knowledge, instructing. "It was like 5:30 in the afternoon, Junior was just waking up," says Dickinson. "I'm sitting at the kitchen table. Mama Rose is cooking him a fish for breakfast. Junior sits down in his overcoat and hat to eat his fish and he's talking to Mama Rose. She's had to deal with three generations of crazy musicians, so Junior ain't nothing to her. She talks in a rough voice like him and Calvin, it's a family trait. She says, growling, 'What do you want for your birthday?' He says, 'I want a pistol.' She says, 'Well, you ain't getting nothing then.' He says, 'You got a pistol.' She says, 'Yeah, but I don't run down the street going "Yeah, yeah, yeah."' She nailed it." Phineas Newborn Jr. never fully recovered his health. He made occasional recordings and performances. On the morning of May 26, 1989, at six A.M. he was found seated on a chair on the porch of his mother's home, dead from natural causes. He was fifty-seven.

"They had these grandiose ideas," says former Ardent engineer Richard Rosebrough, referring to the Memphis pop band Big Star. "It was all a Beatle thing, a Beatle and a Who thing. John Fry was a pilot and so were a few other people at Ardent. At the time, we were all enamored with this plane, the Lockheed Constellation. The plan was for John to buy one and Big Star would tour around the country playing these gigs. They would have this thing above the stage that would drop gold stars on the band while they played and they would get on the cover of *Rolling Stone* and all retire rich and famous. Alex [Chilton] had been a star, and he was disenchanted with the music business, except that he still liked the star thing. And John Fry loved playing the game. He loved radio, and he loved these great pop records, and he always wanted to record his own and have them be great records like Phil Spector and George Martin. But what he needed was somebody to record. And that was Big Star."

The saga of Big Star has to be one of the most unusual in pop history. Although they were unable to reach an audience during their three-year existence, their popularity has snowballed since they disbanded in 1974. Two decades later, they have become so well known and influential that a reunion concert received national publicity, was released as a CD, and the band was invited to perform on "The Tonight Show." Their stardom is a pop culture phenomenon, a word-of-mouth secret that reached Europe, Asia, and Australia without forsaking its intimacy. Music fans bond around informing each other of this talent that, until recently, has been completely overlooked by the mainstream. Big Star's worldwide popularity is the epitome of Memphis obscurity. Not only does the package come with exceptional, durable, bright pop music, there's also a story with it. Hear that lead singer? That's the same guy—*the same guy, man!*—who was the vocalist in the Box Tops. You know, "The Letter," "Cry Like a Baby?" *You don't know the Box Tops? Oh, man* . . . The tale widens to include the Box Tops' producer, Dan Penn, who wrote so many soul hits, and it includes Jim Dickinson, who produced Big Star's third album.

But the heart of the Big Star story is Alex Chilton. On top of the world at sixteen years old, a brilliant pop individualist by twenty-one, and three years later, 1974, he can't get a finished album released, one now recognized as a masterwork. Spurning the industry ever after, he has made a comeback completely on his own terms, a privilege usually reserved for superstars. Unlike most people in the world, Alex Chilton is able to do what he wants with his life. Chilton is his own person, his own artist. Known for being unknown, his independence and unpredictability trap him in the spotlight.

Chilton had begun singing with the Box Tops when he was sixteen in 1967, dropping out of high school to devote himself to the band. When he quit, he was nineteen, free from the state's grip. The band was in England, about to usher in the 1970s with a tour. When it became apparent that the promoter was not going to hold up to his contractual agreements, the singer opted out. He locked his hotel room door, emerging only to catch a plane home. The tour went on without him, but the band, distinguished as it was only by his voice, was effectively over.

Though he could not yet comfortably perform with a guitar while singing, Chilton had become a competent composer. The third Box Tops album included one of his songs, and the fourth and final, with Chips Moman replacing Penn as producer, featured several Chilton compositions. "I Must Be the Devil" drew from the blues that surrounded him. "Together" achieved an anthemic pop feel, revealing a complexity that would distinguish his best Big Star material; the sadness in his vocal, the solemnity of the organ, and the foreboding tone of the fuzzed guitar all belied the joyousness of his lyric. Before departing for the Box Tops' tour that didn't happen, Chilton had begun a solo recording at Ardent, working with engineer and producer Terry Manning. "Ardent was the only place in town that wasn't already locked up with a bunch of Tin Pan Alley writers and these sterile musicians playing all the sessions," he says. The album was completed after he quit the Box Tops; fifteen years later, he released four of these tracks on the self-compiled (and self-titled) *Alex Chilton's Lost Decade*. "Free Again" apparently anticipated his departure: "I'm free again/ to do what I want again/free again/to sing my songs again." Instead of the deep gravelly voice characteristic of the Box Tops, Chilton sang from the top of his throat, the higher register he would employ on the Big Star material.

Returning from England unemployed but with money in the bank, he moved for a brief time to Manhattan, honing a solo coffeehouse gig. "I was just trying to learn how to play," Chilton says. "I was sick of bands. I figured I was going to learn to accompany myself so that I wouldn't even need 'em. It was the first time I'd ever really tried to sing and play guitar together, and sometimes I'd shake so bad that I just couldn't play the guitar at all." Hanging out in various folk joints, he worked up his chops, even jamming with Roger McGuinn from the Byrds. He maintained a working relationship with Dan Penn, writing and demoing songs for his publishing company.

Chris Bell, from an affluent Memphis family, had a friendly disposition, though a tendency toward depression. He'd begun playing guitar at a young age, developing an intuition for acoustical space. He wanted a guitar to sound three-dimensional, and he developed a universality to his voice, a transparency suitable for mass appeal. When the public was not widely appreciative of his talent, he believed himself born out of time and out of place. His mother was British and he used to say he was homesick for England even though he'd never been there. He felt like he should have been a part of the 1960s British Invasion. His fantasy was for the past, but history proved him ahead of his time.

Chilton had known Chris Bell while growing up in Memphis, seen him playing parties since they were in their early teens. They'd worked together briefly in an early band, the Jinx, named in tribute to the Kinks. Chilton remembers, "There was lots of people who were going to parties and people who were having parties. It was a place for young bands to play in front of people. 'Hold It' was a real popular song when we were kids, an instrumental. The Mar-Keys, Willie Mitchell, a bunch of bands recorded it. It's the classic Memphis break song." At his one guitar lesson, Alex asked Sid Manker, a friend of his father's and the guitarist who'd cowritten "Raunchy" with Bill Justis, to teach him "Hold It." "He knew it, and he taught me the swankiest version. There was stuff in there I didn't use until twenty years later." During Chilton's tenure with the Box Tops, Bell had remained in Memphis, playing in bands and gravitating toward Ardent, which had moved from Granny's sewing room to National Street in 1967.

"John Fry had this studio, Terry Manning was working for him, Chris was a hanger-on over there and I became one too," says Tom Eubanks, who quit the band that became Big Star. Eubanks, Bell, and future Big Star rhythm section Jody Stephens and Andy Hummel called themselves Rock City, capitalizing on the tourist attraction in east Tennessee that advertised on the roofs of barns: SEE ROCK CITY. "It was a good scene. When the studio wasn't in use, Fry would let us cut stuff there. That's the way Stax came up with their good stuff, they'd take people off the street and do spec sessions until they got something. We practiced a lot, played every now and then, mostly for rich folks. Everyone else around town was playing soul music, we were doing stuff from *Tommy*, 'Into the Fire' by Deep Purple. I remember we had this job in Ripley, Tennessee, and we were doing 'Shapes of Things' by the Yardbirds, Chris was playing a semi–hollow body guitar, got down on his knees in front of the amp and started getting all this feedback, it sounded like an airplane going over. These country boys stood there with their mouths open, What is this sonuvabitch doing? Another time, we got booked into this building where Sonny and Cher were also playing, in a different room. Somehow, our gig was for a group of American veterans, all these old people. This mafia guy was running the club, and we were drowning out Sonny and Cher, so he started punching our roadie, telling us to turn it down. These old army jerks hated us, they'd come up front and curse us, razz us, so Chris would run over and turn it back up. Here comes the mafia guy beating up the roadie again. But that was Chris too: If somebody insulted him, he'd pour it on."

Drummer Richard Rosebrough played in several bands with Bell and remembers being introduced to Jimi Hendrix records by him. Bell brought Rosebrough to Ardent, and he too became a member of Uncle John's gang. "In 1969, John Fry got sick of us just hanging around there and he decided to teach us to engineer," remembers Rosebrough. "It was me, Christopher Bell, John King, who ran publicity for Ardent, Charlie Hull, who had recorded at the old studio with the Shades, and a few others. Classes were free and held at the studio at eight A.M. Fry would stand in front of a blackboard and teach us. The rule was you could show up drunk, and you could get drunk with the teacher after class, but you had to show up. I like to say that I've got three mentors: John Fry taught me how to record, Jim Dickinson taught me when to record, and Sam Phillips taught me how to make it interesting."

Chilton had already established a working relationship with Ardent, and during a visit to Memphis from Manhattan he encountered Chris Bell at the studio. Impressed with the material Bell was working on, Chilton shared some of his recent efforts. There was talk of forming a folk duo, but Bell was not interested in moving to Manhattan. Realizing the promise of their collaboration, Chilton returned to Memphis. Bell's Beatle fantasy was now complete with this likeness of the Lennon-McCartney partnership. Fry was their George Martin. "We didn't think about doing live gigs," says Chilton. "We thought we were the Beatles and weren't playing live anymore."

Eubanks remembers getting a call from Bell when Big Star's debut was being finished. They had recorded "My Life Is Right," which he'd written with Bell. "Chris asked me if I would let him take my name off the song and put Alex's on, because he wanted to have them all read 'Bell, Chilton' like 'Lennon, McCartney.'" Eubanks's name remains.

Rosebrough, in the meantime, had begun to engineer in earnest. His recording of the Memphis group Alamo, for whom he also drummed, earned them a deal with Atlantic Records. Ardent hired him full-time as an engineer; his next project was the Moloch album. "I was feeling big, an Atlantic recording artist," says Rosebrough, "and when Chris and Alex asked me to play drums for their band, I turned them down. I'd walk into Ardent and I'd see them recording, and I kind of thought they were a kid band. But there was so much energy in the studio when they were around. They were having kid spats, smashing guitars, passing joints when Fry wasn't looking." The Ardent label was blossoming with the infusion of talent. The studio crew regularly marched across the street to the Sweden Kreme for hamburgers and milkshakes, cooling off at a picnic table and dreaming up schemes like traveling in a Lockheed jet. While strumming guitars on Ardent's front stoop, staring at the milkshake palace across the street, Chilton and Bell discussed their group's name. Sweden Kreme didn't have a ring to it, but the supermarket next to it did, so they copped the grocery chain's moniker: Big Star.

Chilton's contemporary view of Big Star is self-deprecating. He's a quarter of a century older now, more worldly and sophisticated, an active artist hounded by past achievements. "The first couple of tunes I wrote in the Box Tops were very simple and very bluesy and very honest. That was easy. It seems like the first song a lot of people write is a good song. But then the more I learned about music and that kind of stuff, the broader the field became, and the more room for error also. So I was really groping around about songwriting and sometimes succeeding. Only about 1975 did I really became self-confident about my abilities, which coincides with the time when I began to write far fewer pieces of music.

"Most of the Big Star stuff was searching for how to get through two verses without saying anything really stupid. Only a few songs really succeeded at that for me. I think 'In the Street' is maybe the best song that I wrote on the first two albums. There are some other good ones. 'Thirteen' is a pretty fair song, but I think the performance on the record is bad. The singing is the wrong approach, but at that time I didn't really know how to make the vocal sounds in the studio that I wanted. 'When My Baby's Beside Me' is a good song. 'O My Soul' is almost a good song, but it was written by a committee, and it's not really about anything. I like the Big Star records okay. There's a lot of nice guitar playing on them, some nice writing and some melodies, and the production's really good. But it's not like I sit around and think those are a phenomenal achievement in recording history. In terms of how they sound, maybe they are. We were doing things in 1971, 1972, and 1973 that sound really good even now. But that kind of guitar playing is something that's there on a guitar neck, and anybody who reaches a certain level of ability is going to play that same stuff anyway."

The Big Star albums have endured. Though technology has changed as much as the global map, these albums continue to reach people. Their immaculate audio quality is largely a testament to John Fry and Chris Bell, who engineered the recordings. But the fact that people still reverberate to the songs is due to the songwriting of Chilton and Bell, and the meaning they convey through their performances. With Fry's meticulous clarity, their sophisticated arrangements and gentle harmonies become gripping, penetrating. Though they are ostensibly a pop band, there's an underlying menace to Big Star's work. They meld the winsome with the twisted. After the soothing tones of "Thirteen" place us like a baby at the doorstep of the next song, we are met by the punch and kick of the electric guitar that opens "Don't Lie to Me," the band's hardest rocker. The song sounds like a domestic quarrel. In the juxtaposition of these two tracks lies Big Star's soul.

"In the sixties, Dan Penn sheltered Alex, kept him from the funkiness," says Randall Lyon. "Then in the seventies, when I met him, he was doing that Big Star stuff and he was absolutely great. I met him through his old man. His father used to play the piano with Bill [Eggleston]. I started going to the Big Star sessions, the power pop stuff with Chris Bell, and it was almost over my head. It was very deep shit. I didn't really know about power pop, had no idea what it was for. It sounded right, but it was way mainstream compared to Sleepy John Estes."

Big Star's 1972 debut (shortly before Ardent cofounder Fred Smith debuted Federal Express) was also the first release on the reactivated Ardent label. Titled *#1 Record*, it confirms the lofty ambitions surrounding the group. Because Ardent was so intertwined with Stax, a distribution deal was easy. By the early seventies, however, Stax was being bought and sold like a Monopoly board property. A month after *#1 Record* was released, Stax entered into a distribution deal with Columbia Records, and Big Star's debut got lost in the shuffle; too much business going on for either company to tend to the actual albums. John King, heading up Ardent's publicity office, was so well organized that Stax was using him for many of their projects. The rave reviews the album received are evidence of his good work. They made the sting from its total unavailability all the sharper. Everyone had given their best effort on this first outing, and they were beaten by an industry gaffe.

David Bell, in his liner notes to *I Am the Cosmos*, the 1992 collection of his brother's work, remembers, "[In 1972] everything seemed to be falling apart with the band, and my brother had apparently tried to do himself in. . . . He was in terrible pain, feeling that he had put forth his best effort . . . only to see his efforts lost in a distribution deal with a record company whose claim to fame had been a score of black Memphis soul products and who obviously didn't know or care how to distribute a white, Anglo influenced rock group. . . . My brother was near rock bottom."

Bell's sense of self-destruction was clearly in evidence during the mastering of Big Star's first album. He went with John Fry to the session where the master stamper was being cut from the tape. Fry worked with engineer Larry Nix, meticulously riding knobs and dials throughout every song, achieving precise tonal qualities. The process took an entire day. When they were done, Bell watched Nix carve the catalog number into the inner groove. "That's the thing that writes on records?" Bell asked. Bell picked up the tool when Nix was done, observed the sturdiness of its arrowlike tip, then dropped it like a dart headlong onto the master, which it pierced. The entire day's work had to be repeated, a session which Bell was invited not to attend.

At Ardent, the group effort in launching the label and running the studio had become a bit cozy. Many of the integral people had been around since the earliest days, working together to advance the studio from a tenth-grade whim to a nationally respected facility. Rosebrough remembers, "We were all drinking, we're taking downs. I start seeing a psychiatrist. I've got a three o'clock appointment and while I'm waiting, [an Ardent employee] and [another Ardent employee] come out from separate doctors. When I come out, Chris Bell is seated where I was, waiting to go in. It's a mind fuck. It was crazy. A lot of crazy situations, competition to make the record company go, people vying for control."

When Bell quit Big Star, he was apparently suffering from paranoia, delusions, and was actually seeing things. Chilton, Stephens, and Hummel threw in the towel as well. But Ardent's publicist John King had conceived of a rock writer's convention to introduce and promote the Ardent label. He had journalists and dealmakers flying in from all over the country, and Big Star agreed to help him out by performing as a trio without Bell. A review of the performance reveals, "They start their set . . . with 'Feel.' And guess what? You could dance to it! By the fourth number the dance floor was packed, and it stayed that way the rest of the evening." Aha! From the days of his preteen parties on through recent shows performed at tiny Memphis clubs, Chilton puts on a great show when the crowd is dancing. It's the shadow of the Plantation Inn, the entertainer entertaining.

"That convention was John King at his finest," says Rosebrough. "He was gaining control at record stations all over the country, and he planned this big show to promote Ardent Records. By then we'd probably released Cargoe's album and were working on a few other acts. So he reserves Lafayette's Music Room, this hip club at Madison and Cooper. [There's that corner again.] The Big Star set was really chaotic, with guitars feeding back, out of tune, lots of people drunk. Big Star was doing T. Rex songs like 'Baby Strange' and 'Jeepster' as well as their own stuff. When they finished their set, Alex put his guitar down and it started feeding back a little. He walked off stage and was gone. Fry and I were in the sound booth and he turned to me and he says, 'Richard, you know the last thing that a captain does on a sinking ship?' I said, 'What John?' He said, 'He sets his ship for normal operation and then he jumps off.' I reach down and I turn all the microphones back on and adjust this one so that it just starts feeding back. John said, 'It's time to leave.' We walked out of the booth, down the steps, all the way around to the back, and as we were walking down the back hall the whole P.A. was really feeding back big-time. John turns to me and he says, 'I love doing this more than anything.' We walked out of there, got in his car, and left."

The reaction to Big Star's set was so overwhelming that the band was convinced to record a second album. The title, *Radio City,* was once again full of romantic expectation. And the music, again, was completely deserving. For album art, Chilton turned to his lifelong friend Bill Eggleston. "I suggested a picture that was radical at the time," says Eggleston, "that picture of a red ceiling. But I thought that picture would look good anywhere. It was modern art, and I thought it was a good idea for a record cover to have a piece of real art on it." Chilton was twenty-three when it was released.

Between Big Star albums, Ardent had moved to the site it continues to occupy, a bigger, more centrally located studio. The corner of Madison and Cooper, a block away, was then being developed as a center for boutiques and nightclubs. Trader Dick's was next to Ardent. Huey's, another hot spot, was a block the other way. "By then, we all had keys," says Rosebrough. "We were going to Ardent at all hours. We could break things and get away with it. Get drunk, take pills, puke on the floor, piss on the wall. Alex and I had become very close then, hanging out all the time, writing and recording together. Three of those songs ended up on *Radio City.* We'd go in at three A.M., just the two of us, recording and experimenting."

When Chilton and Bell parted, they divvied up their material. Though each had contributed to the songs, they agreed on sole proprietorship after the split. So "O My Soul," though "written by committee," bears only Chilton's name; conversely, Chilton's name does not appear on Bell's album. For *Radio City,* Bell also contributed some background vocals and guitar. "The things we did that were unusual, I had nothing to do with," says Fry. "That was Chris and Alex. We had a variety of guitar sounds that played against each other in a kind of pleasing, almost orchestral way. 'September Gurls' used a mandol-guitar that Alex had, a tiny little thing. That real high, piercing guitar you hear is that. We probably featured drums a lot more prominently than it was fashionable to do at the time. And, to the extent that we could, we used a combination of reverb and delay."

Ardent was English in its orientation, subscribing to British studio magazines and mail-ordering records not available in the States. "If they did it in England, our view was that was the right way to do it," says Fry. "Memphis music is peculiar in that it combines so many seemingly contradictory or conflicting elements. You have all this blues and rhythm-and-blues influence, and so much of the recording that we were doing was with various Stax artists, and other people doing similar things. We added an English sensibility to it."

Before the band toured behind the second album, Andy Hummel left the trio; he is today an engineer for General Dynamics. A replacement was enlisted and they drove to the Northeast, where their equipment was promptly stolen. Chilton was the sole guitarist in the band, now confident in his technique. One of their shows was a radio broadcast on a Long Island station, the bootlegged tape of which circulated widely for many years before being properly released by Rykodisc in 1992. In an interview with the disc jockey, Chilton describes "a hard life, out on the road and all, driving around in station wagons. It just wasn't any fun." The band's defiant attitude toward their contemporaries was also manifested in the interview; topping the charts then were Alvin Lee and Ten Years After, Golden Earring, the Mahavishnu Orchestra; the music was self-indulgent progressive rock—songs that were too long, too meaningless, and too boring. Likening the crisp and clean guitar sounds of Big Star to the Byrds and the Beatles, the WLIR disc jockey asked Chilton if they were "anachronistic."

No, Mr. Deejay, they're not from a different time; they're from Memphis, where pop records are not disposable. "Commerciality has always been important to me," Chilton says. "But I don't really approach things from an angle of what's going to get on the radio. I approach things as what I think is appealing. The first time I was in control of the records I was making, the Big Star records, I made them to be commercial. It's so hard for anybody to play what they like in the record business. Big Star was a band playing what we liked to play. It didn't conform to any other corporate crap. After the rhythm and blues and the jazz stuff, the rock and roll that first really captured me was mid-sixties British pop music, and that was all two and a half or three minutes, really appealing songs. So I've aspired to that same format. That's what I like."

CHAPTER THIRTEEN

Stranded in Canton

～✦～

THE 1970S SEEMED A LONG WAY AWAY FROM THE 1960S. EVERYONE WAS a rock star. The music that had earned disdain when the witnesses began playing it was now the soundtrack for a generation. And everyone wanted to be part of it. Musicians who weren't cutting hits in Memphis were cutting demos. Studios and production companies were everywhere. Teenage bands with a riff had no trouble finding a place to record, a place to spend their money. Songwriters who were making demos of their material opened their facilities to the public and found themselves as studio managers. Businessmen were financing sessions with themselves as producers. It was the beginning of modern, corporate rock, when record label offices went from manufacturing and promoting records to controlling artistic direction: The corporate record is now defined before it is even recorded.

The good cheer even spread to the classical musicians. Pop hits have long featured string arrangements, and in the seventies Noel Gilbert, who led the Memphis Symphony's string section, began appearing on records that would make Beethoven roll over. "The first time we used Noel and the symphony's string section," says Dane Sullivan, a staff writer from American who opened his own facility with his wife Gala, "we split the session four ways. Instead of us having to pay the whole session, we paid one-fourth. Four people got records, and the string section got a full session. They could have spent the same amount of time and gotten paid four times the amount, although then it probably wouldn't have happened." The strange bedfellows enjoyed each other.

"You could hum something to the symphony players and they'd work with you," says Gala. "We'd say, 'Can you do something like this?' It was a real

Rogues' gallery. Left to right: Lee Baker, Wayne Jackson's profile and glass, Waylon Jennings, Jim Dickinson, Jerry McGill, John David, Dan Penn. Photo by Randall Lyon.

give-and-take situation. They didn't demand charts, and they really enjoyed it." By then, Ardent had purchased a Mellotron, a keyboard instrument popularized by the Moody Blues which had tape loops of string sounds inside it; it was like a synthesizer for string sections. The union, anticipating the wave of the future, feared that a whole string section would be replaced by a single person. At Ardent, the Mellotron was kept in a locked room because officially it didn't exist.

It was a good time to be a songwriter. Not only were pop stars employing house bands; they were actively seeking outside material to record. The staff writers at American were supposed to have at least one song for every artist who booked a session there. "Every week there was at least one album session," says Dane Sullivan. "Joe Tex, B. J. Thomas, Elvis, Neil Diamond, Petula Clark, Dusty Springfield—every week there was somebody of that caliber." ASCAP came to Memphis to cultivate writers, offering sizable advances.

Memphis was seen as a test market for records. The audience here approximated what the industry perceived as normal, tending toward the fickle. "If you got sales in Memphis, you could get attention, the ripple effect," says Sullivan. "And if you needed to, you could do it by buying all your own records, going across the bridge and throwing them in the Mississippi River. You create a sales figure, it gets reported. You'd make 'breakout' in *Billboard*.

That was happening all over. We had somebody cut a record that we controlled, and we heard that the pressing plant was shipping 40,000 copies. But no royalty statement was forthcoming from said person, who's located in Kansas or somewhere. How are you gonna fuck with them?"

In a 1969 falling-out between Chips Moman and his bean-farming partner Don Crews, the latter left American and bought a studio across town called Onyx. American's house band and the writers remember working in both places. Onyx became a laboratory for engineers from which a few hits emerged. T. G. Shepherd, a 1970s country star, was a promotion man with an office there. Coming downstairs one day he heard someone in the control room asking about a singer to demo a song. Shepherd volunteered, recorded "Devil in the Bottle," and had a new career. The laboratory atmosphere at Onyx was created around the tape vault. Many of the early American hits were stored there. "We'd go in and pull the original eight-tracks on the old hits," Dane explains, "and see if we could remix it the same, see if we could remix it different. It was fascinating. Between that and the activity that was happening up on Chelsea in the main place, sitting in on sessions and mix and remix sessions, there was plenty of opportunity to learn all about making a record." The Onyx spirit has continued, the studio now home to Easley Recording, the city's foremost alternative venue.

The Sam Phillips Recording Service was another place to get a music education. "Before Sam sold Sun," says Randy Haspel, "I'd be hanging out at the studio, Teddy Paige, Knox, Jerry, whoever. We'd be bored, and so we'd go up and check the library. Box after box, everything you could imagine was in that library, and it was all catalogued on a Rolodex. We'd go, Howlin' Wolf, hmm, E-64, and we'd pull out this box of tape that Mr. Phillips had cut during the early 1950s—unreleased master tapes sitting in the Phillips studio—we'd put it on the board, sit there and listen. Ike Turner, Rufus Thomas, all these people. And when Mr. Phillips sold the label, the library went with it."

"I learned a great lesson when I hired Dr. John to play on the Brenda Patterson album I produced," says Dickinson. "I sat down with him and he said, 'What instrument would you like me to play?' I said, 'Well Mac, I kinda thought I wanted you to play piano.' He said, 'Well I could play bass.' I said, 'Yeah, I got Chris Ethridge, Mac.' He said, 'I could play guitar.' I said, 'Yeah, I got Ry Cooder, Mac.' He said, "You want me to play piano? Full piano?' I said, 'Yeah, yeah, full piano, Mac.' He said, 'Well you know, that's my thing.' I said, 'Yeah, that's why I want you to play it. I want you to play full piano and do your thing.' He said, 'Well full piano, that costs twice as much.'" Dickinson laughs uproariously. "I said, 'Right on, Mac, it's fine with me.' After that,

I did it to some teabags who came to Memphis to record Johnny Hallyday, this French Elvis-type. I did the full piano thing, the whole bit.

"Those Johnny Hallyday guys, they learned about cutting a record in Memphis. The first night of their session, I was at Ardent with Alex Chilton, Danny Graflund, and Campbell. They saw Graflund as this bodyguard person, so they thought they could send him out for coffee. Graflund went across the street, got a tray of coffee, filled the cups with Ajax, and took it in there and served it. Before their session was over, they had hired Campbell to do security and they had hired me at double scale to play piano, and it was all basically orchestrated by Graflund. They asked if it was the initiation process. While they were there, they crossed up [a Memphis artist] who was cutting down the hall. He went off on them. He had that producer on the floor at Ardent with this machine gun in his mouth. When he got up, he went out in the parking lot, drove to the airport, and was a star in six weeks. He said, 'Man, I just lived through this, I'm gonna do whatever it takes. I'm through fucking around.'"

Former Mar-Key Packy Axton, no longer encouraged to use Stax, was sharing his healthy cynicism with those around Ardent. He would put together a band in the studio, hum a riff, and create an instrumental in as much time as it took to arrange it. In an afternoon, he could do four or more songs, labeling them according to sound, like "medium tempo garbage" or "fast trash." On one, he insisted on an eight-beat break early in the song, telling the band he'd fill it later. Coming off a bender, he was rooting through tapes for something to sell, and had the engineer put that one on while he went to the vocal booth to fill the hole. A break is common on instrumental records; "Last Night" has one. Packy is dead now and there is no way to know what his intention was, but when the time came for him to say whatever he wanted, Packy took a breath, opened his mouth, and vomited. Puked all over the place, and recorded it perfectly on tape. He named the song "Hung Over" and called the band the Martinis.

Near records. Vanity records. Custom records. With so many hits, it seemed so easy. In Nashville, they call naive, money-spending lesser talents "Tex Nobodies." "That name kind of irks me," says Roland Janes, the veteran from Sun, "because everybody is somebody. Without those people, there wouldn't be any music business. They're the bread and butter, what keeps the industry going while you search for hits. A bunch of smaller studios couldn't survive without them. Those people are spending their good, hard-earned money and you're taking that money, so you have an obligation to give them the utmost respect and do the best job you can. I don't have a name for that except 'Ladies and Gentlemen.' I chuckle sometimes like everybody else, but deep down inside I have only respect."

Others no doubt share the respect, but their chuckling is louder. In a boom situation like Memphis's through the 1960s and into the 1970s, the numbers of these wanna-be records increased exponentially. The grist for such a mill is people way on the outside, or on the periphery of the inside of the business, who do not see that the factors involved in making a hit are so multifarious. With so many aspects under so many different domains, with such a large element of chance, that talent, Q quotient, "it"—whatever you call the quality that makes a record special—that quality alone does not guarantee success. As the radio constantly reminds us, talent is not even a necessary ingredient. It's a hustler's business. Any record could be the next big hit. Conversely, the next big hype could be the next big flop. Janes sums up his point: "There's a lot more money spent in the music business than is made in it. You take away that base, and there would be no music business."

Sam Phillips's original storefront business catered to such a clientele. It allowed him to scout talent, and brought us Elvis Presley. Another producer in Memphis named Red Matthews contracted himself out to singers, recording them in ballrooms of hotels with radio station gear. Roland Janes played for Matthews on a session for one Brother Dave Gardner, resulting in "White Silver Sands," one of Memphis's first million-selling records.

One Memphis entrepreneur devoted his career to near records, establishing several labels and releasing some of the worst records of all time—without a trace of irony. The philosophy of Style Wooten was that he was being asked—paid—to record an act, not to determine how worthy or talented they were. His Pretty Girl series was for female singers and featured a photo of the vocalist near her name on the label. Designer was his gospel label; with the built-in audience at their church, gospel acts made steady clients. Camara, Burch-lo, and a variety of other names—Style Wooten was there to suit your every recording need. He worked regularly at Sonic, where he and Roland could cut six gospel acts in a weekend, four songs on each, from which Wooten could pick A- and B-sides. "Style never tried to cut hit records," says Janes. "He just cut custom records for people that wanted records. For a fee he would see it through from start to finish."

Lee Baker's first studio experience was an encounter with both Style Wooten and Roland Janes. "The Blazers had an original song called 'Hard to Please,'" Baker recalls, a hint of a grin creeping onto his face as the memory comes back to him. "We cut 'Bo Diddley' on the other side. Style was gonna take it to Nashville. God knows where it went. I just remember looking at

Style and going, Man! I didn't know a lot about records and stuff like that but
I knew that he wasn't it. I knew that Roland was cool and Roland and I got
along. The thing about Style, we knew he was bogus—he radiated that he was
bogus—but he used Roland and we knew that's where Travis Wammack was.
So we thought we had a shot."

Near records were expedited by the proximity of Buster Williams's pressing plants. After spending thirteen dollars at Sonic, for another hundred or so
you could get five hundred records pressed by Williams, then take them across
town to his Music Sales Record Distributor, and they might pick up a couple
hundred for jukeboxes, radio stations, and one-stops. "It was a great thing
back then," says Janes. "Everybody worked together and it was conducive to
people getting a break."

All the studios—Sun, Stax, Hi, Fame, Ardent, American—cut the near
records alongside the real ones. "Everybody wants to be in show business,"
says Jim Dickinson. "These guys would hang around Chips or somebody and
they'd see a session and they'd wanna do it. Especially when they couldn't
figure out what anybody was doing. Parks Matthews, I remember cutting his
first session. He'd been hanging out over at Chips's. He came in the door of
Ardent on National and he had these two skaggy-looking broads with him,
two ice chest coolers, and this big orange plastic bag like a trash bag. And he
says to me, 'Jimmy! Jimmy! I'm all ready to cut a session. I got the girls—I got
the liquor—I got the beer—' and he held up the orange package and he says,
'And I got the pills!' He figured that was all he needed."

The Fame studio in nearby Muscle Shoals was achieving such success with
artists like Wilson Pickett, Aretha Franklin, and Clarence Carter that Rick
Hall, who ran the place, opened an eight-track facility in an old grocery store
in South Memphis. A disc jockey from Tupelo, Sonny Limbo, was sent to run
the place. (Limbo discovered country superstars Alabama and also was listed
as cowriter on the schmaltzy hit "Key Largo.") "Everybody was trying to
build a studio situation where they could work on a larger scale than just
booking time on an hourly basis," says Dane Sullivan. "Fame in Memphis was
working on a variety of stuff, a lot of it a departure from what they were doing
in Muscle Shoals. Jerry Lee Lewis and Tarp Tarrant were cutting there,
Bowlegs Miller, even Piano Red." Liza Minnelli came to Memphis and spent
time at Fame, but no recording was made. "There was a woman who cut one
of our songs who had these Vegas people as her manager," says Dane Sullivan.
"Their guy got into some controversy with someone behind them driving
with his bright lights on. The manager got out, told the driver to fuck off, and
tried to slug him while the window was down. The driver rolled the car win-

dow up on his arm and takes off, dropping the window as they curve in front of a semi. The manager was a puddle of blood on the road after that. A lot of projects at Fame seemed to end that way."

The music writer at one of Memphis's daily papers had a bet with Sonny Limbo. The producer claimed he could cut a hit record on the worst singer the writer could find. "Vicky L.?" says Dane Sullivan, his voice rising in a question mark.

" 'Knock Three Times' and 'Muleskinner Blues' were her favorite," answers Gala.

"She had Elvis ducktails and a fifty-seven Chevy."

"What they did was really mean. Vicky was working successfully at some club near the airport when [the journalist] found her," continues Gala. "She had written a couple songs and her parents came with her to the studio. The Chivas Regal was flowing."

"Sonny Limbo literally fell out of his chair, onto the console, laughing hysterically," says Dane. "She's out there singing, thinking she's recording a serious session, and they're cutting in on the talkback, 'Sing it whorey, bitch. Sing it like a slut.' And her parents are back there saying, 'You've got to record her on "All I Want for Christmas" and "Jesus Loves Me." ' "

"I resented the exploitation aspect of the music business very deeply for a long time," says Dickinson, "until I started to understand it. A couple years after I'd worked for Jerry Wexler at Atlantic in 1970, he came to Memphis for some event, and we ended up at this party, quite a party. Wexler, Sam Phillips, Betty Hayes—who'd booked bands with Ray Brown—my wife and I and Stanley Booth. Wexler had just produced an Aretha Franklin gospel record, and he was real proud of it. He had also, not that recently, done a Tony Joe White record. Well, after dinner everybody was kinda laid-back and Wexler kept trying to play this Aretha Franklin record, but every time he'd start it, Sam would take it off and put on the Tony Joe White record. Sam kept playing the same cut over and over, 'Got a Thing About Ya, Baby,' which was a hit. And finally Wexler says, 'Sam! Baby! You know, I'm really hurt that you're not listening to my Aretha record, baby!' Jerry plays it again and so one more time Sam gets up and takes the record off, puts on 'Thing About Ya, Baby' and says, 'Goddamn, Jerry, that's so good, it don't sound paid for.'

"I thought, By God, that's it. They can hear the difference. To somebody at the level of Sam Phillips and Jerry Wexler, that's what they get off on. Not paying for it! I believe that during the recording process, for a successful record, everybody's got to get off on something. Compromise is the nature of the beast. But everybody, whoever he is in the project, has got to get off on something. I had always taken it real personally when they didn't pay me. I'd say, Oh, the bastards didn't pay me again. Now I understand this sense of larceny as an element of production."

One Memphis music entrepreneur, Eddie Bond, had been angling for a break since he'd established himself as a rockabilly artist with the classic "Rockin' Daddy." Being on a label wasn't enough for Eddie, who has created several recording companies of his own. In his search for the right "in" he has also been a disc jockey, owned radio stations, and hosted his own TV hokum variety show, appealing to an audience of mouth breathers—a friend to the people who needed a friend.

Then Eddie Bond discovered Buford Pusser. The *Walking Tall* sheriff had a natural flair for the dramatic; before becoming a lawman, he'd been a professional wrestler. His battle against evil in McNairy Country (about two hours from Memphis) resulted in great injury on both sides: It took the lives of Buford's wife, several of his friends, and finally his own—but not before he lived to see his life story become such a hit film that a sequel was made. Pusser himself was being considered for the lead role in part three when he was killed. "Eddie introduced Buford to the world, did TV shows about him, had this awful album of tribute songs, just wretched shit," remembers Dickinson. "I'll never forget seeing them pull into that alley at the old Sounds of Memphis studio, the blue lights and the sirens going off in what looked like a pimpmobile. It wasn't at all like *Walking Tall*. Buford was this big Frankenstein motherfucker. All fucked up down one side of his face. Eddie thought he was made, and everybody told him, Eddie they won't let you keep it, somebody's going to take it away. Sure enough, Bing Crosby Productions made the films. That was back when, in Memphis, if you had a crooked disc jockey, seriously now, a crooked disc jockey, a drunken brain surgeon, and a used car salesman, you were making a record. Those were the elements you needed to record somebody's girlfriend singing some dogshit song and everybody pay their rent."

As the seventies continued, so did the Dream Carnivals, though their spirit changed. Instead of a room full of people attempting a unified out-of-body experience, it became more selfish. Blame it on the Quaaludes. At the 1975 St. Valentine's Day Massacre, held at an old movie theater a block from the first Dream Carnival, it was obvious something had changed. "That was a horrible night," says Baker. "The vibes were real fucked up. That was during the days when people were taking a lot of downs and drinking a lot. This 151-proof rum was real popular that night, and people were just fu-ucked u-up. There's a picture of Graflund and Campbell on the stage, and we're playing and they're talking and Campbell looks like a fucking beast."

Graflund recalls that Campbell had, indeed, been a fucking beast that night. "Campbell came with his girlfriend and a couple more of his buddies, and they were sitting out in the audience. Right behind them was Dewitt Jordan, a respected black painter. Dewitt said something to Campbell's girlfriend, something like, 'Hi.' And that was just the end of that guy. Campbell beat him up and threw him out in the street. And I think Dewitt came back in and Campbell beat him and tossed him out again."

Even stoic, predictable, beautiful, traditional folk music was getting fucked up in 1970s Memphis. An urban juke joint for artists called the Procapé Gardens opened in Midtown in 1974. Located next to the city's most prominent gay bar (where the floor show was always on when the folk artists were on break), Procapé was an acoustic nightclub that was the inverse of the early coffeehouses, exploring instead of shunning the side of folk music that was wild and unrestrained. Serving hard liquor no doubt helped.

Never having adapted to the electric guitar, Sid Selvidge remained the pre-eminent folkster. For the club's three-year existence, he played Monday through Wednesday nights. "It was great because the only people out on those nights are the ones who want to be there," Selvidge says. Though he usually began each evening alone onstage, rarely did he end that way. Often—regularly—there were too many guitars to fill the stage, so musicians played along from their seats in the audience. "We had a big Bacchanalian time. Everybody would come and sit in, it was quite a scene. Horace Hull, who I'd begun playing in Memphis with a decade earlier, Lee Baker, Alex Chilton was hanging out there. And you could do anything ridiculous that you wanted and nobody would pull your plug."

His last sentence is a definition of the eternal spirit of Memphis music. At Procapé, Memphis photographer Dan Zarnstorff remembers watching Eggleston "try to jump up and click his heels twice. He'd throw his legs straight out, horizontal to the floor, and fall flat on the terra-cotta tile. He bounced himself three times before somebody finally stopped him. You could always go to Procapé and know you were going to see some good friends." Marcia Hare was then hanging out with a wealthy junkie who was trying to die. "Larry would take me to the Procapé when Sid was playing and buy me dinner. It was a folkie scene but I would get up in front of Sid and dance, upstaging him. Larry loved for me to sit beside him and toss beer mugs into the middle of the floor and break 'em. I'd do that every night and it was so much fun." When Larry returned to jail, where he successfully overdosed, Marcia went to the

Sid Selvidge gig at Procapé Gardens. Left to right: Gimmer Nicholson, Larry Davis, Alex Chilton, Horace Hull (back to camera), Sid Selvidge, Lee Baker. Photo by Dan Zarnstorff.

club on her own. "I went in there by myself and started breaking beer mugs and they called the police on me. I said, 'What's the deal, I've been doing this for months.' It turned out that Larry had been paying somebody a hundred bucks before I'd start throwing the glass and this time he wasn't there. Instead of going to jail, I had to agree I would never come back in there. That's when I got my first job in Memphis dancing topless. If I was going to be barred from the Procapé, I might as well be able to go somewhere."

Selvidge remembers Chilton using the Procapé to work though an artistic transition. "Alex was at a juncture," he says. "He'd had a real bad experience with the Big Star stuff and was trying to distance himself from his acceptable past, I felt, because what he would do at the Procapé would chase people off. They didn't understand it. His whole concept was, If I were a thirteen-year-old right now and I were just learning my instrument, how would I play guitar? People don't realize what an accomplished guitar player Alex is, his versatility. He's a consummate guitarist. So from that level of sophistication, he was trying to play without knowing all that he knows. He was trying to play note for note what somebody who doesn't play the guitar would play like. That's a pretty convoluted concept, but that was his idea. And it fits per-

fectly into rock and roll. This was popular music to him, from where he came
at it and got his hits in the first place."

The nights at the Procapé contributed to Chilton's album *Like Flies on
Sherbert* and, before that, to Selvidge's *Cold of the Morning*. Both were released
on Selvidge's Peabody Records. That label was begun by a patron of the Procapé, and Selvidge's album was to be the first release. After the recording and
pressing, but before the release, the patron pulled out of the record business.
"I was handed several thousand of my own records, and that's basically how
Peabody records began."

Cold of the Morning, released in 1976, captures Selvidge's voice in its pristine
glory, the finest silk. It's also a good taste of Memphis in the mid-1970s: It's a
folk album and Memphis was a folk town—the legacy of the blues players prevailed. But it's folk with a glass-throwing edge, the abandon of rocking de-
mons playing beautifully and unrestrained; Jim Dickinson produced. Much of
the album is simply Sid's voice and guitar—"Boll Weevil" is an a cappella field
holler. He proudly interprets George M. Cohan alongside Furry Lewis. On
the two songs that feature the acoustic version of Mud Boy (plus tuba), one
can almost see the players in the studio, nodding to each other, knowing when
to lay out and when to come in. Their work is like an oriental carpet with secret messages stitched into the weave.

Selvidge's earlier LP, a 1970 release on the Stax subsidiary Enterprise, does
not fare so well. *Portrait* catches him in fine voice, but the day it is reissued on
CD, we must question the industry's sanity. Don Nix produced it at Ardent,
and in his defense, it was a very purple period in music, tending toward overproduction. "Children's Suite" epitomizes the sappy, overblown production;
the strings are so thick, Lawrence Welk would have hanged himself. The
couple of songs unencumbered by the cotton candy hold up well, especially
"Amelia Earhart," which is practically the artist unadulterated. "I'm not
ashamed of this album," Selvidge says. "I did my part, I sung these as demos,
and I was young and hot to get on vinyl and somebody walked in with a deal.
I'm still glad it didn't hit big because then I'd be stuck with this type stuff the
rest of my life."

Selvidge has continued to play clubs regularly, garnering rave reviews in
the *New York Times* for his 1977 dates at Tramps; in 1992 he played Carnegie
Hall. He has released two more albums on his own Peabody Records, and in
1993 he released *Twice Told Tales* for the Elektra/Nonesuch American Explorer
series. If you were going to buy just one Selvidge album, hunt for 1982's *Waiting for a Train*, and play the title cut over and over. Simply the way the track
builds from solo artist to the whole band is worth hearing, but you also get a

taste of Selvidge's falsetto howl, Baker's insane slide guitar, and Dickinson's piano beating. The album is less folk-oriented than *Cold of the Morning*; the backing band is essentially an augmented Mud Boy, with Selvidge taking all the leads and Jim Spake blowing some mean saxophone. On "Swanee River Rock," Jim Lancaster plays the rockingest tuba solo I've ever heard north of New Orleans. Selvidge's spare rendering of Fred McDowell's "Trimmed and Burning" will satisfy anyone's folk jones.

The disappointing part of seeing a human being bite the head off a live chicken is the ease with which the chicken's neck disengages from its body. Geeks don't so much "bite" the head off as, with the chicken's head in their mouth, they pull the head and neck loose, kind of like sucking your thumb but yanking it all the way off.

This I learned while watching *Stranded in Canton*, a cinema verité document of Memphis made by Bill Eggleston while the Procapé scene was going strong, while Campbell Kensinger was still alive, when video cameras were decades away from being common. Eggleston purchased one of the earliest Porta-Paks made by Sony. Using his knowledge of electronics and photography, he modified the instrument, enhancing the image clarity, crispness, and value. He wanted to document the moving world around him in the same way he'd approached stills.

Stranded in Canton is the name Eggleston has given the footage he shot during the mid-1970s in Memphis, New Orleans, and the Delta between. A geek grudge match on the street in New Orleans is one of the least exciting events he recorded. "We've got our geek here, and we'll put him against your geek," a not quite sane-looking man announces to the small but accumulating crowd. How the show began is not clear, whether the camera stumbled upon it or whether the show is for the camera's benefit. Once headless, the chicken continues flapping its wings and the first geek smiles a feathery grin. Someone in the crowd yells "Geek power," and the second geek steps forward. He doesn't look cocky or nervous or any different from most of the people gathered around him. He strokes the chicken's beak, calming it, and repeats the act just seen. Somehow his show is better. He gets more applause, and Eggleston brings the camera from the front of the crowd around to the side, up close to geek number two. He removes the soup stock from his mouth, and now the geek is glowing, aware he's the winner. When the camera is upon him, he too smiles, chicken cartilage limp on his lip.

Stranded in Canton is a document of the spirit of Memphis, or more precisely, of Midtown Memphis, 1970s. Using natural light (and later infrared tubes), Eggleston shot unobtrusively in bars, backhouses, fields, cars—day and night. "The electricity generated in a room with Campbell and Eggleston videotaping was amazing," says Mary Lindsay Dickinson. "The maestro at work with what may have been the world's first infrared handicam! People would do absolutely anything to be in the movie." Those few who might have been constrained by the camera assumed it was too dark, or that there was no tape in the camera, or that Eggleston was just looped and playing around. "My idea was to shoot whatever was out there," Eggleston says. "The second I saw the first reel—I believe it was when we were in New Orleans and went back to the Royal Orleans and piped it through a TV and it was beautiful—I was very happy. I knew that it was perfect. I was looking forward to more of it and we just kept doing it."

Eggleston is as dashing a man as God has put on this earth. Always trim and crisply dressed, he is quietly acute. Soft-spoken, the precision in his manner, his expression, and thoughts belies charges that his photographs are mere snapshots. To discuss Memphis, we left the city for an antebellum home he is rehabilitating in northern Mississippi. The appreciation and attention to detail he devotes to the refurbishing of this prized home is the same he gives to his photographs and to his subjects in *Canton*. None is more freaky or more precious; all are prized. "*Stranded in Canton* works because of the way the whole takes came off, unedited," he says. "The way it looked, the way it was paced and things moved. The meter to it. It was as if we were looking at something that had been shot fifty times and this was the best take. And always these were the only takes. It was just that good."

"We knew at the time it was really special," says Randall Lyon, who was Eggleston's assistant on many of the shoots. Lyon had worked in television and understood lighting; he became Professor Reflecto, holding the single light employed when a situation demanded it. Usually, however, Lyon was on the other side of the camera, the subject, his innate theatricality and brilliant spontaneity a driving force of the piece. "We tried to do as best as we could. We knew our technical limits and we tried as much as we could to really kick out the jams."

They succeeded. As the various scenes unfold, whether it's Eggleston's underage black chauffeur sitting on Stanley Booth's lap and chewing bubble gum, a drag queen in New Orleans draping himself in toilet paper to perform for the camera in a tiny bar, or a tanked veterinarian in a seersucker suit (Tony the Tiger looking over his shoulder from a box of Frosted Flakes) doubting a statement made by Campbell Kensinger (to which Campbell responds, "I'm heavier than I am tall"), the viewer is quickly and stealthily brought into this other world.

In one scene, the camera follows Lyon into Jim Dickinson's backhouse studio, where assorted people are sitting around: Dickinson and Mary Lindsay; Jerry McGill, who had recorded for Sun and sang with bands around the time of the Regents; Jim Lancaster, who often accompanied Mud Boy on bass and rock and roll tuba; his wife Jill; Marcia Hare, and a few other people. Some of the musicians are jamming—Dickinson is playing an electric guitar, Lancaster is at the piano. McGill, his gaunt and tapered face resembling a cobra's, takes hold of an acoustic guitar and performs a song. When he's done, Lyon begins spouting a soliloquy, holding a bottle of champagne in his hand. The camera surveys the room, but his words are clear. "This is a dis-ass-trous period in our time. We got to respond to what's going ahn or else we got to hang it up with kinder-goddamn-garten." Dickinson accompanies with apocalyptic feedback from his guitar, and it all becomes too claustrophobic for McGill. The camera whips around at the sound of gunfire—McGill has drawn and fired his pistol. He smashes Lyon's bottle with the barrel and then puts the gun against Lyon's head. The voices that squealed when the bullets caught them off guard have suddenly stilled. The guitar continues, a soundtrack like the Wild West saloon player who knows it's best never to stop. The camera remains focused on the gun, the gun always, because whoever may say whatever, the subject in that room is the gun.

"I'm gonna whip you with this gun barrel," says McGill, whose eyes shine like BB's. "Be nice. Be real nice." Lyon is doubled at the waist, his head, his life, in McGill's hands. Then McGill—he is no longer McGill, he is Pancho Villa, he is Jesse James, he is completely and totally Lash LaRue—turns to the camera, sees that it's pointed right at him (he's still holding the gun), and he says, for the camera's benefit, "I don't care nothing about that." He'll do it for the world to see! In an instant, the pistol is waved, smashing the bottle in Randall's hand, and the following instant, smashing the light. The guitar feedback stops with the sudden darkness and the scene, take one, the only take, is over.

After several years, Eggleston began putting together a similar outfit to shoot in color. The equipment proved unsuited, too heavy to allow the necessary portability. *Canton* came to a natural close. "The piece was finished," he says. "It was like a movie, about ninety minutes, and it doesn't need to be any shorter or any longer or lack or need anything. It became apparent that the material was suited for black and white and when I realized what I had, the piece was done." Shortly thereafter, he was asked to be artist in residence at Harvard University. "I showed *Canton* for a solid year," he says. "Later, I showed it at Yale. The audiences seemed very moved. I see a lot of those people now and they always bring it up. I think some people remarked at the time, 'Are these people acting out something you told them to do?' And I would explain, 'No, I'm just recording them, whatever they're doing. I didn't tell them to do this.'"

Canton, friends, life in Memphis, Tennessee.

While still working on the project, Eggleston showed up one night at the Sam Phillips Recording Service. This was 1974, and the divergent forces in Memphis music came together that night at the post-Elvis studio built by the master around the corner from Sun. It was a session for Jerry McGill, whose Topcoats were the South Memphis hoods that East Memphis mamas were too scared to hire in the late 1950s. McGill's one released recording had been for Phillips some twenty-five years earlier. Jim Dickinson was producing the session, using demo money he'd wrangled from Warner Brothers. Those present included Danny Graflund, Campbell Kensinger, Marcia Hare, and another of the Mud Boy dancers. Impresario Jim Blake was there, as was writer Stanley Booth. Knox Phillips, Sam's elder son, was engineering the session.

Campbell sat in the control room drinking Wild Turkey from a fifth, bouncing the bottom of the glass bottle on the floor as he listened to other people tell stories. "You ever think of 'the Law' as a whole fucking table?" Campbell asked. And he picked up a coffee table, put the corner in his mouth, tried to bite it off.

Stanley Booth, who was practiced in the martial arts, broke the wall with a double karate elbow attack. Campbell, chuckling, passed him the Wild Turkey. Jim Blake remembers Campbell saying, "These guys in my gang walk around with these guns and knives and shit and they think they're tough. I'll show you tough," and Campbell whipped his noonchuks from his back pocket and started hitting himself on the left side of the head. "About twenty times," says Blake, "stuff that would have not only disabled me or you but would have given us permanent brain damage. And he said, 'Now that's tough.' Hey, nobody could disagree with that."

Knox and Dickinson, who was thinly slicing hog tranquilizer for sustenance, kept their attention on McGill, who was overdubbing the vocal. Knox remembers that he was singing "Desperados Waiting for a Train," but Dickinson believes it was a Civil War song called "With Sabres in Our Hands." In the latter number, there is a line that upset McGill every time, a line at the end of the song in which the southern narrator refers to "the lost cause." Dickinson leaned to Knox to confirm that he'd frisked McGill before the session.

"Yes," said Knox, "I got his gun."

"Gun?" said Dickinson. "Guns!"

At that moment, Eggleston was entering the studio floor with his video camera, and McGill's fuse lit. It was bad enough admitting defeat on audiotape, but to have it chronicled on video was too much. Eggleston crept closer as the song neared its climax. The camera was on top of McGill when he said the scurrilous words. The goddamn line sung, the final notes fading, McGill reached into his jacket and stated, "Lost cause my ass," unloading his six-gun into the ceiling. Instinctively, everyone in the control room ducked. When Dickinson looked up, Knox was still at the board.

"What're you doing?" he hissed.

Stated the ace engineer, "The gun needs mo' echo."

With the vocal completed and the place turning into a mad scientist's laboratory, Knox was ready to call it a night. He had to be convinced that they'd never have such vibes again, and to do the song justice they'd need to finish under these unique circumstances. (And here, Knox, take another slice of this.) For the sake of the song, he agreed. Graflund had moved to the couch out front. Campbell was beside him, bouncing the whiskey bottle on the floor. "He was getting cranked," says Graflund. "He was thinking, 'I should be in the limelight, not this guy.' It was getting to that time of the evening. I knew someone was fixing to get it." Graflund's nose, perhaps from the tension in the room, suddenly began to bleed, so he went in the bathroom. Campbell returned to the control room, and a few minutes later, the bathroom door where Danny was washing his face whipped open. It was one of the girls. "Her nose is bleeding like a faucet," Graflund continues. "She opens up this door screaming, sees me lift my head, I've got blood running down my face, and she just screams and runs out the building. I go back in and say, 'What the hell happened to her?'"

"Campbell was very sorry about that," says Marcia Hare, who'd witnessed the event. "He didn't know her and said that in the future we were to introduce him to anyone we didn't want punched."

As those things go, the night ended suddenly. Stanley Booth and Graflund got their background vocals down, the sun was coming up, and so everyone rose to leave. With feelings of satisfaction and wonder, they all walked outside together. Greeting them was a line of motorcycles up and down the street. Campbell's bike had been brought for him and was by the door. Graflund says, "He walked out, cranked his up, they all cranked up, *varooom,* and they rode down Madison in formation with the sunrise." The tapes remain unreleased.

In the Memphis tradition of recording freaks, the great seventies label was

Jim Blake's Barbarian Records, begun in 1974 and struggling along the margins of society through the end of the decade. Blake is a hustler from way back—swapping comic books in grade school—and the principles he learned on the playground trained him for the record business. The Memphis home he rents is overflowing with unidentified but interesting-looking boxes and stacks of papers, magazines, and records. Some might call him a pack rat, but Blake is waiting for the world to catch up with him, to share his ideas of what is valuable. "I feel like the android in *Bladerunner*," he says. "If people could see the world like I do . . ." He shakes his head. It was Blake who was negotiating for the rights to *Conan* eight years before it was made. When he was promoting records, he tried to get his boss to hire Sweet Connie, the South's most famous groupie, because he understood that she could get records played. Blake could as easily have been a Hollywood mogul as a renter in need of dental insurance. The breaks fell against him, a throw of the coin, but he is the stuff of empires.

Down the block from the first Dream Carnival and a year earlier, Blake was the buyer at one of the city's most popular record stores. Utilizing his place at the epicenter, he began an underground newspaper. He went on to open his own store, expanding into head shops and enlarging his publication business. Memphis disc jockeys realized he was riding the crest and hired him to program their shows. His work got several jocks promoted to prime time on both coasts. In the mid-seventies, Blake himself entered the big time. "Jerry Lawler had drawn comics for my newspapers," he says, "and in 1974 I began to manage him full-time. My interest was in Lawler as an artist. I had this background in records and radio and retail, and I understood that the reason the earlier wrassling records had failed was because they were the wrasslers being projected as wrasslers, instead of as recording artists. The wrestlers never saw records beyond something else to sell at the matches."

Blake helped Jerry "the King" Lawler give personality to his career. He'd seen Lawler's fans dip their wrestling programs in his blood. He knew their devotion. "My whole trip with Lawler was to get him and Elvis together. If I'd ever had that picture, it would have been all I'd needed to take Lawler to the next level as a recording artist. I tried to get them in the ring together, wrestling versus karate." For Lawler's first recording, Blake chose "Bad News." He knew Dickinson from a creative writing class at Memphis State; Dickinson did not have to be convinced into merging wrestling and rock and roll. His participation lured a mixed bag of musicians, ranging from the members of Mud Boy to Teenie Hodges, hot with the Al Green records. This recording set the model for all subsequent Barbarian sessions. "Lawler was a bad guy at the time," says

Blake. "We sold twenty thousand of those records at the matches all over the territory and never got a moment of radio play. People were buying 'em for a buck and a quarter and breaking 'em right in front of us. Great! I'll sell you another."

Blake's friendship with Campbell Kensinger kept the biker from attacking the wrestler. "Campbell Kensinger watching Jerry Lawler on television talk about how bad he is? When Campbell knew that he could beat the piss out of him? I told Campbell I needed both of them around because I was trying to get the film rights to *Conan the Barbarian*. Not that I saw Lawler as Conan; I wanted Lawler to be the bad guy. Campbell should have been Conan. The audience would have known he was real."

Blake began to record other wrasslers, and Lawler went on to record a version of "Cadillac Man" and, in 1977, "The Ballad of Jerry Lawler." "Jerry was at my house and we were working on a poster for that record. Our theme was 'The king is dead. Long live the king.' We were getting ready to print it when the news came on the radio that Elvis died. I pulled the record off the market, even though it was the number-one request record in the area. I didn't want to make any money off of a dead man, it was bad luck. My heart went out of the project after that. The Elvis thing was so important. I'd worked so long and so hard to get Lawler and Elvis together."

During that time, Blake had earned the respect of the musicians. He kept his Barbarian label alive with their help. "The reason I was able to cut the records that I cut was because I'd done the wrassling thing. Everybody had laughed at me and I proved them all wrong. I made everybody in Memphis want to come to the matches. Everybody wanted the records, everybody wanted to meet Lawler. Nobody could afford to laugh at me anymore, and that's how I was able to do my other Barbarian projects, crazy as they were. I recorded giants and midgets and transsexuals. I even got Tommy Burk to reprise 'Stormy Weather.' I was set up perfect when punk came in."

When the Memphis musicians had no other outlet, Blake was cutting them. The more extreme the better. "Everybody liked doing Blake sessions," says one musician, "because they were such a party. You never knew what was going to happen."

"I engineered a bunch of Blake records," says Richard Rosebrough, a former Ardent employee. "I saw all this insanity going down, people making tapes in these insane ways, and I was getting burnt out on recording. I thought of Blake records as Blake tapes, because they'd never come out. We were in la-la land, doing crazy things."

Blake's extensive archives dwarf Barbarian's relatively small output. He did, however, release an outstanding Lisa Aldridge record, and a Dickinson single, "Rumble," that Robert Palmer named in the *New York Times*'s top ten of 1980. Aldridge's version of the Velvet Underground song "Story of My Life" was mixed by the Regents' Rick Ireland. He inverted the standard mixing rule of turn up the good parts and turn down the bad parts. In an entirely pleasing way, he made the guitar distortion and the mistakes the focus of the song; these unique sounds suddenly come way up in the mix and the listener gets whiplash, turning toward the speaker, checking for dust on the needle, before realizing it's part of the song. "Rumble" was recorded over several years, a reel of multitrack tape thrown on the recorder at the end of a bunch of sessions, filled up and mixed down to another reel, which is then filled up and mixed down, again and again. Wholly singular, it sprawls from track to track, session to session, studio to studio, year to year. Impossible to imitate, impossible to duplicate, it is a hit that no one will hear, a pinnacle of the underground, recognized by the *Times* and completely unavailable. (Copies of the single, with its intricate packaging, now sell for two hundred dollars.) Symphonic in its chaos, it is unlistenable because it barely exists.

In Jim Blake's vault are a hundred hours of recordings featuring the finest Memphis musicians. He has solo recordings of Sid Selvidge and a duet between Alex Chilton and Jerry Lawler. He has recordings by the Klitz, by Mud Boy, an a cappella cowboy on downs. Though there have been several times when the market appeared ready for his treasure trove, to Blake, it was not ready enough. Helping him try to get the records released, I had to establish a rule that when we were discussing the price for these tapes, the words "a million dollars" could not enter the conversation. Memphis obscurity personified, Jim Blake should be the head of Disney; he should have a multimedia empire at his feet, conduct meetings around his Beverly Hills swimming pool. The world may not yet share the android's vision, but his patience and unwavering faith is clear to those who know him, clear to those sweating beside him as they cart boxes around a Memphis warehouse.

CHAPTER FOURTEEN

Thank You Friends

IT'S EASY TO DESCRIBE THE POSITION IN WHICH ALEX CHILTON FOUND himself in 1974, impossible to fully realize. At twenty-four, he was an eight-year veteran of the music business, wearing a purple heart. He'd been on the top of the charts, heard his voice define the sound of the street, been on the receiving end of tens of thousands of screaming girls. The singing was his, the talent was his, but the Box Tops belonged to someone else. When he'd declared himself his own artist with Big Star, his work was universally admired and almost completely unavailable. It was a long way to fall.

The disappointment surrounding Big Star was fresh when Chilton returned to the studio the same year that *Radio City* was released. This next album was to be his second solo effort; at the time of this writing, the first has yet to be fully released. Chilton never titled the 1974 effort, but when it finally became available in 1978, it bore the name *Big Star 3rd;* Jim Dickinson's production notes reveal some other names they were considering: *Sister Lovers,* because Alex and drummer Jody Stephens were dating sisters, and also *Beale Street Green,* from a line in the song "Dream Lover." Chilton reflects, "Maybe I would call it Alex Chilton's something or other," indicating the solo effort that it is. Yielding to the vernacular, I will refer to it as *Big Star 3rd*.

The first two Big Star albums are exuberant cries of youthful energy, not just of pleasure but also of pain. Chilton had pushed pop lyricism into a new decade by sloughing off love in "September Gurls," singing, "I loved you/well, never mind." The third album is also exuberant, though the proportions of pain and pleasure have been reversed. The lyrics are cocky and existential, anguished and depressed. In "Big Black Car" Chilton sings, "Nothing can hurt me/Nothing can touch me/Why should I care/ . . . it ain't gonna last."

After the failure of Big Star's first two albums, *3rd* is a confirmation of everything shitty about the music business, a sworn testament by an artist who knows.

"That record, to me, is a very unhappy sort of thing," says John Fry, who engineered the recording. "Basically it's a chronicle of all the stuff that was going on in Alex's life at the time, and the thing is by and large pretty depressing. You don't do a record that sounds like that when you are feeling real positive about everything that is going on in your life. If an audience is going to get a record like that, it's bought at the expense of somebody's pain somewhere.

"There were some strange sessions. A lot of it we were hiring the best players you could get and trying to get them to do the worst they could. And then other sessions you'd get the worst players you could and try to see just what they'd do anyway. You never knew whether you were gonna get more than one or two takes. It's almost like a Fellini record, if there were such a thing. It's the juxtaposition of all these bizarre elements, and I guess it makes something that's interesting and it's probably a good thing that it was done and preserved. But everybody certainly was not having a good time while they were doing it."

3rd is a landmark rock and roll album. Alex Chilton, like many blues artists, looks into the abyss of personal turmoil, chronicles an agonized love relationship, and wallows in the darkness of drink and drugs. The audience shares his anguish through the recording; the experience of disappointment is universal, and *3rd* is driven by monumental disappointment. Unlike many such expressions, his is not cacophonous. The album is filled with beautiful melodies and somber tones; Chilton's fine and pure voice is a reed bending with the wind. The mix is pristine, as immaculate as the previous Big Star albums, but more capacious. These songs are not about rock and roll guitar, bass, and drums. They are about texture, contrast, blankets of blackness punctuated by miniature holes of light. Instruments are often not recognizable, words are unclear, and the effect is one of suggestion, impressionistic rather than representational.

"I thought what the guy would be doing with his music was something that might lead to his getting a record deal so he could keep on recording," recalls Fry, who was engineering material he felt he'd be unable to sell. "Though at that particular time in his life, I'm not sure he had any choice about it." Our discussion is nearly two full decades after the fact, yet John Fry is visibly uncomfortable when recalling *3rd*. He fidgets, his lips sort of smack in a grimacing way, his conversation is filled with pauses. "I think some of the things that

Jim and Alex did and some of the technical things were good, but the overall unpleasant aspect of it to me is the subject matter and the content of most of the songs—and what you could see Alex was going through in connection with that, and what leads up to getting somebody to do that. Jim has a reputation, well deserved I think, for being able to work with and get results from difficult people. And he does that in a pretty unobtrusive way. His approach is to capture the moment and then if there's something we need to add or fix we can deal with that later in a little saner climate. But if it's gonna be insane anyway, just let it get as insane as it can get and see what happens. And we did a lot of that."

"When I first met Alex," says Dickinson, "he was living in his mamma's house and he had the gold record for 'Cry Like a Baby' on the wall. It was sealed, like in a glass box, and the label had peeled off the record and fallen, kind of laying over in the corner. And that summed up Alex for me then." Dickinson was an established producer by 1974. One of his projects had been Dan Penn's never-released second album, *Emmett the Singing Ranger Live in the Woods*. The two friends had fallen out during the mix, over a financial matter, and Dickinson took the Big Star project partly as revenge on Penn; Penn was aching to cut another hit with Chilton. Charlie Freeman, Dickinson's best friend, had died the previous year. The record contains some of his own anguish.

"*Big Star 3rd*, to me," Dickinson continues, "is a catharsis, a series of very different emotional responses that Alex is having. You don't get to do very many *Big Star 3rds*, they don't come along very often—thank God. You'll notice that Alex hasn't done another one either. I've been accused of indulging Alex, and some of it was indulging, but you listen to that record, you hear it working. Where people had normally told him, 'No, you can't do that,' I told him, 'Sure, we can do that.' I figured out a way to do 'that' each time. When it didn't work, we did something else. We created the guitar sound by solving a problem. Alex had this big ol' Ampeg amp, wretched sounding, and he wanted to play real loud. So we turned it all the way up and put the mike across the room, where it wasn't supposed to be. There's great big hunks of that stuff that just worked great. I think back on what it actually is—it's 1974!—what we did seems heroic. The synthesizer parts on 'You Can't Have Me' are being randomly triggered off Tommy Cathey's bass. We did the same thing to an upright bass player we hired and he thought we were completely insane. He would laugh openly while he was playing.

"'Kanga Roo' was when I got Alex's trust. He came in in the middle of the night with Lisa Aldridge and he recorded it with his voice and the twelve-string acoustic guitar on the same track, just to make it harder. He said to me, 'You want to produce something? Produce this.' So I started stacking stuff on it. I did the strings first with the Mellotron, then I started playing guitars. Pretty soon Alex was out there with me."

Lisa Aldridge was Alex's girlfriend at that time, later to lead an all-girl Memphis group, the Klitz. Dickinson posits that *3rd* is about her. "She was a real part of the process, and knew it. And put up with a whole lot of shit for the project and for Alex."

"Femme Fatale" is included as a nod to Lou Reed, who in 1973 released *Berlin*, a dark album similar in tone to *3rd*. The song includes Steve Cropper's contribution to the album. Richard Rosebrough was engineer when it occurred. "Stax was failing then, Cropper's own studio TMI had already failed, and he was at Ardent working with John Prine," says Rosebrough. "Typical Dickinson, if there's someone hot in the building that's playing, get 'em on your album. Cropper didn't want to do it. He said he'd do it if he had time. I knew how to get things in red fast, so when he walked in and said, 'I have ten minutes,' I had a direct line waiting for him. He would not enter more than two feet in the door. He put his guitar on, we did a few passes and that was it. Cropper was scared of it. He thought this was scary evil shit."

3rd has been released at least three times, each time with a different sequence, usually with a few extra tracks. Changing the order of the songs radically affects the meaning of the album. It's like giving the same film to different editors. The latest, and probably the most broadly known sequence, was released by Rykodisc in 1992. I saw a young clerk in a record store put on this new CD and when the opening track came on—one of the album's few upbeat songs—and he played a brief air guitar, I knew he was discovering an album different from the one I first heard. "Thank You Friends," now the second track, used to close the album and serve as an appreciation to pals who would stand close even through times as difficult as those represented in the album's journey; it's now just a rock song that helps cushion you against the blackness, introduced by the third cut, "Big Black Car." By the time the 1992 version gets into a series of heavy songs—"Nighttime," "Blue Moon," "Take Care"—the lighter, rock and roll mood has been well established.

Nat King Cole's "Nature Boy" features Bill Eggleston on the piano; he'd recently hurt his foot and the sound right before we hear Alex smile is Eggleston's crutch falling to the ground. "Dream Lover" was not included on the original release and proves to be a piece of the album's core. Harmonizing with himself, Chilton shows no boundaries, wrenching his guts—wrenching our guts—twice. He gives himself over to the song completely. The gnarled guitar is Lee Baker, and it creates a strong tension against Alex's spare piano, cushioned by the strings. It's full of drama and tension. "We didn't even arrange that song," says Dickinson. "Alex said, 'I've played it twice, once when I wrote it and then I played it for Lisa and I shouldn't have done that.' He said, 'If I play it one more time, I'm going to be bored with it.' That's the kind of thing I'm sympathetic to, so I said, 'Okay Alex, sing a little bit of it, we'll find some stuff, then we'll do it.' Baker didn't even know the changes, he just started playing. It got to this point after the bridge and Alex just leans over and says, 'Play it for me, guitarist,' and Baker goes into a scratchy kind of funk solo. We overdubbed the Memphis Symphony on it, and it's really pretty good."

Early into the sessions, Chilton hired a bodyguard. Don Nix was recording down the hall and he had one, Jerry Lee Lewis had at least one, and Alex figured it might keep him out of trouble. Danny Graflund was a large guy, a friend of Dickinson's, and he needed a job. His relationship with Campbell Kensinger, who was still a year from being killed, added a sense of danger. "It got to be where we started hanging out," says Graflund. "Alex would ask if I wanted to do something, said he was picking up the tab, and when he'd introduce me as his bodyguard, I didn't care. I was having a good time." The two remain friends. Back then, they were drinking heavily, eating downs, rubber-legging their way through Midtown. Part of their professional relationship involved the freedom for Alex to bring situations to a sharp edge, when Danny would step in to resolve them.

Graflund recalls one night when the two of them, accompanied by a girl who had a tape recorder in her purse, went to hear Jerry Lee Lewis at a Memphis club built on the site where Beatnik Manor had once stood. Selecting a large table up front, Graflund removed the "reserved" sign and they occupied it. When the reserved party arrived and tried to claim the table, words got heated. On the tape, one man drawls to Chilton, "You'd better tell your friend to settle down because there's a bunch of folks here that want to whip his goddamn ass." Chilton taunts, "If you're not some kind of chickenshit, you'll tell him yourself." But the redneck never has a chance to speak. Graflund, pilled up and drunk, has become his alter ego, Other Man. ("I drank, waiting for that 'click.' Then I'd be Other Man. People might say, 'You went into a bar last night and grabbed this guy's wife and jumped on the bar,' and I'd say, 'I didn't even go to that club last night.' 'No no, about midnight you were here.' I'd tell people *I* didn't do that. The click came, and I was Other Man.") Like a monster cartoon, Other Man rises from his seat, knocking over the table, sending glasses flying, beer bottles shattering. People scream as if in a 1950s Japanese horror film. Jerry Lee kicks his band into double-time. *3rd's* "Whole Lotta Shaking" acknowledges the Killer as a kindred spirit.

"It took so long to do *3rd*," says Dickinson. "And we needed all that time to get what we got." Not only were they cutting under the shadow of the previous Big Star disappointments, but this time the Stax organization was caving in while the sessions were underway. "The test pressing has a Stax master number on it," says Dickinson. "As Stax was obviously going down, and Fry was pulling out with all of his product—they were owing him so much money that he couldn't go any further with them—we just kept on cutting." Fry was becoming more and more disturbed by the sessions. The plug was pulled when, on the third day of a bender, Graflund brought a drinking buddy for his first visit to a recording studio. Slim was not accustomed to the isolation necessary for recording, and three days out, the situation disoriented him. After some time, he was led out to the floor and placed in front of the microphone, given the opportunity to sing or speak his mind. It was a moment to be captured. Tape was rolling. What went on in his mind is impossible to determine, what he saw from the other side of the glass or what was reflected back at him. Whether it was because of the three-day binge behind him or because of the fourth day ahead, Slim, at six feet four, 250 pounds, and weathered like a radial tire, stood in the middle of the production room floor, headphones covering his head, and when given the signal that the world was his, the hulking figure grew silent, paused, breathed in, out, then broke down crying, sobbing with no control, blubbering.

Fry declared the recording process over. Despite the high tension, he agreed to participate in the mixing. "Fry was at the peak of his craft then," says Dickinson. "That's the last project that he did hands on, all the way from cutting it through mixing. That record is a testimonial to the engineering expertise of John Fry. That's why it sounds so good. It still sounds contemporary."

But in 1974, it sounded ahead of its time. Record labels uniformly rejected it. Dickinson remembers sending the tape to Jerry Wexler, for whom he'd worked at Atlantic. Wexler phoned him. "Baby," he said, "that tape you sent me makes me very uncomfortable."

"You knew you weren't turning the radio on and hearing anything like that," says John Fry. Fry and Dickinson shopped the tape on the East Coast and then the West, calling on all of their music biz connections. They were turned away repeatedly. When Fry gave up, Dickinson stayed, banging on doors until he was called home for Campbell Kensinger's funeral. The industry's reaction was enough to drive both Fry and Dickinson from the business. If it couldn't accept an album about the dark side of life, the business wasn't for them. Fry put his studio up for sale and tried to get out of the business; Ardent was bought, the sign was taken down, and the offices changed hands, but the new owners defaulted on their payments. Fry continues to run Ardent to this day; his fourth incarnation of the Ardent label began in 1993, and in 1994, Chilton signed a domestic deal with him.

Chilton says that in 1975, "something clicked in my head and from then on I knew how to write a thing that would please me." Cavalierly dismissing the Big Star albums, he is, I believe, an artist too close to his work. He hears only the "mistakes" in the songs, details invisible to the listener not involved in the creation process. In 1975, he recorded with music critic Jon Tiven at Ardent. Tiven was an early believer in Big Star, writing an extended article about the band in the March 1974 issue of *Fusion*. He developed a relationship with the artist and with Fry and came to Memphis in the fall of 1975. An EP was culled from the sessions for the 1977 release, *Singer Not the Song;* Tiven sold more of the tracks to a German label in 1981, and more again to an American label in 1993. The latter two releases share the name *Bach's Bottom*. Frankly, they're hardly special. The songs sound rushed, Chilton is nearly manic, the chaos distracting instead of invigorating, as on 1979's *Like Flies on Sherbert*. There are only two new compositions on these sessions. "All of the Time" was cowritten with Lisa Aldridge and is pleasant, if the performance is a bit grating.

The other new song is "Take Me Home and Make Me Like It," which came out of Chilton's friendship with his bodyguard. The title was a pickup line Graflund used with women in bars. "I'd be out cruising, being Other Man, and I'd see a chick somewhere. I'd move in and say, 'Hi, I'm Danny,' and then get into this rap, Other Man's version of 'Blue Suede Shoes': 'You can knock me down, drag me in the gutter, you can stomp on me, piss on me, spit in my face but then [through gritted teeth] take me home and make me like it.' Me and Alex used to go to his apartment, he would turn on the tape deck and say, 'I'll play, you sing.' I don't think he thought anything serious was going to come out of me, but he wanted a tape of it because it was good for laughs." Danny was in a bar one night when he was told Alex was at that moment cutting his song at Ardent. "I got some chicks, went down to Ardent, the guard let us in. This one girl looked at the control board and said, 'It's Christmas,' and began changing all the knobs."

Richard Rosebrough picks up the story. "This was the first night of the sessions, and Alex was producing instead of Jon Tiven. Alex would stand in the control room with a microphone and sing, while running the board and playing guitar. We're in red, I'm in the studio playing drums. I saw Graflund come in, go to the back wall and I could see by looking at his back—what is he

Dan Penn (in glasses) and Alex Chilton lounging at the Sam Phillips Recording Service, mid-1970s. Photo by William Eggleston.

doing? I could see this spot on the wall getting larger and larger. He peed on the back wall. I was sort of representing the studio at the session. We finished that song, I put my sticks down, and I threw them out. You can't pee on the wall! I have to use this room tomorrow!"

"When the record came out," says Graflund, "I told Alex it was shitty that I was listed as the fourth writer when Mark James and Dan Penn had begged me for the hook to that song. They were going to give me half-writer's credit for just the hook. Not long back, Alex let me know that he'd amended it and I had first writer's."

Ork Records, one of the nation's first punk labels, asked Chilton to play in New York when they were releasing the Tiven sessions EP. They said they'd help him put a band together up there. "They introduced me to Chris Stamey and Chris and I got along fine and had a good time," says Chilton. "We worked together all that year. That's when I produced his single 'Where the Fun Is.' By the end of that year, I don't think Chris wanted to work with me anymore. Chris had decided I was totally unreasonable. At the time, I was a drunk and I'm sure I wasn't the easiest person to get along with in the world."

Chilton's landmark single "Bangkok" was recorded while he was in New York, with Stamey on maracas and Chilton playing everything else. It's an eerie neo-rockabilly original, a lighthouse in Chilton's 1975–79 fog. During that time, he also recorded some demos for Elektra Records. "I think they're available on that bootleg of my stuff, *Dusted in Memphis*. I like the writing on 'My Rival' and a song called 'A Little Fishy.' I did those and a couple of other straight kind of things for a real record label so they wouldn't think I was totally crazy. I hadn't met anybody who didn't think I was crazy in about five years." Elektra's reaction to Chilton's material: "I never heard any reaction at all. They didn't pick it up, I'll tell you that." "Bangkok" is a turning signal that lead down the path to Chilton's 1979 pseudo-reckless masterpiece, *Like Flies on Sherbert*.

The Cramps were another inspiration for *Flies,* and also for the Memphis band the Panther Burns. Chilton met the Cramps in New York in 1977. They were a band from middle America that had moved to Manhattan and, in the face of the exploding punk rock movement, forged their own sound playing horror movie rockabilly. Such a renegade spirit was a natural attraction for Chilton. "I became a big fan of theirs. I would go see them play any time they were in the city. It turned out they rehearsed in the basement where Lisa Aldridge lived, and one day I went over to her house and there they all were in her apartment. We started talking and I suggested we do some recordings together. I told them I could arrange to do it for free at Ardent in Memphis, and when it's all said and done, they could have the tapes and do whatever they want with them. It's the kind of deal I know I would like. So they said okay, so we did."

The Cramps had built a reputation around a small section of New York and were completely unknown outside of that. Shortly after arriving in Memphis, they performed at a college outdoors. Their regalia was a bit baffling to many of these students who'd never left the Bible Belt. They'd seen movies with bikers, so they had some idea about all the leather, but the flamboyant sexuality, the male singer in high heels and leather underwear; it all added up to something beyond them. "We performed outside," says vocalist Lux Interior, "and all these jocks wanted to kill us. At first they thought it was something from New York where you had to have a program and have read five books to understand what it was. Then they got into it. I put Bryan Gregory on my shoulders and his guitar became unplugged. We ran around the crowd going 'ma-mammamamamamamama' in their faces, while they're hitting their fists into their palms. We won them over, and they were just going nuts. It ended up with them throwing empty beer cans way up into the air and there was just a shower of empty beer cans coming down on us. It was really cool." The Cramps released their Chilton-produced tracks as singles, compiling them onto *Gravest Hits,* which won them international acclaim. They returned to Memphis two years later to record *Songs the Lord Taught Us,* working at Sam Phillips after Chilton had recorded *Flies* there.

When *Flies* was begun, *3rd* was still on the shelf, where it had been gathering dust for four years. "My life was on the skids," Chilton says, "and *Like Flies on Sherbert* was a summation of that period. I like that record a lot. It's crazy but it's a positive statement about a period in my life that wasn't positive." *Flies* began at Phillips, a collaborative effort between Chilton, Dickinson, Sid Selvidge, and Richard Rosebrough. Dickinson produced, Selvidge provided the record label and manufacturing, Rosebrough was a house engineer at the studio. Knox and Jerry Phillips, in their usual sympathetic and philanthropic way, made their studio accessible. Rosebrough remembers, "Alex was getting into his most degenerate mode. He looked really bad, just degenerate enough to where we all wanted to make a tape."

"When I conceived of doing *Like Flies on Sherbert,*" Chilton says, "I thought Jim and I and maybe one or two other people would record. When I turned up for the session, Jim had his whole band there! But I didn't say anything, I thought we should try it and see how it goes. We started recording and I thought, 'Man, these guys don't know the songs,' and I was trying to teach them and they'd go, 'Yeah, we know the songs,' and then they just go and play the first thing they thought of. So we were rolling the tape and doing this outrageous-sounding stuff, and I thought, 'Man, this must sound terrible,' but when I went in the control room and heard what we'd been doing, it was just incredible sounding. Getting involved with Dickinson opened up a new world for me. Before that I'd been into careful layerings of guitars and voices and harmonies and things like that, and Dickinson showed me how to go into the studio and just create a wild mess and make it sound really crazy and anarchic. That was a growth for me."

"I'd been running a bush hog that afternoon before we started," says Lee Baker. "I caught some barbed wire in the thing and it started whipping around. I felt a sharp pain in my leg, got off the thing, got the wire out of the bush hog, and went back to bush-hogging. My leg was still hurting so I reached down there and I had a fucking piece of barbed wire sticking out my leg. I went to the studio that night and I wasn't really feeling too good. And that was the first night of those sessions. I had no idea what we were going to do. Alex had the tunes and he showed us the songs and we played 'em. It was the same as at the Ardent sessions, except with *Sister Lovers* the tunes were weirder. And they were weirder partly because everyone was taking all them damn downs."

Flies is an epitome of Memphis music—a complete rejection of the industry norm. It embraces what traditional studio set-ups reject. It is sloppy, often indecipherable, and very, very alive. *"Like Flies on Sherbert,"* a critic has written, "painfully confirmed the degradation of a once-major talent." Such a statement reveals a dickhead writer with a bad record collection. On the album we hear Chilton bumping into the microphone and then laughing about it—where else but Memphis goddamn rock and fucking roll are you going to hear that allowed onto the finished product? "Fixing" that would have made a super alive moment into stone dead rock. *Flies* presaged the wave of American punk, foretold the return to roots rock, and once again sent out a trend from Memphis that the city itself couldn't swallow until, like a baby bird, it was given predigested versions.

Like Flies on Sherbert was recorded, mostly, over three nights in 1978, mixed over the year that followed, and released to an unsuspecting world in 1979 by Selvidge's Peabody label. While it takes only three minutes to record a song, Chilton emphasizes that sorting it out takes a lot longer, "especially if you cut things that're really crazy." Only five hundred copies of the album were pressed (a British label subsequently pressed a version), and I suspect that through a series of phone calls over a short time, one could locate the individuals who own four hundred of them. Peabody had little distribution, but Chilton's ardent fans managed to acquire their copies.

It's unlikely anyone could have been prepared for what they heard. Like a classic R&B performance, the album opens with a band track, the leader waiting in the wings. The song features drummer Ross Johnson, a librarian with a capacity for verbiage not dissimilar to Dewey Phillips's, and (then) a capacity for beer not dissimilar to a keg's. He and Chilton establish a hard-driving riff, very immediate sounding, upon which Johnson unleashes an extended "Red, Hot & Blue" tale, informing your jugular that whatever else follows will bear little resemblance to the Alex Chilton you have previously known. This was the culmination of the concept that Selvidge saw Chilton experimenting with at the Procapé: If I were a thirteen-year-old right now and I were just learning my instrument, how would I play guitar?

"On *Flies*," says Dickinson, "Alex told me he had gotten too good to play the kind of guitar that he was interested in. Almost all of the piano on *Flies* is Alex."

The Procapé experiment was a success. "You can't pretend to fall together loosely," Chilton says. "You can't know the song really well and then pretend not to know the song and come out with the same effect. Sometimes the first time through on something, people play in a whole different way than they ever play it again, you can hear them learning and hear them thinking the way they'll never think and approach it again." *Flies*, like *3rd*, captures that elusive quality.

There was another quality they were unable to catch. "Alex was real enamored with the way his voice sounded when he woke up," remembers Rosebrough. "So we made these elaborate plans in advance to have everyone at the studio at eight A.M., get the tape on the machine and be ready, and then somebody banged on Alex's door to wake him up. By the time he got to the studio, he was already awake and he'd lost the voice. So he took a handful of Valium. That didn't work, but we tried."

Though Chilton was an established songwriter by the time of *Flies*, fully half the record is other peoples' songs. A similar balance has continued in his work to the present day. But the songs Chilton covers are usually retrieved from deepest obscurity, abandoned gems that serve to direct his listeners along veins of other treasures. Critics who chastise Chilton for not writing all his own material ignore the value of his song scouting. Among the sources for *Flies* are the Greenbriar Boys' bluegrass, the Long Island vocal group the Belltones, and the Carter Family's interpretation of a slave song. If that's not a likely Dewey Phillips set, I don't know what is.

Chilton has written more than his share of great material, so much that it has ensnared him. People don't want Liz Taylor to grow older, they don't want Elvis to be dead, and they won't let Alex Chilton change. But his interpretations are usually his own, and they serve his listeners as signposts to discovering artists that the rest of the world has missed. "I'd like to write some more great songs," he says. "But I'm tired of people bitching at me about 'How come you only write three songs a year?' Fuck it, how many great songs are people supposed to write in a year? If somebody writes one great song in two years—one great song in a lifetime—that's plenty. People are kind of unrealistic about songwriting these days. It's an expectation that the Beatles sort of are responsible for. And if you ask me, the Beatles were stretching themselves way thin." Indeed, the mountains of compact discs that are released every month are a rehashing of old song ideas. The challenge could be not to write your own version of a song, but to make an established song your own,

"Ubangi Stomp" or otherwise. Reinterpretation is a standard practice in jazz, is common in rhythm and blues, and in pop does not preclude a hit. Chilton's interpretation of Ernest Tubb's "Waltz Across Texas" uses a familiar song to create a new message; Tubb's version does not evoke Bonnie and Clyde.

On the morning of Alex Chilton's twenty-eighth birthday, while *Flies* was being created, the newspaper announced Chris Bell's death. He'd had a single-car accident the night before, his 1977 Triumph striking a utility pole at one-thirty A.M. on December 27, 1978. He'd lived to see the rerelease of the first two Big Star albums earlier that year, and enjoyed some acclaim for "I Am the Cosmos," a single he recorded in 1974 that featured Chilton on background vocals. Rykodisc's 1992 compilation of his work, *I Am the Cosmos,* shows an artist in the throes of overwhelming sadness and despair. "Chris had become a very committed Christian by the time of his death," says John Fry. "Nobody really says anything about that." *Cosmos* makes it clear, especially in such songs as "Better Save Yourself" and "Look Up."

"*Flies* nearly killed us," says Randall Lyon, who videotaped much of the recording sessions. "It was a horrible experience from beginning to end. By that time, everybody had a bunch of attitude. It was not a good moment—it's good on record, yeah, but it's because we were all at each other's throats. The music was so heavy. Chris Bell died while Alex was working on that record, and *Flies* to me, is the end process of the whole Chris Bell/Alex freakout. With Chris is where Alex had begun his own individual journey, and when he died, Alex began a period of transformation. It was a crisis. I remember Alex would come over to my place and listen to Tommy James and the Shondells and to Hank Thompson. He was sussing out different parts of things he was interested in. He had to decide what he was going to do, as an artist. He had already been everything. And he turned into this wonderful person. What a survivor that guy is. His influence, his music has been a real motivator. There's so many important movements to him. But he didn't have it easy, he struggled with that shit. I remember when 'The Letter' came out for the first time on a TV collection of the sixties, it was real embarrassing. It really kicked his ass."

"I saw Alex in the parking lot of Goldsmith's department store when some Big Star reissues were coming out along with some new recordings," remembers Mary Lindsay Dickinson. "He was with his mom in his car. He was laughing that he had four records coming out and his mom was taking him to buy some new clothes."

"If you could imagine, even yet, he's a cultural icon and gotten paid damn little," says Selvidge. "Like Furry Lewis would say, Where's my money? Still to this day, Alex gets very little recognition by the labels. They'll put out stuff that's safe, only after everybody's named songs after him."

Perhaps it was *3rd*'s initial release during the punk explosion that refocused attention on Big Star's first two albums. One response to the late-seventies anger was late-seventies melody, and in Big Star's early work, bands like R.E.M., the dB's, and scores of others found inspiration. Rock history now places Big Star on a plane similar to that of the Velvet Underground; it has been said that anyone who heard the Velvet Underground's early records went on to form a band, and the same may apply to Big Star's influence. "I always am amazed that all this stuff has the interest and the following that it does," says Fry. "It's really pretty obscure in terms of the relative handful of records that were out there for anybody to get ahold of. It really strikes me as curious that everybody keeps coming back around to it. I thought the Big Star records were good, and it was fun to be involved in it, particularly the first two, and it was probably worth doing the third, but I didn't expect people to be asking questions about them twenty years later. Music, to me, is essentially an emotional communication, and it either connects or it doesn't connect. I'm not sure why, but all these people resonate to this Big Star business."

Big Star's enduring popularity is intimately related to its obscurity. Their melodic teen angst is a contradiction that continues to reverberate with listeners. But it's not just their music that keeps people's attention. In Big Star's history fans confront the fear of having something important to say that no one will hear. It's taken twenty years, but Big Star has prevailed. The band's cult status helps listeners realize their lives are not in vain.

In 1985, after a long hiatus, Chilton returned to the studio sober and serious, recording the first of a series of R&B-influenced releases. It was a return to his pre-British Invasion roots. That investigation continued right on into a 1993 Big Star reunion CD. Following that, he did not succumb to the obvious commercial step of releasing a new album of Big Star-ish material; instead, he released a solo acoustic disc of vocal standards associated with singers who draw reflexive groans from college kids because they remind them of their parents. *Clichés* forgoes a band for just his voice and acoustic guitar. Drawing on the songs and artists that wafted up the stairwell from his parents' salon below, Chilton creates a direct and personal statement that draws on his past to discuss his present. Unmitigated by other musicians, this effort yields an unusually strong sense of immediacy.

Parallel to Chilton's solo career, Big Star's reunion has assumed its own life. Despite continuing claims of retiring the idea, the band remains in demand, appearing in England, Japan, major cities in the U.S., and finally a homecoming in Memphis. No longer tentative about the material, Chilton and Jody Stephens, aided by two members of the Posies, deliver the old songs with new life. Guitar solos with a 1990s edge enhance the exuberance of Big Star's material, so that fans who may have anticipated an exhibit from the museum of rock and roll history leave the reunion shows with hopes of a new Big Star album.

Alex Chilton is a musician looking to the future, haunted by a following wrapped up in his past. The weight of his achievements creates a dissatisfaction trap: His fans demand, Why don't you do again what you've already done? In the bigger scheme, he does: Big Star was contrary music in 1972, and *Cliches* is contrary to Big Star's latest popularity. The constant is Chilton's aggressive and defiant attitude, while his music, his art, continues to evolve. In this industry, controlling one's own destiny is as difficult as collecting monies owed. His has been a circuitous route, and the path ahead is unclear and unsure — exciting. Despite the naysayers, despite the soothsayers and the imitators, Alex Chilton charts a personal course.

CHAPTER FIFTEEN

Attempted Gawk

MEMPHIS IS A TOWN OF DONUT SHOPS AND CHURCHES. WHATEVER MU-
sical achievements it claims are achievements in spite of the city, not because of
it. A Beale Street merchant, Abraham Schwab, whose family business has been
in the same location for over one hundred years, has a saying: Memphis has
torn down more history than most other cities even have. During President
Nixon's urban renewal program of the 1970s, when the destruction of Beale
left only a shell of its former self, the city tried to make Mr. Schwab leave his
site, for the benefit of the street. He wouldn't budge. They condemned the
building. Today, if he's not too busy stocking items that sell for ninety-eight
cents each, two for a dollar, he will take you on a tour of his basement, pointing out the sturdiness of his structure, laughing about the city's drastic mea-
sures against him. Insensitive destruction is part of what defines Memphis.

The country blues from the Delta, the urban blues that evolved on Beale,
Sun Records, then Stax and American and Ardent—Memphis never embraced
them. Blues were shunned as the music of black people, rock and roll the
music of degenerates. During the 1980s, the civic government made an attempt to support the scene, enticing Chips Moman back to town and building
him a studio a block off Beale. The city learned it had no business in the record
business. The very thing that they're afraid of is the thing that made it work.
"The Memphis sound is something that's produced by a group of social
misfits in a dark room in the middle of the night," says Dickinson. "It's not
committees, it's not bankers, not disc jockeys. Every attempt to organize the
Memphis music community has been a failure, as righteously it should be.
The diametric opposition, the racial collision, the redneck versus the ghetto

black is what it is all about, and it can't be brought together. If it could, there wouldn't be any music."

On October 1, 1978, before Alex Chilton's *Like Flies on Sherbert* had been recorded, Mud Boy and the Neutrons gave a farewell performance in the Orpheum Theater, an old-time movie palace that had escaped death by bulldozer like a Saturday serial's hero. It was not the first time Mud Boy retired, nor was it the last. The Tennessee Waltz, as the show was dubbed (a jab at the Band's farewell appearance, the Last Waltz), was the third event in a trilogy sponsored by Dickinson. These shows commemorated the release of *Beale Street Saturday Night,* an album he produced that demonstrated the fluidity running through the diverse branches of Memphis music. (One of the record's achievements was reaching the unconverted. Paid for by a bank, the album was sold at various society functions, at Schwab's store on Beale, and in the Orpheum lobby. Few were sold through record stores.) The first show was a jazz and blues album release party featuring Furry Lewis, Thomas Pinkston, Phineas Newborn Jr., and Fred Ford. The second was a rockabilly tribute named "Red, Hot & Blue" after Dewey Phillips's radio show. The lineup included Harmonica Frank Floyd, Barbara Pittman (one of Sun's few female artists), and the Mississippi soul man Jerry Saylor. The third show was given to rock and roll. Mud Boy played two sets, acoustic and then with a rhythm section.

Their decision to retire was a response to the plug-pulling incident at the Beale Street Music Festival the previous May. An article previewing the show in the *Commercial Appeal* quoted Lee Baker: "The [festival] promoters treated us like we're second-rate, like we're 'white boys' and we don't know how to play." Sid Selvidge was also quoted: "We've been promoting old black folks for years and never taken a nickel from 'em and at great expense to ourselves. We've been knocking City Hall over the head since nineteen-sixty whatever, and all of a sudden it becomes economically feasible for downtown to rip off 'some old niggers.' It's because it's in their economic self-interest—not because it's in the city's or the artists' self-interest—but in their own, lily-white, East Memphis interest to be downtown, and the old bluesmen can help 'em sell it." Mud Boy was angry.

The Tennessee Waltz was a multimedia affair, a Dream Carnival with respect for the proscenium arch. Bill Eggleston and his two preteen sons were onstage with video cameras, recording the event while displaying it on monitors to the audience. The dancing girls, whose quiver had offended the city in May, were front and center. A few other documentarists appeared, and overall, the musicians were pleased to be outnumbered on the stage. Not long before the music began, a former member of the Big Dixie Brick Company, the Dream Carnival's theater troupe, asked Dickinson if he could perform during the intermission. His name was Gus Nelson, but he was about to birth an alter ego. He was thinking of a country blues revival with a punk aesthetic, and it would become the torchbearer of Memphis music, however dim the coals. He would take the name Tav Falco and call the idea Panther Burn. "He came up to me at the show," recalls Dickinson, "and said softly, as is his way, 'Would it be alright if I sang a song, Jim?' I didn't know he sang. I said sure, I thought he meant with the band. He said, 'That's alright, I'll accompany myself.'" In the audience was Alex Chilton.

"I always like to be set up as an antienvironment to something that's happening," says Tav Falco, applying his theater background to music. "That day there was this rock and roll thing going down, so after Mud Boy's first set I went out onstage and set up a guitar, a big black-and-white television monitor, and a Bell and Howell speaker from a motion-picture projector that I was running the guitar through. And I had an electric chainsaw on a stool and an electric skill saw on another stool." Tav cultivated his Charlie Chaplin looks and donned a tuxedo with fingerless gloves, further separating himself from the swirl of color he followed. "This was my first time singing in public. As soon as I began, all these TV cameras came down front and onstage. I had this strange way of playing guitar—nobody else was playing like that that day, believe me—and I started my treatment of Leadbelly's 'Bourgeois Blues.' There was no band up there, just one person on electric guitar with all this sound reinforcement equipment and it just—*phoom!*—was out there, pretty powerful sounding. I was shocked by it because I had never sung through amplified equipment.

"I got further and further into 'The Bourgeois Blues,' you know, 'Home of the brave, land of the free, I won't be mistreated by no bourgeoisie,' and, 'This is a bourgeois town.' I worked up into the height of this frenzy, when I started blowing this police whistle and laid the guitar between the two stools and got the electric chainsaw and started ripping into this guitar. The sound, man, it was just complete sound. Extremely chaotic. People started screaming in the audience, going crazy. And then I got this skill saw and ripped through that guitar, still plugged into the sound system and it created all these scrunching, tearing, slicing, electronic, bursting, exploding noises. And WHBQ is filming in color and there's all these other cameras and Little Bill's got mine going out to the audience on video and I just kind of collapsed. People had to drag me offstage."

"I saw Tav play 'The Bourgeois Blues' and I was really impressed," says

Chilton. "I was interested in looking at a little country blues then and that was his thing, so I started going over to his house. He had a lot more material, and I began showing him some rockabilly stuff and he was interested in that. We just sort of—I said, 'I know a drummer,' and we called up Ross Johnson and we were a band, bingo." Alex charged Tav with leading the band so he could finally enjoy the role of sideman. His presence sanctioned the Panther Burns. Deriving their sound from Tav's initial performance, the band's name reflected the lore surrounding Panther Burn, Mississippi. This town was menaced by an elusive wild beast that, when finally cornered, was set aflame. Its dying shrieks so horrified the citizens that they named their community for it. The moniker was appropriate for Tav's assembly. He says, "I didn't know music, and Ross didn't. We put Eric Hill, an art academy student, on a very crude synthesizer and he didn't know music. Alex was the only one that had an understanding of musical form, which he thought would make it more interesting. The whole No Wave scene was going on in New York, and the Cramps were playing very fundamental, rudimentary things. Here was an art form I could participate in by just picking up the instrument, like a Kodak Instamatic camera. It was the feeling and aesthetic that mattered, more than musicianship or virtuosity. I didn't feel hindered by my lack of conventional guitar knowledge. I just went into it full tilt."

The Panther Burns sounded like wind howling through the cracks in a house. They took Sonny Burgess's "Red Headed Woman" from the Sun label and made it a Memphis punk statement. Falco sifted through the Moon Records catalog, an early Memphis label inspired by Sun and run by a rocking lady named Cordell Jackson. Their revival of her songs "Dateless Night" and "She's the One That Got It" gave new life to her career. She ultimately found wild popularity in a Budweiser commercial, where her expertise on the Hagstrom guitar smoked Stray Cat Brian Setzer. The Panther Burns booked themselves with Charlie Feathers, introducing rockabilly's most devoted practitioner to another generation of fans. They did the same with north Mississippi bluesman R. L. Burnside. In a fallow period of Memphis recordings, the Panther Burns regularly brought studio work to the finest local talent, including Wayne Jackson and Andrew Love—the Memphis Horns, and trumpeter Ben Cauley who had survived Otis Redding's plane crash. Dickinson and Chilton usually alternated as producers. Nearly fifteen years since its inception, the band lives on, their sound a little more polished, their musicianship on equal footing with their theatricality.

When the Panther Burns formed, Falco was a partner with Randall Lyon in a nonprofit video company. TeleVista Projects, Inc., inspired by Eggleston's work, had released documentaries on rural blues joints, profiles of various bluesmen, and interviews with diverse people—the Memphis painter Carroll Cloar, the former Arkansas governor Orval Faubus (who had defied the federal integration order in Little Rock's Central High School), and with Fred Martin, the first black man elected to public office in Arkansas since Reconstruction. By the eighties, their company was still extant on paper, though most of their equipment had been repossessed. By making the Panther Burns the TeleVista orchestra, they received a grant from the National Endowment for the Arts to participate in a global linkup of videographic slow-scan phone-line transmissions.

Tav secured a spot on a local morning talk show, hosted by the polite, matronly Marge Thrasher. Booked during May, their appearance coincided with the Memphis Cotton Carnival, festivities built around secret societies akin to the krewes of New Orleans' Mardi Gras. Befitting an "orchestra's" appearance, Thrasher arranged to have the King and Queen of Cotton Carnival as guests.

"We built this network with Memphis, New York, Toronto, Victoria, Vancouver, and the San Francisco Museum of Art," says Lyon. "When we were on the show, we were sending the signal through telephone transceivers up to a satellite, down to other television stations. We were using broadcast TV systems, cable TV systems, and phone lines. It was one of the first international cyberspace experiments. Corporations were blown away that artists were going to use this technology. Law enforcement and financial markets were the only ones who'd previously used it. Nobody knew what we were doing. We were over the top. After that, I started talking to people about wanting to play the Mississippi River bridge like a musical instrument."

The episode aired live at nine A.M. This was long before the band's musicianship and theatricality were equals. The fleshed-out group featured a second nonmusician on synthesizer, and a trumpeter who wore a wacky horizontally-striped suit and kept his back to the camera. They were a motley crew. The first song was a treatment of the Burnette Brothers' version of "Train Kept a Rollin'." Instead of caterwauling power-punk, the band was restrained and spare, the tentative search for each next note producing a surreal quality. A melody was evident, though camouflaged. Between shots of the band's performance, Lyon interjected slow-scan stills of the same, black and white, the images being sent to the San Francisco Museum of the Arts, the Franklin Street Furnace in Manhattan, and the other participants in the global linkup. At the first song's conclusion, a befuddled Ms. Thrasher asked questions, to which Tav responded:

Thrasher: This is anti-music, is that right?

Falco: An anti-musical environment. The Panther Burns would like to do one more tune—

T: Wait a minute. Wait a minute. That may be the worst sound I've ever heard come out on television.

F: Thank you very much.

T: That's what you want, I'm assuming?

F: Well, the best of the worst is what we're after.

T: Let me get all this straight. Are you all also part of the federal grant of money?

F: No, we're simply an orchestra to accompany this image-feed. You have a sound track and then you have a picture track. In this case, it's a live situation. So we're the live orchestra accompanying the imagery.

T: If I had realized that I'm not sure I would have wanted you to represent the King and Queen of Cotton Carnival. That would not have been my selection of music. [Cutting off Tav's inquiry] Gustavo, what kind of field are you in, because you are so big on telling me that you are anti-music. I don't understand.

F: I don't think anyone else is playing music like this in Memphis or maybe anywhere else in the world.

T: I don't think they are either.

F: In that case, we're doing something quite different, see, something that is not part of the establishment, not part of our everyday environment. We have to create an anti-environment to make more visible real musicians, people who are early Memphis performers—

T: Why do you have to be anti to do it?

F: Because it's all invisible to us. We can't see what's around us. There are blues people here who don't have exposure, rockabilly artists who don't have any exposure. They don't really exist here, they're part of our environment, we see them every day, yet they're invisible to us. We take them for granted. It takes a group like us to create contrast, to create focus—

T: Do people pay you to play this?

F: Occasionally, but we're not in it for the money. We're in it for something else.

T: Art.

F: I don't know if it's art. It's art damage. It's—

T: You're really very bitter, aren't you?

F: I'm not bitter about anything. I get exhilarated by this kind of music. Highly exhilarated.

T: So if you have an outlet, that brings the exhilaration to the forefront.

F: It brings it to a peak, yes.

T: Do you think there's a market for your kind of music?

F: I'm not sure. We're exploring markets. But I'm not that concerned about the marketplace. I'm more concerned about a stage area, a communications environment in which we can set up and focus on our complete environment which has become invisible to us. So we need other forms of music to be able to see what's genuine and what's authentic in our musical environment.

T: Why don't you introduce the band members to us.

F: [Tav introduces Eric Hill, Vincent Wrenn, Ross Johnson, Rick Ivy, Alex Chilton.] We would like to do one more tune, which is a rock and roll tango—

T: Gustavo, we're not quite ready for it. Okay. We're gonna take another break here on "Straight Talk" and we'll be back in just a moment.

The band was allowed to perform their second song, the tango "Drop Your Mask," after which Thrasher said, "An all-time low this morning on 'Straight Talk.' I want to talk about some of our upcoming guests on the program. . . ."

"Because it's all invisible to us," Falco told her, and it is as true in Memphis today as it was when Robert Johnson was ignored by every white man he passed on the street. A Picasso of the blues, Johnson was made transparent by the cultural mindset. That attitude was clearly evident forty years after Johnson's death when one local TV station tried to rectify the situation, producing and broadcasting a one-hour special seeking "to show the variety of music associated with the city . . . blues, gospel, hard rock, rhythm and blues, pop, country and opera." It preempted the John Davidson show at seven P.M., and the following day, the *Press Scimitar* ran some of the viewer comments noted by the station's switchboard operator:

6:55 When is the "John Davidson Show" on?
7:13 Get that Negro off the TV!
7:35 You won't have anyone looking by the time Marguerite Piazza comes on the program.
7:47 If I want to watch monkeys, I would go to the zoo.

The establishment proffers donuts and churches, ignoring the hole in their middles. Memphis music had come up from the neighborhoods and the neighbors of these diverse musicians, had reached all corners of the earth, breaking down barriers that seemed impenetrable, and Memphians continued to insult Furry Lewis with the basest comments. That same year, 1976, a Memphis disc jockey watched his Estelle Axton-produced comedy song go to number one on the charts; "Disco Duck" eventually sold over five million copies. Rick Dees recently set a fiscal record when he signed a twenty-five million-dollar radio syndication contract with ABC. "Memphis," says Wayne Jackson, "is a tension that expresses itself in music."

On June 5, 1977, Sleepy John Estes died in poverty, and his funeral arrangements were left to his Memphis friends. Bukka White had passed three

months earlier. Gus Cannon died November 16, 1979. He was 104. Furry
Lewis died at eighty-eight on September 14, 1981. The pawnshop scheme was
turned one more time, and invisible Memphians bought him a headstone.

One cold night in the early eighties, the painter Charlie Miller was leaving
a club where he'd been painting the dancers. One of the girls was waiting out
front for a ride that hadn't shown up. "I told her I'd give her a ride home. On
the way, she asked me if I'd stop at one of the convenience stores we passed.
She came out of there, had a box of Faultless Starch and a Coca-Cola. We were
riding along and she opened that box up and started scooping it out eating it.
I said, 'I didn't know you could eat starch like that.' She said, 'Oh yeah, it'll fill
your belly up when you're hungry.'"

While on a world tour with Ry Cooder in 1983, Jim Dickinson reunited
with Memphis entrepreneur Isaac Tigrett in London. In the course of the day,
Tigrett played a tape by a since-deceased Memphis barrelhouse piano player,
Big Sam Clark. "I made some sort of bitter remark," says Dickinson, "and
Isaac got furious. 'You have no right to be bitter,' he told me. 'You were fortunate enough to witness the end of something truly great, and intelligent
enough to understand some of it.' On the road, alone in a hotel room, I
thought about that a lot. He is absolutely right. I'm not bitter anymore. I may
remain pissed off, but I'm not bitter."

The questions about contemporary Memphis are, Where are the hits? Where
are the stars? And the extremely agitating, Why can't Memphis be like Nashville? To the last, one can only respond that Nashville is a company town and
Memphis is for renegades. And the relationship works well for both: Nashville
acts come to Memphis studios to "get away with" what the corporate environment won't allow, and plenty of Memphians regularly travel up the pike to
hawk their talents in the marketplace. The ways of the two cities are as different as New York and Los Angeles, and the comforts of home are as close as a
three-hour drive.

A misconception about Memphis is that all the labels departed. But Memphis has never been a record label town. The companies that thrived here were
independents, Sun and Stax being the most prominent; in the industry picture, they were rebels. They created a distinct sound—in the case of Sun, a distinct genre—and then they died. Sun died as Sam Phillips returned to his
original interest in radio; after Johnny Cash, Jerry Lee Lewis, Howlin' Wolf,
and Elvis, what was left for him to do? Stax died when it lost its focus on
Memphis music. When they tried to play the big boys' game, Stax was unmer-

cifully hacked by record distributors, oil conglomerates, and—the unkindest cut of all—a local bank.

Memphis has long been a studio town, a place where a person with an idea can find a laboratory to experiment, to create. Since soul music, the city's impact on the music world has been spare. But the blues remains the essence of each new generation's ideas. While other cities have flared up—Athens, Georgia; Seattle; Miami's bass sound; Chicago's house sound—the coals in Memphis still burn, even if coated in ash. "It really is as simple as the blues, Sun, Stax, bam bam bam," says Dickinson, "the same basic thing happening. Memphis created a product that obviously was art because art is enduring, and entertainment is transitory. This stuff that's been done here, by people who were often completely unaware of what they were doing, has endured. The Delta blues is going to be one of the most significant western contributions to the twentieth century."

In 1978, after more than a decade of not producing, Sam Phillips returned to the studio. John Prine, who has often recorded in Memphis, was cutting *Pink Cadillac* at the Sam Phillips Recording Service, with Knox and Jerry Phillips producing. "We had been trying to get a good take on a song called 'Saigon,'" says Knox Phillips. "It was a great song, but we were doing it at like a hundred eighty miles per hour. I thought that was the right way to do it. I had told Sam, 'Dad, this guy sings so bad, you'll love him.' So Sam comes down to help us with the album."

Richard Rosebrough, who was engineering the session, remembers, "It took doing a session with Sam Phillips to make me believe. There was a magic that that man had in his fingertips. There was a magic in that man's eyes, they saw forty feet right through you. The words that came out of that man's mouth were bizarre. I had heard this story that when he cut the Yardbirds, he told the bass player to whip that guitar like a mule's peter. Well, now I believe he said it. When John Prine was working on this song called 'Saigon,' Sam says, 'I want you to slow down that song and draaaaag it out.' The way he used this word 'drag' was the whole thing. 'I want you to drag it out like you're dragging it across the street so you can find out what's on the other side.' It was all in Sam Phillips's control, totally.

"He decided he was going to put some echo on this guitar that started out the song. They had live echo chambers then. He put one hand on the echo-send and the other on the echo-return and he cranked it up. You could hear the speaker disintegrate. You could see sparks down the hall. Everyone went, 'No. No! NO!' sort of automatically reaching for the board. It turned out to be the most magical song on the album. A couple days later I was making tape copies of the whole album. Alex Chilton was down there, hanging out in the lobby on the sofa. This was around the time of his *Like Flies on Sherbert,* so it was going to take a lot to impress him. He heard a song go by and he yawned. Then another. When 'Saigon' started, he slowly got up, followed that sound into the control room. He said, 'What *is* this?' That was Sam Phillips. Sam knows something we don't know."

I heard Sam Phillips once say, "Producing? I don't know anything about producing records. But if you want to make some rock and roll music, I can reach down and pull it out of your asshole." Yessir. Sir.

Across from a donut shop in Midtown, a decaying building is sandwiched between a VCR repair store and a dentist who seems to rarely have customers. It is one of Memphis's last bastions of independent rock and roll. The Antenna Club has no sign, its shabby facade expressing all that anyone needs to know. In the late 1970s, the venue was known as the Well, a beer-only joint where the clientele brought fifths of cheap whiskey to while away the daylight. The Well attracted some musicians living cheaply in Midtown's run-down elegance, and they began performing on the club's small stage in return for the cover charge; the regulars did not have to pay. When punk became a fashion statement, the older couple who ran the place sold it for more than they thought their dive would ever be worth.

Tav Falco and his Unapproachable Panther Burns honed their chops at the Well. The Panther Burns, with Alex Chilton's assistance, have cut a swath for others to follow, often restraining branches so those trailing won't get whipped in the face. From the beginning, Tav employed the Burnettes, a shifting lineup of nubile femmes, and as that group stabilized, they formed an entity of their own. The all-girl Hellcats released a couple albums on the French New Rose label, the outlet that was un–record company enough to gain Chilton's cooperation in the mid-1980s, and that subsequently developed a healthy relationship with the Memphis talent around him. Lorette Velvette, now a solo artist, took her first plane trip with the Panther Burns—a twenty-hour flight to Australia.

After living in Memphis for several years, my girlfriend referred to the Antenna Club scene as car crash music, likening it to a wreck on the highway that makes you slow down as you pass, gawking. The Panther Burns were gawk music. The theatrical basis of their beginnings made them a sight to see, and their drama was enhanced by the musical barbs lobbed from the one musically proficient member. Describing a show in San Francisco, Tav says, "We cleared the house. It was great." The Hellcats, and their phoenix offspring the

Alluring Strange—the band includes three of the five Hellcats—work the same tension. The first time I saw the latter perform they were utterly thrilling, each note sounding as if it might be their last, the whole mess lurching forward with a defiant bravura. Rehearsal has tightened their sound, but sparks still fly on the stage, and on their debut recording, *Will You Marry Me?*

The Country Rockers are misunderstood as gawk music. Their visual appeal is strong: A trio with an octogenarian dwarf drummer and septuagenarian backwoods vocalist and guitarist. But their music is as pure as roadhouse whiskey. Tying them to the modern Memphis scene, their bassist, manager, and producer, Ron Easley, is a regular member of Alex Chilton's touring band and also of the Panther Burns. (The Country Rockers' two completely unpretentious European albums are available domestically on a single CD, *Free Range Chicken*.) Some audiences have the same trouble with Cordell Jackson. Her speed and dexterity on the guitar warrant a listener's attention, but seeing it come from "the rocking granny" in her frilly southern gowns causes people to stare.

A punkish guitar-blur band called the Grifters embraces the independence of the Memphis spirit. Their series of singles drew courtship from several major labels, leading to proffered contracts of five figures. The band has so far declined all, opting for a tiny local label where they know their integrity will not be compromised, as surely as they know the same assurances from the majors were bullshit. Neighborhood Texture Jam has converted the washboard to a larger piece of corrugated tin, enhancing the industrial aura of their rootsy modern rock.

Several of Mud Boy's kids lead popular Memphis bands now. Dickinson's two back up their old man playing blues, rockabilly, and river silt, but on their own, as DDT, create a blistering rock with funk undertones. Selvidge's youngest leads the city's most popular neo–hip hop band, Big Ass Truck. They use their urban R&B mindset to reexamine soul highlights, incorporating samples with a live deejay. Lee Baker's children are younger, but they have already shared the stage with Dickinson's and Selvidge's, launching Son of Mud Boy, aka Three-Legged Puppy.

With over thirty recording facilities listed in the 1994 phone book, bands have no trouble finding a place to get their ideas on tape. Ardent remains busy, though focused more on big-budget projects. The preeminent alternative studio is Easley Recording, validated early on by Chilton. Their work has become identified as the sound of alternative Memphis, and people buy recordings solely because the Easley name is on them.

Not all of the contemporary acts are garage bands. One of the most excit-

ing performers in Memphis is the Grammy-nominated gospel artist O'Landa
Draper and the Associates. In his early thirties, Draper commands his sixty-
voice choir like a fine painter works the variegated hues of a color. I knew I'd
seen something when he rippled the voices across his choir and the image of
flowing water was overwhelming. He can command an audience as pro-
ficiently as Rufus Thomas, inspiring hundreds of people at once so that each
feels Draper is speaking only to him or her. But gospel music is ostracized
from popular music, quarantined on specialty stations. Although Draper and
his choir accompanied Billy Joel on the 1994 Grammy Awards, the gateway to
the mainstream has yet to swing open.

Memphis still sits isolated in a large rural region. In less than an hour's
drive, you can be in communities where electricity and indoor plumbing remain uncommon, where juke joints with wood stoves provide a glimpse of
blues roots that all the compact disc reissues in the world could never equal. In
the city, there are cinder block clubs in black neighborhoods that hint at the
old feel—without trying. Outsiders entering either of these types of places
must cross a cultural bridge and overcome a sense of invasiveness not unlike
that faced by the hippies and folklorists of the sixties.

"All in all, it's been a great battle." Randall Lyon is not wistful with his summation. He continues to influence people, writing for a biweekly newspaper
in Little Rock and dispensing advice to young bands trying to get a toehold on
today's modern music world. "The cultural forces that prevail, a totally anti-
racist, anti–high art/low art approach to the blues—that comes from Bob
Palmer's work. People forget there was a school that said there is no African
music in the blues, and Palmer refuted it. If that discussion had to take place,
we added something to it. And it was going to take place because the records
were coming out. People were missing the point. No, these artists aren't playing guitar in a crude manner. That intonation and pitch was worked out in a
context. It made people realize that traditional Western scales weren't really
the most exciting work ever done. It made people hear music in a different
way. The very presence of the artists was inspiring. They had been through so
much more than we had been through. And they had worked it out, as a
lifestyle. They were the troubadours of the heroic furor."

Robert Palmer is today spread as wide as his ken. He is shaping a ten-part
public television series on the history of rock and roll, has codirected a film
called *The World According to John Coltrane,* and was the on-screen narrator for
a film titled after his book *Deep Blues.* He also continues to work on a book
that isolates and follows the strains in music that later became rock and roll.

"It's really surprising," he says, "that some of the major rock and roll bass parts turn out to be from Africa by way of Afro-Cuban music. There's an amazing amount of Afro-Cuban material in early rock and roll—not influence, but actual patterns, riffs, licks."

In John McIntire's twenty-fifth year at the Memphis College of Art, a new administration came in and he was the first faculty member to be let go. He sculpts full-time now, still sifting through yard sales to make an extra buck.

Roland Janes, the Sun guitarist and Zen riddle, is still at the Sam Phillips Recording Service, sipping soda and eating candy bars. The studio doors continue to open and close behind musicians, and as the sound of the street has changed, he has rolled with it. "A lot of people kid me about rap," he says, "and I kid about it myself, but I've worked with enough of it now that I feel like I understand it, the music and the gimmick. It's a message music, really, the message of the streets, told in its rawest form. When most of the musicians first come in here, they're really trying to impress upon me that they're whatever the image they're trying to be. But after they get to know me awhile and they listen to a few of my corny jokes and we get to communicating, then suddenly they become like everybody else. That's the way I see it."

Randy Haspel regularly stops by the studio, greeting Roland, visiting his old partner Bob Simon, who writes in the B room, pushing aside the very board on which Sam recorded Elvis to make desk space. Haspel nearly had a big break in the 1970s, but his audition for John Hammond at Columbia Records was ill-fated. His success as a songwriter is nothing less than a tribute to Dewey Phillips, the artists who have covered his material ranging from Rufus Thomas to George Jones, from Moe Bandy to the Impressions. He still gets a charge out of playing clubs, where the Radiants make filling the dance floor look easy.

As casinos have proliferated in the upper Mississippi Delta, Herbie O'Mell has found himself in demand. He was host of the first one to open, then was hired away by a larger enterprise. He continues to manage affairs for Jim Dickinson, working with O'Landa Draper's gospel choir as well. "Last year I was out at a place and a guy walked up to me, an older guy, kind of rough-looking, and he said, 'You Herbie O'Mell?' And I said yeah, and he said, 'Ya probably don't remember me, I'm a friend of Campbell's.' I said, 'Oh, okay. Nice to see ya.' And he said, 'If you ever need anything, here's my card.' He gave me his card and it had his name, a phone number and it said, 'When in doubt, knock 'em out.'"

Teenie Hodges continues to write crossover hits, recently landing a song on Bonnie Raitt's 1994 *Longing in Their Hearts;* working with his brothers and cousin Roland Robinson, the Hi Rhythm Section released an independent CD, *Perfect Gentlemen,* in 1994. Willie Mitchell is still in the same studio where he cut all the Al Green hits. His control room has been upgraded, but the studio floor remains untouched, the same 1970s carpets and styles oozing feel all over the place. William Brown stays busy as his chief engineer, and Willie's grown children have a rap act of their own, the M-Team, and produce many others.

David Fleischman never got anything national going with Flash and the Board of Directors, but as a promo man for Atlantic, he worked his way into the national office, heading up campaigns behind Ratt, Twisted Sister, Julian Lennon, Mike and the Mechanics, and Robert Plant. He is currently a vice-president at MCA Records.

All the surviving Mar-Keys are still active in music. Cropper and Dunn, along with Booker T. Jones, released a new Booker T. and the MGs album in 1994, after touring behind Neil Young and Bob Dylan. The Memphis Horns (Wayne Jackson and Andrew Love) released a new album in 1992, produced by Terry Manning, who remains active in the studio. Terry Johnson still makes time to write songs. Smoochy Smith has joined Stan Kesler, Sonny Burgess, and a few other friends, performing rockabilly as the Sun Rhythm Section.

"There's something in Memphis that makes people a little crazy," says Don Nix. "Since I moved out of there, I'm not near as crazy as I was. It's something about that town. As far as the music goes, it's always been there, and it always will be, but it's hard to tap it. It will come around again someday, I'm positive of that. It might take another hundred years or it might be next year, I don't know. But Memphis, it's there. It's just there."

"Memphis is the town where nothing ever happens but the impossible always does," says Danny Graflund, sober since evicting Other Man from his life. "People come here and they either love this place, or they don't understand and can't see what's going on. It's its own little thing, and it's always happening." With a video camera at his side, Graflund is attempting to document that which is so hard to see. He is often hired by Mary Lindsay Dickinson, whose latest project is a collaboration with Ardent on a CD-ROM for kids.

Mose Vinson has sobered up since his performance at my high school. He performs every Saturday on Beale Street at the Center for Southern Folklore, and every Sunday at his church. He was featured in 1992 on the National Public Radio program "BluesStage," and in 1994 he entered the studio with Jim Dickinson and recorded a solo CD.

Jimmy Crosthwait performs his puppet show for school kids, working out of the museum system. Recently, he ran an art gallery in Eads, Tennessee, outside of Memphis, where his shows included photograph exhibitions by Stanley Booth and Jim Dickinson. He gave the gallery to someone else when it started drawing too much attention, and he spent two years designing and building a home of his own, progressing from sculptures that move to a sculpture he can move into.

After releasing his major label debut in 1993 and playing Carnegie Hall, Sid Selvidge accepted a commission to write a folk opera, choosing as his subject the Mississippi Delta flood of 1927. Bill Eggleston is the scenic director. Eggleston remains prominent in modern photography. Though some magazines became more fascinated by his lifestyle than his art, his books, including *The Democratic Forest* and *Faulkner's Mississippi,* continue to exemplify exciting modern photography.

Lee Baker still rides a tractor around the lake in Arkansas. He has reunited with several former Moloch members and they play around Memphis as the Agitators. Baker and Selvidge recently played an acoustic gig to an audience of five on Beale Street. During the break, Baker and I talked gardens. He'd been told that ground red pepper would keep raccoons away from his corn, but said it wasn't true. "You know what, though," he said, "you get a radiator leak, put that ground red pepper in your radiator, it'll stop it up. That's good to know, 'cause you never know when your radiator will spring a leak. Might not be near a can of Stop Leak, but they got red pepper all over the country." Five of us heard some amazing guitar that afternoon.

Jim Dickinson remains anathema to the music business, producing several albums a year, some over a matter of days for the smallest companies, others done with more grace and bigger budgets. He insists that most of his projects come to Memphis, removing them from the record company loop and helping them broaden their boundaries. Whenever possible, he spreads the money around, bringing in vocalist William Brown or saxophonist Fred Ford. "As sure as I am that corporate rock is overfeeding the public, I am equally sure that the public will get tired of it," he says. "Sooner or later they get tired of everything, they want the antithesis. Always. And as long as that happens, the corporate mentality has to make a place for people like me. Because they only understand the here and now, they don't understand the possible maybe of the future."

Those energy vectors that drew Robert Johnson and Otis Redding and Johnny Cash and Al Green and all these artists to Memphis, those vectors still point here. Disbelievers say the reason can't be in the earth, can't be a product of the dirt or the river. But they ignore empirical facts: People who come to Memphis notice cultural collisions. Other cities may have similar black and white populations that interact or segregate themselves exactly as Memphis does, but something about this city tunes our antennae to such things. Whether knowing its history we project it, or we are drawn to it by forces we cannot see, race relations, also known as music, is the lifeblood of Memphis. The first song to top the pop, country, and rhythm and blues charts came from Memphis forty years ago, Carl Perkins's "Blue Suede Shoes." Memphis music is a concept, not a sound.

This writing occurs four decades after Elvis made his first recordings with Sam Phillips. Rock and roll is middle-aged and fat. Since the 1970s, when the music passed it adolescence, there has been less risk taking. Despite constant predictions of its death or demise, it still struggles to be the voice of rebellion, sponsored by corporate conglomerates that are the object of the overthrow. But the art of rock and roll has moved from the musicians to the businessmen: it's an art of the bottom line. Mass sales, mass popularity. The globe is the market, billboards dwarfed by the Goodyear blimp, dwarfed by the space shuttle. Having achieved the capacity to sell millions of cheeseburgers and hamburgers dressed all different ways, marketing's next step is to sell tens of millions of one kind of hamburger. Moving hundreds of thousands of pieces of product no longer means success. Upstart artists who score hits are ruined by misguided follow-up expectations; upstart artists who don't score hits are abandoned. The business does not allow time for artistic growth. The cultural relevance of music has been replaced by the cultural relevance of sales.

But all is not lost. The Michael Jackson syndrome does not deny the Jim Dickinson factor. As more of the same is heaped on the public, they will, by nature, become bored by that and demand something else. Memphis lives for the "possible maybe of the future." The city has had its days and years in the spotlight, and in this interim (this long, long interim) between thrusts, there are still many people here making a living through music. The machinery is in place. Recording studios proliferate, bands are signed to big and small labels, writers still get their songs on records.

Not long back on a not very busy afternoon, Dickinson and I were a block off Beale Street at a studio. When the doorbell rang, we walked together to the lobby. Dickinson opened the door and a youngish black kid was there. He said, "Is this building a recording studio?" Yes, it is. "I want to make a record, man," the kid said. Dickinson didn't laugh at the naive ambition of the stranger, and he didn't send him off on a goose chase to other studios. Rather, he gave the young man the studio owner's name and phone number, told him he'd have to get permission from him to come in and work. The stranger left, the ticket in his hand, and may or may not have ever made the necessary call. In the early part of this century, the blues came up from Memphis earth, and later rock and roll and soul music followed. Somewhere in Memphis a kid is channeling that same spirit today, and the world waits for that person to come knocking.

Further Reading, Watching, and Listening

THERE ARE TWO COMPANION CDS TO THIS BOOK, *IT CAME FROM MEMPHIS* (Upstart/Rounder; www.rounder.com) and *It Came from Memphis II* (Birdman; www.birdmanrecords.com). On these discs you can hear Dewey Phillips in action and lots of the bands, songs, and styles of music discussed in this book. Both discs are wildly diverse and both contain lots of photos in the liner notes that I couldn't squeeze into the book. Both CDs are essential listening, but don't take my word for it—let the music prove it to you.

Many insightful writers have written books on Memphis music and Memphis culture. Peter Guralnick's *Sweet Soul Music* (Little, Brown) is a warm introduction to both, with an emphasis on Memphis soul music. Guralnick profiles several other prominent Memphis musicians in his collections *Feel Like Going Home* and *Lost Highway* (both Little, Brown); his two-volume biography of Elvis Presley, *Last Train to Memphis* and *Careless Love* (both Little, Brown), is about so much more than just Elvis and is nearly all that need be read on the subject of Elvis's life (Greil Marcus's *Dead Elvis* [Harvard University Press] rounds out Elvis's afterlife). Stanley Booth has long been a part of the Memphis scene, and his collection of essays, *Rythm Oil* (Da Capo), is a personal account of both well-known and obscure Memphis musicians. Booth's writing is elegant, and his Rolling Stones book, *The True Adventures of the Rolling Stones* (A Cappella; originally mistitled *Dance with the Devil*), should not be missed (Stanley has his own website at www.galleryofsound.com/stanleybooth/). Michael Bane's *White Boy Singing the Blues* can't decide if it wants Memphis obscurity or a broader pop music context, and the vacillation probably works in its favor; don't be fooled by the picture of Elvis on the cover of the reissue.

Greil Marcus's *Mystery Train* (Plume) is a provocative and informative examination of roots music and touches on several Memphis artists. For information about the Sun label, turn to *Good Rockin' Tonight* (St. Martin's) by Colin Escott and Martin Hawkins. Louis Cantor, a former disc jockey on WDIA, has written a history of the station titled *Wheelin' on Beale* (St. Martin's). Rob Bowman collected his encyclopedic knowledge of the Stax label and published it in the book *Soulsville USA* (Schirmer). Gayle Dean Wardlow collected and updated his pioneering essays on early blues facts and figures in *Chasin' That Devil Music;* there's a CD packaged with it that invites you to sit in on some of his interviews.

A handsome pamphlet titled "LXF1" bootlegs two extended interviews with Alex Chilton, from which I drew several quotes. For a history of William Eggleston and his work, the essay that accompanies his *Ancient and Modern* is a good overview. That book, unfortunately, has become hard to find. He gives a pretty good interview in *The Hasselblad Award 1998*, but for photos, the 1999 book *2 1/4* (Twin Palms Publishers) is stunning. Several of Eggleston's students have embarked on careers of their own: Don't miss a photo exhibit by Huger Foote—it feels good to stand in a room of his work. His first book, *My Friend from Memphis* (Booth-Clibborn Editions), is beautiful. Mark Crosby has turned his lens on New York—*New York Christmas* and *New York* (both Universe)—and David Julian Leonard, judging by his recent gallery and museum work, should soon have his own book.

For a solid introduction to the blues, Robert Palmer's *Deep Blues* is outstanding. My own biography of Muddy Waters, which I'm finishing at the time of this writing and which will be titled *Can't Be Satisfied: The Life and Times of Muddy Waters* (Little, Brown), is also good. For a great feel of the Mississippi Delta and the resettlement of its people in Chicago, check out *The World Don't Owe Me Nothing* (Chicago Review Press) by David "Honeyboy" Edwards. Harder to find but a good overview of southern soul is Barney Hoskyns's *Say It One Time for the*

Brokenhearted (Fontana), which focuses on the relationship between black soul and white country music. Amiri Baraka (LeRoi Jones) presents a more sociological approach to blues history in *Blues People* (Quill), and he continues the discussion, emphasizing jazz, in *Black Music* (Da Capo). It took a guy from New Zealand to write a book on gospel groups in the Mid-South—Al Young did a great job with *Woke Me Up This Morning* (University of Mississippi Press).

The larceny and evil of the business behind the music may be an art different from the songs, but as Fredric Dannen's *Hit Men* (Times Books) proves, it's plenty exciting to read about. *The Death of Rhythm and Blues* (Obelisk) by Nelson George reveals the appetite of the pop machine and how it can swallow a whole culture. Jerry Wexler's autobiography, *That Rhythm Those Blues,* is a less dark peek behind the scenes.

For another feel of Memphis, James Conaway has published a memoir, *Memphis Afternoons* (Houghton Mifflin), which is a look at what some other people were doing in Memphis around the 1950s. *Memphis Since Crump* (University of Tennessee Press) by David M. Tucker details how integration came to the city that wouldn't. Joan Beiffus's book, *At the River I Stand* (St. Luke's Press), is an oral history of the sanitation workers' strike during which Dr. Martin Luther King, Jr., was assassinated. Steve Stern has set several of his novels in the Pinch, Memphis's immigrant neighborhood, and they are all fine reading.

Some other companions in spirit: everything by Nick Tosches (once I meet all these deadlines, I'm gonna hole up with *The Nick Tosches Reader* [Da Capo]); *Love in Vain,* a screenplay by Alan Greenberg about Robert Johnson; poet Etheridge Knight's *Born of a Woman* (Houghton Mifflin); *Let Us Now Praise Famous Men* (Houghton Mifflin) by James Agee and Walker Evans; *Juke Joint* by Birney Imes; *Watching* by John Fergus Ryan; *Sermons and Sacred Pictures,* an experimental documentary by Lynne Sachs that uses archival film footage from the Memphis black community as its foundation (Home Use: Center for Southern Folklore [see Chapter One below]; institutions: University of California Extension Center for Media and Independent Learning, 2000 Center Street, 4th Floor, Berkeley, CA 94704).

A good website for these and other books on Memphis is Burke's Bookstore (www.burkesbooks.com) or you can browse their nooks and crannies when you visit town: 1719 Poplar Avenue, Memphis, TN 38104; 901-278-7484. They've usually got copies of *Beale Black and Blue* on sale, and it's a hard-to-find document.

The following recordings—audio and video—are sources for more information about the subjects in each chapter. Some that were mentioned in the text are repeated here, but many are not. For the music that your favorite local mom-and-pop don't got, check with Shangri-la Records (www.shangri.com; 1916 Madison Avenue, Memphis, TN 38104; 901-274-1916) or Audiomania (1698 Madison Avenue, Memphis, TN 38104; 901-278-1166). Other good, used Memphis record stores are River Records and Memphis Comics. For videos, I usually have good luck at Vestapol Videos (www.guitarvideos.com; P.O. Box 802, Sparta, NJ, 07871; fax: 973-726-0568; ph: 973-729-5544) and at Facets Video (1-800-331-6197; www.facets.org).

CHAPTER ONE

Allow me to toot my own horn for a moment. *All Day and All Night* is a documentary I directed and edited that uses Beale Street and Beale Street musicians to discuss points similar to many of those made in this book. Rufus Thomas and B. B. King, among others, tell how the Beale Street community nurtured its artists and, through WDIA, helped them go national. The awards the film has received indicate it is as much fun to watch as it was to make (Center for Southern Folklore, 119 S. Main St., Memphis, TN 38103; 901-525-3655; www.southernfolklore.com).

There is a lot of scattered film footage of Furry Lewis around, but my favorite piece is his performance of "Going to Brownsville" in *Good Morning Blues*, a documentary available through Yazoo at Vestapol Video. Another of their reissues, *Out of the Blacks into the Blues*, is also a good genre overview. For listening to Furry, I'd start with *Fourth & Beale* (Lucky 7/Rounder), recorded by Terry Manning at Furry's home in 1969. *Live at the Gaslight* sometimes surfaces in used-record bins, and it has given me hours of enjoyment. And of course, *Furry Lewis in His Prime* on Yazoo. Adelphi Records recently issued another great 1969 Furry disc, *Take Your Time*, featuring accompaniment by Lee Baker. The Adelphi people came down from Maryland in 1969 and recorded many hours of great stuff on both tape and film. Dig the Adelphi website for info on their other labels (seek out their Harmonica Frank CD), plus great photos and very rare film clips: www.adelphi-records.com.

Mose Vinson went back into the studio in 1994 and was recorded by Jim Dickinson, under the auspices of the Center for Southern Folklore. That recording is available through the Center. Mose, and several of the other 1970s blues survivors, are represented on *The Devil's Music,* an album released in conjunction with a BBC documentary.

The furor of the blues festival incident when the plug was pulled on Mud Boy is evident on a videotape that has no name and is not very widely circulated. The next-best thing is Mud Boy's live album, *Negro Streets at Dawn,* released in Europe. It's a pretty close second, but it's also very had to find; portions of it appear on the domestic Mud Boy compilation, *They Walk Among Us* (Koch).

CHAPTER TWO

The Dewey Phillips album compiled by Charles Raiteri, *Red, Hot & Blue,* is available on CD through the Memphis Archives label (www.inside-sounds.com); it includes the acetates of Dewey broadcasting from his hospital room, which were discovered at a Memphis yard sale and mentioned in this book's previous edition. This album is the best way to get a taste of Dewey's power. Randy Haspel's reflection on Dewey can be found in the June 1978 *Memphis* magazine. Some excellent transcriptions of WDIA gospel broadcasts are collected on the album *Bless My Bones* (Rounder). And Gatemouth Moore, the former WDIA disc jockey, is the eccentric and very entertaining subject of Louis Guida's documentary film *Saturday Night Sunday Morning.* An English CD, *Hey Mr. Gatemouth* (on the West Side label), collects his great 1940s and 1950s sides.

CHAPTER THREE

The 1968 Memphis sanitation workers' strike, mentioned in this chapter and several others, is examined in depth in the documentary *At the River*

I Stand. Three Memphis filmmakers utilized a cache of film footage from the era. It's available to universities and other institutions through California Newsreel (149 Ninth Street, San Francisco, CA 94103).

CHAPTER FOUR

Jim Dickinson's early singles on the Southtown label pop up periodically (one track is on the second volume of this book's companion CD). His 1972 solo album, *Dixie Fried* (Atlantic), has yet to be issued domestically on CD, but it is available as an import from Atlantic's Japanese division, and it sounds great. If a domestic label can wrest the master tapes from Atlantic's vault, they should find bonus tracks there. Dickinson's *Beale Street Saturday Night* album—used bins in Memphis only—is a modern interpretation of old Beale. The outtakes to that project are called *Delta Experimental Projects, Volume 1* (New Rose when it was in business); *Volume 2*, with which it's coupled on compact disc, contains some of Dickinson's solo soundtracks (including two films by yours truly, *Southern Dust* and *Down*). Jim's got a couple new albums in the can, and he's leaked a few thrilling tracks to compilations; when the stars align, we'll have much new Dickinson music to savor. When we thought this book might need a subtitle, Jim had the best suggestion: *The Afterbirth of Rock and Roll*.

For jug band music, a label called Old Hat (www.oldhatrecords.com) is preparing some of the most beautiful packages on the market. Their lavish booklets and careful recording transfers recognize the regal nature of this earthy music; seek out *"Folks, He Sure Do Pull Some Bow!"* and *Violin, Play the Blues for Me*. The collection *Frank Stokes' Dream* is another good starting point (it has some great Furry Lewis tracks), and also *Wild About My Loving* (RCA).

The sound of the West Memphis scene is probably lost to memories and beer, though some hints can be heard on the Hi Records box *Hi Times* (The Right Stuff/Capitol), which includes tracks from Willie Mitchell, Ben Branch, and Bowlegs Miller.

CHAPTER FIVE

No record collection is complete without the Mar-Keys' "Last Night," which is on their debut album, *Last Night* (Atlantic). It's also included on *The Complete Stax Singles 1959–1968* (Atlantic). The next two volumes of the Stax singles, on Fantasy Records, are also great. For those who find twenty-eight long compact discs intimidating, check out the four-CD *The Stax Story* (Fantasy). Some essential Stax listening: Booker T. and the MGs, *And Now!*; Isaac Hayes, *Hot Buttered Soul;* William Bell, *Soul of a Bell*; Steve Cropper, *With a Little Help from My Friends;* and a live revue recording, *Funky Broadway*. Volume 1 of this book's companion CD includes Packy Axton's immortal "Hung Over."

The Stax building was torn down in 1989 for a community center never built, and in the late 1990s, a nonprofit group—Soulsville USA—began buying the land around the site, and finally the site itself, for construction of the Stax Museum of American Soul Music (www.soulsvilleusa.com). Groundbreaking was April 2001, with a projected opening of 2002. In addition to the museum, the project includes a music academy. The work is being done in association with nearby LeMoyne-Owen College, with an emphasis on neighborhood revitalization. Check out the museum on your next visit, at the corner of College and McLemore (try the barbecue and the cheeseburger at the nearby Big S Grill).

If anyone is looking for another theme around which to compile a CD, I suggest collecting the best of Charlie Freeman's guitar artistry. It's scattered from early Memphis studio recordings to the Dixie Flyers and beyond, and would tell a tall tale were it all in one place.

CHAPTER SIX

The Alan Lomax series of field recordings that inspired many of the white artists in this book was reissued as a four-CD box set titled *Sounds of the South* (Atlantic). Since then, that Lomax material and more has been repackaged by Rounder in a continuing series, The Alan Lomax Collection, that intends to get all of his recordings in print. Try *61 Highway Mississippi* and *Voices from the American South*, both from the

Southern Journey series; from the Deep River of Song series, try *Mississippi: The Blues Lineage* and *Mississippi: Saints and Sinners*.

The classic Randy and the Radiants are included on the *Sun: Into the Sixties* (Bear Family) box. They released their own soul CD in the 1990s, *From Sun to Sun*; try writing P.O. Box 771025, Memphis, TN 38172-1025.

CHAPTER SEVEN

Many of the Ardent singles are available in used-record bins around Memphis. Some of the Jesters tracks are included on the Sun Records box *Into the Sixties* (Bear Family). There's a great *Talent Party* video compilation waiting to happen; George Klein has several reels of choice material, including many prominent artists. They span a decade or more and give a great feel for the times.

CHAPTER EIGHT

Some good blues revival listening: Sleepy John Estes, *Legend of Sleepy John Estes* (Delmark), and his *I Ain't Gonna Be Worried No More* (Yazoo); Fred McDowell, *Amazing Grace* (Testament/Hightone); and Bukka White, *Sky Songs* (Arhoolie). The Everest label has proven very trustworthy; though their packaging is deceptively chintzy, their recordings are consistently exciting and intimate, and I've found it worth buying anything they've put out.

I never heard the Hodges brothers' JAMF, but I'd guess it couldn't be far from the Bar-Kays' *Soul Finger* (Stax), which was issued around this time. As the Hi Rhythm Section, the Hodges are best heard on the Al Green *Anthology* box, and also the *Hi Times* box. They've put out some CDs of their own recently, though I've never seen them after the release parties; ask for *Perfect Gentlemen* and *Collection 2000* by name. Probably more accessible, and a real revelation, are their two tracks with Ike and Tina Turner included on the *Bold Soul Sister* CD (Hip-O/Universal).

A lot of blues revival film clips have been issued on video, though they seem to be dominated by spiritless performances in uninspiring college auditoriums. You've got to dig for the bright moments. Vestapol (www.guitarvideos.com), Yazoo (www.yazoobluesmailorder.com), and Shanachie (www.shanachie.com) boast extensive catalogs; the Lomax stuff from Newport is also noteworthy (*Devil Got My Woman* and *Delta Blues, Cajun Two Step*).

CHAPTER NINE

Though each of the Memphis Country Blues Festivals was recorded, only the latter two ever saw audio release. *The 1968 Memphis Country Blues Festival* (London) is long out of print, but I've heard rumors that it was an early issue on CD when the labels weren't yet sure who the CD audience would be. The artists from the 1969 show were recorded in the studio; that double LP, *Memphis Swamp Jam*, has been reissued on two discs as *Mississippi Delta Blues Jam in Memphis* (Arhoolie) and includes bonus tracks. A recent issue of an old Reverend Robert Wilkins session, *Remember Me* (Genes), includes one track recorded at the 1969 show, and it is incredible. Genes is one of several labels associated with Adelphi, the label and website mentioned in Chapter One above. For more information on the blues festivals, seek out Stanley Booth's article, "Even the Birds Were Blue" (*Rolling Stone*, April 16, 1970). There are reminiscences by members of the Insect Trust on the web at http://www.furious.com/perfect/index.html and http://www.furious.com/perfect/insecttrust.html. I've included several tracks from the 1969 festival on Volume II of the companion CD.

CHAPTER TEN

A correction to the text in this chapter. Despite what is written there, the Box Tops did play on more than "The Letter" and the Muscle Shoals session. Unfortunately, my research was incomplete. "Sometimes it was only us, sometimes it was the studio musicians, and sometimes it was a combination," says Bill Cunningham, bassist with the band. "It really depended on who was in town. To give an extreme example, 'I See Only Sunshine' was just Alex and me. They needed a B-side, and everyone else was gone. Alex sings and plays guitars, I play everything else. We did it on the spot

because the need arose." The Box Tops had more of a role in their music
than this chapter indicates, and I apologize for the mistake.

The Box Tops albums and various greatest hits packages are readily
available in used bins (a reflection of their quantity, not quality), and they
remain good listening. To get a taste of the blues background that Dan
Penn refers to, two good starting places would be Bobby Bland's *Two
Steps from the Blues* (Duke/MCA) and Ray Charles's *Genius + Soul = Jazz*
(ABC). Dan Penn's brilliant *Nobody's Fool* was finally issued on CD
(Repertoire); he and Spooner Oldham have been touring together at
their leisure (the only way they do anything), and a recording of one of
their shows is available: *Moments from This Theatre* (Phantom). And Penn
went fishing one weekend in Louisiana in the year 2000 and ended up
catching a good vibe on a home recording, *Blue Nite Lounge*, available
through Dan's website: www.danpenn.com.

It's difficult to pick a place to start for the American Rhythm
Section—other than just turning on the radio, oldies or new country—
but you certainly will not have heard everything until you've heard Dusty
Springfield's *Dusty in Memphis* (Atlantic); the CD does not include
Stanley Booth's original liner notes. The Sweet Inspirations' "Sweet
Inspiration" is another personal favorite. The Rhino compilation *The
Muscle Shoals Sound* presents the diversity of that house section. This just
in: www.chipsmoman.com.

CHAPTER ELEVEN

The hard-to-find Moloch album is finally available on CD, an import from
Japanese Atlantic. Their first single, "Cocaine Katie," from a version of the
group that included the late Busta Jones, is included on volume one of this
book's companion CD. The second volume includes a live track that captures their big, ugly sound. That's Eugene Wilkins on harmonica, accidentally deleted from the CD credits.

The Don Nix albums are a mixed lot, tending toward overproduction,
but several of them have their moments. The double live LP with the
Alabama State Troopers includes a whole side of Furry Lewis, but the
Shelter and Elektra albums are the better bets. His Albert King album on
Stax, *Lovejoy, Illinois*, is great. Ever innovative, Don was behind the Great

Southern Musical Memories calendar—the dates are past but the photos are still great. He also wrote a book, *Road Stories and Recipes*, which is part stories and tales, part photographs, and also includes recipes from various musical luminaries.

The Dixie Flyers need a CD of their own, but until that happens, seek out their work behind Aretha Franklin, *Spirit in the Dark*; Ronnie Hawkins, *The Hawk*; Delaney and Bonnie, *From Bonnie to Delaney*; and Carmen McRae, *Just a Little Lovin'* (all Atlantic). I'm still flipped out by the recent Japanese import of the Flyers backing a Japanese pop band, *The Tempters in Memphis*.

CHAPTER TWELVE

If you can find the cassette issue of Mud Boy's *Known Felons in Drag* on Sid Selvidge's Peabody label, it comes from a different master and has more punch than the French vinyl; don't forget the aforementioned domestic Mud Boy compilation, *They Walk Among Us*.

Two musical entrances to Phineas Newborn's oeuvre: his first release, *The Piano Artistry of Phineas Newborn Jr.* (Fantasy), which also features his brother Calvin Newborn, and Phineas's later *Solo Piano* (Atlantic). Calvin has written and self-published a book about his family, *As Quiet As It's Kept: The Genius of Phineas Newborn, Jr.*; try sending $20.00 to P.O. Box 26307, Memphis, TN 38126-0446. Koch Records recently released a great 1960 recording featuring Phineas's friends Harold Mabern and Frank Strozier in a group called MJT+3, *Message from Walton Street*. Dig James Williams's *Meets the Saxophone Masters*.

Big Star's first two albums have been recently reissued by Fantasy on a single disc and are not hard to find, but beware the import version, which looks similar but has deleted a couple tracks. There have been several live documents issued, the best probably being *Big Star Live* (Rykodisc); *Nobody Can Dance* (Norton) is more irreverent, the spiral toward *Third* having begun (its version of "The Letter" gloriously presages punk rock). Big Star's reunion show in Memphis was professionally documented with a multi-camera shoot and the possibility of its issue remains—Danny Graflund continues to entertain offers.

CHAPTER THIRTEEN

Sid Selvidge's best albums (*Waiting for a Train, The Cold of the Morning*) are on his own label and probably are available through the Select-O-Hits distributorship (www.selectohits.com). There has long been talk of completing *Stranded in Canton;* David Byrne has been helpful and encouraging. Bill Jr. recently shot a feature film in Memphis and, not having seen or heard from him in a while, I believe he's in a cave finishing it. The Barbarian archives remain perfectly preserved and deserving of prominent reissue. Jim Blake has recently been discussing a new round of singles for collectors, and anyone with serious money is invited to contact Blake (I'll be happy to help). In a National Public Radio interview, Sam Phillips said something like, "I believe with sound I could stop wars"; he could have been talking about the Barbarian archives.

CHAPTER FOURTEEN

Alex Chilton's mid-period masterpiece, *Like Flies on Sherbet*, has finally become accessible. I am lobbying the Salvation Army to give away free copies at their missions, it's that inspiring. The Last Call label, the successor to New Rose, put out a version in Europe and Selvidge's Peabody Records (try www.redeyeusa.com) put one out in America, both of which have bonus tracks. Tav Falco has videotape from the sessions, including a full take of the "My Rival" master recording. Fabulous stuff. *Big Star 3rd (Sister Lovers)* is in print again through Rykodisc; play it to your children in their cribs (lots of Alex's post–Big Star stuff is available; one of my favorite performances is on a Chet Baker tribute called *Medium Cool*).

In the mid-1970s, Chilton helped the Randy Band get established. Bandleader Tommy Hull turned out to be one of the greatest pop songwriters this city has produced, though he's totally unknown. Twenty years after the fact, he released some of his songs on *far from this planet* and then released another disc, though I've never found it. Last time I saw him I asked if he was still writing. He smiled, nodded, and said, "Fast as I can throw 'em away."

CHAPTER FIFTEEN

Okay, here's where I plug my own work again: I compiled (but did not name) a cassette called *A Slice of the South*, culling various southern musics from the audio archives at the Center for Southern Folklore (see Chapter One for the address). The tape ranges from a one-string guitarist to fife-and-drum music to a fiddler imitating a catfight. It's good.

Fife-and-drum music is about as soulful as it gets, and no one has a soul deeper from which to draw than fife genius and living saint Otha Turner. Luther Dickinson became a disciple, and his first collection of Otha recordings, *Everybody Hollerin' Goat* (Birdman), contains not only fife-and-drum music but also great dialogue and musical instruction. When Otha coaches R. L. Boyce (a Hill Country legend) on song composition (the track is called "Boogie"), you're as near to the heart of the beast as you'll get without setting foot in Shelby County. Otha's second disc, *Otha Turner and the Afrossippi Allstars*, is drawn from a session with Senegalese musicians; it's appropriately subtitled *From Senegal to Senatobia*.

For modern rural blues, nothing in the world beats the Fat Possum label (www.fatpossum.com). Their R. L. Burnside album *Too Bad Jim*, produced by the late Robert Palmer, captures the sound and feel of a great juke joint. Some of my other favorites include Junior Kimbrough's *All Night Long* and Elmo Williams and Hezekiah Early's *Takes One to Know One*. The label's two compilation volumes, *Not the Same Old Blues Crap*, are good places to start. I'm eagerly awaiting Kenny Brown's Fat Possum album (hunt up his first one, independently released, called *Goin' Back to Mississippi*). Also noteworthy in the modern blues vein is the reissue of the High Water catalog on Hightone/HMG (www.hightone.com). Best place to start is the compilation *Deep South Blues*, which includes Jessie Mae Hemphill, Junior Kimbrough, and Hammie Nixon. Jessie Mae fans should note the reissue of her *She-Wolf*, and Fieldstones fans will be glad to hear that their long-awaited second album, in the can for two decades, should be out by the time you read this. Fieldstones vocalist Will Roy Sanders is the subject of a CD, book, and film, all titled *The Last Living Bluesman* and available through the Shangri-la records imprimatur. Robert Palmer also produced the soundtrack to Robert Mugge's *Deep Blues* film, which someone has got to put back out soon. Mugge's must-see Memphis film is *The Gospel According to Al Green* (he licensed some great preaching tracks to the Al Green *Anthology* that I compiled). A couple more blues documentaries of note: *The Search for Robert Johnson* and *Can't You Hear the Wind Howl*. Rounder's Bullseye label put out some notable Memphis blues in the 1990s, especially their Booker T. Laury and Little Jimmy King CDs. Several good Clarksdale artists can be heard on Rooster Records, namely Super Chikan and Willie King. (A plug for good Chicago blues: Delmark Records. There's good blues shopping of all varieties in Chicago at the Jazz Record Mart, www.delmark.com.)

Deserving of a book unto itself, filled with praise, is the Revenant label, which, like Old Hat, treats its reissue subjects like the gods they are (Revenant was founded by John Fahey). Two of their CDs especially relevant to Memphis fans are *Charlie Feathers: Get With It* and *American Primitive, Vol. I: Raw Pre-War Gospel*. The Feathers package, covering 1954 to 1969 on two CDs (and featuring lost recordings found in Charlie's closet, such as his collaboration with his mentor Junior Kimbrough), is breathtaking and will make you reconsider rockabilly— which is as perfect a tribute to Charlie's memory as any could be. The raw gospel CD stirs dust in unknown caverns of your soul. Another gospel note: O'landa Draper was one of the most charismatic performers Memphis ever produced, and with the Associates he made great music (*Live . . . A Celebration of Praise* being my favorite); since his untimely passing, the Associates carry on his feeling. Another source for older blues is the Smithsonian Institution (www.si.edu), which keeps all of its titles in print. Check out *Leadbelly's Last Sessions, Volume 1*, *Music from the South: Country Brass Bands*, and *Afro-American Music from Tate and Panola Counties, Mississippi*.

My favorite album by the Amazing Rhythm Aces is *Too Stuffed to Jump* (Collector's Choice); they've regrouped recently, and I hope to see them perform. John Prine's *Pink Cadillac* (Oh Boy) is a must, and his album of duets, *In Spite of Ourselves* (Oh Boy), is also great (if I loaned my copy to you, please return it, asshole, I miss it). Reggae meets soul on Toots Hibberts's *Toots in Memphis* (Island), produced by Dickinson.

Essential Tav Falco and the Panther Burns begins with their first EP, *Freni 2000*, and includes *Sugar Ditch Revisited* and *Shake Rag*. Their year 2000 recording, *Panther Phobia*, was a return to tradition; it sounds like the landlord beating on the front door. You gotta search used bins and hear the Cramps' *Gravest Hits*, the Hellcats' *Hoodoo Train*, and the Country Rockers' *Free Range Chicken*. Lorette Velvette, who was so well-received on volume one of the *It Came from Memphis* CD, has finally got a domestic release, *Rude Angel* (Okra-Tone/Rooster), which culls from her three European releases. There's a hard-to-find compilation called *Swamp Surfing in Memphis* (Frenzi/Au Go Go) that documents the diversity of the early 1980s Memphis underground from blues to garage art (is "Girl from Frayser" brilliant or what?). I still dig OFB's *Saturday Nights Sunday Mornings* from the same era. See photos of the Antenna Club at http://www.angelfire.com/punk2/antennaclub/press/music_down_under.html.

Monsieur Jeffrey Evans, a Gibson Brother who found his heart in Memphis, is producing a compilation of contemporary Memphis stuff, *Memphis Push*, for Sympathy For The Record Industry. His band, 68 Comeback, has released lots of great recordings on that label, but I'm currently partial to Jeff's solo release, *I've Lived a Rich Life* (Sympathy For The Record Industry)—it should get Jeff a role as band and sidekick on one of the late-night talk shows.

The aforementioned Shangri-La enterprise has released the self-explanatory book, *Playing for a Piece of the Door: A History of Memphis Garage and Frat Bands 1960·75* (but can you handle the Memphis Goons' *Teenage BBQ?*). Author Ron Hall has also compiled a companion CD.

The Memphis scene at the time of this writing, early summer 2001 with the heat approaching, is really thriving. The North Mississippi All Stars, a band with Jim Dickinson's two sons, have just ended a long tour supporting their first release, *Shake Hands with Shorty* (Tone-Cool), and they're at work on a follow-up. A rap group, Three Six Mafia, have become the biggest-ever selling group from Memphis; their *When the Smoke Clears* has just gone platinum. The debut CD from Lucero is selling briskly; it's on the local MADJACK Records (there's a link at www.memphismusic.org), a label home to several popular regional artists: the Pawtuckets, the Subteens, and Cory Branan. Blue Mountain's *Home Grown* on Roadrunner was one of my favorite CDs of the mid-1990s; their recent *Roots* is evidence the fire still burns. The Grifters, who almost became the Next Big Thing out of Memphis, have regrouped, and now that the pressure is off, the feeling and the fun (or is it the angst?) are all the way on. David Shouse's other project, Those Bastard Souls, continues to release exciting, innovative, and very listenable music, and Scott Taylor's other gig, The Porch Ghouls, are great live. Big Ass Truck continues to play and record with undiminished enthusiasm. Between the two publications of this book, the Oblivians revved up, then exploded; their recordings survive. Greg Oblivian's current project, The Reigning Sound, should foster a complete revival of Sam the Sham and the Gentrys; check out their *Break Up . . . Break Down* (Sympathy For The Record Industry). Metaphysical anthropologists are investigating whether Di Anne Price is the reincarnation of Sweet Emma Barrett or Lil Hardin. Rosco Gordon is in fine form on *Memphis, Tennessee*, his comeback (www.stonyplainrecords.com). The Bluff City is blessed to have Alvin Youngblood Hart newly in our midst; hopefully he and Dickinson will continue to draw from this soil and make records as stimulating as Hart's *Start with the Soul* (Hannibal; the track "Once Again" is a model blues for the new millennium). You'll enjoy recent recordings by these Memphis artists: Lucero, the Satyrs, Charlie Wood, Freeworld, Ross Rice, Tommy Hoehn, and Shelby Bryant/The Clears. Attend their gigs, or those of the Bo-Keys, the Porch Ghouls, the River Bluff Clan, and Curlew (*Fabulous Drop* is my favorite).

Lots of these bands can be heard among the following recent compilations: *Memphis (In the Meantime)*, *Memphis (Ain't Like It Used to Be)*, and *Makeshift: The First Broadcast*. Also, note Loverly Records—the public aural art project that benefitted the multitudes. Ed Porter gave a large number of artists free rein in a proper studio (Easley Recording, 901-323-5407, where Sonic Youth cut their *Washing Machine* and Jeff Buckley cut *My Sweetheart the Drunk*), and he was rewarded with mostly fantastic results (and three double CDs). There's a recent soul compilation that's really pretty good: *926 East McLemore: A Reunion of Former Stax Artists* (High Stacks).

Some other musts: Jerry Lee Lewis, *Old Tyme Country Music* (Sun); Charlie Rich, *Pictures and Paintings* (Sire) and the two-CD collection, *Feel Like Going Home* (Epic/Legacy); *The Complete Blind Willie Johnson* (Sony); *The Soul of O. V. Wright* (MCA); King Curtis, *The New Scene* (OJC/Fantasy); *Memphis Slim with Guests* (Inner City Records); James Carr, *Dark End of the Street* (Blue Side); Larry Davis, *Funny Stuff*

(Rooster) (Robert Cray's soul-blues ain't got nothing on this); Slim Harpo, *Knew The Blues* (Excello); Son House, *Father of the Delta Blues* (Sony); Muddy Waters, *The Plantation Recordings*, any *Best Of*, *Hard Again*, and hopefully there'll be a companion CD to my biography of Muddy; anything by Howlin' Wolf.

The following web pages may be helpful before your next visit, may expand your knowledge on subjects discussed in this book, or may break your computer:

www.memphislocal.com
www.bealestreetextended.com
www.motherbluesvideo.com (includes Mud Boy film footage)
www.memphismusic.org

Before you come to Memphis, you may want to send off for The Lowlife Guide, published by the friendly folks at Shangri-La Records. Send three bucks for your copy (1916 Madison Avenue, Memphis, TN 38104) and be sure to visit their store—they stock lots of this stuff. I published a lot of my favorite Memphis places in a *Spin* magazine book titled *Spin Underground USA* (Vintage/Random House).

When in Memphis, stop by the Center for Southern Folklore, now tucked away off Main Street in Peabody Place. Sometimes their gift shop includes tapes of their films, and you've got to see *Hush, Hoggies, Hush, Gravel Springs Fife and Drum, All Day and All Night*, and most of the others. Around the corner on Beale Street, your visit won't be complete without entering A. Schwab's, a general store from the old days that maintains a great voodoo counter. Your visit to Beale will be enhanced by Richard Raichelson's booklet, *Beale Street Talks: A Walking Tour Down the Home of the Blues*.

Around the corner from Beale, inside the Gibson guitar factory, is the Smithsonian Institution's permanent exhibit, the Rock and Soul Museum. It's a great way to get a real good understanding of the cultural crossroads here. The National Civil Rights museum is also nearby, but to visit you have to cross Jackie Smith's picket line, an act I can't endorse. They displaced small black businesses when they were building the museum, and if that wasn't antithetical enough to the museum's philosophy, such a tribute goes against the explicit wishes and direction of Dr.

King. I've heard it's a real moving exhibit; if you go there, be sure to talk to Jackie (this is being written on the thirteenth year, two hundred and fifteenth day of her protest).

WEVL FM-90 is still the best place to hear indigenous music, and WDIA plays good modern blues on Saturday mornings. On Sundays, scan your AM dial for those old-time, forceful black church sermons. Call Tad at the American Dream Safari and tour Memphis in his pristine 1955 Cadillac; it'll blow you away, and Tad's full of good tips (901-274-1997; www.AmericanDreamSafari.com). For good, cheap southern eats, dine at Alcenia's downtown (hot water cornbread!), at Ellen's Soul Food in South Memphis, or at the Cupboard (downtown and midtown). You'll need a good meal while you're here. Spend enough time in Memphis, and you'll appreciate that, truly, nothing ever happens but the impossible always does.

Index of Names

Barbarian Records 231–233
criticizes Martindale, Wink 24
feelings about segregation 35
Kensinger, Campbell and 180
Phillips, Dewey 17–18
Stranded in Canton 229
Sonny "Harmonica" 1
Blakey, Art 79
Bland, Bobby 13, 161
Blankenship, Jerry 54, 62
Blazers (band)
composition of 74
fading of 185
when the Beatles hit 92–93
mentioned 88, 219
Blind Joe Death *see* Fahey, John
Blues Magoos 139
Bobby Fuller Four (band) 104
Bo Diddley 55, 59
Bolton, Michael 4
Bond, Eddie 110, 222
Bono
Cher 208
Sonny 208
Booker T. and the MGs *see also* Jones,
Booker T.
the art of making music together 169
current work 262
Manning, Terry and 104
Mar-Keys performance was, by mid-
sixties 68
when the Beatles hit 88
mentioned 59, 74, 167
Booth, Stanley
current work 263
Ford, Fred and 204–205
idolized LaRue, Lash 31
Newborn, Phineas, Jr. and 204
Stranded in Canton 227, 229–230
mentioned 79, 151, 221
Box Tops (band)
American Sound Studio 74, 157, 160,
167
buying instruments 89
Chilton, Alex 7, 158–159, 207–208, 210,
234
Oldham, Spooner keyboard playing
163

success of 159, 164–165
while still the Devilles 94
mentioned 88, 166, 206
Boyden
Jack 91
Mrs. (Jack's mother) 91
Branch, Ben
bebop edge to music 51
influence on the Stax sound 52
integration in music 75, 171
King, Martin Luther, Jr. and 52
music described 51
O'Mell, Herbie hires for the Penthouse
63
Plantation Inn 50, 52
Brando, Marlon 30
Brandt, Jerry 140, 142
Brenston, Jackie 51
Briggs, David 164
Broken Wheel (bar) 179
Brothers Unlimited (band) 189
Brown
Charlie
character of 132, 149
hired bluesmen for coffeehouses 84,
131
Memphis Country Blues Festival
134
James 74, 80
Ray 65, 76–77, 101, 221
Roy 5
William 262–263
Brubeck, Dave 155
Brynner, Yul 22
Buckley, Lord (British hepster comedian)
31
Buffet, Jimmy 49, 196
Burch-lo (record label) 219
Burgess, Sonny 47, 262
Burk, Tommy 74, 92, 99, 232 *see also*
Counts (band)
Burkle's Bakery 131
Burnette, Johnny 99
Burnette Brothers 113
Burnettes (female group) 258
Burnside, R. L. 252
Burrito Brothers, Flying 43
Burroughs, William S. 138, 140

look for the companion CD

IT CAME FROM MEMPHIS Vol. 2

1. Come On Down To My House • **Good Kid Robert**
2. Boogie • **Otha Turner**
3. Smokestack Lightning • **Moloch**
4. By Your Side • **Sid Selvidge**
5. Let Your Light Shine On Me • **Mud Boy and the Neutrons**
6. T'aint Nobody's Business • **Hammie Nixon, Van Zula Hunt and the Beale Street Jug Band**
7. Shake Your Boogie • **Johnny Woods and Bobby Ray Watson**
8. Calvin's Boogie • **Phineas Newborn Orchestra**
9. Train Kept A' Rolling • **Tav Falco's Unapproachable Panther Burns**
10. Trip To Bandstand • **B.B. Cunningham**
11. Memphis, Tennessee • **Jerry Lawler**
12. You'll Do It All The Time • **Jim Dickinson and the New Beale Street Sheiks**
13. Going Down Slow • **Soldiers of the Cross**
14. Family Values • **Band of Ones**
15. Back for More • **Lawson and Four More**
16. Special Rider • **Insect Trust**
17. Bottle Up And Go • **Bootleggers Quartet**

compilation produced by Robert Gordon

available where CDs are sold.
©&℗ 2001 Birdman Records — www.birdmanrecords.com
distributed by Revolver USA — www.midheaven.com

Made in the USA
Lexington, KY
05 January 2018